EUROPE WITHOUT BAEDEKER

BOOKS BY EDMUND WILSON

EDMUND WILSON

Europe Without Baedeker

Sketches Among the Ruins
of Italy, Greece and England,
together with
Notes from a European Diary:
1963–1964

THE NOONDAY PRESS
a division of
Farrar, Straus and Giroux
New York

CONTENTS

v

NOTES FROM A EUROPEAN DIARY:
1963–1964

PREFACE TO THE FIRST EDITION

THIS BOOK is the result of a trip undertaken for the *New Yorker* magazine in the spring and summer of 1945. Chapters 1, 2, 4, 10, 11, 12, 13 and 14 were printed first in the *New Yorker*, but here appear in a revised and expanded form. An abridged version of Chapter 3 was printed in *Town & Country*, and parts of Chapters 3 and 9 have been printed in *Horizon*.

The reporting of the things that I heard and saw is as faithful as I could make it, except in the cases of the third and fourth sections of the chapter on British officials, in which I have used fictitious names and shuffled personalities a little, and of the chapter on U.N.R.R.A. in the Abruzzi, which, though derived from fact, is fiction. Since my experience of the Abruzzi is too limited for me to work up imaginary localities which would seem satisfactorily representative, I have resorted to the perhaps questionable device of planting an invented story in real places that are called by their names and are for the most part accurately described. The people are not, however, the real ones, and I must apologize to the U.N.R.R.A. workers at Aquila, to the officer in command of the Aquila hotel and to the *sindaco* of the town of Orsogna for the roles that my characters are made to play. I have no reason to believe that the relations between British and Americans in Aquila were such as I have shown in this story; but the things that I have here invented are the kind of things that often did happen, and I have tried to create a typical situation.

1947

PREFACE TO THE SECOND EDITION

When this book first came out in 1947, it was badly received in England. It was even denounced by Dean Inge. Hawthorne had the same experience when he published his book on England called *Our Old Home,* which was based on the seven years that he had spent there as consul in Liverpool. He was somewhat surprised to find that anything he had had to say in the way of negative criticism was received as outrageous slander. "I received," he wrote at the time, "several private letters and printed notices of *Our Old Home* from England. It is laughable to see the innocent wonder with which they regard my criticisms, accounting for them by jaundice, insanity, jealousy, hatred, on my part, and never admitting the least suspicion that there may be a particle of truth in them. The monstrosity of their self-conceit is such that anything short of unlimited admiration impresses them as malicious caricature. But they do me great injustice in supposing that I hate them. I would as soon hate my own people." This kind of patriotic reaction has seemed more characteristic of England than of any other nation. The French do not resent foreign criticism because they do not know it exists. They cannot even imagine it possible. It was amusing to remember the incessant disparagement to which we had been subjected by the visiting English. On this side of the water, on the other hand, I was scolded for being an Anglophile, and one correspondent wrote me that if I thought so much more highly of England than I did of the United States, I ought to go back and live there.

What seems to me rather curious is that, after having been five times to England—though usually rather briefly —and belonging as I did to a generation that had grown up on English literature, I should have had so little conception of what the English were really like. The point is that when we read English writers in youth, we assimilate them so far as we can to ourselves and treat the rest as a kind of fairy tale. One cannot find out what a people are like from seeing congenial friends who more or less share one's own interests: one has to be obliged to deal with them as they come in business or official relations, when you can see how they habitually behave. My picture is of course somewhat dated. The England that I saw at the end of the war—bedevilled and bombed and deprived—is not the England of twenty years later, resigned to the loss of its imperialist role and trying to adjust itself to a social system less rigidly stratified. What this means for England of today has, it seems to me, been dramatized in a masterly way in Mr. Angus Wilson's novel *Late Call*, with its story of three generations of a formerly lower-middle-class family in process of turning into something else in one of the modern "New Towns." As an outsider, writing at the end of the war, I could only record a few signs of this. But what, rereading *Europe Without Baedeker*, does today considerably embarrass me—to the point of making me suppress one passage—is my plugging of the virtues of the United States in contrast to England and Russia. The Anglo-Irish friend whom I call Bob Leigh was more perspicacious than I then imagined in saying that if the English didn't move in in Europe, the Americans probably would. We have done so, and not only in Europe but also in Korea and Vietnam, and have we done any better by their peoples? I used to make fun of the English assumption that "the wops begin at Calais" and assume, as I say in this book, that we of the United States had sought to coöperate with the natives of the countries of which we had more or less taken possession, and it is true that there was a difference, at the time of which I was writing, between the English and the American approaches—though I learn that in the Pacific the Americans called the natives "gooks" as the English called the Jugoslavs "Jugs," and that that is what they are now calling the natives in Vietnam. How we behave now I do not know. We have earned the slogan, "Yanks, go home!" In any case, after killing and mutilating so many Koreans and Vietnamese, we can hardly be said to have been helpful. Our talk about bringing to backward peoples the processes of democratic government and of defending the "free world" against Communism is as much an exploit of Anglo-Saxon hypocrisy as anything ever perpetrated by the English. And I must, also, now deflate my boast of twenty years ago that we should probably be able to avoid the evils of the modern bureaucratic state. I did not foresee the present development of our huge official bureaucracies, Pentagon, C.I.A., Internal Revenue Bureau, or that a human bureaucracy of clerks and officials, invested with special powers which are more or less mechanically exercised, would resort in the long run to a mechanical bureaucracy of computers.

The three new sections included here also first appeared in the *New Yorker*.

1966

EUROPE WITHOUT BAEDEKER

1

NOTES ON LONDON
AT THE END OF THE WAR

THE ENGLISH WAY OF GETTING THINGS DONE is quite
distinct from the American way. It is quieter, more
orderly, politer. When our ship was about to dock at
London, a British pilot came aboard to take us up the
Thames. The deckhands had been cleaning the deck and
draining the water out of a hole next to the ladder up
which he was to climb, and one of the sailors now closed
the hole. The pilot, as he appeared over the side, said to
the Norwegian sailor, "Good morning, thanks for stopping the water," and went immediately about his business
on the bridge. I was somehow impressed by this and tried
to think what an American would have said. He would
probably have said nothing at all or would have made
some kind of wisecrack. And so, when the officials of the
port came aboard, it seemed to me that one's dealings
with officials in England were pleasanter and more expe-
ditious than with those of any other country. Even when
they are holding you up, there is no strain and no
friction. The officials of other countries tend to behave as
if they assumed you were a crook, but the British officials
look up at you with a candid and friendly eye which
seems to assume that you are honest. I had the impression

3

later, in London, when I saw people getting their ration books and complying with other wartime regulations, that the whole organization of life for the war had been handled in this same calm and careful way. Compared to England after nearly five years of food rationing, fuel restrictions and the rest, the United States, in its first pangs of privation, seemed hysterical, uncertain and confused.

———

I stayed with a friend in London, who had been in the Ministry of Information. There arrived among his mail, the first morning, a pamphlet with the following title: *Address of the Honorable Archibald MacLeish, Assistant Secretary of State, Before the Annual Meeting of the Association of American Colleges, Atlantic City, New Jersey, January 10, 1945*. He amused himself by reading me passages and demanding, "Now, what does that mean?": "If the direct relations of peoples to peoples which modern communications permit are relations of understanding and confidence, so that the men and women of the world feel each other's presence and trust each other's purposes and believe that the common cause of all the people everywhere is peace, then any reasonably intelligent organization of the world for peace will work. If, however, the direct relations of the peoples with each other are relations of doubt and suspicion and misunderstanding then no international organization the genius of man can contrive can possibly succeed. . . . What is unfortunate about the current designation [of culture] is its suggestion to certain minds that a program of cultural relations is a decoration, a frill, an ornament added to the serious business of the foreign relations of the United States. You gentlemen, who know that a nation's culture is a nation's character, would not so interpret it but others do. And when they do, they endanger the best hope this country now possesses of preparing the climate of understanding in which peace can breathe. The people of the five continents and the innumerable islands can only live together peacefully in the close and urgent contact of modern intercommunication, if they feel behind the jangle and vibration of the constant words the living men and women. It is our principal duty, because it is our principal opportunity, to make that sense of living men and women real. Our country, with its great institutions of education and of culture, is prepared as are few others, to undertake the work that must be done. If we will undertake it, believing in it with our hearts as well as with our heads, we can create, not only peace, but the common understanding which is the only guarantee that peace will last."

What MacLeish was trying to say was that radio and aviation could help bring the nations together as well as enable them to make war more effectively; but this idea, already vague, had been expanded to nine pages of sheer verbalizing nonsense. It is like one of those great wads of spun sugar that are impaled upon little sticks and sold to children at Coney Island. It is embarrassing for an American to arrive in Europe and find that this is what we have been sending them. The Atlantic Charter is not much better.

———

There is about London today a certain flavor of Soviet Moscow. It surprises the Londoners if you remark on this and does not particularly please them. But people told me at the American Embassy that several other visitors who had been in Russia had said the same sort of thing. The regimentation and the tension imposed by the resistance to Germany have produced certain results very similar to those of the effort, during the twenties and thirties, to make the Soviet Union self-dependent. The people look rather shabby, but almost everybody looks equally shabby. A great number are working for the government, and everyone has a definite task. There is the atmosphere of emergency and transition to which everybody has settled down; many things are left undone or unfinished—in London the repair of buildings, in Moscow the carrying out of civic projects—leaving what would in normal times be regarded as intolerable eyesores. There is a great deal of getting oneself registered and of having to have passes, and people are always lining up and waiting for hours in queues. There is also the relative democracy of manners —one of the striking changes in London—of people in the same boat who cannot afford to be too rude to one another, all threatened by a common danger and obliged to work together.

The English, since the war, have, also, been somewhat shut in from the rest of the world, as the Soviet Russians were. Their newspapers today are as meager, though not so misleading, as the Russian ones; their sense of what the other countries are like and of what is going on outside England seems to have become rather dim. People who have been living in London through all or most of the years of the war—unable even to go to the seaside: a great hardship, apparently, for Londoners—all complain of a kind of claustrophobia; and young people in government offices who have had to give up to the war five years of that part of their lives which is usually more pleasantly employed, show the same mixture of boredom with devotion as the young workers for the Soviet economy toward the end of the second Five-Year Plan. As in Moscow, there are women in pants and the problem of neglected children. There is also the quietness of everybody, the submissiveness, the patience, the acceptance. The parks, like Russian parks, seem muted. In the evening people lie on the grass or stroll along the paths or go boating on the Serpentine or play a primitive form of baseball called rounders, and are almost as soundless as the rabbits that, in an enclosure, are munching grass. Even the American soldiers playing the American form of baseball are much less noisy than they would be at home.

———

I had forgotten what a pleasant city London was. No doubt it comes to seem more attractive as New York becomes consistently less so. From the moment a New Yorker is confronted with almost any large city of Europe, it is impossible for him to pretend to himself that his own city is anything other than an unscrupulous real-estate speculation—whereas a capital like London is a place in which people are supposed to live and enjoy some recreation and comfort rather than merely to feed the bank-accounts of landlords. The green parks and the open squares that interlace the whole West End seem enchanting after the windowed expressionless walls, the narrow crowded streets, of New York. The best that Mr. Moses has been able to do, admirable though it is, seems pathetic beside, say, Kensington Gardens, which provide a real escape into the country, not a mere space for benches and asphalt walks. The moist air, which softens form and deepens color, gives all these parks a special charm, as one sees them under pearly clouds in the pale-blue sky of an early April evening or, later, fringed with purple lilacs and studded with white-blossoming chest-nuts, amid turf soft and dense like the air. And though a good deal of fun, at one time or another, has been made of the London statues by people like Osbert Sitwell and Max Beerbohm, it is cheering to a New Yorker with a depressed recollection of the figure of Fitz-Greene Halleck in Central Park, to find, within a short walk in London, monuments to four English poets—Chaucer, Milton, Shakespeare and Byron—and even allegorical statues of the conventional public kind which give a certain effect of vitality: the bronze Victory on one of the big arches driving her horses into the sky and the Saint George of World War I killing a dragon with the Kaiser's mustaches. You realize that the English, through such symbols, almost as much as the French, have managed to keep in the air an admiration for human excellence and an imaginative vision of history. There is, however, one mechanical monument which stands out among these human ones as a bleak unassimilable block—a statue to the Royal Artillery in the shape of a huge howitzer gun. This suggests that the war just ended may eventually bring, for its memorials, bronze bombing planes, marble tanks and granite anti-aircraft batteries. You have already, in fact, something of the kind in the great war monument in Edinburgh Castle—which I saw on a trip to the North—where there are yards and yards of bas-reliefs of men with trench helmets, machine-guns and gas masks, all the complicated unsightly accoutrements in use in the last war. You feel here a definite break in the tradition of human heroism: the armored knights with their plumes and beaked helmets were still caricatures of the human animal; but the big age of engineering has reached the point, in England as elsewhere, of getting this animal quite out of sight. An appropriate monument for the next world war might be simply an enormous rocket which would never have been touched by human hands from the moment it had been shot from its stand.

———

The effect of being attacked from the air by rockets and flying bombs must be something quite new in sensations. While our ship was lying in the Thames on a mild and quiet April day, a rocket went off somewhere not far away among the streets of little London houses on which we were looking out; and the pilot mentioned to someone the next morning that another had just passed overhead. When we got off the boat, we were told that the tram-line was now blocked, due to the blowing-up two days before of the bridge at the end of the street. The word "nightmarish," summoned so often to convey the idea of horror, can hardly be applied to these automatic ex-plosions. A nightmare involves apprehension: the terror must always be expected. The Londoners say that, in the case of the Blitz, you were dealing with other human be-ings, could see them coming and could at least try to do something: a relationship between combatants was es-tablished, so that a strategy could be evolved. But the "doodle bugs" or flying bombs, and, even more, the rockets, came as a disruption completely irrelevant, com-pletely unpredictable, in even an emergency pattern of life. With the rockets there was nothing you could do: you could not either hear them or see them, and you might just as well not think of them at all. Though when you walked through one of those pleasant parks or squares that you were in the habit of passing every day, it might be a shock to find there a sudden great gaping ulcer, the crater of a V-2. Or you might, on some other occasion, be knocked flat in the street and stunned and have to be carried away, or you might be sitting at home and have all your clothes blown off and your skin peppered with masonry and plaster, or you might be annihilated. There were no crises of danger, it was constant; and people had to learn to live with it as a strain from which there was no escape. Nothing, of course, could have been further from the attitude of London during the days of the V-2 rockets than the atmosphere of abject panic described by German

propaganda. At the time the V-2's were falling, there was
an exhibition in Oxford Street which showed a diagram
and model of the rocket and photographs of some of the
damage; and curious people were dropping in, very much
as they did on the waxworks and the fortune-telling
machines.

But those who know what the Germans were preparing
say that, if they had gone on with their program, London
would have been rendered uninhabitable. A commission
which visited the Pas-de-Calais, after that part of the
coast had been cleared, found a whole hillside studded
with giant guns, fixed in their positions and aimed at
London and capable of firing five or six projectiles a
minute; and, in another place, a hilltop which had been
scooped out and equipped with rocket sites for some
larger type of weapon than V-2's.

The London theater, to a New Yorker, is amazing. It
used to be very much less interesting than ours, but it is
at present incomparably better. Our stage has been demoralized by Hollywood: no one really, any more, takes it
seriously. We have very few producers or directors who
would even like to do a good job, and these rarely get to
the point of trying. But in London the theater still exists,
and the war has had the effect of stimulating it to special
excellence. With so much of tight routine in their lives,
so little margin for vacation or luxury, and feeling somewhat helpless in their hemmed-in world, the Londoners—
again like the Russians—have needed the theater for
gaiety, for color, and also—what is very important and
what, for educated people, the American films can't
supply—for the vicarious participation in the drama of
personal emotions which is possible only in peacetime,
when men and women are relatively free.

In the first place, they put on in London plays that are really first-rate. During the month that I spent there, it was possible to see three plays of Shakespeare's (as well as a film of *Henry V*), John Webster's *The Duchess of Malfi*, two plays of Ibsen, two of Bernard Shaw, one of Chekhov, one of Strindberg and, on a lower but still respectable level, two plays by Noel Coward, Somerset Maugham's *The Circle* and a dramatization of Jane Austen's *Emma*. Some of these were brilliantly done, and all that I saw were produced with a kind of theatrical competence that is almost obsolete on Broadway. Not only have the Londoners at the present time an appetite for serious plays, they are also connoisseurs of acting. I found everywhere discussion of actors in their roles of a kind that has not been heard at home since the early years of the twenties. I saw half a dozen of London's top actors: Ralph Richardson, Laurence Olivier, John Gielgud, Cecil Trouncer, Sybil Thorndike and Peggy Ashcroft—performing in repertory companies in which they were as likely to play small parts as big ones and had none of the fantastic billing which has done so much to spoil our theater. *Richard III* and *The Duchess of Malfi* were astonishing to me who had just come from New York and who had not for years—if ever—heard Elizabethan blank verse read without losing the rhythm of poetry and yet with every line comprehensible and effective as human speech. With us this tradition has been lost from the time, I suppose, when John Barrymore was persuaded to play *Hamlet* as if it were all in prose. And today a Shakespearean production in New York may combine a variety of accents, American, British and ham, and a variety of metrical or non-metrical conceptions of the rhythm of Shakespeare's lines in a way that does the poet little justice. But Shakespeare in England is all of a piece and quite natural on the stage, as it never is with us. It is

strange to find that the speeches sound more personal and
forcible and practical, more alive at the present time, than
the people of contemporary London, who beside them
seem thin and dim.

Unlikely though it may appear, the Elizabethan *Duchess of Malfi,* not professionally performed in many years,
is probably the most fascinating show to be seen on the
stage in London. It seems to me, in fact, one of the best
productions that I have ever seen of anything anywhere.
You would think that this old tragedy of blood, with its
grotesque horrors and highly wrought poetry, is the kind
of thing of which a revival would be sure to turn out
boring or comic; but this production by the poet George
Rylands is so immensely imaginative and skilful and the
acting at the same time so dynamic and so disciplined that
it holds you from beginning to end. You might have
thought that Webster's style was too precious for the
stage, but every speech has its force and its point. And
they somehow get the emotions of wartime into both
Richard III and the *Duchess:* the speeding-up of crime
and horror, the cumulative obsession with grievance and
revenge. No: *The Duchess of Malfi* is not funny. You
understand what Gertrude Stein means when she says
that she reread, during the war, in France, Shakespeare's
tragedies and historical plays and realized for the first
time that human life could be like that. One sees the fall
of *Richard III* just as Hitler is staggering to defeat; and,
in *The Duchess of Malfi,* the scene where her doom is
announced to the Duchess amidst the drivellings of the
liberated madmen, at the moment of the exposé of the
German concentration camps.

Thus the theater, like everything else, gives the impression of being breathless and strained, of being ridden
by fatigue and fear. One can gauge in a different way
how desperate the pressure must be when one goes to a

contemporary play which is intended to be consoling. *The Wind of Heaven,* by Emlyn Williams, well done though it, too, was, depressed me by attempting to exploit the need of the people for something to believe in, something to assure them that, after all, there is a merciful God behind the world. Mr. Williams makes a Messiah appear in Wales at the time of the Crimean War: a saintly child who can cure the cholera and about whom is heard in the air the sound of celestial music. But you remember, when you go out of the theater into the blacked-out London streets, that there is no Messiah there.

———

In general, what I have seen of the artistic and literary world, dwindled and starved though it is, is impressive through its good faith and sobriety. These people have been living on the threshold of death, and they have had to pursue their work under the threat of defeat by the Germans and the suppression of their free press, and with, in any event, no prospect of immediate reward in either money or fame. There is, however, as in the case of the theater, a real need that they may take pride in serving.

Here the training of so many of them at Oxford and Cambridge has stood them in good stead. If they are not, so far as I know, turning out anything quite first-rate, they are not letting their standards down—whereas, with us, even the people of talent who have escaped Henry Luce and Hollywood have sometimes inebriated themselves with a frenzy of war propaganda. There are several good English writers who do literary articles for the newspapers, but they do them so very badly that one can hardly recognize their hands, and this does not seem to affect their other work. What is fatal to the American

writer is to be brilliant at disgraceful or second-rate jobs.
A man who has been to Oxford is always likely to keep a
certain residuum that is not much affected by change or
by a different intellectual climate. It is a learning that
involves some wisdom: a detachment toward geography
and history and a steady appreciation of those products of
the human mind that outlast societies and periods. You
can talk to him, more or less, no matter what is happening at the moment and whether or not you share his
opinions. But with the kind of American writer who has
had no education to speak of, you are unable to talk at all
once Hollywood or Luce has got him.

It was also reassuring and pleasant to hear Elizabeth
Bowen say that, except for some disagreeable moments
when "one of those humming things" had landed near
her, she had enjoyed London during the war: "Everything is very quiet, the streets are never crowded, and the
people one dislikes are out of town."

———

I listened, at a literary party, to a conversation between
two writers who were comparing notes about their experiences in the volunteer fire brigades. They had both been
to public schools, and they agreed that it was quite
different from "school." I gathered that what was lacking
was the spirit of the school team: the cockneys who were
sometimes in command merely counted on people to do
the right thing in a more matter-of-fact way. Such a
conversation could hardly have taken place between graduates of American prep schools, in their late thirties as
these men were, because even an expensive education
does not usually unfit Americans to work with other
kinds of Americans and also because at that age Americans would not still be looking back to their school days.
This reversion to public school memories is a conspicu-

ous and curious feature of the recent writing of the
English. I cannot remember that the public school background played any important role in the literature of the
earlier period upon which I was nourished in my teens.
That was the generation of Wells and Bennett, Shaw
and Chesterton, Kipling and Masefield. None of these
men had been to Oxford or Cambridge; none, with the
exception of Kipling, had been to a public school—and
the brutal and raucous version of the second-rate Army
and Navy school that we get in *Stalky & Co.* is as
different as possible from the Winchester and Eton that
we read about in later writers. In the first decades of the
twentieth century, the British middle classes had something to say for themselves: they did not feel any need to
identify themselves with the official governing class. But
—what, at first sight, seems queer to an American—these
writers have had no successors unless you count someone
like J. B. Priestley, who does not particularly interest the
people who were stimulated by the earlier crop of writers.
Instead, you had Strachey and Virginia Woolf, E. M.
Forster and Harold Nicolson, Aldous Huxley and T. E.
Lawrence, all of them—except Mrs. Woolf, who had,
however, her university connections—educated at Oxford
or Cambridge, and in most cases deriving from the official
class or actively engaged in its work. All these have a tone
in common, a common social-intellectual atmosphere,
which are not at all the tone and atmosphere of the
Bennett-Wells-Shaw generation. And the following generation of Connolly, Orwell and Auden grew up in that
atmosphere, too, and have never quite lost that tone. The
more vigorous ones, in their various ways, broke away
from the Bloomsbury circle; but, confronted by the coming catastrophe, they tended at first to creep back into the
womb of the public schools—see the memories of Isher-
wood and Connolly and the earlier poems of Auden—of

which they gave rather an equivocal account, inspired
partly by a childlike nostalgia and partly by an impulse,
perhaps childish, too—one noticed it first in Strachey's
essay on Arnold—to blame the schools for their own
inadequacies and for everything that was wrong with
England. On the voyage over, I read a book by a young
man named Denton Welch, a good deal of which is
occupied with his school days and which presents an
extreme case in point. Denton Welch was desperately
dissatisfied with school and kept trying to get away, yet
he loves to remember his boyhood and seems to want to
remain a baby. When I inquired about him in London, I
learned that he lived in the country and had continued to
write about his teens. There was a certain amount of
dispute as to what his age really was, some insisting that
he has always pretended to be very much younger than
he is. At any rate, he seems to represent the final stage of
this regression toward childhood. He is not at all a bad
writer, but he has never been able to find any other
theme than that of his own attractive youth and its
quarrel with the horrid people who broke in on its
bemused self-consciousness by rudeness or admiration.

It is thus as if the code and the glamor of the traditional upper-class world were the last things to survive in
English letters. You find them in a different form in the
later work of Evelyn Waugh. Beginning, in *Decline and
Fall,* with the comic misadventures of a naïve young man
who has set out to study for holy orders but is first se-
duced and then destroyed by aristocratic friends, he has
ended, in *Brideshead Revisited,* with a bedazzlement by
great houses and noble names that reminds one of romantic lady novelists. The middle classes here occur only
as overbearing *nouveaux riches* or as ill-bred and boring
upstarts. And what, indeed, has become of that old
middle class of which the writers mentioned above were
the spokesmen? Even in the Bloomsbury phase that came

between these generations, the only first-rate non-upper-class figure was D. H. Lawrence, the coal-miner's son, who had almost as little in common with the Bennett and Shaw point of view as he did with Virginia Woolf's. Must we conclude that that articulate middle class which thought it was working for democracy and freedom is now almost completely dead, having failed, in the time of its prosperity, to create a lasting civilization, so that there is nothing today left but a laboring and shopkeeping people, more and more equalized by the pressure of the war services and of wartime restrictions, over whom hangs a fading phantom of the England of the public school?

———

Certainly this new lower middle class, which may be destined to absorb the others, supplies an eager and growing market for the worst—in movies, radio and journalism—that the United States has to send them. Our Hollywood stars are already their stars, our best-sellers their best sellers. To an American, these signs of Americanization seem mostly stale and depressing. The British feed themselves on our banality without catching our excitement and gusto. Many of them now chew gum.

———

The influence of America on England had already gone pretty far when I was here in 1935, and a reaction against it was evident in the humor of the London revues, which were ridiculing the United States at the same time that they were borrowing American jokes and exploiting American methods. Today the influence is more perva-sive, and, though criticism on the stage and in the press is restrained by our relations as allies, the rebellion against it also seems stronger.

Everybody goes to the American films, and everybody

under forty-five of whatever social class seems to say *O.K.* and *That's right,* and the American use of *fix* in the sense of *mend* or *arrange* has also become very common. People, I believe, more often begin statements with *Look* than with the old *I say;* and an American is sometimes startled at hearing a phrase like *het-up* pronounced by an English voice. But the English, as a result of all this and of their recently having been swamped by the American Army and Navy, seem to have become rather neurotic about Americans. They look back on the descent of our troops as an ordeal of almost the same horror as the Blitz or the robot bombs. It must, of course, be a dreadful nuisance to have the people of some other country dumped suddenly upon one's own, and the English have had cause for complaint in the uniformed hillbillies and hoodlums who took advantage of the blackout in London to snatch purses and attack women. In the case of the American officers, whose sometimes obnoxious behavior has astonished as well as outraged them, they cannot understand that in a country like ours, without permanent class-stratifications, there is no section of the population from which officers may be drawn who can be counted on to play the same role as the officers in European countries. A man who gets a commission in wartime may be a well-conducted person or he may be a rough diamond. If he is a blackguard, he will be less trained to conceal it than would be the case in England. This is one of the results of our system which must be faced and accepted for better or worse.

But now that the Army is mostly gone, I had assumed that this resentment had subsided, and was therefore surprised, in London, to hear a good deal of bitter criticism of practically everything connected with America. I had begun by being deprecatory about those products of the United States—*Time* magazine, movies, etc.—to which I objected as much as they did. But I soon found that this was not understood: it is a part of the Englishman's code, probably derived from school games, never to criticize his country to outsiders, and he thinks that if you criticize yours, it is an admission of inferiority. I first became aware of this attitude some years ago at home, in meeting a visiting English scientist who told me that he hesitated to say that he had enjoyed Sinclair Lewis's *Babbitt* because he feared that we might not like it. This seemed to me odd at the time, but I realized, when I came to England, how different in such matters the English point of view is from ours. They do not publicly engage in self-criticism; they are too intent on keeping up face. And I felt that, in comparison with England—or, in fact, with any European country—we were not a *nation* at all—that is, we were not an entity which perpetuated its local breed and had to compete with and protect itself among peoples of other breeds; but a *society* in course of construction, composed of the most diverse elements, in which it was the way of living and not the national existence and occonce that people considered important. Thus the admission of a weakness to a foreigner is, for an Englishman, an act of treason, whereas a satire on Babbitt, for us, is merely a comment on a social tendency.

But eventually I became rather irritated. If the people I met in London did not, as they often did, attack America and Americans directly, they would resort to the old offhand methods which one reads of in books of the last century and for which it seemed to me, in 1945, a little late in the day. One man who had been in the United States pretended to think that Vermont was a town in Florida and that it was pronounced as if it had the same root as "vermiform," and another, an Oxford don who had lectured for a year or so at Harvard, a scholar of enormous reading who quoted lyrics in Portuguese and had the Russian poets all at his fingertips, remarked that he had never read Walt Whitman, who was considered, he understood, a great writer in South America. When I said that *Leaves of Grass* was probably the greatest American book, he asked me whether I thought it even more important than the writings of Whyte-Melville. I did not actually talk with people who believed—though I heard that the legend was current—that the long legs of the American women were due to the prevalence of Negro blood; but I met several well-educated persons who had ideas that were almost as fantastic. George Orwell, for example, believed that the language was being impoverished in America: that we had, for example, few separate names for the different kinds of insects, but called everything "some sort of bug."

With the more offensive people I presently took a tougher line. I would retort that the American soldiers who had committed misdemeanors in England were our revenge for the obnoxious British propagandists who, from the moment the English had realized that they needed us against the Germans, had been sent over to put pressure on us, and I cited examples, in this line, of British atrocities in the United States. The first rebuttal I got was an unperturbed retort that in general the diplomatists and agents who were sent to New York and Washington were not out of the top drawer: when a man did not come up to scratch, he was usually assigned to the States. But my new tactic was not ineffective. The British, though impassive, are pugnacious: they have always stood four-square in their own little country with their fists clenched against the world. They understand giving blow for blow—again, the school-games idea. When the challenge of rudeness was offered, I would take it up in conversations that went more or less like this: "The

English," I would declare, "are fantastically incurious and ignorant about the United States. A friend of mine in Scotland who knows America well was saying that they see North America on the single page of an atlas so that it looks about the same size as England, and so assume that it is a small homogeneous place." "One of the things," my English friend will reply, "that make it difficult for us to learn about America is the inferiority of American books, which are usually so badly written that it is impossible for an Englishman to read them." Or: "The social classes in England are quite different races of beings, who even speak different languages. Perhaps the jargon of the American movies may prove to have this use in England: that it will give them a common medium by which they can communicate." "What about the American Negroes? They seem to be excluded from privilege as no group in England is. And though I am used to talking to Americans, I often find it very hard to understand what a Negro is saying."

This attitude of the English toward America is, of course, partly a wartime phenomenon: a symptom of exasperation, of the peculiar state of mind produced by being penned up at home for five years, and in uncertainty, since 1940, about England's surviving at all. I provoked an immediate resistance whenever I expressed the opinion that Europe, after the war, would have to be governed by somebody or something; but it took me a little time to realize that the English at once assumed that I meant that *we* ought to run it. When I had done so, I would explain that the difficulty would be rather, once the Germans were defeated, to induce the United States to take any further interest in Europe. Yet the British, though they shudder at the notion of any other power's dominating Europe, shrink also from the idea of coöperating, for purposes of international control, with the other great Western countries. They used to reproach us, with reason, for creating the League of Nations and then refusing to take our place in it, but, during my visit, I got the impression that the average educated Englishman is still thinking of the future of the world in terms of old-fashioned balance-of-power, for which nations are irreducible units that can associate in pacts and alliances like the combinations of molecules in chemistry but cannot cohere to produce a new structure by a process of crystallization.

The great difference that one finds between England and the other English-speaking countries is due perhaps mainly, I have come to see, to the fact—of which, obvious though it is, I had not fully appreciated the importance—that the English inhabit an island, whereas the rest of us are spread across whole continents and, with wide spaces of sea around us, unconstrained by menacing neighbors, have acquired a certain nonchalance, a readiness to get on with people, that make the non-English Anglo-Saxon something distinct from the native of England. The Englishman sits tight on his island and makes forays into the outside world which are adventurous or predatory but do not establish friendly relations.

———

I had never before fully grasped what was meant by "British rudeness." The point about it is that what we consider rudeness is their form of good manners. In other countries, manners are intended to diminish social friction, to show people consideration and to make them feel at ease. In England it is the other way: good breeding is something you exhibit by snubbing and scoring off people. This is of course closely connected with their class system, and it is partly a question of accent, vocabulary and general style, which your inferior cannot acquire. I have been told that, when a way of talking begins to pass into common use, the higher people evolve something new which will again fence them off from the lower. Certainly I heard interchanges in London of which I could hardly understand a word. But their competitiveness is also involved: it is a game to put your opponent at a disadvantage, and if you succeed in saying something blighting in a way which makes it impossible for him to retaliate without a loss of dignity more serious than that which he incurs by accepting it, you are considered to have won the encounter. You have the status of King of the Castle till somebody else comes to pull you down. Nothing in this respect seems to have changed since the days of which Henry Adams wrote in his *Education*, when what he had heard described as "the perfection of human society" required that a man should be able to "enter a drawing room where he was a total stranger, and place himself on the hearth-rug, his back to the fire, with an air of expectant benevolence, without curiosity, much as though he had dropped in at a charity concert, kindly disposed to applaud the performers and to overlook mistakes."

For all that with other peoples is understood by politeness or courtesy they have a special word, *civility*, which is spoken of as something exceptional and rather unimportant. To say that a person is *civil* is usually patronizing; to complain of someone's *incivility* usually means that a vulgar person has made himself offensive by breaking the rules of the game and not accepting the inferior position to which you have tried to assign him. They have also as a part of their rudeness what may be called mock considerateness, which may well be described in the words of a distinguished Russian artist with whom I once had a talk about the English. "They're at their worst," he said, "when they're being kind! They scratch you and scratch you and scratch you—and then they take

out a little bandage and graciously bind you up—and
then they begin to scratch again." You find it all in the
Alice books, those wonderful studies of English life and
character. Alice is a little lady; she is supposed to have
been very well brought up; and it is a part of her good
breeding to have learned how to make other people
uncomfortable without ever losing the pretension of being a thoroughly tender-hearted person: " '*Où est ma
chatte?*,' " she addresses the Mouse—"which was the first
sentence in her French lesson-book. The Mouse gave a
sudden leap out of the water, and seemed to quiver all
over with fright. 'Oh, I beg your pardon!' cried Alice
hastily, afraid that she had hurt the poor animal's feelings. 'I quite forgot you didn't like cats. . . . Don't be
angry about it. And yet I wish I could show you our cat
Dinah. I think you'd take a fancy to cats, if you could
only see her. She is such a dear, quiet thing,' Alice went
on, half to herself, as she swam lazily about in the pool,
'and she sits purring so nicely by the fire, licking her paws
and washing her face—and she is such a nice soft thing to
nurse—and she's such a capital one for catching mice—
oh, I beg your pardon!' cried Alice again, for this time the
Mouse was bristling all over, and she felt certain it must
be really offended. 'We won't talk about her any more, if
you'd rather not.' . . . 'Are you—are you fond—of—of
dogs? . . . There is such a nice little dog, near our
house. . . . A little bright-eyed terrier, you know . . .
and it belongs to a farmer, you know, and he says it's so
useful. . . . He says it kills all the rats and—oh dear!'
cried Alice in a sorrowful tone. 'I'm afraid I've offended it
again!' For the Mouse was swimming away from her as
hard as it could go, and making quite a commotion in the
pool as it went." Lewis Carroll meant this to be funny,
and he knew that the nice little English girls to whom the
book would be read would love to hear about the Mouse

being frightened and finally making an unseemly commotion while Alice remained perfectly cool. Yet Alice, with her brutal good manners, was of course constantly jostled and crowded by creatures that were brutal in a more overt way. They were not by any means all mice: she had to stand up for herself among Mad Hatters and Ugly Duchesses, and any English child who read the book would have thought her a little fool if she had not given as good as she got.

Yet they usually seemed rather shocked when I said that the Soviet Union, England and the United States were three very different social systems which had little, among the three, in common, and which were only united at the moment by the accident that they were all afraid of Germany.

The President died April 12; and I went to the House of Commons to hear Churchill pay his tribute to Roosevelt. His speech was, however, held up by a curious and unexpected incident which turned out to be more interesting to an American visitor than the little oration itself. A new M.P., a Dr. Robert McIntyre, who represented the Scottish Nationalist Party, presented himself to be seated without the customary Parliamentary sponsors. Now, it seems that a Member of Parliament, when he first takes his place in the House, is supposed to be sponsored by two other members, who escort him on either side, as, stopping three times to bow to the Speaker, he walks down between the benches. Dr. McIntyre, the spokesman for an intransigent group, had decided to appear alone, in order, as he said, to dissociate himself from "the London party game"; but the result was that the Speaker, in his very high chair and wearing his shoulder-length wig, immediately challenged the Doctor's procedure and, when he began to explain his position, cut him short with, "You have no place to speak from. You cannot make a speech." He was sent to sit behind the bar—that is, to a kind of limbo consisting of a "cross-bench" at the back of the room; and he retired, walking backwards and making the Speaker two more bows. A spirited debate now took place. A Scottish member, Mr. Buchanan, with a strong Scottish accent, urged that the old rule be suspended for a day. Dr. McIntyre, he said, had been "duly elected after fighting both party machines," and was certainly entitled to his seat. Other members objected that the rule had a very important purpose: if sponsors were not required, there would be nothing to prevent any vagabond of the streets from walking into the House of Commons and taking his seat as a member. It turned out that this regulation, in force since 1688, had come in question only once before—in 1875, when a certain Dr. Kenealy had been personally so unpopular that he could not get anyone to sponsor him—on which occasion the requirement had apparently been waived. The supporters of Dr. McIntyre were unable to make any headway. A Conservative member, Earl Winterton, even inquired indignantly whether the House were obliged to tolerate Dr. McIntyre's remaining in the room at all, and provoked from Mr. Buchanan a counter-question addressed to the Speaker: "Could you not order Dr. McIntyre's execution just to satisfy Lord Winterton?" The question of whether or not Dr. McIntyre was to be seated had to be put to a vote. "I could not," said Mr. Churchill, "advise the House on this occasion to depart from tradition and custom. On the contrary, when the British House of Commons is under the gaze of the whole world, and the admiring gaze of a large part of it, we should not in the least shrink from upholding the ancient traditions and customs which have added to our dignity and power."

I had that afternoon been very much impressed, amidst the carvings and the gilt of Westminster, by the spectacle of the opening of Parliament: the huge gold mace, the Speaker framed in his wig, the attendants with their necks rigid and their chins stuck out, all proceeding through the solemn portals while the crowd was made to stand at attention. I had never quite felt before—since we have nothing in the least like this—how dramatic and how compelling these anachronistic rites could be, how much that power and dignity of England of which the Prime Minister spoke still resided in a mystic core of which such things as crown and mace and woolsack were the most conspicuous symbols but which lived and provided an orientation for almost every British subject. As our ship was docking at London, I had been struck when the British stewardess, born in India and married in the States, who had been but once in England, had observed, looking out at the grassy shores: "There's something *worthy* about it, don't you think so?" And yet, now that the Prime Minister was appealing thus for the continuance of an obsolete custom on the ground that it would be a good thing for British prestige abroad—in a word, that it was better publicity—I felt that the power and the glory were perhaps ebbing out of these symbols, that the old virtue was no longer quite there.

I later read in a paper the program of the Scottish Nationalist Party, which included the following points: "The breakup of large landlord states among farmer-owners responsible to the Nation; Government ownership responsible to the Scottish people alone; a central bank and control of private and municipal banks, customs and excise; the curbing of combines by immediate legislation making it illegal for a Scottish firm to sell a majority of its capital to non-Scots and by a differential tax on chain-stores; national ownership of the coal reserves of Scotland"; and, as "war aims," "national freedom for Scotland and all other nations." To an American, these demands of the Scots had a certain familiar ring. I do not know how important this party may be or how legitimate its grievances are. The Englishmen I asked about it smilingly brushed it off, conceding sometimes that it might be a good thing if the Scots had a parliament of their own, which would prove to be merely, they said, a sort of "glorified borough council." But the more open-minded kind of Englishmen, toward the end of the eighteenth century, must have smiled in very much the same way about the demands of the American colonies. At any rate, the oration for Roosevelt was held up while a division took place. The members went out to vote; Mr. Churchill had to withdraw with his speech in his hand. The decision was overwhelmingly for the government, against the seating of the Scottish member: 273 to 74.

———

This quiet laughing-off of the Scottish M.P. and the derouting of his challenge by Parliament led me to reflect on the methods which the English have invented and perfected for warding off inconvenient questions. A favorite device is the False Issue. This is best handled in the tone of light ridicule. They acquire the technique so early that I think they must be trained in it at Oxford. If you do not want to stand by the Poles, you make fun of them for their effervescence, thus implying that they are quite irresponsible; if Gandhi is becoming too powerful, you are amusing about his loin-cloth and goat. Only in more aggravated cases do you resort to moral indignation. If the

Americans expect loans to be repaid, you denounce them as "Uncle Shylock"; if the Irish are becoming importunate, you raise a hue and cry against Parnell on the ground that he has committed adultery. When something atrocious one does has not merely to be defended, but to be perpetrated in the presence of the victim, a special skill and address are required. This demands that the thing be presented either—on the ground of gentlemanliness—in such a way that, if the victim objects, he will appear to be behaving badly; or—on the ground of a manly idealism—in such a way that, if he does not subscribe, he will seem to confess sordid self-interest. I saw later, in Italy and Greece, this game worked again and again on inexperienced and unsuspicious Americans. The point is that, unless you are used to it, you are unable to imagine that a person so correct in appearance and tone as the well-trained British official can be up to anything really outrageous. In America, external crudeness usually goes with a lowness of motive. But in England it is mostly with the humble that the straightforwardness and decency reside. The Norwegian captain of our ship told us that when he was making his first voyages, he was warned by other Norwegians that everybody would try to cheat him, with the single exception of the English. I am sure that this was quite true of the English with whom the captain came into contact; but it is certainly not true of the people who make and carry out British policy or in the higher reaches of British business.

I may mention here, also, a device much in vogue among British intellectuals for the purpose of taking down a rival without sacrificing outward dignity or the semblance of generosity. I forbear from quoting actual examples, but the kind of thing I mean is as if Fletcher were to have said to Shakespeare: "You know, I don't think you ever did anything better than *Love's Labour's Lost*. You had a real lyric gift," etc.

————

Thus an American of English stock, coming to England at a time when we are supposed to be working in close alliance, finds himself estranged from the English more than ever before. We have always, I suppose, an instinct to make connections with the English past from which we have been cut off; and this instinct, at the present moment, finds itself up against a blank wall. It has been brought home to me, certainly, more sharply than it has ever been before, that the real English social revolution occurred, not in England, but in America; and that the United States stands to England in the relation of England's own modern history, as if the first French Republic had been detached and set up in another country, where it was able to prosper in a material way far more than it could have done at home, while the old regime in France continued fighting the old kind of wars with its neighbors and adapting itself, as it had to, to a moderate industrial development.

But the English will not recognize this: they go on pretending that it never happened, and the more the success of the United States is forced upon their attention, the more determined they are to ignore it. It is difficult for an American to grasp the persistence and completeness of this British refusal. We take a friendly interest in England, and we remember the past without rancor; we cannot understand to what lengths the English go in order not to know about us. It is a shock for the American visitor to read in Westminster Abbey the inscription to Major André, and to realize what his monument implies: "Sacred," the legend reads, "to the memory of Major John André, who was raised by his Merit at an early period of Life to the rank of Adjutant General of the British Forces in America, and, employed in an important but hazardous Enterprise, fell a Sacrifice to his zeal for his King and Country on the 2 of October A.D. 1780, aged 29, universally loved and esteemed by the Army in which he served, and lamented even by his Foes. His Gracious Sovereign KING GEORGE the Third has caused this monument to be erected." You would never get the impression from this that André was hanged as a spy, and that his name, in America, was indissolubly associated with the betrayal of Benedict Arnold. The man who died at our hands and was buried at Tarrytown had been dug up and brought to the Abbey, and one could not even get a glimpse through his epitaph at the violent page of history in which he figured. I was not surprised afterwards to notice, in a review of a book by an Englishman who had visited the United States, that he had gone there quite ignorant of the defeat of the British in the War of 1812 and had not known that the British Army had at that time burned the Capitol and the White House—quite unnecessarily and simply, as Henry Adams wrote, "because they thought it proper, as they would have burned a Negro kraal or a den of pirates." Naturally one does not want to keep sore a feud based on ancient injuries; but an American is bound to feel that it is the British themselves who nurse it. We are the only one of the British colonies which has completely got away from the system. We have escaped being exploited like Canada by having our raw materials all taken by England and being prevented from building up our own industries; we were not left disunited like Ireland (though the British hoped to see our disruption at the time of the

Civil War). We broke away from the English and beat them and sent them back to their island; and they have never forgiven this.

———

Altogether this visit to England has been for me almost as much of a revelation of an alien and little-known world as my trip to the Soviet Union in 1935. Though I have five times before been in England, it has been usually just to pass through. I have never before stayed here for any length of time except in the summer of 1914, when, with American college friends, I took a bicycle trip from Scotland to Cornwall, mostly making the rounds of the cathedral towns and consuming large teas in country inns. We saw nothing, except casually, of the people, and the English I had since got to know I had seen mainly in the United States. Now I am having some firsthand experience of that tough-rooted and densely-branched English life which I had learned about principally from books and which seems so unexpectedly different from our looser and shallower growth. I see now that those appalling novels which we read for amusement in America and which seem to us half fairy-tales like Homer, the myths of a remote and archaic world—*Vanity Fair, Bleak House, The Way of All Flesh*—are true pictures of English society. They do not represent, as we tend to think, merely the cynical worldliness of Thackeray, the grotesque imagination of Dickens, the grievances against his family of Butler: they portray basic English qualities, with which, after nearly two hundred years, Americans have to reckon again: the passion for social privilege, the rapacious appetite for property, the egoism that damns one's neighbor, the dependence on inherited advantages, and the almost equally deep-fibered instinct, often not deliberate or conscious, to make all these appear forms of virtue. I have lately often thought of these books. When you know that they deal with realities, they become so much more powerful and terrible than the criticism of irreverent outsiders. Beside them, Bernard Shaw seems a popular Irish entertainer and his satire mere persiflage. A more deadly description by a foreigner is that by Henry James in *The Wings of the Dove*, which has also been much in my mind where the relations between Americans and English are concerned. Here the American disinterested idealism, indiscriminate amiability and carelessness about money, along with the aimlessness and petering-out of Americans who have made themselves rich and their helplessness outside of America, are contrasted with the desperate materialism that is implied by position in England. *We* find making money exhilarating, but we also find it exhilarating to spend it. Money for us is a medium, a condition of life, like air. But with the English it means always property. A dollar is something that you multiply—something that causes an expansion of your house and your mechanical equipment, something that accelerates like speed; and that may be also slowed up or deflated. It is a value that may be totally imaginary, yet can for a time provide half-realized dreams. But pounds, shillings and pence are tangible, solid, heavy; they are objects one gains and possesses. And in England every good value is bound up with the things one can handle and hold.

———

I stayed for a time at the Hyde Park Hotel, which still managed to keep up the appearances of a Victorian comfort and grandeur. The waiter asked me what I wanted to order for breakfast in my room the next morning. When, in reciting the meager menu, he mentioned scrambled eggs and sausages, I said, "That's fine!—

bring me that." "That's not what they usually say when they see it, sir," he dampeningly replied. I should have done well to take his warning, for, when my breakfast came, the eggs turned out to be concoctions of egg-powder, and I saw what someone had meant when he told me that sausages in England were now a form of bread.

———

The strain of the war has made the English irritable, and it may be that these notes are affected by the atmosphere of general resentment in which Americans, too, are involved.

I had dinner one evening with a Labour man who had a job in the Air Ministry and with a journalist who had fought for the Loyalists in Spain and was now an anti-Stalinist radical. It was the moment, near the end of April, when the Americans and the English had nearly completed their hideous work of ploughing Germany under, and the conversation, over the coffee, was becoming quietly ghoulish. The official archly remarked that, when the Germans went home after the war, they would find their country "rather changed." The radical, in reminding us that Warsaw had been "completely wiped out," gave a kind of involuntary grin—but presently caught himself up: "Who could have imagined," he said, "six years ago, that we should soon be talking in this frivolous way about the destruction of whole popula-tions?" I had often thought of this myself. Through the whole of the previous war some humanitarian feeling survived and continued to assert itself: it was assumed that the misery and slaughter were abnormal and unde-sirable. There had been Harden, Rolland, Barbusse, Ber-trand Russell and Bernard Shaw, Upton Sinclair and John Dos Passos—to say nothing of Lenin and the socialists of the Zimmerwald Conference—to protest against the war as a bad thing in itself. But today it is perfectly plain that human life is no longer an issue. No one pretends to give a damn any more—unless they are one's close friends or relatives—whether people are killed or not. After the first shock of the German bombings, we in America followed the contest between the Royal Air Force and the Luftwaffe as if they were football teams. After we ourselves became involved, nobody but an occasional old liberal like Oswald Garrison Villard, to whom nobody paid attention, seemed to feel any scruples whatever. The newspaper reports of our bombings were designed to make them sound quite jolly. "Smiling skies," one would read in the dispatches, "sent out flying squadrons"; when our planes destroyed the monastery at Monte Cassino, the building "blew apart like a house of cards," and the Germans ran out "like ants"—as if they had not been human beings. When we began to smash up Berlin, people said that it was an ugly city and that its buildings were no great loss. We have, to be sure, had to be treated, like the Germans, with a certain amount of indoctrination to arrive at this point of indifference. We have had to be convinced, as they are, that the enemy are not really people. Just after the official reports of the Japanese atrocities had been published, I went to a movie newsreel which had been made to arouse the public. First you were given a dose of the dead or still writhing bodies of Chinamen slaughtered by the Japs; then you heard one of the American officers who had suffered at the hands of the enemy and who declared that he had been convinced that the Japs were no better than "animals"—at which point the announcer took it up and pounded it home with ferocity: "You hear what Captain So-and-So says. He thinks that the Japs are animals. And now we must fight these *animals*! We must buy bonds to defeat these *ani-*

mals!" Goebbels hardly used a different technique in working up the Germans to the point at which it seemed to them quite natural to attempt to exterminate the Poles and the Jews; and our efforts have been equally successful. We can contemplate now with equanimity, with a cheerful self-satisfaction, a kind of warfare that crushes whole cities and that brings down agony and death on thousands of women and children.

Yet the long-continued concentration on killing people whom we rarely confront, the suppression of the natural bonds between ourselves and these unseen human creatures, is paid for by repercussions, the spitefulness of fear and stifled guilt, in our immediate personal relations. Our whole world is poisoned now, and we must recognize that outlawing the enemy makes it easy to dislike one's allies.

———

When I was finally leaving England, the officials were equally polite, but it turned out that, from the British point of view, my papers were not in order. By that time I had the status of a war correspondent, and I had not been provided by the American bureau with a permit from the Allied Forces office, so I was not allowed to fly that morning but made to go back to London to equip myself with the necessary document. The American authorities, when I returned to them, insisted that I did not need this passport, that my papers *had* been in order, and a certain amount of animated argument was carried on over the telephone. I had a glimpse, in the course of all this and of some later complications, of the conflicting tendencies, in Europe, of the British and the American methods. The British handle their formalities entirely without fuss, but they are very exact about them. They were quite correct, I found, in telling me that the permit they insisted on my having would be asked for when I arrived in Italy. On the other hand, if I had not had it, the Americans would certainly have let me through. The point was that a new kind of credential had just gone into use with the Americans without the British having had notification. But the American officials thought that the fact that they sent a man to an airport provided with American credentials ought to be enough for the British.

The Americans like to act for themselves and to do things with a freer hand. They do not always take the routine of their paperwork quite so seriously as the British do. To the latter, they doubtless seem hit-or-miss, and they probably make annoying mistakes of a kind that is rare with the British. It is the result of having more space to move in, more margin of resources to dispose of. With the British every penny counts and every link in the chain must be tight. They do not understand our looser methods—the methods of a big gang of men working together with a minimum of formality to get something quickly accomplished, so that they can sit down and eat a good dinner.

2

ROMAN DIARY: ARRIVAL; A VISIT TO SANTAYANA

From the air, the green and deep-chocolate fields make intarsia like the floors of Herculaneum. Then a countryside that has lost its rural pattern to the scrawlings of attack and defense and been left notched with boomerang-shaped trenches and perforated with the craters of shells. Some of the houses still keep their pink roofs, but many are stove-in or broken barnacles. The cattle look as small as lice. Even after you have landed, it is hard to grasp that you have really come to Rome. You are still in the world of the air, as, from the airfield, you watch sturgeon-snouted planes taking off like fish surprised in shallows.

The man who drove me into Rome turned out to come from Massachusetts, and we talked about the cranberry crop on Cape Cod. They had written him that the warm spell in March had brought the cranberries out prematurely, and he was worried for fear a frost would kill them. The freshness of the campagna in the morning, with the donkey-carts going to town, excluded any idea of its antiquity. I asked the driver about some old stumps of Roman ruins—fragments of brown brick masonry, with weeds growing out of them like hairs on warts—and he answered, "I guess that's the old water line." They seemed sordid and completely irrelevant to the beautiful clear spring morning and the familiar-looking American gas station where we stopped to fill up our tank.

———

Rome astonished me by its brilliance and cleanness. I had not been here since 1908, when I was thirteen years old, and what I remembered was rather an ignoble modern city, dirty, commonplace and somewhat provincial, with enormous ancient monuments embedded among hotels and shops. What I found, at this bright end of April—as we ripped into the Piazza Venezia and caught a view of the Colosseum behind the dazzling and dripping white frosting of the immense Victor Emmanuel Memorial—seemed, amazingly, as smart and as sparkling as any city of pre-war Europe. Mussolini *had* evidently done something for Rome in policing it and building it up. Flimsy and rather chichi though so much Fascist architecture is, the solarium-like modernist buildings of light-tinted plaster and glass give the city a kind of *élan;* they are much more cheerful and perhaps no more jerry-built than the same sort of thing in Moscow.

One feels in the air, after London, the freedom and exhilaration of a people who, earlier than the rest, have escaped from the repressions of the war; and, after Naples, it is reassuring to find Italians who seem self-respecting, well-washed and well-dressed. There are many people riding bicycles, which have gleaming handle-bars and spokes and all of which seem to be more or less new. The women are remarkably handsome, and it is wonderful how they have managed, with materials so poor and scant, to get themselves up so effectively. Their short skirts always seem well hung, and their raised wooden pattens with straps at the heels, in which they walk with bare feet, are the only attractive footwear that I have seen

since I came to Europe. They also know how to do their
black hair so that they always look tempting from behind
even when their faces, as one passes them, turn out to be
long-featured or coarse. One feels that these Roman
women have a natural ineradicable chic that is common
to all sections and classes. And the bookstores and newsstands are fizzing and frothing with the covers of new
books and reviews, of which the white or pink or green
paper-backs have kept that lavish Italian touch—in ample
spaces and ornamental typography—that is so different
from the sober prose elegance of the yellow-backs of
Garnier or Calmann-Lévy. I have never seen so many
bookstores, news kiosks and wandering book-carts in any
city, even Paris, and the quantity and variety of translations, as well as the modern French classics reprinted in
French, would give, if nothing else did, a cosmopolitan
tone to the streets. American and English novels that one
knows in their original native boards get a flavor of Asti
Spumante from their lively Italian titles: *La Via del
Tabacco, L'Amante di Lady Chatterley,* and (James M.
Cain's) *In Due Si Canta Meglio.* I am surprised to see
the vogue of Herman Melville, all of whose novels they
seem to be translating. The walls are covered with
posters, remarkably well designed, exhorting the public to
buy war bonds; declarations in fine black-and-white, full
of rhetoric against the Fascists; and—gashing the surface
of the city, keeping open the recent wounds—the reiter-
ated outcry of the Communists: a hanged man on a
gallows, with the slogan *"Vendichiamoli."*

The little cakes in the *pasticcerie* looked appetizing and
perfectly normal—I had tried some in Naples, which had
been gritty and gooey and depressingly deficient in sugar;
but when I went into one of the most tempting of these
places and sat down at an outside table, it proved to be
embarrassing and uncomfortable. You found yourself not

far from a group of pallid and ragged people who were
waiting to get into a door where the Americans were
giving them a handout; and you were buzzed about by
little dirty kids with an eye on the sweets you were
eating, whom the waiters shooed away like flies but who
were always back the moment after.

———

Just before I had left New York, I had received, with
surprise and pleasure, a copy of *Persons and Places*,
inscribed to me by George Santayana, so I thought it
might be in order for me to look him up in Rome.

The Colosseum was terrific as I came upon it, or rather
as it came upon me, out of antiquity and out of my
childhood. I had forgotten how big it was. On the first
day, when I had merely had a glimpse of it behind the
Victor Emmanuel Monument, I had seen it, at the end of
a vista arranged by Mussolini which took it down from its
full stature and made it look, as someone said, like a man
on his knees. But now that it rose to its imperial height, it
seemed gigantic even by modern standards, and I felt
dazed and almost incredulous at finding myself suddenly
dropped down in Rome and going to see Santayana
behind the Colosseum. I walked around the old Madison
Square Garden, which, so unlike the American building,
embodied, in its grimness and grandeur, a human attitude
that made it an official mask; between it and the Arch of
Titus; and along the cobbled Via Claudia, with, on the
one hand, a scratched yellow wall and, on the other, a
dense texture of purplish-pink brick, the rubbed and
eroded remains of some long-demolished ancient building,
that showed holes like a crumbled sand castle and looked
dishevelled with dry dusty shrubbery bristling down from
the top. Then a tunnel of low acacias that overarched a
quiet street; another old wall that screened off what?—

there were so many kinds of things in Rome, all mixed up yet with walls between them. Then a street out of the eighteenth century, with high pediments over the windows and brown shutters spread wide on the gamboge walls. Then the Via di Santo Stefano Rotondo. Here, among the dead relics of the Caesars' Rome, there had grown, through the Christian centuries, convents and churches that are still intact and evidently more or less living. The street, with no footpath, all cobbles, that slopes toward undulating old gutters, follows the curve of another wall, grass-grown and of irregular height, with, here and there, deep gouged-out scars and the arches of bricked-up doors. Below an antique iron lamp on a black iron arm that contained an electric bulb, a man and a girl were silently kissing.

There was an entrance through this ancient wall to the Hospital of the Blue Nuns, to which, after the outbreak of the war, Santayana had come to live. The order was Irish, and their convent enjoyed some sort of extraterritoriality: an English-speaking non-citizen like Santayana was presumably safer here than elsewhere. Inside all was snug and decent in rather a non-Roman suburban way: the straight cypresses, the well-trimmed lawn, the green-shuttered orange building, the little tinny dome that looked as if it belonged to a small college observatory. I inquired at the gatekeeper's house and was told by a little girl that there was *un dottore, un professore,* who must be the person I asked for. The Blue Nuns were decorative and fantastic, for they actually wore great starched head-dresses that had been dyed with some deep bluing. They were English and said at once that the professor was always glad to see people. They wanted to take me right in, but I thought they had better announce me and make sure that he wanted to receive me, so I waited in the dark little parlor, very British and middle-class with its sentimental modern Catholic pictures, till the nun appeared again and led me out and down a long corridor.

Santayana came to the door in a plain brown dressing-gown, with a cord like a Franciscan friar's. I had not expected to find him so slight. Never tall, he must have shrunk with age, and the smoothness and blandness of the face that one sees in the photographs has faded and lost its mold; but his round black Latin eyes have remained alive and attentive. His complexion is more swarthy than I expected and his nose, seen in profile, more pointed. He received me with simplicity and courtesy and excused himself for reclining on a little chaise longue with a blanket over his legs. He occupied a single room, in which he both worked and slept. There was a table at his right, with papers and books, and, at his left, a small bed, concealed by a screen. There was almost nothing else in the room.

I thanked him for sending me his book. "Did I send you a book?" he asked. "I don't think I sent it to you," he said gently when I replied that he had and told him my name. "You wrote in it," I tried to remind him. "The publishers sent out copies," he suggested. "They must have written in it." "No," I insisted. "It seemed to be your writing and it was dated Rome." "I have a poor memory for names," he murmured. He seemed to want to slip away from the subject, but I was nonplussed and embarrassed at coming to see him when he did not know who I was. I said something more in an attempt to establish with him the right connection, and in a moment the explanation had occurred to him. "An American soldier came here," he said, "and asked me to autograph some copies. Perhaps you got one of those."

With a freedom that surprised me, however, he at once began talking about his recent books: *Persons and Places* and *The Middle Span;* and so about his career and his family. He was evidently rather dissatisfied with the form in which his memoirs had had to appear. He had wanted to include illustrations, but the conditions of war had made it impossible to collect or transmit the photographs (the manuscript itself had had to be smuggled out of Italy); and there had been things in the second volume about certain of his American friends which, against his own inclination, another friend had induced him to omit. The third volume, though already completed, couldn't, for personal reasons, be published till after his death. As he spoke of the people he had known in connection with his portraits of them in these memoirs and in *The Last Puritan*, his small mouth would occasionally twist in a mischievous little smile, as if he had been still a clever boy at Harvard. Except physically, he seemed hardly to have aged: he had none of the pomp of authority, none of the arrogance of reputation, but merely an old-fashioned politeness that was cool and yet quite informal. All he felt he had to know about me in order to talk of himself was that I was one of his readers.

His position—between two civilizations—had been, he went on, unusual, and he had dealt with it in an unusual way. His mother and father, both Spaniards, had been more or less identified with the Philippines, and he had never been sympathetic with the idea of Anglo-Saxon domination. Yet he had lived in the United States through the period—the nineties and the early nineteen-hundreds—when this ideal had been in the ascendant and, in associating himself with American institutions, had in a sense been "taking the side of the enemy." He had never been willing to "coöperate," to propagandize in any form for the Spanish, any more than for the American, side. It seemed to me, indeed, as I talked to him, as it had in reading his books, that he was perhaps the most international—or, better, the most super-national—per-

sonality I had ever met. I told him that the United States
was less predominantly Anglo-Saxon now, and he said
that he knew that was true: he could see by the literature
they sent him from Harvard that the University was
"reaching out tentacles" in a way that was very unlike the
old narrow Anglo-Saxon conception of Harvard. And
now the United States *had* been called upon to play a
great role. America and Russia had emerged as the
principal powers in the world. People had used to talk,
when we were annexing the Philippines and Cuba, of the
"Manifest Destiny" of the United States. It wasn't Manifest Destiny now, but a demand that had been made
upon America in the natural course of things, and he had
always believed that when it happened that such demands were made upon one, one had to accept the
responsibility: not to do so was to make *"il gran rifiuto."*
And the situation of South America was thus, also, now
to be changed. We, and not Spain any longer, were to
become the chief influence there. Well, he had always
been against the idea of Spain's influencing South
America, just as he had been against the idea of England's influencing the United States.

I said that I had just been in England and started to
speak of the exacerbated antagonism of the English toward the Americans. "You don't have to tell me!" he
stopped me. He had talked often with an English colonel
who had escaped from an Italian prison and had been
hidden by the nuns—"it was courageous of them"—for
months in the hospital there. He had seen that this
colonel was troubled about England's losing her place in
the world. He had himself lived in England and he liked
the English; they had taken him in in a friendly way,
and, if he had been given a chair at Oxford, which had
seemed possible at one time, he might have spent the rest
of his life there. But eventually, as usually happens, he

had, I gathered, been rebuffed or frozen. He had delivered, he said, two public lectures. At the first one—a
reading of a chapter from *Character and Opinion in the
United States*—the people had responded: they had
laughed (at the expense of the Americans, no doubt).
But at the second there had been certain things—he
touched on them rather gently: something about the bad
lighting and the way he had been introduced—and he
had known, when he sailed for the Continent, that he
would never go to England again. The English were like
the French, he explained. He liked France very much in
some ways, and, if the French had not been so narrow, he
might perhaps have lived in France. But they were
occupied with their own interests to a degree that made
real intercourse with them difficult—everything else was
only politeness. "And the English are not polite," I
suggested. "The English are not polite," he confirmed. I
was struck both by his sensitive feeling in his relations
with other people and by the contrasting or compensating
detachment with which he seemed to have passed the
cities in review and chosen the one that fitted him best.

It was somehow a little uncanny to hear him talk about
the outside world and show a grasp of what was happening there. I had felt, when I first came in, that the
atmosphere of the convent was spooky, and, while we
were talking, it had begun to rain, so that the room had
become rather dark. It was at the same time respect-
inspiring and disturbing to one's wartime preoccupations
to find this little husk of a man, at once so ascetic and so
cheerful, sustaining at eighty-one so steady an intellectual
energy, inhabiting a convent cell, among the layers of
historical debris that composed the substance of Rome,
intact and unmoved by the tides of invasion and revolution that had been brawling back and forth around him;
and when he talked about these outside occurrences, it

was as if he attached them to history: the war was an
event like another which would presently belong to the
past.

I think that he fancied himself in his role of monastic
sage, and that his drab Franciscan dressing-gown was not
perhaps altogether an accident. He told me, as if it interested and pleased him, that he had lived there for two
years without money. He had not been able to get any
from America and the nuns had given him credit—
though he now paid like any other inmate. He believed
that the war had prolonged his life by forcing him to
come to the convent. Before that, he had been growing
fat, and his friends had been rather disapproving of what
they considered his too comfortable life, which they felt
was doing damage to his spiritual side—they thought that
his condition was becoming "quite vicious." But now the
diet had made him thinner. He had little to eat but the
vegetables that were raised by the nuns in their garden—
with, usually, an egg for dinner. Even the colds he used
to have had disappeared since he had been eating less.
And if it hadn't been for the war, he would certainly
have travelled and worn himself out sooner "not that it
matters now," he added. He had had something like a
stroke last winter. He used to walk all over Rome, but he
was forced to be careful now. He had intended to go to
Avila, because he had friends and near-relatives there,
but, if he had done so, he would have had certain duties,
have had to occupy himself with family affairs, and it had
been rather a relief, after all, to be obliged to stay in
Rome. And then, he would have had to speak Spanish,
and he did not really speak it well. The Spanish they had
spoken at home had always been rather mechanical—his
mother had never spoken any language really well. (It
seemed to me extremely characteristic that he should thus
have felt the necessity of speaking Spanish as an objec-

tion to visiting Avila. It was not merely, I thought, the shrinking of age from the trouble of doing something not habitual but partly a reluctance, toward the end of his life, when he had shown himself a master of English, to try to express himself in a medium which he was not able to handle brilliantly. He had remarked that it was a great advantage to be able to speak English in the hospital—though, of course, he spoke Italian, too.) He would also like to go to America, but he wouldn't, because he would have to be entertained, and he knew that he could never survive it. I thought that he was proud of his reputation in America and of his American career and connections. In his earlier days, he said, his work had not been known at all, but now even his earlier books were being read. Yet his point of view, he added, was unfashionable, since he dealt with things not in the modern way but rather in terms of the mediaeval categories.

He had evidently, during his stay in the convent, accomplished an immense amount of work—though he spoke of having written, or of wanting to write, "something," as if it were merely a method of passing the time. I felt, as I had done already in reading his later books, that he was a writer of passionate vocation; that this writer had been in abeyance during the years of his academic service, when he had had to play the specialized philosopher, but had been fledged on his emergence from Harvard and had triumphed in the solitude of his later life, when, even more than through his early verse, he had revelled in a poet's power. He had just done a small book about Jesus, which was a result of his seclusion in the hospital, where, failing other reading matter, he had had to fall back on the books of the nuns. He had been through the whole of the Bible, a good deal of St. Thomas Aquinas and a number of Catholic novels, which he had found of a certain interest. Besides his memoirs and this book on the New Testament, he had been writing a long treatise on politics, of which he showed me the high stack of manuscript on the table beside his chair. He had not dealt with the two world wars in his memoirs because he had been discussing them there. He had been much concerned, he said, with the first one, and written books that had been inspired by it directly; but he had only been aware of the second as he was of the Battle of Cannae.

He touched on a number of subjects with the blend that one finds in his books of sympathetic appreciation and a skepticism that was slightly mocking. When I spoke of the relative freedom that I had felt in the atmosphere of Rome, as if the people had been really revived when they got rid of the Fascist machine, he said that the regime, at its best, had had certain very admirable features. For one thing, they had done a lot for the young people. And they had been helpful—to him, I gathered—in a way that was characteristic of Americans, but ordinarily unknown in Europe. And then his irony began to creep in. He had received a letter one day inviting him to become a Roman citizen. He had gone to the bureau indicated and explained that he was a Spanish subject and that that was what he preferred to remain. They told him that becoming a citizen of Rome would not interfere with this. What were the obligations involved? he asked. Very simple: you paid so many lire. So, he said, he had declined the honor and had not availed himself of this chance "to become *civis Romanus.*"

He thought that it had probably been thanks to the Pope that Rome had not been bombed, and he went on to discuss with much interest the Church's internal politics. No new cardinals had lately been appointed: there were only forty now where there should be sixty-nine (the seventieth is never appointed). The Pope was waiting till after the war so as to get them from both sides: some from Germany; the Archbishop of Westminster, undoubtedly; some from the United States. I said that the Catholic Church at home was playing, as a pressure group, a new and rather sinister role. It also worked the other way, he answered America was a pressure on the Vatican. They depended on American money, as everybody in the world now did. Then the irony set in again. "A very great man," he said—with a pleasantry which deftly diminished this man's inflated reputation—"is coming to see me here." He named a celebrated Catholic convert on an official mission to Rome. "I think there's something of the Calvinist about him," he said when I asked him his opinion of this man. "He's unforgiving with his enemies. I like the Catholics better when they're charitable." Someone, he remarked in the conversation that followed, had said about him, Santayana, that he himself was a Catholic in everything but faith. I remembered that a friend of his had told me of Santayana's once having said: "There is no God, and Mary is his mother."

I thought that I was staying too long and made a move to go; but "Don't go unless you want to," he said, and I saw that he was really glad to talk. I had gotten, from people who had known him, the impression that he was rather inaccessible, but I had found that the opposite was true and that what they had meant was something else, which I shall try to explain in a moment. One of the wonderful things about him was, on the contrary, the readiness and grace with which he played a classical role: that of the sage who has made it his business to meet and to reflect on all kinds of men and who will talk about the purpose and practice of life with anyone who likes to discuss them—as with me, whom he didn't know from Adam—since these are matters which concern us all. On his dignity and his distinction he did not need to insist:

he let them take care of themselves; and his attitude toward a visitor—an attitude rather rare with the literary and the learned—was simply that of a man in the world who was trying to make some sense of it as you were. He now developed, at some length and with a vividness which I cannot reproduce, a theory that Western philosophy had made three crucial false steps in its history. The first had occurred when Socrates had "put the physical world under the heel of the moral." Socrates himself, in the beginning, had limited himself strictly to the moral, but his followers had made things worse by bringing in the metaphysical. The second *"faux pas,"* as he called it, had been the mistake of the Reformation when it had taken and perpetuated all that had been bad in paganism instead of reviving, like the Renaissance, the elements that had been good. The third had been the mistake of the German idealistic philosophers like Kant (and not merely of the Germans, but also of Locke, Hume and Berkeley) in adopting the impossible position that the order of discovery of objects comes before the order of their genesis—as if (he laughed) the idea of our grandfather came before the fact of our grandfather! He talked about the German philosophers—as in his witty and deadly book, *Egotism in German Philosophy*—with an instinctive antagonism, which he tried, not entirely successfully, to temper with detachment and humility. Schopenhauer and Nietzsche, he said, he had never had any difficulty in following, but the others he could not follow. Not that he criticized them on that account: he felt that it was his fault and wished he could. But the point of view of the idealistic philosophers was completely inacceptable to him. "For me," he said, "our conception of the flaming sun is a sensation of the same order—an essence [in the special sense that he has assigned to this word in his system]—as the older conception of Apollo with his golden rays. Neither is an object that we know, as the idealistic philosophers believe."*

When at last I arose to go, I made another attempt to get to the bottom of the mystery of the autographed book that had been sent me. I asked him how he had come to know my name. "Oh, I didn't know it," he said mildly. "The man who brought the books had a list of names of people that he thought would like to have them." I felt, as I left, that the philosopher derived a certain satisfaction from treating me with amiability but not knowing or caring who or what I was. I remembered Gilbert Seldes' telling me that he had taken a course with Santayana at Harvard and that, at the end of the final lecture, when they had given him a great ovation, Santayana had dropped his eyes and seemed for a moment on the point of making some acknowledgment of it, but then had apparently thought better of this and allowed the class to leave without a word; and it came back to me, also, that Logan Pearsall Smith had written of Santayana: "How he gives himself to you, pours out the rich stores of his mind, and forgets all about you the moment you leave the room! He doesn't dislike you, and doesn't like you or anyone else." I had mentioned in our conversation having recently met two persons of whom he had once seen a good deal, and had been struck by his total failure to show even a conventional interest in how they were or what they were doing. In Rome, I discovered, he was person-ally not known, had never even been met, by American and Italian residents who seemed to know everybody else

* When *My Host The World,* the final volume of Santayana's autobiography, came out after his death, I found that he had simply been repeating to me something he had just written: "He [Bertrand Russell] seemed one day astonished and horrified when I said that the image of the sun as a luminous disc, sometimes (if you squint) with rays round it, is as fictitious and imaginary as the idea of Phoebus Apollo with his golden hair and arrows."

in the intellectual world. The only time I ever heard of his having been seen by anyone but me was when he came to the Embassy one day to attend to some necessary formality. Yet I do not think that Pearsall Smith is right in declaring that he "doesn't like anyone." On the evidence of his memoirs, it is obvious that some of his friendships have been deep and lasting. He spoke to me of certain complaints on the part of the reviewers of these books that he had written at too great length about people of little importance; but "I wrote about them," he protested, "not because they were public figures but because they were important to *me*!"

It would not be precisely true to say that Santayana is narcissistic, but he is interested in his own thought as a personal self-contained system, and in his life as a work of art which owes its integrity and harmony partly to a rigorous avoidance of indiscriminate human relationships. The objective materials with which his mind works have been the systems of other thinkers and the assumptions underlying civilizations. It is easy to see, when one meets him, how his attitude toward the world has derived from his personal characteristics and from the circumstances of his life. A pure Latin of small stature, with fastidious taste and a subtle mind, it was his fate to spend most of his formative years living among Anglo-Saxons. In another man this position might have produced an alternation of the defiant with the propitiatory; but Santayana has subjected himself to a self-discipline which has kept him both firm and, as he said to me of his relations with the English, "discreet." The discretion is self-protective, the mockery a tempering of insolence. I felt occasionally, in his tone about other people a suggestion of something feline which was perhaps not quite congruous with the true Socratic irony; and he seems always to have found it difficult to resist a display of virility. Unsympathetic with the Germans, he yet admired the officers in uniform that he saw in his student days; and his weakness for Mussolini may partly have been due to a similar reaction.

But to say this is merely to say that the books of George Santayana have been written by a human being; and one is, if anything, even more impressed by him after meeting him than one had been in reading these books. The image of him came back to me afterwards in the course of the solitary evenings that I spent when I was first in Rome: alone, with his plain table and his narrow bed, so far from Spain and from Harvard, yet with all the philosophies, the religions and the poetry through which he had passed making about him an iridescent integument, the manners of all the societies in which he had sojourned awhile supplying him with pictures and phrases; a shell of faded skin and frail bone, in which the power of intellect, the colors of imagination, still burned and gave out, through his books and his gentle-voiced conversation, their steady pulsations and rays, of which the intensity seems even to increase as the generator is more worn by use. I do not imagine he is troubled by the thought of death or that it even impinges as a shadow: his present so triumphant functioning appears to absorb and enchant him. Nor is he really alone in the sense that the ordinary person would be. He is still in the world of men, conversing with them through reading and writing, a section of the human plasm that, insulated by convent walls and by exceptional resistances of character, still registers the remotest tremors. He has grown, it seems, almost immune to physical or emotional shock. While others, in these years of the war, have been shaken by the downfall of moralities or have shuddered under the impact of disaster, while they have been following the conflict with excitement, his glass has scarcely clouded or brightened; but the intelligence that has persisted in him has been that of the civilized human race—so how can he be lonely or old? He still loves to share in its thoughts, to try on its points of view. He has made it his business to extend himself into every kind of human consciousness with which he can establish contact, and he reposes on his shabby chaise longue like a monad in the universal mind.

3

ROMAN DIARY: SKETCHES FOR
A NEW PIRANESI

SET DOWN SUDDENLY IN ROME TODAY by an American
army plane and still feeling yourself a part of the American war-machine that has clamped itself upon Europe,
your first involuntary reaction to the Forum is likely to be
that all that irrelevant old rubbish—the broken stones
and the chunks of brick—ought to be cleaned up and
carted away and the place turned into a nice public park.
The columns, single prongs or small clusters, that have
lost their companions or mates, give the impression of
useless old teeth that ought to be pulled to make room for
the bridgework of a modern colonnade. A playground for
the Roman poor is what the Forum just now mainly
serves for. Little children with gray clothes and dusty legs
climb up on the loosely piled marble or play train, astride
a fallen length of column, while their mothers sit around
on scattered fragments. It is difficult to focus your mind to
the consciousness that these rounded flags—with enormous lacunae among them, like the gaps in an ancient
text—are actually the Via Sacra, where Horace met the
bore. But the Temple of Faustina wrenches you up to
confront that giant world, as it lifts out of the dirt and
debris its tremendous steep brick steps and its façade of

stupefying grandeur, a huge intact block of antique Rome. Below it, the Allied Commission has put up, for the instruction of the troops, a large sign in dubious English, which mixes Latin with Italian names:

Temple of Antonio and Faustina

Begun 141 AD following the death of Faustina, wife of Antonio Pius and who was declared a goddess by the Roman Senate. When the Emperor died he was made a Joint Patron Deity of the Temple.

Beyond, on the Palatine Hill, stretches the shapeless agglomeration of the Palaces of the Caesars, with empty eyeholes in their grass-sprouted brick and, at the top, a fringe of pine and cypress that seems to have grown like the weeds, with no tending. Faceless though they have mostly become, the old sallow arches and fractured walls have the look of faded old men with tufts of hair growing out of their noses and ears. When you explore the stripped carcases of these structures, with their entrails laid open and their naked ribs, you find them ugly and rather repellent: it is hard to make head or tail of what was once organization and splendor. Descending into the dark vaulted chambers, you find nothing but human excrement. And the elegances and luxuries of later times first gladden and then depress, as you find them defiled and neglected. You climb to a still thriving garden, enclosed by a low box hedge, which has roses hanging garlanded on stakes and plantings of red gladioli, yellow lilies and magenta dahlias, and think at first sight that this part has been kept up; but, entering the maze behind it—box paths with a palm in the middle—you discover that it is now a latrine and that the little walls of hedge have been broken down, where people have forced their way out. A grotto that must once have been charming, matted with a great growth of vines from which water continually drips, enshrines a green and limpid pool, the clearness of which, however, reveals only a pulp of old papers. The Renaissance stone lion that guards it has one front paw broken off and is scribbled all over with initials.

The Palatine Hill is a favorite resort for the black British Basutoland troops. The Italians are afraid of these Africans, and they herd away here by themselves, sauntering along the paths or milling quietly among the ruins. One finds groups of them, mingled with Sikhs, with whom they do not, however, associate, on a summit where a big arc of masonry opens to the empty sky, and where an unprotected gap in the walk discloses, in the bowels of a vanished palace, a great underground length of gallery: some cellar for stores and slaves, which, laid open, after a thousand years of darkness, by a recent collapse of the roofing, inspires, for the history-read visitor, a feeling of dread and awe. But, for the Africans—who have been recruited by being told that the White Father was in danger and who have been surprised to find other Negroes who say they live in the United States—the splendors of the Caesars, Italy, Europe itself, cannot mean very much more than they did to Attila's Huns. The only consolation they find in Rome seems to be the low class of prostitutes who meet them toward nightfall in this part of the Forum. The girls take them to a part of the ruins that has a row of little compartments: just the thing for an informal brothel.

———

I found in the Allied Commission, in the department of food distribution, L.M., whom I knew from college, and I had from him a very realistic and highly entertaining account of the day-by-day workings of his organization.

He had been trained, when he first came over, at a place called Tizzi-Ouzou near Algiers, where there was "a so-called school of military government." Here American and British officers were for the first time quartered together and confronted with the problem of getting on. The tone as well as the routine were, however, set by the British. Instead of American reveille or roll call, they had British morning parade. They would line up in a huge courtyard, and the British commandant would appear on a balcony, look at his wrist-watch and announce: "Gentlemen, the time is now eight forty-five. Parade dismissed!" The Americans and British were mixed in the ranks and at the moment when they broke formation, the Americans would walk straight away, but the British had to execute a "right turn," salute, bringing their hands down smartly, and march forward with a military step. They would thus run right into the Americans and a scene of confusion would result. The same thing took place morning after morning. And they were out of tune in other ways. The movements of British drill are usually calculated to make a sound in order to keep the men in unison: the British wore hob-nailed shoes and were always snapping their heels, whereas our men wore rubber heels and sometimes felt like ineffectual phantoms. Then there was the issue of tea: where Americans and British had a mess together (we had the same situation at our correspondents' hotel), it always annoyed the former to be forced to wait till seven-thirty for dinner because the latter liked tea at five. Both sides, in this phase, however, were making efforts to be amiable together; but "the cleavage began from the moment when they got on the ship for Naples—and they've been cleaving ever since. The A.C. is a shot-gun wedding. There was a certain amount of fellowship at mess when we first arrived in Rome and we were all mixed up together, but later the Americans and the British separated out from one another completely." (This, too, was true at our hotel, where, eating three meals a day in the same dining-room with the British, I heard only once of an English correspondent sitting at the same table with Americans.) The two armies, in the Allied Commission, were supposed to be represented equally, but they were equal, he said, only in the sense of the story about the wartime rabbit stew, in which it was discovered that "one part horse, one part rabbit" meant one horse to one rabbit. The proportion of British to Americans was actually something like sixty to forty, but the former, through various devices, had acquired the real control. Our army promotion system played into the hands of the British because it worked on a rationing basis: we could have only so many colonels, so many majors, and so forth; but with the British, the rank went with the job, so that, though any given department might be organized with equal numbers of equal ranks, the British could and did soon promote as many of their own men as they liked, and now outranked the American element. The real power behind Colonel Clark, the nominal head of the Commission, was an Englishman who told him what to do. We had become civil servants for the British, who treated us like colonials, "playing Santa Claus with our food, oil and man power. As Sumner Welles says, we're the tail to the British kite!"

He had some amusing stories of Naples. The Neapolitans would take paving-stones out of the streets in order to slow up the American trucks and get a chance to steal the bags of flour. They would also slit the sacks in the trucks, and then later, when these had been taken out, the little boys would come around and scrape the flour off the floor. In the station at Naples there were two little boys who worked together in the following way. When they saw an American carrying bags, one would stick a hatpin into him while the other grabbed the bags, as he dropped them. At Civitavecchia, he said, a considerable amount of salt had been stolen with the connivance of the carabinieri—salt is a government monopoly—who, as their price, took a cut of the shipments. Someone had told him that the same thing was mentioned in one of the classical Roman historians.

But these were merely the pettier peculations. He knew of an American officer who had been offered a handsome villa to live in after the war if he would agree to let a load of supplies be diverted to an improper destination. In Sicily, a British officer had been living in a castle with a local countess and levying a personal tax on every cargo of wine that went north. He was now in Italy proper and the authorities were supposed to have the goods on him; "but did you ever hear of an officer—especially a British officer being convicted by a court martial?" L. himself had had one experience which had struck rather a sour note. He had got to know an Italian family whom he had liked and to whose house he had sometimes gone. It was a kind of palace made of white soap. The father was a splendid old figure, with a pair of enormous *baffoni* and a great shock of thick white hair. He had the concession for making records of all the music that was played in the Vatican—the big organ, the Sistine Choir; but at the present time none could be made and the family were rather hard-up. One evening he had proposed to L., in the blandest and most natural way in the world, that L. should supply him with the flints that the Americans were shipping in for cigarette-lighters for the soldiers. He would sell them, and they would split the price. L. has decided, he tells me, that he can't go to the house any more.

———

The Borghese Gardens—into which you pass, at the top of the broad Via Veneto, through the old chipped reddish weedy Roman wall and the stone gates with the modern eagles. Here one always finds an atmosphere of gaiety, of leafage, of light bright color—everything both larger and more casual than in a park in London or Paris, and enchanting with a freedom and felicity that are characteristic only of Rome—all a little not precisely tinselly, not precisely flimsy, but slightly both tempting and teasing the foreigner by a careless disregard of plan, a cheerful indifference to purpose, that, nevertheless, derive a certain insolence from blooming among the monuments of so much solid civic building, so much noble and luxurious beauty. With all this behind them, these immense rambling grounds can afford to lack foundation, be perishable—like D'Annunzio's *Elegie Romane* and Respighi's *Fontane di Roma*.

I found myself almost every afternoon, when I had been to call for my mail, wandering up into the Borghese Gardens to read it and the Italian papers in a little out-of-doors café called La Casina del Lago. You went inside a special enclosure, shut off from the rest of the park by a little black iron fence, behind which were posted at intervals, whitish and dim in the shadow, a set of small antique statues, and walked along a gravel alley vaulted with fine straight green oaks, which seemed marvellously cool and reposeful after the dirty main drive and the meridian heat. The strange blend of informality and grandeur that is so much the quality of Rome! Outside, one would have passed a wall, loaded down with midsummer vines, which just revealed sculptured griffins and the flank of an embedded sarcophagus; and now one met a gray ducal stone lion grasping a sheaf of stone arrows in his paw but pedestalled on some makeshift brickwork which on one side it overlapped. The *casina* resembled a temple: a small portico with classical columns. In front of it were little round tables sheltered by ample umbrellas and surrounded by wicker chairs, and wide-branching pink rhododendrons growing out of large clay jars. A radio, concealed over the portico, was always warbling romantic opera or concert renditions of Mozart, often announced, as rather surprised me, to emanate—I suppose on records—from the Metropolitan Opera House in New York or the Boston Symphony Orchestra. The waiters were unobtrusive, sympathetic: they soon appeared, brought you apricot ice and little pink *paste* in frilled paper cups, then drifted into the background and let you alone.

I read letters from G. when I got them, and wished she were with me to go around with. Rome—even for Italians, apparently: the lovers in D'Annunzio's *Il Piacere* —ought to be seen as an historical pageant and in company with someone else. I haven't gone to many churches or museums. My idea has been that, sometime later on, I shall bring my children over to see them, as I was brought in my teens; and in the meantime, I have felt this spring as if the whole past of Rome has been pushed by the war into a history that is now finished. My attention is always on other things: on the phenomena of Anglo-Saxon, Germanic, Russian Soviet civilization that is taking over the world. The old routine of the tourist, reading up the earlier chapters of the story which is to culminate in his grandfather, his father and himself, seems relegated to the archives now, like the final instalment of a serial bound up in the completed volume of a suspended magazine.

One Sunday I was asked for lunch to a place in the country some distance from Rome, and was driven there, in an official limousine, by one of the other guests, a rather important man from the British Foreign Office.

There was also a uniformed English girl, whose father was a well-known diplomat, then at the San Francisco Conference. They engaged in a conversation so low-voiced, laconic and private as to become almost telepathic. The first part of this peculiar interchange was more or less intelligible to a stranger—we were all sitting together in the back seat: Captain D. told Sir S. what she had done during the war with masterly matter-of-factness: she had apparently, in some capacity, been connected with the firing of anti-aircraft guns; and they talked about the effects of quinine—she had just "come out" to Italy—which you were supposed to take to ward off malaria, but which, the girl said, would turn you yellow, so that she felt she'd rather risk malaria. But then their voices sank still lower, and there was nothing but Christian names and nicknames, monosyllabic questions and answers in a kind of private code. The only name that I recognized was "Winnie," who, Captain D. explained, lay in bed in the afternoon—"which nobody else is able to do"—and so came out "full of beans" at night, when the cabinet ministers were tired. And there leaked through to me rather dimly one of those inevitable British stories about someone who had snubbed someone else in a sharp and satisfactory manner. Sir. S. would occasionally raise his voice and address a remark to me, as if I were sitting in another room.

All this time we were passing through a region that had been absolutely laid waste by the fighting. Of whole villages there was nothing but rubble and empty walls—though the women still went back and forth, balancing jars on their heads, and the children played by the roadside, climbing on the old rusty guns that had been camouflaged with green dappling and now lay about, sometimes belly up. Spattered and speckled walls; balconies hanging in shreds. The pink, white or yellow houses looked almost too soft for real buildings: a railroad station presented the aspect of a partially gnawed graham cracker, and one was reminded by other ruins of loaves of bread with the crusts rather clumsily sliced off or of dilapidated cardboard boxes from which most of the paper coat had been ripped and the gray underneath partly torn. One house, with its staircase exposed, looked like a broken conch-shell which shows the interior spiral. Another, with the staircase destroyed, had been equipped with a long ladder which gave access to some still usable upstairs rooms. In another, on an upper story, a family of little children were sitting around in their Sunday clothes —black suits, green and red dresses—in a room of which only two corners were left: below them dropped a precipice of ruin; but they had brightened what remained of the room with little pots of flowers, and seemed to have got used to living in the open and in the danger of breaking their necks. In the main square of a fairly large town stood a headless unidentifiable white statue—with one arm still pathetically upraised in a gesture that had no longer any meaning—which perched on what looked like a rockery but was really a blasted pedestal.

Sir S. pointed out to his companion that the women were "very well-dressed compared to the women at home." His tone about the Italians was invidious, but his opinion was not borne out by my own observation in England. The women in these roadside towns *did* look better than English women, but only because they had more chic. The bright little short dresses which they were wearing with bare legs were more vivid but less substantial than the clothes one saw in England. This was Sir S.'s only comment on the scenes through which we were passing till we came to a badly shelled cemetery which had once had a wall around it and which bore still, over its battered gate, the legend "IN CHRISTO QUI-ESCENTES." "Sad to see that shattered!" he murmured.

We were on our way to lunch at the country place of a Roman prince, whose family went back to ancient Rome. I believe that he was still repaying, or had only lately repaid, a loan that his house had made from another equally ancient house sometime in the Renaissance. He had married an American woman, who was a patron of literature and the arts and had been particularly kind in guiding me to useful connections in Rome. The small castle, which, we were told, had been built about 1300, consisted of a low house and a square brown brick tower, with little rectangular windows and saw-teeth along the top; swifts and some kind of crows were flying in and out of the crevices. Rienzi—the popular leader, the Mussolini of the fourteenth century, who first carried all before him, then was murdered like Mussolini by the populace: the appearance and extinction of such leaders has been a recurrent feature of Roman history—had cut fourteen meters off the top as a punishment to the nobles, who, the Prince said, "doubtless needed to be punished, as they had in other cases." Behind the castle, flat as a backdrop, granite and dark shrub-green, rose a mountain wall that looked quite sheer. At the top of this, on the right, one saw the old brown square buildings of an unlikely-looking town, which the American-born Princess never seemed to have got over regarding as rather quaint. There were a very swiftly running brook—the water here was filtered through the granite—and a little river, also rapid, at once dark and quite limpid—there were trout in it—with great beds of watercress, and across, on the opposite bank, gigantic elephant ears of some coarse mullein-like plant.

The effect of this water was lovely and, like the little old castle, queer.

The Princess, though so active and generous in her efforts on behalf of the arts, had something of the dehydrated quality that Americans are likely to get when they have lived a long time in Europe. When I had met her first and asked an Italian who knew her whether she were intelligent, he had answered, "Not quite." I felt that, in spite of her competence in the role she had chosen to play, she was somehow rather sadly displaced. Her only son had been pointlessly killed in the Italian invasion of Greece. The other guests made upon me an impression distinctly theatrical. They reminded me of the national types that had been caricatured so crudely in an early Soviet play, Sergei Tretyakov's *Roar, China,* in which representatives of the capitalist countries were shown exploiting the East. Sir S. could not have been more the official Englishman. He did not take the foreigners seriously or pay very much attention to them, but went off and took photographs of the landscape and the castle. (The young girl who had been with us in the car was a somewhat deceptive case. She was actually not English but the daughter of a well-known Balto Russian family, yet from lifelong residence in England she had come to have the attitude and appearance of a sturdy upper-class Girl Scout.) The Frenchman had no cultural nonsense and talked of nothing but commercial affairs. There were three other Americans besides myself: one of those supposedly important lawyer-banker-industrialist executives, conspicuous for their bulk, who get into public life, with his wife and a male assistant. He had been sent to Rome by the President on a diplomatic mission. The wife was the soul of a lack of tact and seemed a perfect example of the European idea of a vulgar rich American

woman. She wore a small navy-blue sailor hat on her soft
slightly curly hair that might have owed its yellow tint to
peroxide, dark blue sun spectacles like horses' blinders,
large gold and blue rosette earrings on either side of her
rectangular face, a string of pearls on the wrinkled neck
under her square jaw and a row of large plain buttons
down the front of her white dress. She complained that I
was being called Wilson when I had been introduced to
her as Warren, and when I was sitting next to her at
lunch, passed her husband's assistant a note asking him
what my name was. He replied in the same way, and she
then addressed a remark to me as Wilson but soon relapsed
into calling me Warren. She announced at one point that
she did not approve of international marriages, and when
the daughter of the house laughed and said that she was
the product of one, the non-internationalizing American
lady said ungracefully, "You're an exception." The assistant to the big executive had a black spaniel that swam in
the river, then shook himself and jumped on people and
had to be shut up. There was a good deal of fuss about
this in the tiresome American way.

The Prince excused himself after lunch. He was trying
to get the estate into shape again, and he had to oversee
things himself. He was worried about the four months'
drought. He had remained in his country place all
through the occupation. The Germans had brought in
salt water to encourage the spread of malaria, and when
German soldiers had pitched their tents on his property,
he had not made any complaint, knowing they would
have malaria. Later on, he had expressed surprise that
they were not camping there again. "Oh, no: everybody
came down with malaria." "What a pity!" I found the
Prince more sympathetic than anyone else. He was a
musician, had composed an opera; there was a cultural
tradition in the family. Stendhal had come to stay at the

palazzo in Rome, and the grandfather of the Prince was said to have made the authoritative map of the three worlds of the *Divine Comedy*. Having been led to imagine the afternoon in terms that were almost as crude as those of any Soviet writer, I cast our host as the very best type of cultivated Italian noble, much concerned with the care of his lands and his people. I learned later that his mother was English and one of his grandmothers Polish, and I was prevented from continuing to idealize him when I was told that, at the time of the war shortages, he had been mean about providing his peasants with food. Friends told me that on one occasion when they had lunched there during the war, a local station-master who was out of work had come to the Prince to ask him for some corn for his wife and children. The Prince had refused—he explained that he had had to give all his corn to the *ammassi,* the government pools. The Princess had attempted to intercede, and when her plead-ing had failed, had suggested that her husband might be able to get the man moved to another station where the trains were still running. But the Prince had said no: that there was plenty of work to be done on his own place—that the peasants now wanted three hundred lire a day but would soon be forced to work for a hundred. I recalled that he had expressed the opinion at lunch that people ought always to be a little underfed: he had, he said, been reading about Byron's dieting, which had apparently stimulated the poet's mind. The light and delicate food had, however, been perfect: ravioli, lettuce salad, sheep's milk cheese, some sort of rice dish with honey, fruit compote and white wine.

The company were subdued about politics and more or less resigned to the inevitable Leftist tendencies. I had seen the hammer and sickle scratched on the Prince's Roman palace. An Italian journalist who was present said to me that there had been nothing like this in Italy since the days of Belisarius in the sixth century, when they had had to fight the Goths and the Ostrogoths. He talked with interest about Walter Lippmann.

———

But the longer you live in Rome—and as the charming and chilly spring gives way to the smothering summer—the more you feel the stagnation and the squalor that are the abject human realities left by the ebb of power and splendor. You notice, in a little side-street such as the Via dei Cappuccini, the stopped-up urinal that overflows the cobbles and the melancholy old sprawling black sandals that lie in shreds in the road; and you become unpleasantly aware of the long accumulation of excrement in the corners of the great grass-grown back stairs of the Church of Santa Maria Maggiore. The beggars begin to get on your nerves. Corrado Alvaro, the novelist, who has done a series of articles on them, tells me that they have a bus of their own, which brings them into town in the morning. The supposedly crippled paupers jump briskly out of the bus, make water against the wall, then go into their professional act, becoming paralyzed, bent and pathetic. Not all are fakes, however, he says; and this soon becomes all too obvious. One sees in the streets many people who are wasted with malnutrition or suffering from various infections, some of them not even begging, but lying on curbs or in doorways in fevered stupors or with bloated feet. There are women with tiny ugly children whom they expose all day to the sun. Near the entrance to our hotel in the Via Sistina is a woman with a limp shut-eyed baby that always seems doped or dead: we try to think it is a fake made of rubber. One of the most ambitious begging efforts is a remarkable family orchestra which is absolutely indefatigable and always to be found in some public place. The father, with an accordion, is the principal performer, and around him cluster seven children, tooting and piping on instruments that look like miniature saxophones. One of the boys doubles with cymbals. The mother stands keeping time, holding a pale heavy-lidded nurseling. Sometimes they play *Lili Marlene,* sometimes the *International.*

The street boys, the *"ragazzini,"* are all intent on illicit business. They are the visible communications of the network of the black market. If you so much as glance at one, he slides up to propose to you a woman and a room or to offer to buy your cigarettes. Cigarettes are the great medium of exchange, and their price goes up or down in proportion to the number of Americans who happen to be in Rome that week. The normal price of a package seems to be two hundred and fifty lire, that is, two dollars and a half, but it once sank to one hundred and twenty-five, when there were a lot of soldiers here on leave. The boys buy from the American soldiers food, clothing and cigarettes, and take them home to their parents, who sell them at central exchanges. On one occasion, a white G.I., who found himself with a dead-drunk Negro, asked a band of *ragazzini* whether they wanted "to buy a black man." They paid him twelve hundred lire, and the boys took the Negro off, stripped him and sold everything he wore at a profit of several thousand lire.

The nights in Rome are unlike nights that I remember in any other city. It seems queer, in the midst of a town that is populated as densely as this, to hear roosters crowing at dawn and the persistent moan of a screech-owl. It came back to me that the Latin word for screech-owl was *strix,* and that there must always have been screech-owls in Rome since the Romans had first called them that. I couldn't at first imagine where these chickens and owls made their homes, but came to the conclusion later that they must be in the Villa Medici. The absence of nocturnal traffic, due to the lack of oil and light, makes the city unexpectedly quiet, so that the noises seem terribly loud: a shopkeeper pulling down his tin shutter startles you with a shattering crash, the exploding exhaust of a truck gives the effect of a ten-inch gun, the yowling of starved and exacerbated cats seems to emanate from souls in Hell, and the songs howled by drunken G.I.'s are not very much more cheerful or pleasant. There is no way of missing a note of the depressing and interminable pounding of somebody playing the piano in the British Other Ranks hotel a few doors down the Via Sistina: he knows only two or three tunes, but he occasionally attempts to vary them by starting on something new, always, however, giving it up, after groping out the first few bars, and returning to the same old melodies.

And there is the desultory whistling of trains that do not sound as if they were really going anywhere. One seems to see them just standing in the station and peep-peeping at the sight of a brakeman, as a dog will start suddenly yapping at the sound of a passerby—but futilely, annoyingly, pathetically. They make you feel as nothing else does that there are no more communications in Italy and that you lie there imprisoned in this pit of the past, where the flimsy constructions of the Fascist regime—which was supposed to have made the trains run on time—have collapsed and joined the rest.

———

Under the clear pale-blue innocent dome of the sky, the swallows, at certain times of day, go flickering and twittering in swarms. There is a revue called *Ma le Rondini Non Sanno,* and, according to its eponymous song, what the swallows are fortunate not to know is "what's going on down there." As June turns into summer, the atmosphere of Rome seems to become more corrupt and turbid. The mess in our correspondents' hotel, the rations assigned to which are obviously being sold to the black market, has recently been getting so bad as to be sometimes completely inedible. The correspondents take it out on the waiters, who have been shifting from servility to surliness; and one day an American officer, who has something to do with the management, threw an unappetizing dish on the floor, provoking, by this overdemonstration, the suspicion that he himself is responsible for our not getting the proper food. In order to escape these meals, we have been going to the Fagiano in the Piazza Colonna, once one of the best restaurants in Rome and now a dining place for Allied personnel; but the Fagiano itself is deteriorating. As one drifts out, after a hot afternoon, into the tepid air of evening, down gray avenues where the slow apathetic people are spreading all over the pavements or through the dark cobbled pavementless side-streets where brawlers are shouting at the top of their lungs, one feels that there is nothing left of the bright and varied surface of Rome but a brackish iridescent scum. At the Fagiano, with its old Roman columns embedded in a modern façade, one has a fancy that the respectable dinners which were still being served there this spring have been actually dematerializing, vaporizing, into the murk of the summer dusk, itself the foul emanation of a humanity decaying and crawling, like slugs in a fisherman's jar that has been left too long in the sun. The space around the Marcus Aurelius column is the Bourse of the black market. You cannot sit down in one of the cafés of the square without someone's sitting down beside you and making you some sort of proposition. Now, you note, we have put up a barbed-wire barrier in front of the Fagiano to protect the army cars and keep the bickering and haggling crowd at bay. The little boys get in, however, and stand at the open windows, and sometimes people hand them out bread.

————

With the stultifying atmosphere of Rome in June has come to be associated a book that I have been reading through these summer days: *Roma 1943* by Paolo Monelli. This is a political and social history of the demise of the Fascist regime, and so full of the jokes, the slogans and the jargon of the streets and the papers, with which I was unfamiliar, as well as so complicated in its chronicle of duplicity and confusion, that it took me rather long to get through it. I would apply myself to it after lunch and usually fall into a dead and perspiring sleep—so that the book, with its gray wartime paper and the queer stale flavor of its prose, seemed saturated with exhalations from the Roman streets in summer, as the *popolo romano* of these streets is given a character for me by Monelli's account of their behavior in the last days of Mussolini's reign.

Paolo Monelli is an able journalist, and *Roma 1943* is an historical document of value. Monelli worked, during the Fascist regime, on such papers as the *Gazzetta del Popolo* and the *Corriere della Sera*—journals which had some tradition of independent political thinking, though they eventually succumbed to the official line. Monelli, in any case, is anxious to let us know that he was not always uncritical of the government and sometimes tried to take a line of his own, and his book has obviously been prompted by a feeling of political guilt which makes the reader, too, rather uncomfortable. In order to write such a book, as he says, in order to perform an autopsy on Fascism, one has to conduct an examination of conscience. But, to a foreigner, this is a little repellent. He shows the abject servility of the Fascist press, which he saw from the inside, with a detail which we cannot think funny because it is so disgusting, and he exposes the faults of his countrymen with something almost like complacency, declaiming and waving his hands over the national humiliation, yet he snatches with an embarrassing eagerness—wherever it is possible to do so—at the courage of an Italian regiment or the industry of an Italian colony.

What is most curious to the foreign reader is the style in which the book is written. Giovanni Papini once said that the trouble with Italian prose was that it had never gotten away from the ornamental periods of Boccaccio; but if one has just been reading Silone or Moravia, one has come to expect a style that has escaped from mandarin requirements and come closer to the colloquial language. Now, Monelli, in spite of his journalist's slang, is still enmeshed in the ancient rhetoric of festooned sentences that go on for pages, show-pieces of literary vocabulary that accumulate adjectives and nouns with a minimum of "functional" effectiveness, convolutions of statements that grow up inside statements, like the whorls of a navel orange, and that give the impression at once of exasperating deliberation and of eyebrow-heaving vehemence (there is in a single sentence of *Roma 1943* one parenthesis two pages long that contains a subordinate parenthesis of over a hundred words). This is a style that one associates most readily with the intrigues of a Renaissance court or the maneuvers of the Council of Trent, and which it seems at first queer and absurd to find used for a critical analysis of the backstage of Fascist politics and for the history of military movements that one has read of in press dispatches.

But then, as one reads on, one has to accept the fact that modern Italy is still partly like this. It is precisely

Monelli's style which explains why he was able to live through Fascism and more than half swallow its grandiose pretensions. While Mussolini was spoiling and wobbling, while his associates were conspiring against him, distrusting and double-crossing one another, while the generals were slipping away, evading their responsibilities and leaving Rome open to the Germans, they still talked a language of literature, still fell back on heroic poses. Among the consequences, writes Signor Monelli, of the "intellectual laziness" of Italians are "the habit of making everything into literature—ideas, theories, feelings, and social and moral behavior, so that we want our action to be literary as well as our writing. And since love is one of the favorite themes of our literature, we import an amorous point of view into our opinions and our activities in the field of international politics." Of the first of these tendencies there are many examples among the events recorded in *Roma 1943*. When, in the summer of 1943, the opposition to the war was mounting and it was plain that Italy had to withdraw, the King is supposed to have said to Badoglio of the old anti-Fascists like Bonomi and Orlando, who had been proposed to form a new government: "But they are all ghosts!"—to which Badoglio is said to have replied: "Your Majesty and I are also ghosts." And in the second of these tendencies Monelli himself indulges in a later passage: "It was not all at once that tyranny revealed itself at the beginning of the dictatorship; it only matured slowly, in the course of a series of arbitrary acts on the dictator's part and a series of concessions and abdications on the part of the people, who, as happens in the case of the concessions that the man in love makes to the woman he loves, believed itself to be perfectly free while it was allowing itself to be robbed of its freedom and its privileges."

The book ends with the account of an incident which,

to the friendly American visitor, cannot fail to be moving as he reads it. Monelli tells how, after horrible weeks of futile fighting and general demoralization, the Allies arrive in Rome. The Piazza Barberini is empty and bright in the moonlight. "An enormous armored car has stopped at the corner of the Quattro Fontane; when we get there, we see a line of other cars which have also stopped further up the street. A curious and eager little crowd is making a hum of voices about them, but does not shout or acclaim them. A lean and very tall soldier is standing in front of the first car and chewing something. The people stare at him but do not speak. I call out [in English]: 'Where do you come from?' 'From Texas,' he replies. I feel myself suddenly giddy amidst limitless open spaces which receive and dissolve the pain, the anguish of nine months, and in which relief itself is lost. Two little girls come up with a tricolor flag in their hands and give it to the soldier. He turns and looks up seriously at his comrades, who are sitting on top of the car and dangling their legs: 'Here's a flag,' he says. One of them stretches out his hand, and takes the flag, and hoists it on the turret."

But even this proves depressing when one has finished the book and reflects how little freedom our "tricolor" has brought them.

———

The young Italians who have come to manhood just before or during the war and who have fought in the resistance movement do seem to make a race quite distinct from any of the older people who have had in one way or another to adapt themselves to the Fascist regime. A young man of this kind, whose acquaintance I have made, a poet and teacher of literature, strikes, by his spirit and candor, a note that is at least hopeful. He points out that there have been always in Italy the same sharp and startling contrasts of character. The people of a city like Rome are predominantly distrustful and cynical; the men lend themselves to all kinds of servilities and frauds, the women all too easily become prostitutes. It is difficult to make them believe in ideas; but their indifference is always redeemed by the emergence of heroic individuals who are willing to die for ideas. Even in the sixteenth century, when Italy was ruled by Spain and under the heel of the Inquisition, when the self-respect of Italians was at one of its lowest ebbs and Italy mainly a field for the battles of alien armies, you had a man like Giordano Bruno; and then later, Garibaldi and Mazzini. (I had realized, since coming to Italy, that my friend Carlo Tresca had been made in this mold. I remembered how the coldness and rigor with which he had talked about politics had contrasted with the bombastic language of the articles in his paper, *Il Martello,* through which he had harangued his followers. Such men were incorruptible, and, except by execution, as in Bruno's case, or by assassination, as in Carlo's, absolutely indestructible. They revived the antique virtue which had never quite died in Rome.) And now, my friend went on, it was not altogether impossible that Italy, having sloughed off Fascism earlier than the rest of the world and finding herself in ruins again, as she had done so many times before, might produce, as she had done before, some new movement that would lead the world. But the Mazzinis and Garibaldis of the future would have to think, not as Italians, but as Europeans.

———

At that time, though I did not know it, the Italian moving picture, *Città Aperta,* based on the resistance movement, had just been finished in Rome; and, as I put these notes in order, it has just been shown in New York.

This picture is very much to the point in the connection of which I have been speaking. How could we correspondents, drowsing and grumbling about Rome in our antiquated tourist hotel, have imagined that a work of such power, at the same time intense and restrained, had been produced in the Via del Tritone, where the prostitutes thronged every evening and through which we walked to reach the Fagiano, out of a patchwork of old lengths of film bought in the black market and with no kind of studio light, so that everything had to be shot during the daytime; or that the Roman Anna Magnani, that brilliant and intelligent actress, whom we saw in the revue *Cantachiaro,* impersonating a D'Annunzio duchess in the manner of Beatrice Lillie and satirizing the Allied occupation, had just given her marvellous performance as the mistress of an underground worker. It is the antique virtue again, and you can see it come to life in this film.

4

TWO SURVIVORS: MALRAUX
AND SILONE

DURING THE DECADE BEFORE THE WAR, when the tradition of Lenin was still alive and Marxism had still its prestige as a moral and intellectual force, there appeared in Europe two first-rate novelists who, though quite different in other ways, both presented the contemporary world in terms of the Marxist class conflict: the Frenchman André Malraux and the Italian Ignazio Silone.

Malraux and Silone belong to the same European generation: there is only a year between them, Malraux having been born in Paris in 1900 and Silone in a little town of the Abruzzi in 1901. Malraux, who studied Oriental languages and went to the East as an archaeologist, became interested in the Chinese revolution, in which, from 1925 to 1927, he played an active role. He worked with the Communist Kuomintang and was a member of the Committee of Twelve, which organized the Canton uprising. He wrote, out of this experience, his two novels *Les Conquérants* and *La Condition Humaine,* and the first of them brought him to the attention of Trotsky, whose acquaintance he made in the years when Trotsky was living in France and who tried to correct what he regarded as Malraux's out-of-date French romanticism and reconstruct him as an unambiguous Marxist. Later, in the Spanish Civil War of 1936–39, Malraux took part on the Loyalist side as chief of an escadrille and accepted the direction of Moscow in its strategy and policy for Spain. Otherwise, in a way exceptional for a participant in far-Left revolutionary movements, he has managed to remain independent of both Trotskyist and Stalinist influence.

Silone, on the other hand, had been an active revolutionary worker from 1917, when, at the age of seventeen, he became secretary of the peasant movement, syndicalist in its political complexion, which had been launched in his native Abruzzi. Soon thereafter, he went to Rome, where he was, first, editor of a Socialist paper and then one of the founders, under the inspiration of Moscow, of the Communist Youth International, and where he took part, in 1921, in organizing the Italian Communist Party. In the years between 1925 and 1929, he was a member of the Central Committee of the Party, doing underground work in Italy under the Mussolini regime and representing the Party in Moscow during a period when its leader was in jail and at such times as Silone himself did not happen to be in jail. When it was evident, at the end of the twenties, that the Russians in the Communist International were beginning to dictate policy from the point of view of Russian interests at the expense of the freedom of the Communists of the parties of other nations to determine their own lines of action, Silone resigned, with a group which included about half the Italians; nor did he afterwards associate himself with the followers of either Bukharin or Trotsky, who had set up split-off Communist groups, for he felt, as he says, that these groups had all the defects of the Stalinist parties without the power of Moscow behind them. He left Italy at the end of the twenties and went into retirement in

Switzerland, where for the first time he began to write novels and where he remained until 1944, when, after the fall of the Fascists, he returned to live in Rome.

The temperaments of Malraux and Silone present in certain respects a very sharp contrast. Malraux, though he served in Spain in the army of international Communism, has had, especially in his earlier career, an element of the international adventurer—part explorer of the ancient Oriental world, whose most exciting sensation was to find there the twentieth-century class struggle; part Byronic egoist and actor, driven by an obscure compulsion to assert his will for its own sake—whereas Silone, since he has broken with Moscow, has been assuming a personality which combines in a peculiar way the traditional severity of the Communist with the compassion of a parish priest. For Malraux, the conception of the class struggle gave him a vision of the drama of history, in which he could play a role, fierce, courageous, perhaps noble; for Silone, it drew clear moral issues which showed him how to direct his energies toward ends that would benefit his fellows. Malraux is largely preoccupied with the tactics and significance of action, Silone with ethical problems. But both, during the critical years of their youth, accepted the Marxist assumptions as a guide to the contemporary world and worked for the Communist objectives, and this phase of their lives has supplied the themes of their most important books.

Now, for the sincere Marxist revolutionary who was able to think for himself and not afraid to follow his judgment, further belief in the Soviet Union as a power that worked for international socialism—if it had not been discouraged already—did definitely become impossible with the signing in August, 1939, of the Hitler-Stalin pact. There is an observation in Malraux's new novel which, though there applied to something else,

sounds as if it had been inspired by the illusions of
foreign Communists and Communist sympathizers about
the conditions of life in the Soviet Union: "It is as
impossible," he makes one of his characters say, "to see a
country which embodies a myth in which one believes as
it is to see a woman with whom one is in love." And the
horror of the destruction of Europe and the degradation
of human values, protracted through the five and a half
years of this war, made the realization of the socialist
hope seem more and more remote and doubtful. For
writers like Malraux and Silone, their natural line of
development was broken; but, confronted with the scene
of wreckage—living in the debris of defeated France
under the German domination or isolated in Switzerland
in an exile which must at moments have seemed likely to
be permanent—they had to lay hold on the new situation
and find some way of making something of it for the
honor of their old ideals; and what they have made is of
exceptional interest.

Malraux's novel, *La Lutte avec l'Ange* (evidently refer-
ring to the ordeal of Jacob in Genesis 32, which was
published in Switzerland in 1943 in an edition of but
fifteen hundred copies,* is offered as the first section of a
larger work—a work which could hardly have been
finished, given the historical immediacy of the subject,
before the war had come to an end, and which Malraux,
who after the expulsion of the Germans was on active
duty as colonel of a regiment, could hardly have had a
chance to finish. It is impossible, thus, to judge this
instalment in any conclusive way, since it is concerned
with presenting situations of which we are not yet able to
see the upshot and propounding far-reaching questions to
which the answers have not yet been found. The book

* Later published in France as *Les Noyers d'Altenburg.*

develops a double story of two generations of an Alsatian family: the career of the German father, a diplomat in the German service, who has seen something of World War I, and the adventures of the half-French son, who, in World War II, fights for the French. It is this son who is supposed to put together the whole rather complicated chronicle. Taken prisoner at the fall of France and sent to a concentration camp at Chartres, he goes back over his own experience and reflects on his father's exploits as he has learned of them through a set of notes which has come into his hands after the latter's death. The father, a capable and clever man, has that insatiable love of adventure, half-quixotic and half-perverse, which is characteristic of Malraux's heroes. Malraux analyzes his motives in a passage which explains his interest, passionate though apparently gratuitous, in the Young Turk movement of the beginning of the century: "His need to get away from Europe, the solicitation of history, the fanatical desire to leave a scar on the earth, the fascination of a project which he had contributed not a little to shape, the fellowship of combat, and friendship." (It is worth noting that the protagonist of an earlier book, *La Voie Royale,* a superman explorer with very little interest in politics, says also, in explaining the impulse by which he has been driven in his exploits: "I want to leave a scar on this map.") In Turkey, this accomplished Alsatian comes under the influence of the propaganda of the Pan-Turanian movement, which aimed at uniting in a great Turkish empire all those peoples who were assumed to be of Turkish stock; but as he travels in Afghanistan and finds only a "people of sleepwalkers" quite unconscious of their Turanianism, the whole myth suddenly fades away. He returns and gives up his mission and presently lapses back into working for the Germans, with whom he is always a little restive. Just before the First World War he is present at a cross-examination, by the head of the Secret Service, of a supposed Russian woman spy, when they bring in her little son to try to make her betray herself, and later, when the war has begun, he assists at a pioneering experiment with the use of poison gas. The German soldiers, on this occasion, finding the Russians asphyxiated, yield to a primitive human instinct and, instead of taking the Russian position, try to rescue the dying men. The Alsatian, himself half-intoxicated with gas, is soon irresistibly impelled to behave as the others are doing: he picks up a gasping Russian and starts to carry him back toward the field hospital. In him, as in the soldiers, there is something which revolts and balks against the cruel methods of warfare that the German General Staff is developing. But the scene now shifts back to his son, and, following immediately after the episode of the gas attack, we get an episode out of World War II—a tank advance by the French—in which the young man had figured before he was captured by the Germans. We are taken inside the tank; it is lumbering and groping at night through a heavy barrage of shellfire, and it slumps into an unseen trench, where it seems to lie heavily helpless. Modern warfare has gone on getting worse, more crushing and more abasing. Nothing has been done to curb it, and the human race itself seems to have fallen, like the men in the tank, to the bottom of a dark ditch, imprisoned and overwhelmed by a great mass of anti-human machinery. Nor does there appear in the second of these episodes, as there did in the gas attack, any sign of a fraternal solidarity between the soldiers of the hostile armies.

Here the volume ends, but a larger vista of interest has been opened up for the reader than this bare outline of the action would indicate. The narrator has a remarkable great-uncle, an intellectual, rather a dilettante but in a serious German way. He has been a correspondent of Nietzsche's and sometimes entertains Freud. At his house he holds periodical conferences, to which he invites a varied company of savants and at which set subjects are discussed. The father of the narrator, returned from his travels, arrives in time for one of these conferences, at which a great German anthropologist, who has been working for fifteen years on a book, is expected to explain his views in a revelation of special importance. But it turns out that he has just decided not to publish the book. This had been an Hegelian affair which led up to the proposition that the civilization of the Germans was the supreme end-product of history; but the author has now ceased to believe this because he has ceased to believe that what he calls "the human adventure" has any consistent significance. The more he has come to examine the various kinds of society which the human race has produced, the more he has been driven to question the continuity of human history and the logic of human effort. He tells the company about the people who were for centuries firmly convinced that the person of their ruler was the moon, that his power waxed and waned with it and that when the moon went into eclipse the king had to be strangled by his subjects; and those natives of the Melanesian Islands who have never made any connection between childbearing and sexual intercourse, refuting attempts to enlighten them by pointing out that it is by no means true that the former always results from the latter. Just as the narrator's father has lost the racial conception of Turanianism in the presence of the Afghan tribes, so the German anthropologist has been losing the sense of the unity of human ideals and purpose among the mutually exclusive delusions on which human civilizations have been based. And are we not still, Western man, he asks, enveloped in some such delusion, and no

more capable of realizing this than is the goldfish of con-
ceiving its aquarium, which to the goldfish must give
the illusion of comprising the whole world, though it is
nothing but a small glass box? And if this is our true
situation, what, then, *is* our basic delusion? Nationalism,
someone suggests. No, not merely nationalism—our false
but all-pervading and inescapable notion may well be our
idea of history and the conception of Time that goes with
it. "Has the notion of man a meaning? In other words:
beneath the beliefs, the myths, especially under the
multiplicity of mental structures, is it possible to distinguish a permanent idea or direction [Malraux uses the
characteristically French and essentially intellectual word
donnée], which retains its validity through history and
upon which a concept of man can be based?"

The question is never answered. These perplexities,
one supposes, are the struggle with the angel, which left
Jacob, it will be remembered, a prince who had "power
with God and with men"; and the whole discussion,
though not very typical of the time at which it is made to
take place, the early years of the century, when the
nations seemed to be prospering under capitalism and few
doubted the inevitability of progress, serves to bring to a
clear formulation the kind of misgivings that has been
tugging at our minds during these years which have upset
our assumptions. Malraux has here sidestepped completely all the obvious melodrama of the triumphs and the
defeats of the Fascist regimes, which our novelists in the
United States, comfortably far from the battle, have been
exploiting with so much fervor and cashing in on with so
much success. Malraux's hero is half-French and half-
German, and his theme is not the struggle with the
Nazis, or even any longer the Marxist struggle of classes,
which gave the confrontation of forces in his earlier
books, but the justification of man himself.

La Lutte avec l'Ange is not, from the point of view of architecture and writing, one of the most satisfactory of Malraux's books. It seems rather to show the marks of having been written, against pressures and under difficulties, only by dint of determined application. Both the style and the mode of presentation give sometimes— through overwriting or congestion—a certain effect of effort. An admiration for English literature has apparently been responsible here for some results that seem awkward in French. Malraux has been praised by Gide, in deploring the femininity of French fiction, for writing books which, by their masculine qualities, come closer to such Anglo-Saxon novels as *Tom Jones* and *Moby Dick,* and he is said, during the last years of the war, to have become a strong Anglophile. Certainly, in *La Lutte avec l'Ange,* he has managed to reproduce—though usually with bad effect—some of the most flagrantly non-French traits of his favorite English authors: Kipling's knowing international allusiveness, Meredith's elliptical expression and Conrad's discontinuous narrative method. Malraux, who is said at one point to have escaped getting shot by the Germans by impersonating an English officer, thus almost appears, in a literary way, as one of those "displaced persons" whom a department of the Allied Commission is now making efforts to repatriate.

But any effort to get outside the formulas which, in preserving the French classical elegance, have tended lately to keep French literature stereotyped and thereby rather provincial is undoubtedly an excellent thing, and one finds in *La Lutte avec l'Ange* passages of sinewy and searching thought, strokes of dramatic imagination, of which only a man of genius would have been capable. Above all, there is a seriousness, an undulled perspicuity, about the large problems of human destiny, that has become the rarest thing in the world. This novel is both the most impressive and the most exciting piece of literature that I have yet seen inspired by the war.

The typical heroes of the novels of both Malraux and Silone have been workers for Marxist revolution, but the two writers have strikingly differed in their attitudes toward what the Communists used to call "the masses." Certainly, Malraux himself did not reach the revolution primarily through sympathy for the underdog, but rather, like his protagonist in *Les Conquérants,* through disgust with the bourgeoisie—to which, in the author's case, must be added the motivation of a very strong sense of what non-Communists call "human decency." All the main characters in Malraux's novels are more or less extraordinary or exceptional men, and the Communist's self-identification with the hardships and interests of the working class has been the aspect of the social struggle which was least adequately rendered in his novels. Now, however, in *La Lutte avec l'Ange,* he has taken some special pains to try to make the common man sympathetic; yet these scenes are not his most successful. The conversations between the soldiers just before the gas attack seem a little gotten-up and labored, the reflections to which they give rise on the narrator's part a little self-conscious and sententious; the whole thing has a suggestion, at moments, of a pastiche of the Barbusse of *Le Feu.* The gas attack in which the German soldiers show their human solidarity with the Russians is not so effectively done as the tank battle in which the man of intellect loses control of his monstrous machine.

Silone, on the other hand, has tended to be mainly preoccupied with the relation of the dedicated revolutionist to the people whom he is supposed to be serving. When the Communist line loses touch with the people, he comes to the conclusion that there is something wrong, and though his protagonist, Pietro Spina, in his novel *Pane e Vino,* never wearies of renewing his efforts to make connections between the peasantry and the Communist Party, his failures bring him constantly closer, at the expense of the Marxist doctrine, to the point of view of the peasants. Pietro Spina, impatient of the exile into which he has been driven by the Fascists, returns, disguised as a priest, to his native Abruzzi mountains in an attempt to rouse the people against Fascism and to build a revolutionary movement, but he finds himself baffled at every turn by the primitive mentality of the Italians, who see the world in terms of sins and pardons, saints and miracles, prayers and rites. He finds that, in spite of his efforts, he can make his only contact with them, not through his appeal to their class-consciousness, but through his natural sympathy for them, the sobriety of his life in their midst, a moral rectitude and a spiritual candor which they recognize and to which they respond.

And just as the false priest of *Pane e Vino* is, in the course of his relations with these peasants, half transformed into a real priest, to whom they look for forgiveness and guidance, whom they believe to possess powers of healing, while he, on his side, is coming to preach to them less as a mere political agitator than as a militant disciple of Christ, so Silone himself has drawn closer to the conceptions of primitive Christianity and has been trying to make a kind of merger between the ideals of modern socialism and these. "In the modern drama," he writes in the foreword to his new book, "a new element has appeared as a protagonist: the proletarian. Not new in the sense of not already having existed in antiquity, but because his ordeal and his destiny were not then considered suitable subjects for history, thought and art. If to us moderns the situation of this character seems the nearest to the human truth, it is because, in the last analysis, between the ancients and us there has been Jesus." This new book, first published in Switzerland in 1944 and now just brought out in Rome as the first of Silone's productions to be published in his native country, is a long play called *Ed Egli Si Nascose—And He Did Hide Himself*, a quotation from John 12 (it is interesting that both Malraux and Silone should have gone to the Bible for titles), in which it is recorded that Jesus withdrew and disappeared from among his followers, after preaching: "Walk while ye have the light, lest darkness come upon you: for he that walketh in darkness knoweth not whither he goeth. While ye have the light, believe in the light, that ye may be the children of light." *Ed Egli Si Nascose* develops, on a larger scale and with a different implication, one of the incidents in *Pane e Vino*. In that novel there was a young man from the country who had gone to study in Rome and who, falling in love with an anti-Fascist girl, had associated himself with a revolutionary group. When his small supply of funds gave out, he resorted, in order to finish his courses, to taking money from the Fascist police for information against his companions. But he has been horribly tormented by conscience and, when he is caught in the country by the local police, who believe him to be a real revolutionist, he allows them to kill him on the spot. His death is thus an expiation and, in the account of it and the scene of his funeral, there are echoes of the Last Supper, the Passion and the Crucifixion. Now, in *Ed Egli Si Nascose*, Silone has made this episode his central theme. The young man is here driven to redeem himself by the much more positive gesture of actually printing and distributing a proletarian manifesto, and his murder at the hands of the Fascist police proves the stimulus—where Spina has failed—that rouses the people against the regime and leads them to organize a united opposition. His death brings the play to a climax with a kind of liturgical drama, which has its Joseph and Mary, its Magdalen, its John the Baptist and its Holy Communion, all worked out in a systematic parallel. Silone has explained in his foreword his belief that "the revolution of our epoch, which has been promoted by politicians and economists," presents "the appearance of a 'sacred mystery,' in which the very fate of man is at stake." "In the sacred history of man on earth, we are as yet, alas, only at Good Friday. The men who 'hunger and thirst after righteousness' are still being derided and persecuted and put to death. The spirit is still forced to hide in order to save itself."

In *Pane e Vino,* Silone had already had Pietro Spina ask the same question as Malraux's anthropologist: "What is man? What is this human life?" "Every revolution," he tells young Murica, the informer who is to expiate his treason, "always turns on this elementary question." And, "in this horrible society," where man is "mutilated, disgraced, deformed, insulted," the problem is to become "a new man," or, rather, to become for the first time "a man in the true sense of the word." Silone's way of finding a continuity in the vicissitudes of human history is to conceive it as a vast enactment of a drama to which the life of Jesus has given the symbolic clue.

Ed Egli Si Nascose, as a work of art, is less successful than *Pane e Vino.* The novel, in its chronicle of the adventures of Spina and its procession of Italian characters, had something in common with the great panoramas like *Huckleberry Finn* and *Dead Souls,* and Silone has not shown in this play a dramatic sense comparable to his narrative one. The emergence, furthermore, of the mystery play from the milicu of the modern Abruzzi may be found distasteful by readers who are remote from the Catholic religion; certainly it will be found dismaying by the old secularist type of Socialist. But the piece is full of excellent things: particularly the post-mortem discussions of the psychology of Communist activity in the period before the war. "The underground character of the movement," the young renegade is made to explain, "offers to the weak man the important and deceptive advantage of secrecy. He lives in sacrilege and shudders at it, but this is all concealed from the world. He is outside the hateful and terrifying law, but the guardians of the law do not know it. His denial of the established order remains an intimate and secret thing, as if it took place in a dream, and precisely on that account is likely to run to ideas that are drastic, catastrophic and bloody; but his external behavior remains unchanged. In his habitual relations this kind of weak man remains as timid, silly and nervous as before. He conspires against the government in the same way that he may be in the habit of dreaming that he is strangling his father, with whom he will sit down to breakfast in the morning." And there is an equally merciless passage on revolutionary work as a drug. The Communist's life is so dangerous and hard, one of the underground workers explains, that the only way to accomplish anything is to eliminate the strain on your nerves, and to do this is to induce a narcosis. "But," one of the women characters objects, "excuse me if I ask a stupid question. How can we be true and brave fighters for the revolution and be drugged at the same time? Shall we turn into a movement of sleepwalkers? . . . If we come to the revolutionary cause precisely through our sensibility—because our sensibility has been wounded by the savagery, the injustice, the brutality which we have found in present-day society? If we neutralize our sensibility, aren't we destroying in ourselves the very feelings that have brought us to the revolution?" The narcotized revolutionist may become unscrupulous and cruel and lose sight of the ends that he set out to serve, and the weak man who loves concealment may find it easy, under pressure of terrorism, to betray the underground movement and to keep this betrayal concealed. When young Murica has turned stool pigeon for the Fascists, he begins to be tortured by the notion that, if no one ever finds him out, he will never be punished for his treason, and it is a horror of this idea that good and bad may be mere matters of practical expediency which drives him, in moral protest, to do something that will get him into trouble. For Silone is here grappling with a problem that is one aspect of Malraux's problem: the justification of a human morality at this moment when the religions are losing their force and man, who now finds himself alone on the earth, has to recognize that it is he who decides what should and what should not be done. The situation of the German Nazis was precisely that of young Murica: why worry about moral principles if you are never to be called to account?—and, unlike Silone's young student, they could not see that they did have to worry.

Silone, confronting this question, has reverted to the Christian religion in a special non-ecclesiastical form, a version which one may find it easier to sympathize with than the formal and official versions of some of the recent Protestant converts to Catholicism. His point of view is a curious one. He makes one of his characters speak of "the new idea of good and evil" of "those who do not believe in the death and resurrection of Jesus but do believe in his agony," and he has explained to the present writer that he does not accept what he calls "the mythology of Christianity," that the liturgical form of his play and the analogies with the Gospel in his novels have come to him, in the most natural way, as a result of having known in his childhood no literature except the Bible and of never, till he was seventeen, having seen any drama except the

Mass. Yet certainly the life of Jesus has still for him a mystical meaning, and, in a paper read recently in Rome before the Associazione per il Progresso degli Studi Morali e Religiosi—I quote from the newspaper account—he dissociated his present position from that of the Russian ex-Socialist "God-seekers" after the defeat of the 1905 revolution, but asserted that he belonged among "those of whom St. Bernard speaks, those whom God pursues, and whom, when He overtakes them, He tears to pieces and chews and swallows." All this does not, however, prevent him from taking a very active part in the work of the Socialist Party as a member of its Central Committee.

Malraux and Silone thus seem to stand today almost alone in Europe as writers of first-rate talent who have continued to take imaginative literature with the utmost seriousness and who have never lost their hold on the social developments, larger and more fundamental, that lie behind national conflicts. They have survived the intellectual starvation, the spiritual panic of the war, and they are among the most valuable forces still alive on their devastated continent. Still they are trying to perform through their writing what Malraux makes one of his characters describe as the function of art: "a rectification of the world. . . . It seems to me that the cardinal confusion has arisen from our having assumed—in our conception of Greek tragedy it's striking—that to represent a doom is to suffer it. But that's not true: rather, it's almost to possess it. The very power of being able to represent it, to conceive it, allows it to escape from its real fate, from the implacable divine scale; brings it down to the human scale. In what is essential, our art is a humanization of the world." This is a much humbler point of view than that of the defiant Romantics of the first half of the nineteenth century or of the professional

Titans of the second half, but it trusts in human strength and vindicates human pride as the writers of our day have not always done. "The greatest mystery," says Malraux in another fine passage of his novel, "is not that we should have been thrown up by chance between the profusion of matter and the profusion of the stars, but that, in this prison, we should produce from ourselves images sufficiently powerful to deny our insignificance."

5

THROUGH THE ABRUZZI WITH
MATTIE AND HARRIET

WHEN MATTIE NUGENT WENT OUT TO THE ABRUZZI, she
expected something pretty rugged and brought along a
blanket-roll and rations. She was amazed to be put up at
Aquila, her headquarters as an U.N.R.R.A.* worker, in a
magnificent new hotel, which had been built under the
Fascists as a skiing resort and had been lately commandeered by the Allied Commission.

She was received by a good-looking young major, with
a small smartly-clipped dark mustache, who, though he
wore an American uniform, gave the impression of being
British. "I'd love one!" she declared enthusiastically, when
he suggested she might like a cocktail even before she
washed off the dust; and he guided her through high-
ceilinged chambers that, palatially cool though they were,
had a little that pasteboardy appearance which she had
noted in the big office buildings put up by the Fascists in
Rome: a lobby, where a woman—an Italian, she thought
—very quiet but rather chic—looked up from the book
she was reading; a spacious lounge with yellowish marble
walls that opened pleasantly out on a garden, full of sun
but devoid of flowers, in the center of which, on a

* United Nations Relief and Rehabilitation Administration.

97

pedestal, stood a black bronze of a naked young girl clasping behind her an enormous fish that seemed to Mattie, like so many things in Italy, not sensual merely but almost obscene; and, beyond, a soft-carpeted soft-lighted bar that reminded her of the latest thing in the "intimate" and the "modern" in the Statler hotels at home, but which was lined with a series of murals of English and Scottish soldiers amusing themselves in night-clubs or active at outdoor sports. "These decorations must be new," Mattie remarked, as they waited for drinks. "Yes, it was crawling with young Fascists on skis when the A.C. took the place over. But there's a very clever chap here who paints and he dashed off these muriels for us." The "muriels," which was meant as a joke, rather amused Mattie. She wondered whether the Major were Canadian.

"This is a rest-home, you know," he went on. "It's the first big attempt that's been made to get the Americans and the British together. Churchill's watching it, and so is F.D.R." "How is it working out?" "Oh, swell. The first one, in Sicily, was not a success; but this time we're going to swing it! We've actually got the Americans playing cricket and the British playing soft-ball." "Those soldiers in the pictures are all British," said Mattie, when she had studied the panels. "It was a Britisher that did them. But don't worry: we're holding up our end. I'm in charge here, and I'm an American." He smiled gracefully with self-assurance. He was obviously enjoying himself, making good, as he felt, at a greeter's job. "Where are you from?" she asked as a man would ask. "Buffalo. Where do you hail from?"—he had caught up her hearty note and was being somewhat more American. "I originally came from Vermont, but I've lived mostly in New York and Washington." "Well, we have plenty of Yankees here— New Hampshire and Massachusetts. Just about the whole English-speaking world is represented in the hotel now! We've even got a couple of New Zealanders." "Oh, it ought to be so *easy!*—if they'd just get used to each other's accents. It's principally the difference in pay that makes things difficult, isn't it? They don't like to go on parties together, because the G.I.'s have more dough." "That isn't an obstacle here," he assured her. "Everything's free except drinks, and we've made prices that are well within everybody's means." "What about women?" "There are plenty of girls." "But money's quite a factor there, isn't it?" "They come to dances that we give at the hotel here and that are joint affairs, of course—and then we have our snappy U.N.R.R.A. workers!" Mattie had noted, and now she reminded herself, that his gallantry was at least partly professional—that his raising of his left eyebrow and smiling on one side of his mouth had obviously been carefully acquired and that he exploited them for effect; yet she couldn't help feeling pleased. She hadn't ever had enough of this kind of thing to be scornful or blasé about it: men liked her and were always all right to her, except when, as sometimes happened, she frightened them by trying to run them; but her normal role was that of the pal who, if she did not always pay for her dinner, never slipped into a position of dependency; and it was nice to be treated flirtatiously, especially in this situation—doing U.N.R.R.A. work out in the mountains—where you would not have expected to be.

"Let me know if you want anything!" he said, with a fascinating special twinkle, as he later sent her up to her room, with a boy to carry her baggage. "I'm sorry it's such a climb, but we hope to have the lift working soon. I think you'll like the room—it's got a swell view." They ascended soft, ample and shallow stairs that swept imperially around three curves; and she was shown into an attractive bedroom, very new, very light, very blond, in which the twin beds with blue blankets and the glass-topped tables and bureau were of pale unpainted wood, and the tall blinds of the big French window opened portals to a blue mountain landscape. It was a place so much created for winter sports that she seemed to herself out of key, until, resisting the pressure of solitude, she began to assimilate herself to a girl who should have come there for that. She had once been a pretty good skier, before she had hurt her knee, and she imagined young Fascist couples—those dark-haired vivacious young women with their flashy but handsome young men—revelling insolently in privileged holidays: their dashing ski-runs and deep relaxed evenings, their intimate laughter, exciting love. In happier conditions, she thought, she could have done with a little of that. Her most serious love-affairs had never quite carried her off her feet and had always in the end let her down. There had been, first, a Jewish settlement worker; then a middle-aged businessman who was unfortunately permanently married; then, most recently, a liberal journalist, who had become a New Deal official and afterwards a captain in the Allied Commission, assigned for duty to Rome. Though their amorous relations had petered out, she had looked forward to seeing him there, and had not been able to help feeling hurt when she had found him inhabiting an apartment with a pretty Italian girl of nineteen—Mattie was thirty-four—who kept house for him as if they were married. No: she had never had the kind of devotion or been given the kind of good time that a girl had a right to expect.—Unless of course those young Fascist blades had been all fundamentally phony.

But yes, Aquila did seem romantic as she stood gazing out the window. She had never been in Europe before, and this was turning out so much more like a pleasure trip than she had expected it or thought it ought to be.

She had only been in Italy a couple of weeks, and she had found herself thrilled no end when, setting out in the jeep from Rome, she had first become aware of the fine layers of hills, one rising behind the other, in their delicate and varying tints of gray, and then had seen, under low-hanging clouds of a silver dullish and pure, the lovely silhouette of a mountain so dim and yet outlined so firmly that it might have been drawn by an artist and washed in with watered ink. Later they passed wide-skirted women balancing baskets and jars on their heads, unexpected little statues of the Virgin bricked-in over stable-doors, and a tonsured Franciscan monk riding a bicycle with his robe fastened up; and it had made her a little giddy to see the almost sheer olive groves and vineyards cultivated with such precision on what seemed such precarious slopes, and by those hill-towns, all in one formless piece and riddled with their tiny square windows, that seemed so much of the same brownish-grayish substance as the barren rocks on which they were based that they might almost have been the mere caves of cliff-dwellers or even the nests of birds. To an American, they were hardly acceptable as habitations for human beings, and, though she tried to think them picturesque, her first instinct was to find them repellent: one especially that had crumbled to rubble under bombing or artillery attack inspired her with utter disgust like a clay wasps'-nest incompletely swept down. Then there were landscapes that would have taken her unbelievably into a mediaeval story-book world—with their steep hills, crowned with little walled cities, spiked or specked with various plant-ings or circled with vegetation and ribboned with dry white roads that wound down from the town to the plain— if she had not corrected the fantasy by recognizing that the quaint old pictures which she had seen in museums at home had been perfectly realistic: the country really looked like that. And now, as she stared out the French window at these impressive Abruzzi ridges that combined in so special a way hard temper with soft color—as if there were steel underneath blue silver, yet a blue so etherealized that one peak, with its pencilled veins of snow, seemed to merge into the slate-blue heavens; as she looked, she felt lifted and freshened just the way she had sometimes been when she had gone back home to Vermont for a visit and had seen her own mountains again. And these mountains were so clean and upstanding!— how could the people who lived among them not be so? How could Italians, who were descended from the Romans and had that beautiful and hard-boned country, allow themselves to get roped in by such an obvious fraud as Fascism? And yet it must have given them something they liked. Had she not, in imagination, been sharing their fun in that skiers' hotel? They were *simple,* after all!—they had been misled. It both exasperated her and broke her heart! And her fancy now made her a leader who was warning them and forcing them to fight for their rights.

There was a knock. Mattie opened. A tall girl in a blue dress stood there. "I'm Harriet Locker," she said. Miss Locker was the field head for U.N.R.R.A., to whom Mattie had been told to report. She came in and gave Mattie a handshake which consisted of a single pump, after which her hand dropped to her side. She had a small ruddy gray-eyed face and bare reddened roughened legs, and wore a dark-blue béret on one side. She seated herself on a bed. "Are you all right?" she asked. "Have you had some lunch?—There's nothing to be done till five." Quickly and quietly she went through her briefing. Mattie was sure she was going to like her so much! She had always admired the English: she herself was long-faced and athletic, energetic and not easily daunted; and she had hoped to get along with them well. It was true that her friend in Rome had made bitter and indignant complaints about their policy with the Italians and their treatment of their American colleagues; but at the moment she was rather in reaction against his whole point of view—he had done such a lot of talking, always making someone else to blame, and had never really lived up to his principles!—and she was quite willing to find the British friendly. How she loved the informal authority, the casual-seeming firmness and sureness, with which Miss Locker mapped the situation and indicated Mattie's duties! An American would have been more assertive— either as a career woman imposing herself on you or a "character" inviting you to share with her her amusement, her impatience or her enthusiasm; and how much more impressive it was not to exhibit your zeal or your competence, but simply to do a good job without calling attention to yourself or confusing the problem with personal feelings! And how this girl seemed to be hitting all the nails on the head! The only thing that she had not made clear, Mattie realized when she had questioned her about the scope of their work, was her own very responsible position as the sole representative for U.N.R.R.A. in four wild and inaccessible provinces.

"Of course they're supposed to do things themselves," said Miss Locker, "and one is here merely to supervise." "But you have to crack down on them sometimes, I understand." "Oh, things have been going quite smoothly." She seemed to hesitate a second—then went on drily to an official confidence: "There's one lot of food that hasn't turned up, and it may have gone astray." "Sold to the black market?" asked Mattie. "One can't be sure what's happened. I've been prodding them about it, but can't get a clear story. It ought to have been distributed two weeks ago, and they keep on making excuses. But they've promised to produce it tomorrow, so we'll see. It's not always easy to know what's being done, because the stuff doesn't go through our hands." "But still"—Mattie affirmed with great confidence the democratic policy of U.N.R.R.A.—"they've got to learn to take *hold* and handle their own affairs!" "They're complaining," Miss Locker replied, "that we don't give them enough direction. They say they got on better with the Germans, because they told them exactly what to do." "But then, they've been taking orders from the Fascists so *long!*—and the whole regime was so crooked that they take to the black market like mad!"

It was not until a minute or two after she had expressed herself so strongly that it occurred to her that it might not be quite proper, the very moment of her arrival, to lay down such positive opinions. Miss Locker had changed the subject, and Mattie saw that she was rather shy and that it cost her a certain effort to put their relation on a natural basis of two young women working together. She tried to meet the nice girl halfway, and when her new chief addressed her as "Mathilda," she said, "Everybody calls me Mattie,"—adding, with a quick grin: "I'm not going to call you Hattie, though!" But the other did not smile in return: the look in her gray eyes was blank, as if she did not know how to take it. "I must watch my cracks, I guess," thought Mattie. "I'm going to have a bath," she said, "and then, if you don't need me till five, I think I'll go out and get a load of the town." Harriet looked at her without replying. Then, after the brief pause, "You can go in the jeep," she said. "I'll show you about, if you like."

Mattie, as they drove through Aquila, was dazed with wonder and sun. The town looked as if it were constructed of hard planes of light and shade that made the most violent contrasts. Above white blinding sidewalkless streets stood façades built of local stone that had a richness despite their austerity, with their juxtaposed orange and sepia, burnt sienna and café au lait, neutral liver and greenish gray, that made a double scale of colors, one darkened and cold, one glowing. The tall doorways were impressively hooded with heavy ornamental architraves, and the windows, well-proportioned and brown-shuttered, were capped with a variety of pediments that resembled now triangular crests, now crowns with twin peaks, now coronets, and contributed to a standard of dignity that—surprisingly, she thought, in that mountain town—attained something akin to grandeur. It did seem queer and not quite comfortable to keep driving through a place of that size and never once to pass a corner drug-store or a Woolworth's or an A. & P.; but Aquila had a unity and harmony which made it seem all to have been built in one piece like those wasps'-nests in the hills that had given her the creeps, but which here imposed themselves upon her and compelled her to respect and admire. This, she saw, was what architecture could do—not merely lay out a plan as at Washington, but dominate a whole city and actually provide the medium in which human beings lived.

"It doesn't seem to be much damaged," she said. "There was an Austrian in command," explained Harriet, "and he evidently behaved very well: he didn't blow things up when he left. The Germans shot him for it. The electrical plant was mined, but the inhabitants dug it out." "They look as if they had guts," said Mattie. Straight, hardened, lean and tall, they were quite different from the Italians of Rome: why of course! they were mountaineers, like the people of Vermont and New Hampshire. She wasn't sure they weren't a tougher breed, because the New Englanders had been certainly degenerating, and these people seemed to have remained the same for hundreds and hundreds of years. "One can't always depend on them," said Harriet, lowering her voice to a murmur, so as not to be overheard by the driver, though he apparently understood no English.—"That's where they wander up and down," she glanced at a long domed colonnade, with attractive-looking cafés and shops displaying unfamiliar objects that Mattie would have liked to examine.

"Go to the right," Harriet ordered the driver. He half-turned, but did not answer. "To the right," she repeated. Mattie helped her out: *"A destra!"* she said loudly and clearly. *"Più lontano,"* he replied. " 'More something,'—I don't get it.—Oh, 'further'!"—as he flapped with his right hand forward. "They always want to do things their own way," said Harriet. "What does *più* mean? They're always saying it." Mattie explained to her the driver's phrase. "Then there's a *poi,*" her companion went on, as if to ease off her momentary interest by slipping into a lightly derisory attitude toward a language full of babyish monosyllables. "And something that sounds like *po.*" *"Poi* means 'then,'" said Mattie,—"and there's a *può* that's the third person singular of the verb that means *can.*" "Is that what it is?" said Harriet, her voice now quite devoid of interest; and she somehow made Mattie feel that she had been a little showing off and that the meaning of Italian words was not a subject in which it was suitable to evince too keen an interest.

The Fascists, it became apparent, had done a good deal for Aquila; an influential Fascist had come from there and had seen to it that the town was well-equipped. Harriet pointed out a stadium and a swimming-pool, with a faint smile which indicated amusement at the idea of Italians' pretending to go in for real sports like English-men and to which Mattie found herself responding with

a little ironic twist of one corner of her wide and good-
natured mouth. "Our men are using them now," said
Harriet. Then they drove up before the G.I.L., the
Gioventù Italiana del Littorio: a long building, with a
shrimp-pink façade and a triple row of slotlike windows,
from the roof of which were flying, side by side, the
British and the American flags. It was pretty perhaps
rather than imposing, but you had to admit, she thought,
that the Fascists *had* given them *something*. She
rather admired the ramplike stairways (on one of which,
however, she noted, with reprobation for what it implied,
a big decorative map of l'Africa Orientale Italiana); the
verandah that stretched at the back, furnished comfortably with steamer chairs and commanding a marvellous
view; the dining rooms and school-rooms, into which they
looked, full of unpainted "functional" furniture, in which
children were still being taught and fed; and the club-
room hung with photographs of old school groups. A
number of these photographs had been destroyed, an
American soldier told them, because they had had Fascist
slogans underneath. "It seems kind of a shame," said
Mattie, "that some of the kids should lose their class
pictures." "They can't expect anything else," said Harriet
quickly and firmly.

"Drive to the castle," she told the driver. This was a
word he could understand. The castle was a flat gray
stone fortress, surrounded by a dried-up moat and guarded
above the door with the eponymous Aquila eagle. "Pretty
grim!" commented Mattie. "I don't think we can use it as
a country club!" Harriet made no response: "I've lost her
again!" thought Mattie. They walked back to get into the
car, and Mattie smiled at the driver. *"Ecco il Gran Sasso
d'Italia,"* he gestured in the direction of the mountains,—
"dov' era imprigionato Mussolini." *"Lei è allegro,"* she
asked, being careful to use the polite form, *"che Musso-*

lini partito?" "Era un buffone, vigliacco," he answered,
starting the car. "They drive like Jehus," said Harriet, in
a way that Mattie couldn't help feeling was intended to
detach her from the driver. "Where is San Bernardino?"
she asked. "I'm afraid I don't know," said Harriet. "The
Major says it's a beautiful church,"—Mattie took out a
guidebook he had given her,—"that it's something you
ought to see." The driver made a sudden sharp turn and
stopped before a square stone façade—announcing, *"Ecco
San Bernardino."* Harriet was plainly annoyed, but she
did not express her annoyance. "Do you want to see it?"
she asked. "I'd like to go in for a minute, but if we have to
get back, it's not—" *"I'll* have to go back, I'm afraid, but
if you don't mind walking and will be on hand at five."
"I've got an hour and twenty minutes,"—Mattie briefly
flashed up her wrist-watch, "and—" "You won't get lost?"
—her chief again cut her short—"It's just down that long
street we were coming to before we turned off here.
Since you speak Italian so well, you can ask if you go
astray." She left Mattie feeling, for a moment, a little
silly over her efforts at Italian and somehow a little guilty
for her desire to stop off at the church. She wondered
whether Harriet Locker—who had, after all, been to see
the castle—were not some kind of clergyman's daughter,
so that she shunned the monuments of Popery on principle. Yes: she might perfectly well have come from some
vicarage or rectory in the country such as you read about
in English novels. She was very provincial, of course, and
that was the reason, poor dear, that she hadn't learned a
word of Italian. And Mattie pushed open the dark old
door and invaded San Bernardino.

Inside, the deep cool shade was wonderful; and, though
in Catholic churches at home she had always thought of
cheap perfume, the sweetness of the incense here seemed
disinfected by the ancient stone, and the candles burning

in silence conveyed sanctity as well as peace. She made the rounds, at first a little self-consciously, of the tombs with elaborate carvings which were confusing and too fancy to please her; a crowned madonna that she thought really touching: that idea of the Queen of Heaven so full of love for her child!; and a big terra-cotta panel of the Resurrection, in which seraphs and saints and angels seemed to be foaming and coagulating like curds and which she was thrilled to discover from the guidebook was supposed to be by Della Robbia, the man who had made the cherubs: a dear travelled aunt in Topsfield, Mass., had had them in her dining-room. But what Mattie had not at first taken in, going from one of these sideshows to the other, and what suddenly lifted her spirit as she stood in the aisle and looked up, was the magnificent gold-and-white nave that opened before and above her. An arcade of high white arches, between each two of which, as if inlaid in the woodwork, stood a white column with a gilded Corinthian top, gave way to a white windowed clerestory and supported a gold-coffered ceiling which had a sword-raying sun in the middle and which framed, on either side of this, a succession of sacred paintings of which the colors seemed softer and more charming, the figures more appealingly human, for the great wrought ornate brooches that encased them. And this white panelling, this sober design, that arrived at felicity through purity, was close enough in tone to the old Congregational churches in which, on New England "greens," she had sung hymns and listened to sermons, to make her feel now half at home; and, as she slowly moved down the aisle, she had almost the reassuring sensation of having just stepped out of a marsh onto indubitable solid ground. Here was something that had kept strong and comely, that had sustained the dignity of man, till it did seem to touch that Divine which, in the days before bombings, before settlement work, before statistics on unemployment and wage-scales, the human race had not hesitated to postulate. What did it mattter if religion was not really true? You were grateful enough for something like this—which had been spared, in these days by the merest chance, through the compassion or good taste of one Austrian, who had perhaps admired the little mountain city and who had paid for its survival with his life!

She approached the foot of the nave and saw before her an open back-door, of which she had not been aware at a distance. Set thus in the dark wall of shade, a small rectangle, clear-cut and bright-lit, it gave a view, above a hillside that dropped sheer below, of the hillside that rose higher just opposite: a sudden vivid green-and-blue vista, that seemed itself a kind of church picture, painted devoutly in the age of faith and placed there where it could always be looked at, where it could always be seen at its best. She stood still, and tears came to her eyes. So in those days they had humanized, had focussed for art, even the sun and the trees and the grass, even the towering mountains, and, in humanizing them, had offered them to God!

And now it was time to go back to the hotel.

II

They had a friendly breakfast together, comparing notes about settlement houses, and got off in good time in the jeep. Mattie remarked on the strange lack of odor of the Italian countryside, which caused her something like a feeling of frustration, as she missed the American humidity that always brought out so heavily the smells of vegetation and earth. Harriet agreed to this: you smelled things much more strongly in England, too. "There are no dogs either," she added. "They've eaten them, I suppose," said Mattie,—"or else had to let them starve." "It's been hard to feed them in England," said Harriet, "but the people would never eat them." It turned out that Harriet possessed two dogs, which she evidently adored. One was a Sealyham and one was a sheep-dog. Her mother was looking after them at home, but she was lame and couldn't take them for walks. Harriet was afraid that they weren't getting proper exercise. Mattie had had two Scotties, one of which—"oh, he was so cute and such a *scrapper!"*—had been killed by a car, it had broken her heart, and the other of which, given her later, she had had to leave with her sister when she had gone to do war-work in Washington.

Harriet paid no attention to the scenes among which they were passing—she had of course had plenty of time to get used to them—and the effect of this impassivity on Mattie was somewhat to check her exclamatory impulses. Yes, you had to take the ruin for granted; this hideous and dismaying prospect was where your work began. There was no nonsense about the British, even on an errand of mercy, and that was the way to be. But all this country had been a battlefield, and almost everything connected with peacetime had been blown into smithereens. Frivolous villas in pink or blue that had once been frilled with little iron balconies and red crenellated roofs, had been crushed in like brittle molluscs, and the pretty terra-cotta statues that had sometimes posed in niches outside had had their heads and their hands snapped off. In one place, a grand iron gateway, flanked by large marble urns, led to a fragment of pretentious façade with a doorway of carved marble and the grillwork of two up-stairs windows, but nothing whatever behind it—though a plain little mud-colored church had somehow remained

intact. The bridges had all been blown up, so that the car
would have to bump down a bank, where a precarious
path had been broken through, and would find, among
the pale dusty pebbles of the dried-up river-bed, chunks
of masonry, crumbled and dusty, that could hardly be
told from the dirt. Among the only things still in good
order were the supplies of unused shells and bombs piled
up here and there beside the road and, in one place, a
whole field of German tanks that, pointing their guns like
proboscises and mottled with dirty green, looked—as
Mattie refrained from remarking—like a herd of queer
grisly cattle.

But the road had the appearance at certain points of
having had enormous mouthfuls bitten out of it, and she
remembered that the driver, on the way from Rome, had
told her that there were still some live mines and that
it was better to avoid the shoulders. Their present driver
was definitely reckless, and, as Harriet did nothing to
restrain him, Mattie assumed that, since the day before,
her chief had given up hope of controlling him. "I'm
going to tell him to keep in the middle," she said in a low
voice and began to consult her pocket lexicon. Harriet
made no reply and let Mattie expostulate and gesticulate;
but when she said afterwards, "I think we're quite safe,"
she made Mattie wonder again whether she hadn't made
a fool of herself.

They spent the night in a town called Chieti, which
was a good deal less civilized than Aquila and seemed to
Mattie quite mediaeval. The cramped and offal-strewn
streets had no pavements, and they were raucous with
shouts and howls. It was the first thing that had scared
her a little. At the hotel, which was also small and dirty,
the old room-clerk looked like a rat. When she and Harriet
separated to go to bed, Harriet gave her some bug-
powder. "You'd better keep your door locked," she

warned her. "I missed a garment once after I stayed here."
And Mattie, rather nervous for her, was kept awake most
of the night by bands of young men who prowled the
streets singing at the tops of their voices. At one point, she
got up to look at them. They did not seem to be swag-
gering so much as she had thought they were, but slowly
drifting arm in arm, so that she felt more sympathetic
toward them. Was it some kind of politics, she wondered,
or merely some youthful whoopee? But why were so
many of them abroad on a weekday?—and why did they
keep going all night? Was it something so romantic and
gratuitous that a New Englander couldn't grasp it? In any
case, it was evidently something not directed by the
Allied Commission.

The next morning they went on to Orsogna, the place
where the food supplies had disappeared. Though Mattie
had now seen already a good many smashed or battered
buildings, she was not quite prepared for Orsogna. Here,
what had once been the public square was a barren
expanse of dust, no longer surrounded by houses but
vaguely bounded by piles of bricks and plaster and a few
upright morsels of walls, with the shutters hanging askew
by one corner and the wiring of fixtures and balconies
shredded like spiders'-webs. Inside these wrecked human
cells, the swifts had stuck their cell-like nests, and they
were flitting in and out, busily intent on their households
and delighted with the new quarters thrown open to
them, while the only sound to be heard was the incessant
bleating of a goat, tied up near the place where the car
had stopped. The goat seemed badly diseased: it was raw
in great patches of a horrid pink, and Mattie tried to
exclude it from her consciousness.

A handful of people who had been hanging around
gathered quietly near the car, and others emerged from
the ruins. They were barefoot, and such clothes as they

had were ill-fitting and patched and discolored, yet they made a fairly decent appearance. They were not voluble, Mattie noted, but seemed rather restrained and sober. An official called the *sindaco* came out, evidently a kind of mayor—wearing a well-curled white mustache and dressed in formal bourgeois black. Harriet talked to him through an interpreter, whom she had brought along from Chieti: a girl from Bridgeport, who had married an Italian and gone to live in Italy. Harriet tackled the food at once. It was known to have got there two weeks ago: why hadn't they given it out? They had been waiting, the *sindaco* explained, for instructions to come from Rome. But they had had their instructions from Rome. Yes, but only a few days ago. Then why had the distribution not been announced at once? It had been: they had put up posters. He handed her something written in longhand, very archaic and clerical-looking. But where were the announcements?—she looked around: there was nothing on any of the walls except clumsily painted-up slogans of *Viva Lenin* and *Viva il Comunismo*. That had been several days ago, he said, and they had taken them down since. "They've never posted any announcement, you see," Harriet murmured to Mattie. Well, why weren't they distributing the food? They had said they would do it at half past ten, and she had come expecting to find them doing it. The *sindaco* said he was sorry—there had had to be a little delay: some of the people worked in the fields and couldn't be there in the morning. The distribution would take place this afternoon. "He says that they'll positively do it," the American interpreter explained. "Tell him," said Harriet, "that I'll come back at three." Mattie understood the *sindaco* when he replied, *"Alle tre precise!"*

In the meantime, they went on to another town. Mattie felt sorry for Harriet. If the food had really disappeared and they were unable to produce it that afternoon, she would have to raise Cain with the *sindaco* without knowing any Italian and would then have to take it up with U.N.R.R.A. headquarters in Rome, who might think she hadn't been on the job. Mattie was just going to try to say something helpful when Harriet said something herself: "Tell him we're sure to need petrol before we get back from Tollo. Tell him to get some here." Mattie asked, after a moment's silence: "Are there many towns in as bad shape as that?" It was the first time she had ventured to comment. "About thirty in this province," answered Harriet.

Tollo, though it figured on the guidebook map as a name the same size as Orsogna, made the latter seem a thriving metropolis. Whatever had been there once was now pulverized level with the road and of exactly the same color. The only thing standing was a kind of shed, which had been recently knocked together, and to which a few women and children who had been living under haystacks or in huts in the fields had come to apply for the handout of lard, flour and sugar, dried codfish, dried milk and dried beans, so meager that it had had to be limited to expectant or nursing mothers and to children under the age of eight. When the U.N.R.R.A. workers appeared, everybody smiled and applauded, and Mattie could not help feeling pleased. She tried to talk to the women, and the interpreter helped her out. One of the burstingly pregnant ones had already, it seemed, had ten. The mother's face proudly beamed as if she expected congratulations. But Harriet only said: "One would think they wouldn't want so many." "Oh, lo-ok!" cried Mattie, delighted, over a tiny two-year-old girl, who was practicing to carry the big earthen jars, for which, it seemed, the word was *conche,* by balancing on her head a little aluminum bowl. Harriet was too much preoccupied with her position of responsibility to do more than give a fleeting smile. "Yes: she *is* rather sweet," she said.

On the way back, they stopped for a moment and ate some sandwiches that Harriet had brought along, and Mattie produced some American chocolate, to which Harriet seemed to react with more eagerness than Mattie had seen her show about anything but the thought of her dogs. "You're lucky," she said, "to have your PX's. We haven't had any proper sweets in England for ages." "I must give you some of my peanut brittle,"—Mattie tried to explain what this was, and Harriet replied by describing how their nana used to make them taffy—Harriet called it "toffy"—"It was awful fun," she said. She seemed to feel so much interest in this subject—"It's the Camp Fire Girl touch," thought Mattie—that her lieutenant did not hesitate to pursue it. "And marshmallows!" Mattie exclaimed. "They have them now at the PX in Rome. I'll get you some and show you how to roast them. It's quite a trick, but when you get them just right, they're absolutely delicious. They have a sort of golden-brown toasted crust, and inside they're all melted and goozily!" But then she was pulled up short by the thought of the dried milk and codfish that they had just been giving out at Tollo. "Well," she declared, "it'll be interesting to see what we're going to find at Orsogna!" "It will indeed," said Harriet—"*jolly* interesting!"

But at Orsogna things seemed quite in order. The distribution did not begin at three; but barrels were being rolled out and upended in a low dark room that had a counter and looked like a general store. A large pair of old-fashioned scales was being set up on the counter; and lists of names were submitted to Harriet, written out in the same ornamental hand as the pretended distribution announcement. The *sindaco* went through some motions of checking up on the contents of the barrels to show that the right quantity of everything was there.

Harriet got somewhat confused between pounds and kilograms, and Mattie tried to straighten her out; but she felt that her attempts to be helpful were resisted, perhaps resented, by Harriet, and she finally gave it up, though she had the impression that Harriet was not getting her problems right. *"Alle quattro precise!"* the *sindaco* declared, holding up four fingers.

"When they say *precise*," said Mattie, "you're supposed to add an hour and a half." She glanced around and caught the eye—brown and friendly, not blackly foreign—of a small man in a khaki shirt. "You're American?" he asked her in English. She was delighted: he had spent sixteen years in the States, and what a relief his straight way of talking, his garage-mechanic's Jersey accent, were to Mattie's expansive nature after the diffidence of the rag-swathed and gaunt-faced natives! A great many people from Orsogna had gone to America, he said—about a thousand out of a population of six thousand. The town itself had been built up, in the years before its destruction, mainly by American money that the emigrants had sent back to their families. "He asks"— he interpreted the question of another man standing by—"why you don't make Italy the fiftieth state." "The forty-ninth," Mattie corrected. "I wish we could," she answered. Harriet had turned away, and Mattie, who had not known how to include her in the conversation, had for a moment a twinge of feeling that what she had said might have been in bad taste. "Do you want to take me around the town," she suggested to the nice little man, "and show me what's happened to it?" "Sure thing!" he eagerly answered. "Would you like to go around?" she asked Harriet. "This man's been in the States and speaks English." "I don't think so," said Harriet hastily, swallowing her words, Mattie noted, like a character in a Noel Coward play. "I'll just stay here and keep an eye on things." "You don't mind if I go?" "Not a bit." Mattie felt a shade of disapproval, but did not allow this to stop her. "Great Scott!" she thought, "it's certainly important to see how these people are living." And she went off with the little man.

Orsogna, he told her as they walked, had been held for some time by the Germans, and besieged and bombarded by the British, who had driven the enemy out and then allowed the Italians to take it themselves. But by that time there had been little to take. The Germans had ordered the people to leave, but some two hundred had stayed behind, and the Germans had killed almost all of them. He showed her one of the rare houses that were still intact. A man and his wife and daughter had lived there, and they had refused to go away, so the Germans had taken them out and shot them. But in other cases they had simply put bombs in the cellars and blown the families up with the houses. A hundred or so had been killed by shells, two or three hundred by mines. Some had gone to live in Padua; others were lodging about the countryside with friends. The people who were left in the town had established themselves in such basements as still had roofs or in the very few habitable rooms, or, as at Tollo, they slept in the fields. "They live like pigs," he said. "They raise a little corn and wheat, that's all. They haven't got no farm implements nor nothing." If they could raise a certain sum in lire for the purpose of rebuilding the town, the government would supply the rest; but even the smallest house cost about a hundred and fifty thousand lire, and that was a lot of money now. In the meantime, the town administration, he said, had been Communist and now was Socialist, and he seemed to have a typically American contempt for this un-American kind of politics: "All they do is bum around and drink. They fight with each other—that's all they do," he said. "And who gets the graft?" asked Mattie. "Who sells the U.N.R.R.A. supplies?" He shrugged and stuck forward his underlip. "We don't know if it's somebody in Orsogna or somebody in Chieti. Nobody knows where the clothes have gone. They're sent and they never get here!" "I thought it was the food," said Mattie. "The food came, but they don't give it out till today. If you didn't come, maybe they never give it out. The clothes don't come at all." "Is the *sindaco* a Socialist?" "He's a Socialist, yes." "Then I suppose he isn't a crook." Her friend gave another great shrug and protruded his underlip.

They were walking toward the end of the town, amid a brownish desolation of masonry that was melting into the pale mud. What had evidently once been a wide street presented but a few scraggy splinters of trees. A carpenter was working on the roof of a house that had not been too badly wrecked: the only attempt at repairs that Mattie had so far seen—perhaps the only place where repairs were possible. And, as they moved toward the edge of the town, she found that she had, more and more, to struggle with a peculiar reluctance, an impulse to rescue herself from an abyss of disgust and horror into which she seemed to be heading. Though she had dealt sometimes, in her settlement-work days, with the last degradations of poverty, these had at least been a recognizable element of the pushing and pulsing city, and, though she had often seen revolting diseases, she had been able to cheer up the patient, or, at least, to cherish the faith that science would discover a cure; but here, she was abashed to realize, it was only by an effort of will and a warning to herself to be lucid, that she could contemplate the carcase of an organism, this city where people had lived, so completely crushed down and ground out, that she could admit to her conception of the world in which she herself had lived the actuality of this wholesale negation practiced by man on man. Something in her did not want to be there, did not want to know about it, only wanted to get away! Among the shapeless and monotonous clay-colored mounds and the less frequent still-upstanding fragments —about which she found herself reflecting that, if they had been eaten away by the sea, the effect would have been more symmetrical—you could look out on the blue Abruzzi and the green hills that rose beneath them. "This is a nice view from here," she remarked. "Yes: people used to say that Orsogna was the most beautiful town in Chieti Province."

On the way back, he showed her the school. This was a creation of the late regime and seemed to her, as a public building, a very pronounced improvement on anything else of the kind of which she had seen the remains. Well, the Fascists *had* been modernizing Italy: you couldn't blame people for being impressed by them. She looked in at the roofless white walls of some large auditorium or common-room and deciphered inspirational texts from Cicero, Saint Francis and Ovid: *"L'anima umana si sente ispirata verso la campagna perchè è il simbolo della libertà"; "Fanciulli, voi siete l'aurora della vita, voi siete la speranza della patria, voi siete sopra tutto l'esercito di domani."* There were only four or five rooms left now— none of which had any glass in the windows—that could possibly be used for schoolwork, and in the bigger ones two or three classes were being held at the same time. The children were taught in shifts, and those who were not in the classrooms waited their turns outside. Here, among the barbed-wire brambles, this youngest genera- tion of Italians, who had been told that they were the dawn of life and that the countryside was the symbol of liberty, amused themselves by playing with unexploded bombs as if they had been nursery blocks. "Gosh!" Mattie exclaimed. "Is that safe?" "They take off the caps,"—her guide smiled—"so they can't go off any more."

Would she like to see the house, he asked, where the Germans had made their headquarters? It had survived because the German soldier who had been left behind to blow it up with its stores of ammunition had failed to obey orders and had tried to buy his own security by surrendering himself to the Italians. They went in, and Mattie's first impression chilled the back of her neck with horror, but she compelled herself to be objective. The point was that the German lookout had been in the top floor of this building, and, in order to prevent the enemy from identifying it by the smoke from the chimney, they had broken a hole in the flue, so that the smoke had all poured through inside, and several rooms had been blackened—with startling white patches where the plaster had chipped—so that they looked like chambers of Hell. Every room had its dirty pallets: a dozen or more people now lived there—glad enough to find place for a bed in this hideously transmogrified dwelling, which the invader had seized and made use of for the purpose of turning the pretty little town into a strategic point on a battlefield and a center of oppression and torment, and which still kept the flavor and, as it were, the shape of the aliens who had now departed. It was with queer fascination and repulsion that Mattie stared, in the abandoned mess-room, at a wall scrawled with jokes and cartoons, of which she couldn't always quite make sense: *"Kamerad! Kennst du Knäckebrod?," "Schön war die Trat in Orsogna," "Was macht die Fussball Braut am Sonntag Nachmittag?"* The drawings depicted the local life: a lazy native lounging crosswise in a basket on the back of a donkey, and a woman with a *concha* on her head. All the figures had potato-noses and looked, not in the least like Italians, but like the types in German comic papers. This was what they had thought of Orsogna, and this was how they had amused themselves. They were human, it was good to remember:

first no doubt, bored and badly fed; then surrounded by an embittered enemy, suffocated and smoked like herrings, and lodged above an ammunition dump, they could hardly have enjoyed Orsogna. But then she thought how they had gone through the street, planting bombs under all the houses and blowing them up one by one. She was glad to get out of the place and not sorry to see daubed on the front: *"Viva Stalin!" "Viva Matteotti!"*

The British had not found this look-out, but, since the tower of one of the churches was the highest point in the town, had assumed that the Germans had been using it, and had shot it down, wrecking the building. Mattie was asked if she wanted to see it—she had an escort now of several men, all of whom had been in America. She waded in among the debris and looked about at the white plaster and naked bricks, and up at the three round domes that were cracked through like the shells of boiled eggs. The broken places showed the pure blue sky, and the swallows, incessantly chirping, were flying in and out. There were mutilated plaster cherubs, still perched over empty niches, from which the saints had in time been removed, and the figure of a bishop, with mitre and staff and two fingers upraised in blessing, which had miraculously remained unbroken. But the confession-boxes were shattered, the top of the pulpit was gone, and underfoot lay a scrambled gray mass of fallen beams, flaked or crumbled plaster, bits of gilt, and wrenched-out wires. Mattie thought about the church in Aquila and wondered what this one had been like. What was left seemed so pretty and touching. An old woman came in with a basket full of some kind of wild white flowers. She had brought them, it seemed, for the bishop, who was the patron saint of the town. They explained to the woman that Mattie was an American who had come to help them. *"Portateci in America!"* she cried in a high voice.

"*Portateci in America!*" "We want that the United States should take Italy," said one of the men who had been there. "If you don't take us, the Russians will take us!" "I wish we could," said Mattie. A brick fell a few feet off with a sharp rather wicked crack. They went away, and left the old woman praying. "Well," thought Mattie, "those paintings and things are certainly a darn sight pleasanter than what you have to study for social planning, but there doesn't seem to be any other way to get through to the Good Society!"

They were walking in the opposite direction from the end of the town which they had first explored. This had evidently been the smarter section, where the well-to-do people lived. There was a wide alley still lined with small lindens, which must have been a kind of park where people came to stroll in the evenings, but where they met now only a morose looking man driving in a flock of sheep. He acknowledged her guide's salutation without the least sign of friendliness or interest. So this avenue which had once represented a certain degree of refinement and luxury had been sent back to the most primitive countryside. The remnants of the tinted façades, with their satyr-masks or little nude nymphs, were evidences, cheap though they seemed, of the cheerful ubiquity in Italy and of the survival through two thousand years of an ideal of pleasure and elegance, and it rather depressed her to realize that, with everything smashed up like this and herself come as an angel of mercy, she would never be able to taste it. Suddenly she felt as she had at the humbler end of the town: choking with dust and death. "It's time for me to go back," she said.

She found Harriet standing by while the last preparations were made—her businesslike and boyish béret drooping a little above one shoulder and one foot stretched out to the side, so as to rest on the edge of the sole and, by a posture as inconspicuous and as far from the feminine as possible, to take the weight off the other leg. She had, Mattie noted, her usual air of an authority so completely indifferent that it sometimes seemed hardly to make the connections that were necessary to activate people; and yet there was something about it that Mattie could not help admiring. She wrote down the name of her guide, and thanked him and said goodby; then, incapable of Harriet's calm, she went in behind the counter and examined the gigantic scales. One of the sides was dropped with a load of the round brass weights, and when she lifted these off, she discovered that the balances did not hang even. "These scales are cockeyed!" she said. "Look," she called Harriet over—"they're about a quarter of a kilogram off!" She spoke directly to the American interpreter: "Tell him these scales don't balance." The two men who seemed to be presiding came up and inspected the scales. They were extremely quiet and grave. Mattie watched them, making vigorous suggestions. When they were about to take the whole thing apart, she appealed to the interpreter to stop them: "Oh, why don't they just use a makeweight? We've been held up so long already! If they fool with it, it may never work." "I don't think that will do," said Harriet. "None of the weights makes the difference quite right. It ought to be made to work properly.—Yes," she directed the interpreter, "tell them to go ahead." But their tinkering did not help, and eventually Mattie supplied a stone that exactly made up the difference.

The distribution now began. Mattie had occupied herself, while waiting for the scales to be fixed, in transposing pounds into kilograms for the quantity allotted of each of the commodities; and she now began checking the number of women who were to be served in the various categories. Harriet stood looking on, and presently, to Mattie's surprise—it had hardly been three-quarters of an hour—murmured almost inaudibly but decisively that there was no point in staying any longer. "You don't want to check?" asked Mattie. "I've done that," she briefly replied. They departed, Mattie feeling dissatisfied and Harriet, she thought, out of humor. "But then," she explained to herself, "she doesn't know where she is with the Italians, poor lamb! It's just as if she were in darkest Africa!"

III

That evening they were sitting after dinner in the interpreter's house in Chieti, in which Harriet had her local headquarters and in which she kept a room—drinking a bottle of whisky which had been given her by a brother. Though she answered Mattie's questions about him in the offhand British way—he had been all through the war, it seemed, and had lately been sent to Bari—it was plain, Mattie said to herself, that she absolutely worshipped this brother; and, warmed by the genial gesture and the idea of family affection into forgetting a slight previous tension, she soon let herself go with her chief. "I don't see," she suggested heartily, "why it wouldn't be a good idea to get some of those Americanized Italians that can really be depended on and put them in charge of things out there." "Florence's husband has been in America,"—Harriet dropped her voice—"but he wasn't very reliable about the food. He was the person who told me it was gone." "I guess he had something there"—"Do you think he was interested in some way?" "What? No: I mean that there was something in what he said." "But they did have the food, you see." "The man who took me around said it wasn't the food that had disappeared, but that a shipment of clothes that was supposed to have come had never been even seen." "The clothes have been distributed," said Harriet. "How do you know? Were you there?" "I had to go to another province —but they showed me the announcement and the lists." "I wouldn't say that that proved much of anything, judging by our experience today. If you hadn't gone out there just now and put them on the spot, I don't believe those nursing mothers would ever have had a smell of those things. I'll bet those scales were that way because they had them rigged. I don't see how we can even be sure, for that matter, that they gave out the whole amount—because we didn't stay to the end, and we don't know that those barrels weren't padded. I gathered from that man that I talked to that there was some skulduggery going on." "They always expect too much. They're quite childish about it," said Harriet. "In one town, a man found a dollar in a suit that had been sent from America, and the others were all complaining that they didn't get dollars, too—they thought they'd been stolen." Mattie laughed, but said inwardly, "She's sidestepping the issue." "One of us," she went on aloud, "ought absolutely to be on the job at every one of those distributions. We could each of us take two provinces. We ought to see that the signs are put up on time and we ought to be right there on the spot when the stuff is supposed to be given out—but I don't think it's any use to try to get anybody to do anything in the early afternoon—nobody works in the middle of the day." "I don't see why we should encourage their laziness." "But they've evidently *always* gone to sleep after lunch. They must have been doing it for thousands of years. I suppose you might just as well expect them to give up eating spaghetti." "They might have a sounder diet. They don't get enough meat and greens. The tuberculosis rate is frightfully high, you know." "Well, in any case, *we* can't expect to make them change their habits about things like that—just a couple of U.N.R.R.A. workers!" But Harriet would not be downed: "We've had to show them the error of their ways," she said, "as far as politics were concerned. I don't see why we should let them expect to idle away half the day when there's so much work to be done. That's not the policy of the A.C.—they make them be on duty all day."

Mattie did not reply at once. For the first time in her relations with Harriet, she was brought up against something that gave her pause. She put out her cigarette in an ashtray and was glad, for some reason, to see that it had been bought in Atlantic City. She glanced toward her empty tumbler. She could have done with another drink; but it was perfectly evident that Harriet drank slowly and only took one. "If anything goes wrong in Orsogna,"— Harriet picked up the thread—"I think we know whom we have to thank." "That *sindaco*, you mean?—I wouldn't trust him around the corner." "I'm afraid there's a hooligan element that's been getting rather out of hand." "Who are they?" Harriet lowered her voice, though it had already been a scurrying mutter: "They're Communists, I believe. You saw the things they'd written up on the walls. I suppose those signs that say 'W Stalin' mean 'We want Stalin.' " "Those are two V's, not a W," Mattie explained. "They stand for *Viva, Long live,* it seems.—But it comes to just the same thing," she added, not wanting to appear pedantic. "The fact that they're Communists, though, doesn't mean that they're going to steal things. In fact, I should say that Communists were more likely to be conscientious about handling supplies like that than the ordinary politicians." Her lover, the New Deal official, had been also a fellow-traveller, and had persuaded her on one occasion to vote for some Communist candidates; and, though she was now out of harmony with him, nothing had ever upset her assumption that the Soviet Union and its leader had the interests of the masses at heart. "The *sindaco* told me," said Harriet, "that the Communists about here are ruffians." "He would," Mattie took her up knowingly. "He's a Socialist, and he represents the bourgeoisie. You can tell by the way he dresses. I'll bet he used to be a Fascist!" "I don't see," demurred Harriet, "that it's any use their trying to be Communistic now." "No: they won't have much of a chance with the Allied Cmmmission here. But who knows what they may do when we go? Unless you want to stay on indefinitely, as I know some of the English do." "One can't let the Russians dominate— because that's what it would come down to," said Harriet. "Well, all I can say," declared Mattie, "is that if I were one of those young guys in Orsogna"—she couldn't help contrasting her ideal of them with her disillusioned view of her New Dealer—"and I'd seen Mussolini flop and then had had my whole town wiped out by a couple of foreign armies fighting back and forth across it, I'd be saying '*Viva Stalin!*', too. I certainly wouldn't go to the priest to have him tell me to submit to God's will. These churches are perfectly lovely, but if I lived in a place like Orsogna, I'd certainly come to the conclusion that my patron saint wasn't much help, and that, if I wanted to keep a roof over my head, I'd better do something about it myself." "Their saints *are* rather absurd, aren't they?— But Communism would mean a dictatorship, wouldn't it?—and that's just what we want to get rid of." "Well, I suppose, if I were an Italian," Mattie answered, "I'd think the A.C. was a dictatorship and that I'd rather be told what to do by a Communist Central Committee that was at least made up of Italians. Our tiny little U.N.R.R.A. handouts aren't going to put them on their feet: they're only a drop in the bucket. It's just like settlement work, and there are moments when it gives me the same futile feeling!" "It helps to keep them from anarchy," said Harriet. "Listen, honey," Mattie warmly exhorted,—"it's not going to be enough just to keep them from having riots. We've got to back the progressive elements and help them get a democratic set-up or they'll decide to do something themselves."

"They'll have to be taught first," said Harriet, "to recognize what's for their own good.—I'm afraid I must turn in now." She picked up the bottle to put it away. "We ought to get off at nine tomorrow—we have to drive all the way to Pescara. Florence's husband will take you over." "God knows," declared Mattie, as she got to her feet—"I'm not for dictatorships any more than you have to have them. As a matter of fact, the people I talked to over there seemed to be much more full of the idea of having Italy annexed to the United States." "I should think," suggested Harriet mildly, "that that would hardly be practical from your point of view." "It does sound rather silly," said Mattie, "but they actually told me in Rome that there was an Italian organization with a fairly large membership that is trying to arrange to have Italy made a part of the United States—and, after all, I suppose that Hawaii will be admitted to the Union soon, and that's almost as far off as Italy."

"Did you sleep all right last night?" inquired Harriet, as Mattie was leaving. "Don't you want to take some bug-powder?" "Well," she answered, "there was a certain amount of racket on the part of some roistering blades that paraded the streets all night—but I didn't particularly mind it.—Communists, maybe," she added with a grin. "When I spent the night there," said Harriet, "there were incredibly rowdy Americans, who had struck up an acquaintance with some women and were trooping about the halls all night." Mattie returned to the repellent hotel, feeling rather annoyed with her chief, but not sure that she really deserved it.

The next day, however, an incident occurred which definitely and, she thought, on good grounds, discouraged her sympathy with Harriet.

At Pescara, on the Adriatic, they supervised the giving out of U.N.R.R.A. food by the nuns of a local convent to the children of the fishermen and sailors. As usual, they were met with the applause which warmed Mattie but now made her embarrassed, because she felt they were doing so little and living so well themselves. The nuns ran a regular soup-kitchen and they seemed to be doing a pretty good job. The kids were lined up outside with little tin cups in their hands, singing a piping little song about supper that had been taught them by the nuns. They certainly needed food. Mattie had read in books about children that looked like little old men, but she had never actually encountered this phenomenon, and some of these children were horrifying in their resemblance to senile goblins. Never, probably, having known for a day the well-being and freedom of childhood, they were shrunken and bony and stooped, and their faces, staring-eyed and creased, seemed never to have expressed any-thing but anxiety. She studied them, but she could not help turning away to a pale but somewhat healthier little girl, who, afraid to go in with the crowd, was clinging to the black skirts of her mother. Mattie talked to her and tried to encourage her, but either her Italian was inade-quate or her way of talking too brusque, for she only made the child shyer.

And, as usual, she soon became interested in something that did not interest Harriet. She and the American interpreter got into a conversation with two nondescript-looking young men who turned out to be engaged in removing mines. They could not have been shaved for a week and were bristling with dark wiry beards; and they were dressed in the queerest assortment of odds and ends of clothes—one was barefoot and had nothing on but an undershirt and a pair of shorts, while the other wore sneakers, a béret and a dirty white knitted sweater that suggested old-fashioned football. But they were tight-knit and strongly built and burnt to an African bronze, and Mattie found them attractive. The one in the undershirt had a leathery unyielding face and talked entirely inside his mouth, as if he had set up a rampart against the mines and tried to keep himself behind it; but the other, with his juvenile garments, gave the impression of a bearded school-boy, and he had evidently grown up during the years of the war, for his eyes had that same curious glaring look, at once desperate and lacking in purpose, which she had seen in the starving children. With him she had a long lively talk, and, assisted by energetic gestures, she seemed to be making great progress in understanding and being understood. This young fellow was the kind of male who peculiarly appealed to Mattie: a little guy with all the guts in the world—it was so that she always saw them—yet vulnerable and needing help, a good kid not quite equipped to take care of himself in the world.

It was *"un lavoro molto pericoloso,"* he confessed when she said, "What a job!" They had an American mine-detector, which was a thing like the handle and hoop of a nettingless butterfly net. They would walk with it, holding it out, and when the hoop came above a mine, it would set up an electric buzzing in a telephone clamped over their ears. Then they would try to dig down on one side and get at the mine from below. But the detector only registered for metal: it was no good for the wooden or bakelite mines; and they had only this one detector.

Otherwise, they just had to look out for the places where
the earth was depressed and probe the ground with a rod.
If the rod struck on something solid, they would make a
big circle around it and take out a whole chunk of earth.
Everybody, both Germans and Allies, had exercised the
utmost ingenuity, and this made it very hard for the
diggers. The Germans had even mined their own ceme-
teries, rightly thinking that this would be the one spot in
which the enemy would assume that there were none.
The worst kind were the ones that jumped: a first
explosion sent the thing up in the air so that the charge
had a clear field, and the second scattered the mine. When
they had got them out of the ground, they first had to
make them safe by sticking a piece of wire into a hole just
below the pin. They showed the ladies—Harriet had now
come up—a bomb that they said was still live, the size
and shape of a dingy brick, and Mattie's friend, while she
inwardly gasped, pulled the cap off with his teeth, then
took out the wire and exploded the cap with a bang that
made her jump and left her heart beating. Harriet walked
away without comment, taking the interpreter with her;
but Mattie allowed the men to conduct her to the place
where they lived. It was a little shack next door to the
convent, and so wretched that it made her sad. All they
had were knocked-together board beds, with no mattresses
and dirty old blankets, and a few pin-ups from Italian
papers plastered on the cracking wall. They told her that
they got for their mine-digging only twenty lire a day, the
equivalent of ten cents, and Mattie wanted to give them
money but felt that this would not do. If she could only
supply them, she thought, with some more glamorous
American pin-ups, say some of the big colored spreads
from *Esquire*!

It was so hot that they were able to work only up to ten
o'clock in the morning and after six in the afternoon, and

now it was time for them to get back on the job. And Harriet was approaching the jeep. Mattie said goodby and grinned and wished them all kinds of luck.

"Those boys have got nerve!" said Mattie, when at last, after some delay, due to the driver's having disappeared, they jolted off on their homeward journey. "After all," Harriet firmly demurred, "they've got an American mine detector, haven't they? When our men were fighting through here, they had to take their chance." "But the war's all over now—and they get only *twenty lire* a day!" A dull detonation stopped her, and it was followed, in another second, by a louder and uglier one, which thudded point-blank on the cardrums. "I hope that isn't those boys!" said Mattie. "There'd be nothing we could do," said Harriet. But Mattie was deeply disturbed: "I think we ought to stop and make sure, though!" "The nuns would be able to look after them. They must be prepared for accidents. They have a hospital in the convent." "If you don't mind, I'd like to go back and see. There might be *something* we could do, and we wouldn't want to—" Harriet cut her off: "I don't think we've got time, you know—we have to make another stop."

And Mattie for the first time was made to feel, freezingly and indefeasibly, the force of Harriet's superior authority. She stiffened; and, after a moment, her companion added priggishly, crisply: "I don't think they can be frightfully careful—the way they were showing off." Mattie made no reply. Rigid and tense with anger, she was silent all the rest of the way.

At Aquila, two evenings later, just as they were finishing dinner, Harriet announced as if casually: "I have to make a trip tomorrow, and I'm going to leave you here to look out for some trucks that are coming. Rather than have us both making these jaunts, I think it will be much better for one of us to stay here all the time. You can go over things with Mr. Morelli and keep tabs on the hospital and the convents. You know, I'm not sure that that Mother Superior who gesticulates and rolls her eyes is giving the boys all they're supposed to be getting. That place isn't so clean as the others, and I don't have much confidence in her. You're so good at getting to the bottom of things—I think it would be worth looking into."

On the way out, they ran into the Major, who invited them to have a brandy. Harriet declined and went up to her room, but Mattie let him take her to the bar. It would be a relief, she thought, to talk to another American, especially since she knew that he and she were companions in frustration now. During her absence, a British colonel had been assigned to the staff of the rest home, and the Major, now outranked, found himself superseded. "Well," said Mattie, after glancing at the soldiers standing up at the bar, "I suppose that all our boys will be playing cricket now!" "Not so bad as that," he maintained. "Well," she declared, "if they don't mix, it certainly isn't *our* fault." "They do, up to a point," he answered. " 'Up to a point' is good," she interjected. "We're getting satisfactory results," he mechanically, officially, insisted, and it touched her to see how his enthusiasm had dropped since she had left the hotel. She had learned from a conversation with one of the G.I. guests—but restrained herself from bringing it up—that there was hardly a case on record of a soldier, either British or American, who had chosen Aquila for his furlough; they had had to be ordered there. "You and me, too," she bitterly said. "I'm just going to be an office-boy, it seems. She wants me to stay here and take telephone calls while she travels around and does all the real field work!" She told the story of the food and the clothes. "This is strictly between ourselves," she said, "but I'll bet that if I went over to Orsogna and jabbered pigeon Italian to them and made them see that I really meant business, I could get things straightened out in no time!—And it's mostly *our* money, too!" "She's a little bit dim," said the Major. "If you must use those British expressions,"—Mattie, by a sudden revulsion, found that to be an American meant being anti-English. "Wishy-washy is what I'd call her—and downright stupid, too! I must have frightened the liver out of her when I was talking to her about Communism the other night." "That's the worst thing you can possibly do—give the impression that you're what they call a Bolshie." "I tried later to make it clear that I was just an old-fashioned American who wanted equal opportunity for everybody and trusted in F.D.R." "The trouble is that a lot of them think that being American itself is some kind of Bolshevism. You have to make them realize that Americans can be just as good-mannered and quiet and just as conservative in many ways as any English person." "That's not my type, I'm afraid," said Mattie. She finished her cocktail and flared up again: "And when we do that, they just take advantage of it. I think that we ought to go to the mat with them and have something to say about things in Italy." "Don't ask me to agree with you," the Major warned, with his smile on one side of his mouth, which had formerly contributed to his charm but which now had a crestfallen wryness. "I'm here to promote cordial relations.—You're wrong about her, anyhow: she admires you—she told me so when you first arrived. You're what they'd like to be but don't get a chance to be." "So in the meantime," she persisted pugnaciously, "they want to keep us down!"

The ranking British colonel saw them and came over and was introduced to Mattie. He sat down with them and had a manhattan. "I really don't know," he said, "how we'll get on with our stuffy old whisky-and-sodas

after our diet of American cocktails—though, like so
many other excellent things that come from your part of
the world, I do think they sometimes let one down after
starting one off with a rush." He beamed in the com-
placent way that the British invariably have when they
feel that they have scored off a foreigner who will be
helpless to defend himself. But he had reckoned without
Mattie. "Just a red-faced old lush," she was thinking,
"who was no use to them anywhere else!" "What do you
mean: we let you down?" she demanded. "Not in any
serious way, my dear lady." "I'd like an example of what
you mean!" "Well, well," interrupted the Major, auto-
matically conciliatory, "nobody has let anybody down."
"We're both letting the Italians down, if you ask me,"—
she switched the subject,—"after all our talk about the
Four Freedoms. We don't let them form a government of
their own—we don't even let them make speeches!" "As
for the Eye-tyes," the Colonel pronounced, "I think they
deuced well get more than they deserve when we send
them such charming young ladies to minister to their
needs!"

"I wanted to say, 'Nuts'!" growled Mattie, when the
Colonel had excused himself and left them. "It wouldn't
have helped," said the Major; and, confronted by his
Anglicized trimness, she was seized by that fierce impatience which had always at last overtaken her with the
men she had begun by loving, and which supplanted the
instinct to protect and prop: the indignant conviction that
they were not the men that she would have been in their
place, that they did not really have what it took. There
must be American men with passion and with backbone,
she thought, but not only did her own bad luck always
involve her with the other kind but she had so often had
to sympathize with her girl-friends for being married to
that kind, too! The drinks had gone a little to her head.

"Oh, come on!" she taunted the Major. "Are we men or are we mice? Did we beat the hell out of these limies at Lexington and Bunker Hill just to let them push us around after we've saved them from being chewed up by the Germans?"

But the Colonel and two other British officers needed a fourth at bridge, and the Major was obliged to join them.

6

ROMAN DIARY: RUSSIAN EXILES

A RUSSIAN FRIEND IN THE STATES had suggested my looking up, in Rome, a cousin of hers who had been living there since the Russian Revolution; and, having located her with a certain amount of difficulty, I went one day to see her. Her house was somewhere out on the Janiculum, almost at the edge of the city, and I had recourse to a P.R.O. jeep, driven by a reckless Italian, who, till I made him restrain himself, hurled the car through the streets like a missile, ferociously cursing the pedestrians and forcing the bicyclists out of the road by pretending to run them down. His attitude was evidently based on the fact that he was working for the winning side and felt he had nothing to fear, and it gave me an idea of the insolence which the people must have had to put up with from the underlings of Mussolini.

On my first visit, I made the mistake of letting him drop me at the foot of the hill and walking up the long succession of flights of steep and backbreaking stairs. Approached in that way, the address proved peculiarly difficult to get to, and when I did find the little villa, it seemed to me that I had penetrated to something very remote from my correspondents' hotel and the offices of the Allied Commission. When I was face to face with the household, I saw that I had had no idea of the condition, during the years of the war, of the ordinary civilian in Rome.

But these Russians represented, also, privations not of recent date. Mme de L., whom I had come to see, had left Russia in 1919, with her husband and her adopted son, and in company with a friend, the Countess R., whose husband had been killed in the Revolution and who had had with her her four children. The family of Mme de L., I learn from a Russian history, had been at one time the richest in Russia. They had benefited, in the eighteenth century, by the extraordinary favor of the Tsar, who had made them immense grants of "inhabited estates," and by the middle of the nineteenth century they had owned three hundred thousand serfs. The country place of Count M., one of the splendors of eighteenth-century baroque, had had as a rival in Russia only the Arkhangelskoe of Prince Yusupov and had been comparable, "if not with Versailles, at least with Potsdam or Caserta." Mme de L. and her husband had lived a great deal in Rome before the Revolution, and they returned there in 1919 to make a household in common with the R.'s. Mme de L. took in "paying guests," and they lived mainly on the proceeds from this. They had to practice the severest economy, and the younger generation suffered. Three of the Countess's children, who had had years of inadequate feeding, died of tuberculosis. Mme de L.'s son had married and gone to America. Her husband had died during the Second War. In the war years, there had been no more boarders, and they had moved to a smaller villa.

I did not, however, know all this at the time, and I was not quite prepared for the state in which I found Mme de L. and the R.'s. It was true that Mme de L., as she told me, had been afflicted for years with ailments which partly accounted for her emaciation; but the thinness of the Countess R. and a sister of hers who now lived with them, the paleness of an R. daughter and grandchild, showed how desperate their fasting had been. Mme de L. used the phrase "dire hunger" but said that things were much better now: she had weighed only forty-five kilos and recently she had put on five. But Mme de L. stood six feet tall, and her figure was now almost a skeleton. Her skin was yellow as if she had jaundice, and it had wrinkled in a peculiar way which seemed due, not to old age merely, but to a collapse from the shrinkage of flesh. Her great gray eyes were blocked out in her face by the straight eyebrows that ruled above them a dark rather majestic line and by the discolored patches below them; but they reminded me—in that atmosphere of Russia that so persistently though fadedly endured there—of Push-kin's description, in *Evgeni Onegin,* of the eyes of the young Lensky when he is dying after the duel and they become like the windows of an empty house, blinded-up and covered with chalk, when the owner has gone away —save that one of Mme de L.'s eyes was also swimming in blood as if a vessel had burst. When I saw her from the side or behind, she had the look of an old black crow, with her long back and her humped bony shoulders, her thin straight black-stockinged ankles and her slippers which she had worn so long that they were heelless and gave the impression of her feet's not being shod but merely, like the feet of a bird, composed of some hornier substance. On the furniture were shabby prints; a screen shut off her narrow bed; on the wall hung a Genovese tapestry. I did not see anywhere the "ikon corner" that such old-regime Russians usually have; but in the corner where she had her chair she had put up a picture of the Tsar, photographs of members of her family, and a view of some mountain landscape. On the table beside the chair were a volume of Dickens in English, a carafe of very harsh red wine and a box of loose tobacco and papers, out of which she made her own cigarettes. This was one of the few parts of Rome that had been rather badly bombed, and the windows of the house had been shattered. In Mme de L.'s room, some of the gaps were patched with a glass that was completely opaque and others had been boarded up. Through a pane that was still intact, one could see the house across the street, which had had one whole side sliced off, and, beyond this, one could look away over a newly-built-up part of Rome, in which the principal objects of interest were a big Benedictine monastery, a yellow arc of monotonous apartment houses and the cypresses of the Protestant Cemetery, where Keats and Ronald Firbank lay: those two Englishmen of brilliant plumage, escaped from the coop of England and dead pathetically, still young, in Rome.

Yet, against this desolate background, her tone was quite cheerful and stout. She showed humor and a sharp good sense, and her voice had an agreeable timbre which combined the gentle Russian humanity with the full throated deep Russian register. After two months of the Italians and the British, I found it rather a relief to talk to her, for an American, in certain ways, seems much closer today to the Russians than to any of the Europeans. Up to the beginning of the First World War, Americans and Russians both, however much they loved their country or however strong their faith in it might be, tended to occupy a provincial position, or acquiesce in a provincial attitude, toward the civilization of Europe. But, to an American in Europe at the present time, it seems just the other way. The little European nations, among which England now must be counted, have fallen into the provincial role in relation to the larger societies of the Soviet Union and the United States. This had already begun to be evident before the recent war, and it is even more striking today, when England and Germany are no longer formidable. Each of these countries, during the years of the war, had been locked into its own boundaries, compelled to feed on itself, and kept concentrating all its attention on the defense of its national existence. Even the Germans, who overran the other nations, could bring them nothing but the bullying and plundering inspired by pure spite. If they had possessed any creative ideas, they might have been able to impose their "New Order," since Europe needed so badly to be unified; and their failure marked the definitive bankruptcy of old-fashioned nationalistic conquest. We are left with a lot of small nations that seem barbaric and ridiculous nuisances, with their traditional family feudings: the quarrel of France with Germany, the competition of Germany with England, the dispute between the Italians and the Yugoslavs, etc., etc., etc. The United States and Russia today, with all the defects of their civilizations, do constitute more advanced systems to the extent that they have succeeded in organizing, in more or less synthesizing, a great variety of kinds of people—so that men find themselves here in a position to think at least about what kind of *societies* they want instead of about how they are to manage to maintain themselves as autonomous nations. But the Russians have always had it in common with the inhabitants of the United States that they were half outsiders in Europe, visitors and curious observers; and I had particularly felt during the last ten years with all kinds of intelligent Russians how far our two peoples were emerging out of the ancient compartments of prejudice into bigger associations that were capable of wider and more lucid views. Even White Russians in exile have felt this—since their starving self-confidence has been stimulated by the Russian defeat of the Germans and by the recent imperialistic tendencies exhibited by the Soviet Union. With Mme de L., at any rate, I found that I could talk more freely about Europe and the Europeans than with anybody except an American.

She understood what one meant about Italy. Yes, the tourists had spoiled the Italians: they had encouraged them to be idle, to live on their past. There was far too much of the past in Italy. You couldn't pull down an old building in Florence that was rrrotten, rrrotten, rrrotten! without letters from English spinsters protesting at the destruction of the picturesque. The Fascists *had* wanted to do something about cleaning up and modernizing Italy, and they had been better, she believed, than the Nazis because they had wanted to encourage the individual. She had approved of the Germans, though, too, up to the time when they had invaded Russia and she had realized how brutal they were.

She would like, she said, to go to America: the only thing she had now to look forward to was seeing her family again. Her son wrote her every day, but the letters took a month or more, the packages of food even longer. She asked me, her face lighting up, as it did not do often, with an eager smile, whether my family were good correspondents. I suggested that, since she knew our Ambassador, he might possibly be able to help her if she wanted to go to the States; and she startled me a little by replying, "There'd have to be some dirty work at the crossroads first!"—though I was later to find out that her talk was sprinkled with Americanisms, which she had picked up from her "paying guests," students at the American Academy. They contrasted rather queerly with a mannerism which I had noted before in the Russians from the upper ranks of the old regime. Russians, when they are speaking their own language, are likely to say *yes* five times—as the French tend to say *oui* three times and the Germans *ja* twice—if they are hurriedly affirming something that somebody else is saying; and Mme de L., if one told her anything, would do this with a note of impatience, as if it were not possible or not proper to inform a person of her position of anything she did not know. This was not, in Mme de L.'s case, in the least impolite or unamiable; it was a trait like her towering stature that she had not been able to help carrying with her.

Distressed by her starved appearance and remembering how much more comfortable were her Russian friends in America, I tried to encourage her to make the trip. But she said it might be better not. She knew she couldn't live in America on five hundred dollars a year, which was what she could just do in Rome; and she could go about here in rags, which she shouldn't be able to do in New York. Somewhat curbed by her *yes yes yes yes yes,* I left most of the talking to her. The room was getting darker with twilight, and her voice gradually dropped to a murmur. She had to spend most of the day in bed, and I suppose that it had cost her an effort to get up and receive a visitor, for she now seemed to relapse from the admirable poise, the quick perception, with which she had greeted me. It was a little as if she were talking to herself, but pursuing a train of thought that had been started by the consciousness of herself suggested by the coming of a stranger. She was saying, as I sat in silence, I rather tardily realized, that it might be that "the ones who had been killed" had been "more fortunate than the ones who survived." But then—she picked herself up again—with a Russian, after all, it was different than with people of other kinds: when one happened to find oneself badly off

on the physical and material plane, one could go on to
another plane.

I did not want to tax her too much and soon left.*

But she insisted on my coming to dinner, and I called
on them several times. "The Italians and the French are
conventional," Mme de L. explained. "They won't ask
you to dinner to eat what they eat. But we don't mind
asking people to eat what we have ourselves." I think that
they must, nevertheless, have made some special preparations for me; but their menus indicated the limits of
persons who live as they do: on one occasion, borshch,
stuffed tomatoes, plums, a little loaf of gray butterless
bread; on another, a bowl of spaghetti with pale pinkish
sauce, a salad of chopped-up lettuce, and little preserved
cherries, with the usual bread and wine. I enjoyed it after
the mess of the Hôtel de Ville, which was betraying
every day more outrageously the depredations of someone
or other to the advantage of the black market and coming
to consist exclusively of leaden and greasy raviolis and
unidentifiable cuts of cartilage.

Before dinner, we would sit and have sherry in the
living room which was also the dining room, between
walls that, in the Russian fashion—like the Hermitage
gallery in Petersburg—were completely plastered over
with pictures: the inevitable Russian water-colors,
painted, no doubt, by some member of the family, and
the usual long Russian engravings of the endless perspectives of the Neva and the barracks-like palace at Oranien-
baum. After dinner, we would sit out of doors in a garden
behind the house. Here they had planted some carrot and
beet seeds which had been sent them, by an old boarder,

* I found out later that she had been taking drugs, and I suppose that her serenity and detachment were partly a result of this.

from America, in a poor soil in which things did not
always grow.

I now encountered the other two old ladies, whom on
my first visit I had barely met. They had the appearance
of good fairy godmothers—though one of them, of whom
I learned afterwards that she had been in her time a great
beauty, gave restive little signs, almost childlike now, of
what must once have been a wilfulness of coquetry. We
listened after dinner one evening, just before the British
elections, to a radio speech by Clement Attlee, which
came through to us rather dimly, interrupted by strains of
dance music and spasms of voluble Italian; and they
commented, as if to reassure themselves, on Attlee's
unexpectedly well-educated voice. The British Labour
Party, said one, wasn't really Socialist, was it? In any
case, said another, the Socialists were much milder than
the Communists. She had always, she asserted, believed
that the public utilities ought to be nationalized—and,
after all, if all that money that the governments had just
spent on explosives had been put into hospitals and
schools and parks! . . . They were puzzled by the failure
of Fascism: the people had been satisfied with it, and the
government was not really intolerant: they had sent out
to the malarial region a sanitary engineer who was known
to be anti-Fascist (there had been, I learned later from
U.N.R.R.A., but one sanitary engineer in Italy), only
exacting from him a promise that he would not make any
criticism of Fascism. I suggested, though I knew it was
futile—they had grown up in the world of the Tsar—that
freedom of criticism was a cardinal issue. It seemed cruel
to tell them that socialism was what Europe certainly
needed. Their lives had been so difficult and frightening.
Having escaped from the Bolshevik terror, they felt the
enemy again threatening them here. They had established themselves in Rome on a meager but stable basis;

they had made, with their children and grandchildren, a solid little Russian group that had weathered the rigors of exile. And now, in their old age, they found themselves pressed by want even beyond the narrow restrictions to which they had accustomed themselves; and anarchy seemed creeping in around them. They told me—what I had already heard elsewhere—that there had lately been gangs in the streets who had been catching well-dressed people and stripping them. A man was supposed to bring twenty thousand lire, a woman fifteen thousand. This had happened, not far away, to a professor of their acquaintance.

The phrase "displaced persons," in one of our conversations, caught Mme de L.'s attention. She considered, she said with a laugh, that *they* were displaced persons. I wondered, as I saw them there, whether they wouldn't have been better off in America. Certainly, I thought, the young people would. A daughter of Countess R. was giving Italian lessons; a boy wrote plays in Italian. Neither seemed Italianized; they were simply uprooted Russians—for a Russian cannot become an Italian. But in America he can become an American on the same footing with everybody else. (Since this was written, the grandson has married an American girl and come to live in the States.) The conception of the American system as a solution to the social problems which had disrupted and tormented their lives loomed even to the two old ladies who were closer than Mme de L. to the order they had left behind. There had been people, one of them said, even in the old days at home, who had had the idea that Russia ought to be governed like the United States.

———

I had dinner with Bill Barrett from our Embassy, and he told me that he had lately been called upon to

interview some hysterical Russians who had come in from
the Displaced Persons Camp just outside Rome. They
were engineers and school teachers and such people who
had been living in Poland before the war and who had
fled and come down into Italy. They now had the status
of displaced persons, and the Soviet authorities had
claimed them and were going to have them sent back to
Russia. Barrett had looked into the matter, and his inquiry had led him to the desk of a British officer of the
Allied Commission whose function it was to deal with
these problems. There he learned, to his astonishment,
that the Americans and the British had, at Yalta, made
with the Russians an agreement according to which we
were bound to hand over to the Soviets any Russian who
had left Russia since 1929. Such people, for reasons not
clear, had been assigned to the status of prisoners of war.
This agreement had never been published (and might
never have been made known to the world if the Vatican
had not got wind of it and "broken the story" to an
American correspondent in March, 1946). Intended os-
tensibly for the rounding-up of Russians who had fought
with the Germans, it could be used, also, to secure the
deportation of mere disaffected persons of the kind who
had been appealing to the Embassy and of the members
of unorthodox political factions and people who had fled
from the purges.

I reflected that a man like my friend the ex-Soviet
official Alexander Barmine, if he had landed among the
displaced persons, might have been, at the insistence of
the Soviets—since he had left Russia after 1929—surrendered by us for certain execution. Fortunately he had
come to America and was now a United States citizen. I
had just seen him before I left New York, and he had
warned me, not entirely in jest, that, since I was known
to have criticized Stalin, I should, if I went into territory

where the Russians were in occupation, be careful about exposing myself to the hazards of standing on the platforms of moving trains. In the course of the voyage over, I had read proofs of the new English version of Barmine's autobiography: *One Who Survived: The Life Story of a Russian Under the Soviets;* and had admired the concreteness, the compression and the feeling for human realities which had enabled him to cover in a minimum space so extensive a field of experience and at the same time to give so definite an impression of everything on which he touched. In this and in its moral sincerity it had seemed to me in the great tradition of Russian revolutionary memoirs, the tradition of Herzen and Kropotkin. A child of the Revolution but now confronted with a new Russian despotism, he had written an exile's book which might well become a classic; and his career and the conclusions one drew from it were vividly present to my mind.

Barmine, born in 1899, was the son of a schoolmaster and a gamekeeper's daughter. His parents had divorced and remarried, and he had grown up without a real home and soon found himself embroiled in the happenings of a period of Russian history chaotic to the last degree. He fought in the civil war on the side of the Bolsheviks, and at nineteen was made a commissar on the basis of his success in getting the villagers to give them food by persuasion and honorable dealing at a time when Red Army soldiers rarely came back from such errands alive. He attended the Red Army Academy in the years when old tsarist officers, recruited to the Revolution, were attempting with a certain skepticism to transform "a lot of young peasants and workmen into infantry officers in six months," while their training was at any moment likely to be interrupted by the necessity of going away to take part in some actual fighting. He was later, at one time or another, as assigned by the Communist authorities, a soldier who held several commands, consul general in Persia, official Soviet agent in Belgium, Soviet director general of imports in Italy and France, and president of the trust that controlled the exportation of the products of the motor and aviation industries. He thus saw a good deal of the business and the officialdom of the Soviet Union; but, though a member of the Communist Party, he played no political role. At the time of the Stalin-Trotsky split, he was content to leave everything to the higher-ups, on the principle that it was always correct to back the findings of the Central Committee. Rather unusually non-political for a Russian, his assumptions were still based on the methods of the first years of the Revolution, when, for example—in 1919, "the most critical year of the Civil War"—it had been possible, fifty miles from the battle, for a public debate to take place, without "passing the bounds of courtesy," between Bolsheviks and Mensheviks; and it was not till very much later that he could see what a "decisive part in causing the final downfall of all Lenin's real companions-in-arms" had been played by the blocking of every attempt to organize an opposition with the argument "that any weakening of Party unity might provoke a crisis of which the forces of counter-revolution would take advantage." In the meantime, as he discovered with amazement on returning to Russia from service abroad, the big officials of the Stalin government had acquired splendid country houses, with tennis courts, Rolls-Royces and servants, while the ordinary Soviet workers in whose name the Revolution had been made were still compelled to spend ninety per cent of their wages on food which, from the point of view of the countries in which Barmine had been living, was miserable in the extreme.

In the summer of 1937, Barmine was chargé d'affaires

in the Russian Legation in Athens. The political purge
was in progress, but in Athens they knew little about it.
All they knew was that dozens of ambassadors and heads
of government departments were being arrested and shot.
Their own chief had been summoned to Moscow, and it
was now a very long time since they had had any
instructions from him. One day they received a com-
muniqué which informed them that Tukhachevsky and
seven other Red Army generals had been executed for
treason, and Barmine learned a few days later from a
friend who had arrived from Moscow that some twenty of
the younger generals, former classmates of his at the
Academy, old comrades of the civil war, had also been
summarily shot. The staff in the Greek Legation had
been listening to the radio in silence, and they pretended
to accept the charges that had been brought against all
these men; but it had suddenly become apparent to
Barmine that Stalin, in his passion for power, had set out
to destroy systematically all the Soviet officials and officers
who represented the Leninist generation and who could
possibly oppose his policies or contest his leadership. He
expressed to one of his assistants his astonishment and his
horror, and the outburst relieved his tension. But soon
after this conversation the assistant was recalled to Moscow, and Barmine became aware that his friends in the
Foreign Office were no longer communicating with him.
An order to seal the minister's papers and have them sent
to Russia was put through over Barmine's head, and one
day he surprised his code secretary rummaging among his
papers. He wrote to the Foreign Office asking to be
relieved of his duties, but received no reply from Litvi-
nov. Instead, he was invited one day to dine on a Soviet
ship which was lying in the harbor at Piraeus. He
declined and went fishing, but the captain of the ship
with several other men waited for him on the dock, and

when he returned, he had to sidestep a second attempt to get him on board the ship. A man from the Legation, however, whose real function was beginning to dawn on Barmine, insisted on spending the evening with him and talked to him suggestively of the ease with which it had been possible in China to frustrate or murder officials who had attempted to run away from the Embassy.

Yet for some reason the mesmerism of Moscow did not succeed with Barmine as it had with so many other officials—though this spell had behind it a tradition as old as Ivan the Terrible with his bellowings of "I am your God!" "My sense of personal dignity," he writes, "was revolted by the alternatives: to submit to kidnapping or to walk out. After the stories I had just heard, I knew what was in store for me. I had to decide where I would be of more help to the Russian people—perishing in one of Stalin's prisons or living as a free man somewhere in the world, knowing the truth and speaking it out." He eluded the maneuvers of the G.P.U., wrote a letter of resignation to Moscow, walked into the French Legation and got a visa as if for a holiday, and boarded the train for Paris.

In Paris he wrote to the Central Committee of the French League of the Rights of Man, reporting the step he had taken and explaining the reasons for it. "For nineteen years," he said, "I have been in Soviet government service. . . . I have fought for the Soviet regime and dedicated all my energies to the cause of the Workers' State. . . . It is quite obvious to me that a reactionary dictatorship is now in control of my country." And he wrote and published in France—in 1939—the book which is now, for the first time, appearing in the United States.

These memoirs—what is altogether exceptional in the writings of Russian Communists—contain no political apologies, no casuistry of the Party conscience. They are

all the more comprehensible and all the more convincing
to the English-speaking reader for their freedom from that
rather creepy atmosphere of Marxist polemic and theory
in which we do not find ourselves at home. So practical
and so direct all his acts and reactions have been, so sensible the conclusions he has drawn from them, that one
feels, as one does not do always in the case of Russian ca-
reers, that, in the circumstances, one would not have behaved differently or arrived at different views; and it
seems almost inevitable that Barmine should (at the end
of 1939) have gone on to the United States.

I had seen something of Barmine in New York and had
been struck by a certain convergence of the Soviet with
the American type. It was not only that the new Russia of
the Soviets, in spite of its socialist beginnings and of its
supposed disapproval on principle of our capitalist business and our bourgeois democracy, actually envied and
aimed to emulate our industrial organization, our brisk
methods and our material prosperity; it was also that a
man like Barmine, tall, straight and well set-up, sanguine
in the physical sense, bred out of what seems quite
another race than that of the ordinary Moscow pygmy,
had behind him, as have so many Americans, a tough and
vigorous rural stock. For both of these reasons, perhaps,
he approximates—though rather more accomplished than
most American executives are—to an ideal at the opposite
pole from the old-fashioned type of Russian official, a type
of which many examples are still to be seen in the Soviet
Union. Barmine is not nervous, not volatile, not theatrical, not evasive; he is not even, for a Russian, very flexible
or very sensitive to psychological atmospheres—as was
shown by his not grasping sooner the full implications of
the purges and the danger of talking about them. He is in
some ways much like an American, and he perhaps finds
himself more at home here than the modernized Com-

munist official can sometimes be in the Soviet Union among conditions often nearly as primitive as that life of the sixteenth century which, to the Elizabethan travellers of Hakluyt's *Voyages,* seemed barbaric in comparison with England.

Yet the product of Marxist schooling and the Soviet commissar have marked characteristics of their own that are unlike anything in America and perhaps quite new in the world. Barmine has been cast in a mold and can hardly now be remelted. The proud self-confidence of the Communist official, taught to believe that the future belongs to him and set off from the common herd almost as much as a member of the old upper classes—an assurance which has come more and more to present a hard mask of arrogance—appears in Barmine as a challenging dignity, a brusquely ironic tone, an air of knowing all the answers; and the tradition of Communism betrays itself in the bad habit which he sometimes reverts to, when his own point of view becomes hard to defend, of trying to talk his opponent down by sheer emphasis or loudness of voice, instead of conducting a sober discussion; and in his resorting to what is technically known as the "bedfellow" line of argument, which relies on producing the illusion of having put you irremediably in the wrong by associating you with some odious person who holds either a similar opinion to yours or an opinion which may be confused with yours. The indoctrination of Leninist Marxism which such Russians as Barmine received went deeper perhaps than the teaching of any of the Protestant churches usually does at the present time and almost as deep as the Catholic dogmas. To us who have first seen the world through the windows of the bourgeois economy, the Marxist view must always come as a heresy and require a certain effort to be valued and understood; but to Barmine it was the social cosmogony,

the story of history and the basic morality, which it
required an effort to correct. He has told me of the shock
that it was to him to discover, in the collective nurseries,
where the toys which had been brought by the parents
had been pooled and made common property, that instincts of acquisitiveness appeared in these children who
had never had contact with the bad appetites of capitalist
society; and of the disquieting doubts suggested by his
realizing at last in the factories that disunion and sabotage
were not invariably and inevitably due to motives of
political obstruction, but could also, all too obviously, be
prompted by jealousies and personal ambitions. Of late
years I have sometimes heard him talk as if he were
disillusioned, not merely with the government of Stalin,
but with the ideals of socialism themselves; yet it is a little
like the pupil of the Jesuits who, emancipated though he
may think himself, can never lose either the conviction of
sin or the intellectual discipline they have given him. So
Barmine, by a conditioned reflex, will respond to certain
kinds of stimulus by plugging the old Communist line of
insisting on the permanent scandal of the contrast between rich and poor in a capitalistic society—only to pull
himself up with the admission that the poverty of Stalin's
Moscow is in just about the same proportion to the
standard of the privileged groups as the poverty of Tam-
many's New York; or—the other way around—he will
start talking of international affairs with the incisive and
cynical realism of Lenin during the First World War—
only, influenced by our own propaganda, by the pressure
of the American newspapers, to fall flat into some ready-
made attitude, to my mind quite unrealistic, dictated by
the supposed desirability of our following the line of the
British.

He is, I think, less out of place in the United States
than he would be in any other country. He can say "we"

as an American citizen in a way that would hardly be possible for a Russian in England or France—in a way that is not wholly different from the way in which the Soviet official talks about the Soviets as "we": in the sense that—as in the case of both countries—the "we" are not an old-fashioned nation but a great geographical unit which is engaged, to use the Communist language, in a project of "social engineering." "We" are trying certain forms of government, going ahead on certain assumptions, rather than straining to save something that is simply there, like the hierarchy of an English county or a set of French peasant holdings. But he, too, is a man uprooted like any exile of the old regime, like any emigrated "displaced person"; and that position is an extremely uncomfortable, an extremely frustrating one. A former officer of the Red Army, a former worker for Soviet prestige abroad, he was not, in the recent war, any more able to defend his country than if he had been an old tsarist general; he could no more serve the State with his brains than if he had been an excommunicated Menshevik. Nor has he, still a foreigner in the United States, still suspect from his Soviet origin, had the chance there to work at a job that gave anything like full scope to his abilities. He cannot, to be sure—as he could be, if he were a displaced person in Europe—be deported to the Soviet Union; but the injury he has suffered through exile must remain beyond a certain point irreparable. And his commissar irony, his Marxist reactions, persist, like Mme de L.'s imperious *yes* and her authoritarian instincts, as the insignia of former power, to remind us of the fate of those who, having been trained for positions of leadership, have not been allowed to fill them.

———

Coming back from Mme de L.'s one day, I saw chalked up on a wall the following ungrammatical legend: *"Viva*

*l'anniversario di novembre 7 quando la libertà è stato dato
al popolo russo."* Well, I reflected, if the Bolshevik terror
had bought the freedom of the Russian people, one could
not, after all, complain. But the truth was that, thirty
years later, the Russian people were a good deal less free
than the man who had scrawled up that slogan and who
at least did not run the danger, even under the rule of the
Allied Commission, of being executed or imprisoned for
life, as he certainly would have been in Russia if he had
been caught making public an opinion equally subversive
for the Stalin regime. The Russians are today not free
either to talk, to print or to vote: they have to do, and
they are supposed to think, whatever the government tells
them, and they have no means of changing the government. They cannot even have recourse to strikes. There is
so little freedom in Russia that even persons of heroic
character and irreplaceable talent are no more safe there
if they differ from the dictator than they were in the days
of the Tsar. First there was Alexander I, who exiled
Pushkin for an ode to liberty; then there was Nicholas I,
who exiled Lermontov for praising Pushkin, who
mounted the throne over the corpses of the Decembrists
with their petition for constitutional government, who
imprisoned and expelled Herzen, and who sent Dostoevsky to Siberia; then Alexander II, who shut up Kropotkin
in the Peter-Paul Fortress and transformed a geologist
into an anarchist, and who would have imprisoned Tol-
stoy if he had not been lucky enough to have an aunt at
court; Alexander III, who turned the student of zoölogy
Ulyanov into a conspirator and would-be assassin and
hanged him when his plot was discovered, and who
prevented his brother Vladimir from graduating at the
university; and Nicholas II, who sent to Siberia Lenin
and Trotsky and a whole generation of the ablest and
most brilliant young Russians. Then there was the first
Bolshevik government, which executed or drove into

exile, for technically different reasons but in the same autocratic fashion, hosts of Mensheviks and Social Revolutionaries, aristocrats, landlords, officials and representatives of the various departments of the professional bourgeoisie (many of them, in all these categories, just as capable and just as public-spirited as the intransigent Marxists that turned them out) and who bedevilled the men of genius that had believed in the Revolution and tried to help do its work till the life of a Mayakovsky had become even more unhappy than those of Lermontov and Pushkin had been; and finally the satrapship of Stalin, who deported and murdered Trotsky, executed Tukhachevsky and conducted a wholesale massacre and imprisonment of everyone who still held to the Leninist faith and so was likely to question his tyranny. For more than a hundred years the world of the West has been strewn with Russians who have represented the brains and the conscience of Russia—men and women who could rarely be so useful abroad as they would have been at home. And, in spite of my liking for the Russians, my sympathy with the hopes and principles with which the Soviets started out, my admiration for their exploits in the recent war, I remembered with impatience how ridiculous it was for them to think themselves civilized, or for others to think them so, so long as a change of government is allowed to involve in their country the slaughter or extirpation of everyone who happens to oppose it, so long as it is still made a crime to differ from the head of the State.

7

ROMAN DIARY: BRITISH OFFICIALS

I WANTED TO FIND OUT something more definite about our pledging ourselves at Yalta to give up to the Soviet Union all Russians who had left there since 1929, and I called on the British major with whom my friend at the Embassy had talked. Like all the British, he was leery of journalists and very firm about refusing information. He admitted that it was true that Russians of whatever age or sex could be claimed by the Kremlin as prisoners of war, but about the precise terms of the agreement he said he was not authorized to speak. He was, however, extremely loquacious. He could, he declared, "write volumes" about what had been going on, if it were not for his official position; and he proceeded to parade for my benefit a personality which he obviously conceived as both formidable and fascinating.

He was an Irishman, superficially Anglicized but furiously exhibitionistic. His accent was completely English, but his eloquence unmistakably Irish. He had the build and the crouch of a bruiser and a British beefsteak complexion, and he fixed me, as if to hold me petrified, with a pale-blue but glaring eye—stopping after every statement to watch for my astonishment or approval. His talk was full of dark intimations. "I thought we were fighting for freedom, didn't *you?*" he demanded. "But I've never seen so many dirty tricks in my life!" He evidently referred to the Russians. He had been twice in the Soviet Union as a Metro-Vickers engineer, but he hadn't, he said, when I asked him, been involved in the 1933 trials: he always kept his politics in his pocket! But these trials, he said, had hardly been political, and many of his comments left me blank. He talked as if, on matters of politics, he entertained the strongest sentiments, but I was totally unable to find out what these uncompromising opinions were. He said challengingly that he hadn't voted once in the last fourteen years, because there had never in all that time been a candidate who was the kind of man he'd like to see run things. This dated his abstention from the moment of the apostasy of Ramsay MacDonald; but when I tried him on the subject of Churchill, usually a touchstone for pro-Labour men, he promptly and emphatically answered that "everything would immediately collapse" if Churchill were to die or be defeated. I came to the conclusion at last that he had no real opinions at all, but merely an overwhelming impulse toward self-assertion. When I later asked L.M. about him—they messed in the same hotel—he answered that the Major was "a child of nature."

I soon abandoned any effort to interview him and simply listened while he let himself go. He had been in all the countries, he gave me to understand, and had mastered all the languages—he could learn any language in three months. In the East, he said, they called him "the wild Irishman"—unquestionably I knew, he propounded, how fast a reputation travelled? But they all knew that he was completely honest and that when he said he'd do a thing, he did it. He had once held five thousand blacks at bay absolutely singlehanded. If an Arab came into his office and didn't wear a hat, he wouldn't say anything to him but would simply get up and kick him, because his not wearing a hat was a sign of disrespect—and the Arab wouldn't do it again. In the Sudan, he assured me proudly, he'd been fined twice for beating natives—£25 and £50. He didn't like to beat people up, but sometimes it had to be done. It was no use trying to punish them by holding out on supplies, because they'd always manage to get some food and to "enjoy their vices" anyhow, and it would only mean that somebody else would have to go without food. He'd asked the judge, on one of these occasions, how much it would have been if he'd killed the man, and the judge had said £5. (I learned later from a reliable source that it was true that the penalty was less for killing than for beating a native: if the man was still alive, he had to be taken care of and gave rise to more trouble and expense.)

I finally tore myself away from his eruption of talk and his magnetic gaze, which were at the same time pugnacious and coquettish. He was a perfect example of the Irishman who, escaped from the old problems of Ireland, no longer oppressed and a rebel, finds himself in a position to bully. He reminded me of New York police captains and of that Irish General Dyer who gave orders for the Amritsar massacre and later boasted that he had meant it to be worse.

———

At a dinner of the Ritrovo, a "cultural" club for bringing Allies and Italians together, I sat across the table from an important South African general. He was young-appearing, tall and blond; talkative, waggish, a good fellow. He told me at once that he was an Afrikaaner and would keep saying from time to time, in the course of our conversation: "I'm not an Englishman, you know." There was something a little pathetic about it, because his accent was completely English and that rather lower-

middle-class English which seems to condemn British
colonials to an irremediable inferiority (the Australians
are better off in speaking cockney). And he was certainly
pro-British enough. I was told afterwards by another
South African that he was supposed to be "socially
ambitious" and wanted the post of South African ambassador to England.

He surprised me by a line of attack that I had not had
to withstand before. He assured me that the United
States was really a British dominion and that all the
British dominions would now have to stand together for
the principles of "fair play" and to "see to it that people
like the Germans didn't go about bullying people." I
denied our dominion status and replied that, in any case,
wars were not really fought for the purpose of defending
moral principles. He readily admitted that this might be
true, but immediately returned to his propaganda. South
Africa and the United States had, he insisted, one great
thing in common. We had both rebelled against England,
and the English had never forgotten it. The Boers had
fought the English just as we had, but then they had
made peace with England, and England had stuck by the
terms of the peace, and the South Africans knew they
could trust her. The implication was that the English had
learned their lesson and dropped their old methods, and
that we need not be afraid of them now. Yes, he went on,
the United States had a lot in common with the dominions—everything but a king (giving me a broad wink)—
and it would be a good thing for us to have one! We gave
our president more power than a king. The king, in the
case of South Africa, was powerless to appoint a prime
minister except on the advice of the South Africans.

I talked after dinner to an intelligent marchesa who
had long been an earnest republican and was supposed to
have played a role in getting rid of the Fascist regime.

She had heard my conversation with the General and expressed her amazement that an American should have taken so calmly the suggestion that the United States have a king. But I had been getting used to British impudence. She, I suppose, as a patriotic Italian, had been suffering from it acutely.

I was told that a lady wanted to meet me who was a descendant of Dante's Count Ugolino. The story of Ugolino della Gherardesca makes the climax of horror of Dante's Hell. He was from Dante's point of view a political traitor and is consigned to the lowest depth. Ugolino had been locked with his sons in a tower by the Archbishop Ruggieri degli Ubaldini, and, when these sons had starved to death, was reduced to feeding on their bodies. But the Archbishop was also a traitor and both are placed by Dante in the lowest circle of Malebolge, where, frozen together in the ice, Ugolino gnaws forever at his enemy's scalp. When I asked why this lady wanted to meet me, I was told that she was interested in writing for the *New Yorker*. This amused me; I was curious to see her, and was sorry that I never did.

Bob Leigh rather relieved me by declaring that Sir Osmond Gower was a "story-book Englishman," and that if you gave him a comic hat, he could make money in a music hall any day. Leigh himself is part English, part Irish. He went straight into the army from Oxford, where he had specialized in Classics and studied some kind of academic history about which he was now indignant because, he said, it had nothing whatever to do with the history he had found himself involved in when he came to serve in the war. He has had a heavy dose of the war; has been all through it from France to Italy. At one time he tried to write something about it but lost his manuscript with his baggage somewhere—which very much discouraged and depressed him. He is intelligent and well-informed and his Irish element constantly stirs in him a satirical point of view on many things that the English take for granted. He is particularly amusing about Sir Osmond, whose accommodations he had to provide for on the occasion of the veteran proconsul's arriving for a brief stay in Rome. He had heard of Sir Osmond's brilliance— he has been praised by Lawrence of Arabia—his dexterity, his tact, his languages, his knowledge of the Near East, his appreciation of literature and music; and the young major rather looked forward to meeting him. But though Sir Osmond's accomplishments were undoubtedly great, his personality turned out rather wearing. He had stopped, on his way from the East, with the intention of delivering a lecture on his memories of T. E. Lawrence. It happened, however, to be V-E Day, and it was intimated that this was an occasion when the troops might not care to come to lectures; but nothing could deter Sir Osmond. He was deeply offended and indignant when only fourteen people turned up—he had brought with him a Roman princess—and said at first that he would not speak at all, but allowed himself to be persuaded by the Princess and the Major to give them an informal talk. The next day he peremptorily demanded that an audience be produced. The Major did his best to point out that the men were recovering from their festivities and might be almost as little interested as the day before; but Sir Osmond, with bland insistence, asked whether the officer in charge of entertainment were not in a position to command attendance, and, as he seemed to be in a position to command the entertainment officer, several hundred rather sulky men were detailed to listen to the lecture.

I met Sir Osmond one evening at dinner, when Bob Leigh was also present; and was astounded by his preposterous vanity. He was now anxious to realize a further ambition of delivering a third lecture—this time on "The Four Great Books of the World"—and inquired of an Italian professor, who had also been invited to meet him, whether the school with which the professor was connected would not care to arrange for this. When Sir Osmond learned that the school was designed for a different purpose: to provide instruction on Italian subjects for American and English soldiers, he did not—though elaborately affable—take it in very good part. Well, since they wanted only to *insegnare* not to *imparare* —since the school was only *senso unico!* (he introduced the Italian words as if he were dropping into some local patois, toward which one's attitude was bound to be humorous)—he saw there was no chance. But, after all, the *Divina Commedia* was one of the great books!—and he told us that he had just been reading it in the plane in which he had flown to Rome. He read it, he said, once a year, and his manner seemed to suggest that it was a work with which nobody present could have any very great familiarity—and, especially, gave us the impression that there was some sort of peculiar merit in relishing Dante in a plane. I brought up the only passage I could think of that could possibly connect Dante with aviation: his account of his flight into Malebolge on the back of the monster Geryon, in which he anticipates the sensations of circling down in a plane by noting that it was only by the wind on his face that it was possible for him to tell how they were moving; and the effect of this upon Sir Osmond was to impel him to recite at length the description of the appearance of Geryon, which was not the passage in point. He then went on to remark that he supposed that Dante's admiration for Virgil was one of the most curious instances in literature of a great man overrating a much lesser man—an opinion which seemed to me to weaken the legend of Sir Osmond's taste, since it is difficult to see how anyone who really appreciated Dante could fail to see the greatness of Virgil or to understand the debt—in the accent and texture of the writing, in the staging of the dramatic effects—of the later to the earlier master. And he told us of the classical honors which he had won in his youth at Cambridge, and declared that there had been a time when he could recite any ode of Horace if you fed him the first line—he believed he could do so still. (Bob Leigh had to restrain an impulse to take Sir Osmond up on this and try to stump him with the opening of an epode.) He had been to see the Holy Father, and the latter had expressed surprise that an Englishman should know the classics so well. Sir Osmond had explained that Horace went with port wine and was highly esteemed in England.

Our hostess being an American married to an Italian prince, Sir Osmond now proceeded to a waspish little poem by Dunsany on the absurd inappropriateness of the American Mrs. Simpson as the inamorata of Edward VIII, and announced that he considered it equal to the Greek epigrams of Leonidas of Tarentum. This was followed by a humorous anecodote about "the then head of my family, Lord Bramwell." Lord Bramwell had been sitting after dinner and had been disturbed by a servant, who said to him: "There's a fire in the library, sir." Lord Bramwell had answered: "I'm quite warm here"; but the point was that the house was on fire. He must have thought, from our reception of this, that we had failed to understand the point, for he repeated: " 'There's a fire in the library, sir.' 'I'm quite warm here.' The house was burning down!"

The whole thing was a sort of performance, and I saw what Leigh meant about the music hall. While Sir Osmond sat back, being brilliant and wagging his white mustaches, the audience were supposed to applaud and laugh: that was the only use he had for his companions. On foreign affairs, in general, he was everything that was most correct from the point of view of British interests and of giving the right impression, but with a guile which could hardly have imposed on babies—though that was what he seemed to take us for. He assured us that the insurgents of E.A.M. in Greece, who had been ruthlessly put down by the British, were disreputable ruffians and brigands; and in denouncing Marshal Tito, whom the British were trying to dislodge in Jugoslavia, he brought out as a triumphant clincher: "Why, Tito's not even his name! His real name is Josip Broz!"

I found later a little paper-bound book containing chapters from Sir Osmond's memoirs, reprinted for army reading—chapters which told of his years in Palestine and discussed the Zionist movement. In preparing this popular edition, intended for the use of the army, Sir Osmond had not taken the trouble to eliminate the Hebrew and Arabic—to say nothing of the Greek and Latin—with which, to use Bob Leigh's phrase, he could not resist throwing his weight around; and the twisted allusive style made rather hard reading in any case. But I got out of his snarled-up narrative a clear perception of something which Sir Osmond, though he tried to obscure it, could not help allowing to come to light. I closed the book with the realization that the British had brought the Jews into Palestine solely for the purpose of providing themselves with an ally against the Arabs, who were menacing their access to the oil wells. And I saw that Sir Osmond himself was simply a British imperialist agent, playing the British game and disguising it with his Greek and Latin, his cultivation of poetry and music. Was not he himself, I asked myself now, sometimes embarrassed by this? Was that the reason for the confused presentation of the Palestine question in his memoirs? Did he take refuge from a sordid episode, of which he knew the underside too well, in the memory of his tripos at Cambridge? Was he prouder of having known Lawrence of Arabia than of the whole of his work in the East? Yet were Englishmen of this sort, I wondered, ever really embarrassed? An outsider could never know. They have been making it for so long a habit to establish themselves in foreign countries, keep the natives at arm's-length and gather up, along with solider loot, the cultural possessions of the region, which they take carefully back to England and deposit in museums and libraries—as Lord Elgin did the frieze of the Parthenon—somehow creating the impression that the English have a much better right to these languages and literatures, these works of art and facts of archaeology, than the people who originally produced them, while these nations themselves are dealt with strictly according to the dictates of British commercial policy.

Later I learned that when Sir Osmond had been governor of a Greek island that had been made into a Crown Colony, the inhabitants, recalcitrant to British rule, had rebelled and burned Government House, destroying Sir Osmond's library. But in those days it was still very hard to make any impression on the English. When the news of Sir Osmond's loss reached England, another distinguished scholar-diplomat, retired, shipped his travelling library out, with an apposite quotation from Virgil, so that Sir Osmond's equipment was again complete and he did not lack for classics.

———

Young Leigh, as I say, seemed to react to Sir Osmond in much the same way in which I did. Yet, in talking to him, I would feel in him, from time to time, in spite of his sensitivity and humor, what seemed to me the well-defined sproutings of the very same mental traits which in Sir Osmond had flowered so flamboyantly as to become rather unusually conspicuous, but which were evidently the inevitable armament for the business of imperial domination. I was perfectly aware, for example, of the weakness and corruption of the Romans, and Leigh, who was the officer in charge of the public utilities of the city, came into much closer contact with them than I did and was in a position to be more annoyed by them; but I thought that he was inhibited by his official position from exploring and enjoying Italian life in the way that would seem to be normal for a young man still in his twenties. He read up modern Italian literature, but found it uniformly unsatisfactory; he went about a good deal socially, but complained that it was impossible to have any fun—to go anywhere or talk satisfactorily—with well-bred Italian girls, because they were guarded so grimly by their parents (it never seemed to occur to the British that the parents of young girls in countries which had just before been occupied by the Germans might regard them, too, as invaders to be resented and never trusted). Italy, he said, was like the frog in the fable which, in an effort to compete with the ox, had blown itself up and burst—and now they talked about their rights and ambitions! And in certain connections, it seemed to me, he instinctively resorted to the method, which I have noted in an earlier chapter, of diverting attention from some matter in which the British were open to criticism by denouncing the injured party on grounds that had nothing to do with the case. Thus the appointment of Count Sforza as Foreign Minister in the Bonomi government had been vetoed by Churchill the winter before, apparently for the reason that Sforza was not prepared to submit to the terms demanded by the British; but when this young major talked about Sforza, he took the line that he was simply an impossible person: egotistic, high-handed, wrongheaded—a description which did not tally with other accounts of Sforza I had heard.

One evening when we met at the Silones', just before I went back to England, I decided to try to smoke Leigh out, to get him down to the basic assumptions which underlay the cleverness and tolerance that these Englishmen from Oxford and Cambridge so agreeably display on the surface and which I usually found so genial that I did not want to prod below them. This proved to be a difficult task, and it took the combined efforts of Signora Silone, Bill Barrett and myself to make him admit his position. When I questioned the British policy of clamping a military government on such countries as Italy and Greece and frustrating their natural political development, he answered that the English troops were sure to be withdrawn soon from Italy, because the soldiers wanted to go home and forces would be needed for Germany; but, in the meantime, it was a good thing, in any case, for them to keep on holding down the North, where the Partisans had become so unruly—since, if political meetings were allowed there, there would surely be horrible riots and a lot of people getting killed. Barrett pointed out that there were a lot of people getting killed anyway: the Partisans went gunning for Fascists at night. To this Leigh replied that, if they assembled at meetings, people would be massacred wholesale. It was his echo, I thought, of the traditional attitude, all too familiar to me, that everything done by the English abroad was done at great inconvenience to themselves and for the benefit of the natives. But did not the English, I asked, have an interest in what they were doing in the Mediterranean countries? Well, the English, he explained, were busybodies who couldn't see strife or confusion without wanting to restore order. There had been the other day, for example, a brawl in the Piazza Barberini. The Americans had gathered about and egged the combatants on, whereas the English had been worried, felt responsible, thought that something ought to be done to stop it. I reminded him that the British—as in Syria—had never hesitated to instigate violence if they could obtain any advantage from doing so. Yes, he said, but they'd begin to be uncomfortable if they found there were more Syrians than Arabs—he seemed to imply that this feeling would be due purely to an instinct for fair play. In any case, it was easy, he said—becoming more realistic—for Americans to be impartial about what was going on in Europe because, Germany now being beaten, they had nothing important at stake. Americans were just as hardboiled as anybody else when it came down to things in which they did have an interest and they were capable of talking, on occasion, their own kind of hypocritical cant, which was just as repulsive as the British brand.

With reservations, we assented to this; but asked why it seemed so difficult for enlightened young people like him to contemplate the position of England as a member of a European federation. Signora Silone urged in her soft and gentle voice that England, with a Labour government, could play such a wonderful role of leadership in organizing a socialist Europe! He replied that conversations like this were conducted on two levels: an idealistic level and a level of political realities—I interrupted, insisting that the international socialist movement was one of the fundamental political realities, and that, if it did not seem so to him, it was because he had not come into contact with it. He admitted that this was true, but said he was going to vote for Labour—in spite of the fact that he didn't believe that they had any chance of winning, and thought that, if they did get in, they wouldn't be able to accomplish much.

Silone had come in during the conversation, fatigued and rather *abattu*. As a member of the Central Committee of the Italian Socialist Party, he had been struggling with the crisis, now protracted for days, over forming a new interim government. The aim was to swing the balance away from the monarchist bloc to the side of the republicans; and what with the five political parties of the Committee of Liberation that were always combining in new alliances and what with the vanity and rivalry of the leaders, the problem was a complicated one. The delay, said Signora Silone, was making Italy look ridiculous, but no one even got to meetings on time. Rome in summer, said Silone, reminded him of Smyrna. Like most serious and energetic Italians, he seemed thoroughly disgusted with the city, where the Vatican was lodged like a polyp and where all business got bogged down and obstructed. He had sunk to a couch and had begged us to go on talking English, which he did not understand: it would enable him to rest a little. From time to time he smiled politely, and at one point he made connections and intervened in the conversation. I had brought out a malicious idea which I had worked up to tease the English: the suggestion that England might comfortably survive as a small agricultural country, with little industry and a reduced population, very sound and clean and trim like Denmark, strong in democratic schools and wholesome rural coöperatives; and he quietly broke in to curb what he took to be naïve illusions about the economic innocence of small "independent" countries. The good Swiss, he pointed out, sent their capital abroad for investment in Swiss-Italian and Swiss-South American companies and thus were living, without working themselves, on the sweat of other people's labor just as much as the more obvious beneficiaries of colonial exploitation. Lenin had pointed this out in his book on imperialism.

At any rate, we made Leigh confess that he could not face with equanimity what he called the decline of England—which implied, by inexorable logic, the breaking-up of the British Empire, since the immediate consequence of that would be a decline in the standard of living. But he added that we Americans were criticizing Britain today "from a very comfortable position." And how were the British to know that America wasn't going to swoop down and possess herself of profitable fields which the British had been induced to relinquish? Hadn't we let down the men of good will like him by coming to Europe in the guise of liberators without having any line of our own that could be opposed to the old policies we complained of?

The British under Churchill, I knew very well, would have fought any liberal aims that we might have tried to bring to Europe, and done their best to prevent us from carrying them out. But that wasn't young Bob Leigh's fault, and he was right about the weakness of our foreign policy. I told him, as we were leaving the Silones' and walking down the many marble flights from the floor on which they lived, of an evening I had recently spent with the late journalist Dorothy Thompson, who had disturbed me by crying up the Christian Democrats, the most ambiguous of the Italian parties, evidently knowing very little about them and attracted, so far as I could see, merely by the benign connotations of the two component parts of their name. She had also, toward the end of the evening, announced challengingly that the foundation was long overdue of the United States of Europe, and that we ought to go straight home from the restaurant and design an appropriate flag. This was the kind of thing, I admitted, that we were sending to Europe just now, at the same time that our occupying army wanted to get home as quickly as possible and take as little responsibility as possible and sometimes offset this lady's benevolence by raping and racketeering. I was dissatisfied, I said, with all this. "We've had it!" Bob Leigh grinned ruefully, as if to wash his hands of the whole thing. This—like "The natives are hostile"—is one of the British catchphrases of the war which illuminate their state of mind. It has, however, come to be used by both armies for such everyday situations as the exhaustion of PX supplies or the end of sorting-out of the mail, and I had never heard it applied before to the downfall of Western civilization. Once, he went on, he would have talked like us. It had seemed to him that the other countries had ideas and ideals and movements that would come to the rescue of Europe where England was deficient or failed; but he had now seen quite a lot of the world—French, Italians, Americans and Russians—and they were just as much out for themselves, just as limited and crass in their objectives, as the British could be accused of being. I told him that this showed an advance, because it meant that he was beginning to learn not to take national differences seriously and that he was ripe for international socialism. Otherwise, I declared, he might be well on his way to becoming a Sir Osmond Leigh. He retorted that I ought not to be sure that I was not myself going to end by becoming a Sir Edmund Gosse—a gibe which was probably deserved if it was aimed at a certain complacency which I fear I had been displaying.

I found one morning a remarkable item in the British army paper, the *Union Jack*. It was an article called *An Idea* by a man named Peter Wilson, which began by explaining that, having defeated Germany, the question now presented itself as to what was to be done with her next. "Many revolutionary theories," the writer said, had "been suggested and discarded. But I have not seen a return to a theory which worked . . . in the eighteenth century—the Mercantile System. . . . America then as now was a big producer of cotton. But Britain insisted that she did not manufacture her raw cotton into finished goods, but exported it by means of British ships back to the Mother Country. [The non sequitur of tenses here matches the logic of the historical argument.] In Britain the raw cotton was spun and woven into goods of all kinds, manufactured and designed by British craftsmen. These were then transported back to America, their country of origin, and were sold to the settlers there." He believes that this system was a huge success, and that it ought to be adopted with Germany.

8

LONDON IN MIDSUMMER

I FLEW BACK TO LONDON in the middle of July and, being attached to the Army now, was given an army billet. This was a dreadful little hotel in Half Moon Street, which accommodated both Americans and British. The elevator was so tiny that you could hardly get into it with another person and so flimsy that you could feel the boards of the floor giving under your weight. I took to walking up and downstairs, though in the confusion of dark stairways and corridors that were shut off from one another, I would sometimes find myself in a *cul de sac* and have to go all the way back down and start up another flight. My room, which looked out on low chimney-pots, was a cubbyhole of yellow walls that contained a little prisonlike daybed, with the greasy marks of heads above it and a horrible brown cover impregnated with pounds of dust; a wooden washstand that had no towel: you were supposed to supply your own; a brown carpet with a rhomboidal pattern, also much stained and full of dust; and, in one corner, a small dung-colored coal grate which contained small and dismal gas-logs. In the other corners large piles of dirt had been swept up and left in plain sight. Down below in the dining room, the clothless tables seemed never to have been wiped, for they were soiled with innumerable spillings of soup, gravy, eggs, jam and tea;

and you were waited on by slovenly skivvies so pallidly unappetizing that they made the meager food seem more tasteless.

I soon discovered that this odd little nexus of streets just off the Green Park was one of the headquarters of the London whores. Most of the three- or four-story hotels are evidently *hôtels borgnes,* and the obvious conclusion is that my billet is a converted brothel. In the middle of all this, at the foot of the street, you find a little Christian Science church, which manages to look almost as old and gray as any other church in London.

It is nearly as hot here as in Rome; and the worst of it is that, whereas in Rome you can at least go around without a jacket—since in summer a shirt with insignia is regulation in the Mediterranean—here in London, as is characteristic of onerous British convention, you have to do all your walking and travelling in a buttoned-up and belted uniform, with your shirt always soaked in sweat.

At night there is still almost as little light as there was before the end of the war, and a section that has been badly blasted, like the Tottenham Court Road, looks gruesome in the late-gathering darkness: its bare and wry trees with tufts of leaves at the tips of the branches like the legs and necks of plucked fowl; its masklike fronts of bombed-out houses, with their dark eye-sockets and gaping jaws. There is a peculiar desolation and horror about finding these carcases of streets unburied in the midst of an inhabited city.

Piccadilly is crawling with life, but equally repellent in its different way. The summer murk, stagnant and tepid, is eddying with the aimless movement of the British and American soldiers and the deteriorated London tarts that circulate slowly or clot in groups. The purposes of the fighting accomplished, the tensions of wartime relaxed, these uniformed and dog-tagged men now find themselves immersed like amebas in the swampy backwater of England. What has the war worked up to?—nothing, vacuity —to these young males afloat in the foreign streets, with no training in directing themselves and with no strong impulse toward self-direction, merely responding to a rudimentary instinct to adhere to these floating females whose faces they can hardly make out.

———

How empty, how sickish, how senseless, everything suddenly seems the moment the war is over! We are left flat with the impoverished and humiliating life that the drive against the enemy kept our minds off. Where our efforts have all gone toward destruction, we have been able to build nothing at home to fall back on amidst our own ruin. Where the enemy are roofless and starving, where we have reduced their cities to rubble, we get now not even useful plunder or readily exploitable empire, but merely an extension, a more wearisome load, of harassing demands and duties.

The novelist Graham Greene said to me the other day that they sometimes thought to themselves, now that the war was over: "If one could only hear the hum of a robot bomb!" Life had been dramatic because dangerous. Everything one did was pointed up, was lived with a special awareness, because it might be the last thing one did, and now they missed this: life was safe but blank. No doubt Greene's rather saturnine nature, his addiction to the peculiar excitements of pursuit and persecution, count for something in his nostalgia for the buzz of the V-I's; but then, Greene himself and his themes are partly products of the conditions of the period, of which a fundamental insecurity has been so much a permanent feature that, once having adjusted themselves to it, the English do not know how to live without it.

G., a London girl whom I very much liked, struck the same sort of note when she complained that the headlines were dull. One was used to reading of cities in flames, infernal concentration camps laid open, German officials killing themselves and their families; the murderous and crushing revenge, like the progress of a gigantic tank, for the assault on one's own cities. And now the crescendo had ceased: the nerves no longer felt the stimulus that had been shocking them every day like the insulin and electric current which, applied to schizophrenic cases, was supposed to give them lucid spells. She had written me of the disappointing flatness of the V-Day celebration in England and of her own depression and apathy at the parties where people had tried to be gay; and now she told me ghastly stories of men she knew who, after years in German jails, had just got back to England. One of these had turned Communist in prison, and was now so appalled and unsettled by what he found at home that his first reaction had been to long to go back to prison, where he had at least known which side he was on and had been able to remain true to his principles. Another had come back to his wife and had stayed with her only two weeks. During his absence, she had had a lover, to whom she had become accustomed, and had taken rather badly to drink. He, on his side, had always been a gambler, and imprisonment had encouraged this taste. In prison he had done nothing but gamble and even used to bet with his friends on which and how many prisoners were going to be converted by the Roman Catholic priest. He found he could not get on with his wife, left the country and came to London, where he completely gave himself up to gambling. A third man had been playing the women's roles in the shows that they had put on in jail, and his companions, who had not seen a woman for years, began behaving toward him in daily life as if he were an attractive girl to be treated with consideration, relieved of unpleasant tasks and courted—with the result that he had gradually developed, in response to the pressure of this attitude—he was apparently not a case of congenital homosexuality—a feminine personality of which he found that he was unable to rid himself. He hardly knew to which sex he belonged.

(I later met, in the United States, a young man who had spent five years in prison-camps and had talked with a woman but once, and then only the Mother Superior of a convent, of whom, through a little grating, he had been able to see only the hands. On rare occasions when they heard women's voices, these had sounded extremely queer. After so long a confinement, he said, during which one had been always under orders, with every moment of one's time assigned, it was incredibly painful and frightening to find oneself at large in London and to have to do things for oneself. It required a great effort of thought and will even to bring oneself to the point of walking down the steps to the Tube, buying a ticket and boarding the train.)

———

G. herself, who is always wound-up and looks physically rather frail, seems to have felt the nervous pressure increase instead of lessening since the end of the war. She has a job in the department of "economic propaganda" and has worked in London all through the bombing, when, as she says, you sometimes thought you "couldn't stick it." A house a few doors from her flat was blown up when she was at home one night. But, now that the war is over, she suffers more than ever from claustrophobia—feels oppressed by day in her office and is dismal with people at night. In between her regular work and dinner, she takes lessons in Italian and Turkish, in the hope of getting herself sent out to Italy or the East.

She is an extremely bright and able girl, with the same sort of all-around competence that the young Englishmen from the universities have. The English women I have met in London have been in general a pleasant surprise. The clever ones are more sympathetic than the same kind of people at home, because they usually have quiet manners and do not try to compete with the men. When they are beautiful, they are beautiful in a feminine way that is a relief after the dashing and aggressive "style" which is directed, on the part of our women, almost more, perhaps, at women than at men. At the same time, I note that G. has one habit which American girls have and which I have come to regard as significant of a change in the status of women. When she is standing and wants to rest, she puts forward one foot with the toe up, resting it on her heel, where the more maidenly older pose involved bending in one knee and leaning one thigh against the other. But these English girls talk the men's language: the crisp laconic schoolboy code that makes everything matter-of-fact or droll, and that has its own kind of charm after the challenging wisecracks of our women. G. combines this with something else which seems to me extremely old English, a more formal turn of phrase in a style probably characteristic of her clergyman father, now dead, which is matched by her beautiful handwriting, with its distinctly detached letters, its deftly twisted ampersands and its incised serifs and shadings. "I think I talk like a don, you know," she says; and she tells me that she can never decide whether to regard herself as "the gamine type" or "the serious type."

She has also—what does seem to me unusual here—along with her matter-of-factness, a volatility of mood and expression of a kind that always enchants me in women; the beauty that seems to derive from a spirit which inhabits the body rather than from the body itself. This spirit, in G., sleeps or wakes, fades or flushes, is *méchant* or merry, flits about through a repertory of several roles, and has its moments of strength and of weakness. Sometimes she looks frightened or a little out of focus, with the two sides of her face not in harmony: one pert, the other chagrined; sometimes on guard and alert, like a keen-eyed quiet baby fox that makes quick silent darting movements; sometimes lovely with delicate coloring or electric with the kind of intensity in which feeling and intellect mix. Sometimes, dressed to go out, her hair caught up from her forehead and ears and done in a knot at the back of her head, she looks grown-up and very handsome, with the hard English chic.

One evening, just before dinner, I made her keep still and wrote down a little sketch of her as she sat in her living room: "Pale slight figure in gray suit and white collar, with slim legs that show pink through gray stockings and too-large old white high-heeled shoes that are the best that can be had in wartime. Against yellow lamplight, her profiled face shows grayish-pink, too. Very fine though rather irregular features. Sharp and longish nose, with a hump and dip in the bridge, that is assertive and shows curiosity. Sharp shoulders, perhaps mainly due to tailoring; soft, delicate and palely-veined neck under pointed little forward-thrust chin, with slight rounded flesh underneath. But the lower part of her face, with its very small mouth, is less strongly developed than the upper. Soft yellowish hair that grows low on her forehead and—worn thus with a feminine tossed effect—has a suggestion of lion's mane; it is balanced in color by the gold of the bracelets on one of her wrists, as she sits with her capable non-tapering fingers clasped about her knee.

But the features that give her face its chief accent are her little diamond-bright blue eyes that might almost be used to cut glass or as points for Johanssen gauges. Beneath her finely drawn-in eyebrows, they look sometimes cold and sharp-pricking, sometimes twinkling and cute."

Her figure has disproportions of largeness and longness with smallness and shortness, which, instead of being disconcerting, are altogether a part of her attractiveness—because they seem to correspond with her complexity. I found, for example, on this visit, when I had bought her some silk stockings from Italy, that her feet, which I had remembered as tiny, were several sizes bigger than I had thought. And this discovery at once disappointed me in that it seemed to destroy the image of an exquisite little figure that I had carried from my previous visit, and pleased me because it added to her piquancy and revealed a firm base in substance for solid qualities of intellect and character with which I was coming to credit her.

Her way of receiving these stockings and some other things I had brought her from Italy seemed to me very English and, especially, very post-war English. There were an antique veil for the hair and an antique black lace fan, two pairs of earrings, the stockings, the new book by Silone, whom G. greatly admired, and an Italian magazine that had in it a short story by Moravia called *L'Ufficiale Inglese,* which, perhaps with a certain malice, I wanted people in England to read, a carton of cigarettes from the American PX and two bottles of some sparkling Italian wine—which were received with a coolness and a minimum of comment that might have made me feel that I had overdone playing Santa Claus if they had not at once been whisked away as if sucked up by a vacuum-cleaner. It would be beside the point, with the English, to complain of ungraciousness of manners since what they aim at is a dryness and curtness that has nothing to do with grace; but it was interesting to note the difference between G.'s way of receiving presents and the transports or emphatic approval of the ordinary American girl. The attitude of Leonor Fini, the painter, whom I had got to know in Rome and who had asked me to bring her some paints and brushes from London, was also quite different from G.'s. In the magnificent Italian way, she offered me my choice of her drawings, any one of which was valued at more than the materials I had bought her; and, when I hesitated between two, insisted on my taking them both. When I afterwards showed an interest in a handsome new album of Pollaiuolo, she made me take this, too, declaring that she had two copies, and, as I was leaving, remarked that she would send me some new books in which she thought I might be interested. I do not in the least, by these contrasts, intend to be invidious at G.'s expense. The incident was one of many which made me see how the privations of the war had intensified to a ravenous voracity the appetite for property of the English, for whom permanent family possessions, tangible personal belongings, a steady supply of food and goods, have always been important in a different way than they are to Italians or Americans. It was not, I am sure, that G. had not appreciated my gifts—she later, in the same inexpressive way and with no suggestion from me, did me a great service, which I shall tell about further on; but, even aside from her "British phlegm," she was too dead serious about things like silk stockings to put on a polite little act.

———

When I had just come to London in April and was taken one evening by English friends to dine in a first-class restaurant, I ordered "roast duck" as a dish that sounded attractive and normal. I noticed, however, that the Londoners approached the menu with a certain quiet wariness, and that none of them selected duck. The duck, indeed, when it came, turned out to be disappointing: it consisted of little dry and tough slivers from a bird that seemed incredibly thin for even a poorly-fed barnyard fowl. The other day, when I was walking with G. through one of the narrow streets near Holborn, we found ourselves inhaling a foul stale smell, and, looking round, saw a little market, on the shelves of whose open windows were laid out rows and rows of dead crows. That was apparently all they sold in that shop.

———

I took G. somewhere in a taxi in the rain and, as I was dropping her, saw a well-dressed woman who was waiting to get a cab. I was going in her direction and took her to Oxford Street. Seeing my war correspondent's insignia, she asked me where I had been, and, when I said that I had just come from Italy, she inquired how things were there. In very bad shape, I told her. "But they're very light-hearted about it, aren't they?" I replied that this was not my impression. She said at once that she had understood that the Italians were "very unwilling to do anything for themselves." I don't remember whether I answered that the Allied Commission in Italy were making it extremely difficult for the Italians to do anything for themselves; but it seemed to me that this lady's remarks were typical of the attitude of the English toward the damage that has been done by our side. It is true no doubt, as was said to me by an Englishman on my earlier visit to London, when the Allies were advancing on Berlin, that the English so hate destruction that they have been made to feel uneasy and guilty by the ruin they have wrought in Europe; but it is equally characteristic of the English that they should always try to present the picture in such a way as to make it appear that their opponents don't really mind having their buildings and people blown up or that it is somehow the fault of the negligence of those foreign and inferior races that one should find them in such a mess.

———

I was a little taken aback one evening for which I had had vague other plans to find that I was going with G. to a new opera by Benjamin Britten which was being done at Sadler's Wells. She had bought the tickets herself and said nothing about it in advance. The only thing I had heard by Britten had been a *Requiem* that had not much impressed me, and I did not feel particularly eager to sit through an English opera called *Peter Grimes,* based on an episode from Crabbe. G. did try, with her usual lack of emphasis, to get me to read the libretto, of which she had procured a copy, but she did not explain that this work had been something of a sensation in London, where the critics, who, like me, had not at first expected anything extraordinary, had been roused from their neat routine to the point of hearing it several times and writing two or three articles about it. But she knew that I ought to hear it, and it is one of my debts to G. that she made me go to *Peter Grimes,* which I should unquestionably otherwise have missed.

For, almost from the moment when the curtain went up on the bare room in the provincial Moot Hall—which no overture had introduced—where the fisherman Peter Grimes was being examined at a coroner's inquest in connection with the death of his apprentice, I felt the power of a musical gift and a dramatic imagination that woke my interest and commanded my attention. There have been relatively few composers of the first rank who had a natural gift for the theater: Mozart, Musorgsky,

Verdi, Wagner, the Bizet of *Carmen*. To be confronted, without preparation, with an unmistakable new talent of this kind is an astonishing, even an electrifying, experience. The difficulty of describing *Peter Grimes* to someone who has not heard it is the difficulty of convincing people whose expectations are likely to be limited by having listened to too much modern music that was synthetic, arid, effortful and inadequate, that a new master has really arrived; of conveying to them the special qualities of a full-grown original artist. In my own case, I am particularly handicapped by lack of technical knowledge and training, so that I can only give an account of the opera's spell without being able to analyze it intelligently. The best I can do, then, is to report my impression —subject to expert correction—that Britten's score shows no signs of any of the dominant influences—Wagner, Debussy, Stravinsky, Schoenberg or Prokofiev—but has been phrased in an idiom that is personal and built with a definiteness and solidity that are as English as Gilbert and Sullivan (one can find, for an English opera, no other comparison in the immediate past). And the result of this is very different from anything we have been used to. The ordinary composer of opera finds his conventions there with the stage; but, when you are watching *Peter Grimes*, you are almost completely unaware of anything that is artificial, anything "operatic." The composer here seems quite free from the self-consciousness of contemporary musicians. You do not feel you are watching an experiment; you are living a work of art. The opera seizes upon you, possesses you, keeps you riveted to your seat during the action and keyed up during the intermissions, and drops you, purged and exhausted, at the end.

The orchestra, in *Peter Grimes*, plays a mainly subordinate role, and the first effect on the hearer, during the opening scene in the Moot Hall, is of a drastic simplification of opera to something essential and naked, which immediately wakes one up. There is no Wagnerian web of motifs that tells you about the characters: the characters express themselves directly, either conversing or soliloquizing in song, while the orchestra, for the most part, but comments. The music is a close continuity, though articulated rather than fluid, of vivid utterances on the part of the personages and—except in the more elaborate interludes—sharp and terse descriptive strokes, in which from time to time take shape arias, duets, trios and choruses. These—almost never regular in pattern and never losing the effect of naturalness—have their full or fragmentary developments, and give way to the next urgent pulse of the blood-stream that runs through the whole piece. In the same way, the words of the libretto, by the poet Montague Slater, which are admirably suited to the music and which the music exactly fits, shift sometimes into the imagery of poetry but never depart far from the colloquial and are sometimes—with no loss of dignity—left perfectly bald and flat. But we soon come to recognize in the music the extraordinary flexibility, the subtlety and the variety, which are combined with a stout British craftsmanship that has a sure hand with mortise and tenon and that knows how to plant and mass a chorus, and with a compelling theatrical sense, an instinct for tempo and point. And—what is most uncommon with opera—we find ourselves touched and stirred at listening to an eloquence of voices that does not merely charm or impress us as the performance of well-trained singers but that seems sometimes to reach us directly with the emotions of actual people. Nor do these voices find their expression exclusively through the singers' roles: one of the most effective devices of *Peter Grimes* is the use of the orchestral interludes that take place between the scenes while the curtain is down. Thus at the end of the

first scene in the Moot Hall, where you have just been
seeing Peter Grimes consoled by Ellen Orford, the school-
teacher, the only being in the town who cares for him,
the orchestra develops a theme which seems to well up
out of Ellen's heart, and then rises and falls with a
plangency that, sustained through the long passage with
marvellous art, conveys, as if her spirit were speaking, her
sympathy and pain for Peter. And at the end of the scene
that follows, when a storm has been heard coming up as
Balstrode, the retired captain, has been trying to remon-
strate with Peter over his plan to take another apprentice
and prove to the town that he is not a monster, the winds
and the waves break loose the moment the curtain falls,
fiendishly yelping and slapping in a way that represents
with realism—Britten was born on the Suffolk coast—the
worrying raving crescendo of an equinoctial gale but that
howls at the same time with the fierceness of Peter's
rebellious pride and of the latent sadistic impulse of
which he is half unconscious but to which the new
situation will eventually give free rein. The sea's restive
and pressing movement has been all through the scene
that preceded, and in the next, in the local tavern to
which the people have resorted for warmth and cheer, the
hurricane wildly intrudes whenever the door is opened
and at last, with the entrance of Grimes, rushes into the
room to stay. This long act, which is brought to its climax
by the silence that greets Peter's appearance and that con-
centrates the hostility of the town, and by the arrival of
the orphan whom, the carrier refusing, Ellen has herself
gone to fetch and for whose welfare she hopes to make
herself responsible—this act has an intensity and an
impetus that carries one through, without a moment's let-
down, from the opening to the end. Nor is what follows
much less effective. The whole drama is a stretching of
tension between the inquest and the inevitable crisis

when Grimes will, if not deliberately kill, at least cause
the death of, the second apprentice; and I do not remember ever to have seen, at any performance of opera, an
audience so steadily intent, so petrified and held in
suspense, as the audience of *Peter Grimes*. This is due
partly to the dramatic skill of Britten, but it is due also to
his having succeeded in harmonizing, through *Peter
Grimes,* the harsh helpless emotions of wartime. This
opera could have been written in no other age, and it is
one of the very few works of art that have seemed to me,
so far, to have spoken for the blind anguish, the hateful
rancors and the will to destruction of these horrible years.
Its grip on its London audiences is clearly of the same
special kind as the grip of the recent productions of
Richard III and *The Duchess of Malfi*. Like them, it is
the chronicle of an impulse to persecute and to kill
which has become an obsessive compulsion, which drags
the malefactor on—under a fatality which he does not
understand, from which he can never get free, and which
never leaves him even the lucidity for repentance or
reparation—through a series of uncontrollable cruelties
which will lead, in the long run, to his being annihilated
himself. At first you think that Peter Grimes is Germany.
He is always under the impression, poor fellow, that what
he really wants for himself is to marry Ellen Orford and
to live in a nice little cottage with children and fruit in
the garden "and whitened doorstep and a woman's care."
Above all, he wants to prove to his neighbors that he is
not the scoundrel they think him, that he really means no
harm to his apprentices and that he will make a good
family man. But he cannot help flying into a fury when
the boy does not respond to his will, and when he gets
angry, he beats him; and his townsmen become more and
more indignant. At last, shouting, "Peter Grimes!," they
go on the march against him, determined to capture him

and make him pay, just at the moment when he has paused and relented, and when their approach will pre-cipitate, in his dash to escape, his pushing the boy so that he falls over the cliff, which is finally to settle his fate. (A comparison of the text of the opera with the story as told by Crabbe in *The Borough* shows that Britten and Montague Slater—though they have used here and there a few lines from Crabbe—have put Peter in a different situation and invented for him a new significance. The outlaw fisherman in Crabbe is married, though his wife does not figure in the story, and he has no connection with Ellen Orford, who is the heroine of a separate episode. The mainspring of the original version is Peter's rebellion against his father: he is in Crabbe completely anti-social and has no hankering for middle-class de-cency.) But, by the time you are done with the opera—or by the time it is done with you—you have decided that Peter Grimes is the whole of bombing, machine-gunning, mining, torpedoing, ambushing humanity, which talks about a guaranteed standard of living yet does nothing but wreck its own works, degrade or pervert its own moral life and reduce itself to starvation. You feel, during the final scenes, that the indignant shouting trampling mob which comes to punish Peter Grimes is just as sadistic as he. And when Balstrode gets to him first and sends him out to sink himself in his boat, you feel that you are in the same boat as Grimes.

———

Every night when I walked back to Half Moon Street, I ran the gauntlet of the innumerable prostitutes that lined Piccadilly and the Green Park. They would brush you with "Come heah, Sweetie!" or a simple "Hullo!" in their low quiet London voices that, with their pale dimly-looming forms, made them seem a part of the night like moths. There was one of them who gave me the impression of being more or less well-bred, for she talked the schoolboy language like G. and would say to me, "Can't I tempt you?," as if she were offering me a cake or a drink. One night when I had lost my way in the queer little tangle of streets behind the Christian Science church, a tough, short and stocky blond wench, almost like some hussy of Rowlandson's, of whom I had asked the way and who was going in my direction, steered me good-naturedly to my sordid hotel. She tried to take advantage of the occasion to do a bit of business, but I replied, in an attempt to discourage her, that I had just been to see a friend. "In other words, you've had it," she said. "Charming!"

One night, wandering back at loose ends, I picked up a really good-looking girl who accosted me in French. She was the only such woman that I had yet seen in London who was not frankly down-at-heels and disreputable. A vigorous well-filled-out brunette with a bright smile of strong white teeth, she was wearing a brown suit, a béret and relatively little make-up. She came from Montmartre, she told me, and had been in London since 1939. Her aim was to go back to Paris and open a lingerie shop. During the day, she worked wrapping up parcels at the French Red Cross; and for the purposes of her traffic at night she did not use the harlots' hotels, but had a well-kept room in a house that was inhabited entirely by French girls. It was impressive, as a feat of French character, to see how these girls stuck together and how astutely they had organized their affairs. Everything here was on a higher level of decency than among the native prostitutes of London. I was talking about this, when I got back to Rome, with Alberto Moravia, the novelist, who had lived for a time in England, and he said truly that the point was that in France prostitution was a recognized profession which did not involve the loss of self-respect, whereas, in England, a woman who took to the streets was consigned to the dregs of society and could no longer keep up any standards. She was now simply a *tart* or a *whore*, which is quite different from being *une petite femme*—what Odette, my French friend, always called herself. The English girls, as a rule, looked blowzy and behaved vulgarly, and they mostly gave the impression of being diseased. But Odette was in good shape and handsome, and conducted her commerce with men with the same sort of efficiency and dignity with which she would have run her shop. She was scrupulously hygienic, and had availed herself of every resource to eliminate both squalor and risk.

It was all like a little chunk of Paris embedded in darkest densest London. Though Odette had been in England six years, she had learned only a few words of English and talked French in a polite and conventional way that would have done perfect credit to the proprietress of a *pension de famille*. She had on tap all the correct formulations, and when she used, as she did not do often, a word of argot that she saw I did not understand—as when she tactfully remarked, in connection with the outburst of de Gaulle against Britain over its attitude toward French interests in Syria, that she "didn't know what de Gaulle had taken into his *ciboule*"—she would immediately explain what this meant. She described to me with clarity but discretion the characteristics of the various nationalities as she had encountered them in the course of her business. The English were very cold: unbuttoned, buttoned up, and then goodby! the Canadians were *"ordinaires."* Some of the Poles were nice. But *"il n'y a que les Français, les Belges et les Américains pour faire l'amour."* The Americans were rather *"bruyants,"* but then they were *"loin de chez eux"* and no doubt

behaved better at home; and, in any case, they were gay
to go out with and really liked to have a good time. She
would have nothing to do with blacks, and one night
when she had been spoken to by an officer who turned
out to be a Negro, she had said she had another engagement.

I saw her several times and used to pay her to stay on
and talk, but merely talking made her nervous and
restless, and she would begin knitting energetically on a
sweater that she told me she was making for the director
of the French Red Cross. If she had had to buy it, she
said, it would have cost her several pounds, but this way
it cost only a few shillings. She discussed her expenses
and savings with exactitude and in detail, and declared
that, what with the rental of her relatively high-grade
room, she wasn't able to save very much; but I am
perfectly sure she saved something.

———

I had lunch in an old London club, full of dark
staircases and antique engravings, very pleasant in its
privacy and comfort, and quite different from the elevator-
served and more hotel-like clubs of New York. The lunch
was much the best and the most abundant that I had had
anywhere in London. They had managed to keep themselves supplied with excellent vegetables and cheeses and
various kinds of meat, as not even the best restaurants
were, and seemed secure in their privileged position.

When I left with the friend who had brought me, we
stood on the curb for some minutes trying to catch a taxi;
but at last, just as we thought we had one, a man
snatched it under our noses, and we decided to give it up
and walk on. My companion must have known the man,
for he remarked: "It's a kind of Hell—eternally waiting
in the street while one watches all the people one most

loathes getting into taxis and driving off." He was not naturally an unamiable man, and it seemed to me that his comment was typical of the general state of mind to which England was now reduced: a combination of competitive spitefulness with exasperated patience.

I looked up Harold Laski and went around with him to some Labour meetings in the industrial towns outside London. From the houses of gray "roughcast" or yellow brick, with their small bay-windows and dull red-tiled roofs, the pale men and women and boys and girls emerged in gray or blue or khaki to sit quietly and listen to the speakers with concentrated and anxious attention. These occasions seemed a great deal more serious than anything else of the kind that I remembered to have seen in America, including even labor-union meetings and the rallies of the Left-Wing parties. The routine of a presidential campaign looked, beside them, like perfunctory clowning.

Laski put on a very good performance, and he received a resounding ovation. People crowded around our car to get a glimpse of the professor from Oxford who was working for their side and who was just then being denounced by the Beaverbrook press. The situation was that Churchill had invited Clement Attlee to be present at the Berlin Conference, and that Laski, the chairman of the Labour Party, had announced that, if Attlee attended, it would be as an observer only, and that the decisions made by the Conference would not affect the future foreign policy of Labour. This statement had been seized upon by Beaverbrook as a pretext for raising an alarm against the sinister hidden hand of Socialism, which, in the event of a victory for Labour, would be manipulating puppet officials. But he had apparently made no impres-

sion on the supporters of the Labour candidates, for
whom Laski had now come to speak. These people were
much too badly off and had much too grim a prospect
before them to be excited by the antics of journalists. The
only thing that mattered to them was that the Labour
Party was promising quick action on housing, education
and jobs. Churchill, as Laski reminded them, had said
that he was "in favor of the traditional Britain, with a few
measures of practical construction"; and now Laski was
declaring that "mass unemployment was incompatible
with democratic institutions," and that they "must never
again allow such a degradation of conditions as had
occurred between the two wars." As for foreign affairs: he
was loudly applauded when he told them that the people
of Europe and Asia, "bound in chains," were "reaching
out for the Four Freedoms," and that the Labour Party, if
elected to office, could not undertake to follow the policies
of the party that had allowed China and Spain, Czecho-
slovakia and Ethiopia, to fall victims one by one to the
Japanese and the Fascists, and which was still, in Italy
and Greece, backing the reactionary elements and trying
to reinstate the very kings who had delivered their countries over to the Fascists and who had no longer any
popular support.

He reminded them that, in the "traditional Britain"
which Mr. Churchill wanted to perpetuate, one per cent
of the population owned fifty per cent of the wealth; that,
in the Army, only one per cent of the officers came from
working-class parents; and that in 1939, at the time war
had broken out, sixty-seven per cent of the diplomatic
corps had gone to school at Eton. Well, they all knew
that the Battle of Peterloo had been won on the playing-
fields of Eton and that the Battle of Sidney Street had
been won on the playing-fields of Harrow! (References to
the Manchester Massacre of 1819, when soldiers charged

with sabers a meeting held to petition for parliamentary reform, and to an incident in the twenties when Churchill, as Home Secretary, went personally, pistol in hand, after some foreigner, a political refugee, who was supposed to be a dangerous character.) Yet I noticed that the speaker did not hesitate to call attention to his own upper-class education. I heard him explain more than once, in connection with social inequalities, that he himself, in being born, had "had the good sense to choose rich parents," who had sent him to a public school; and he made a conventional joke about his coming from "the best university—by which I of course mean Oxford." (I remembered that he had been telling me, on the train coming down, about a book by some liberal peer, who showed brilliantly how impossible it was "to get a real education at Oxford.") Well, this kind of thing, I reflected, would never have gone down in America from such a speaker before such an audience; but I imagined that Harold Laski knew perfectly what he was doing, and that he was not merely aiming to create prestige by appealing to the deep-rooted snobbery which is supposed to prevail in England, but also, or perhaps solely, to disarm any possible resentment of his Oxford manner and accent. The alternative would have been, I suppose, to pretend to be apologetic about them—which would have been found a good deal more objectionable. In America, the differences in the way people talk, though considerable, are less noticeable than in England; and where the factory worker's son may very well go to some college, there is no clear issue of education. But in England the consciousness of class seems omnipresent and everlasting, and even in a campaign where the speaker is advocating "government ownership, under socialist control, of land and raw materials," this factor has to be exploited or circumvented.

But I felt about Harold Laski, as, in Europe, I had already felt in connection with certain other figures, literary, artistic or political, whom I had met since the end of the war, that the processes of disintegration had now gone so far over here that people, if they were capable of seriousness, had now to be serious in a way that our well-fed and well-defended intellectuals had never lately been forced to be in America. If one was capable of good sense and courage, those qualities were aroused, were demanded, by this hour of moral slump; and they emerged with a moral dignity that differed from the heroism of wartime. There has always been in Harold Laski an element of intellectual vanity, of self-indulgence in his own virtuosity, of a confidence in his own resourcefulness which plays sometimes into a boyish sense of mischief, sometimes into the irresponsibility of taking himself, or letting others take, the appropriate and ready legend for the outlying uncivilized fact (as in his willingness to ignore or not to recognize the totalitarian tyranny of Stalin or in his habit of casting himself for a role in all his anecdotes of illustrious contemporaries). At these meetings, his cleverness and his competence, his quick wits in dealing with the problems of the moment, combined with his long-range capacity for absorbing and retaining data as well as for sticking to principle, were displayed in a striking way. He was adroit at disposing of hecklers—of the hired and coached kind, set up by the Conservatives and the Communists; marvellous at answering questions—he had the answer on the tip of his tongue the second that the questioner had finished; admirable in the homes of the Labour people, with whom and with whose wives and children he had no stiffness and knew just what to say. But I felt now as I had not done before, merely in talking to him or reading his writings, that he was more than an intellectual radical who formulated plausible positions. I felt that there was something in him of the real fighter for human rights, and that this had survived, through two wars, an era of chaos and panic, in rather an impressive way. At one moment—I was sitting on the platform and in a position to study the audience—I caught sight of an elderly woman (she may not have been so elderly as she looked), who sat with chin and nose thrust forward, eyes intent yet staring, and with a peculiar kind of hungriness and gauntness that caused one to recoil from the suggestion of something that was just on the edge of not being quite familiarly human—as if she belonged to a breed that was distinct from even the poor people of peacetime communities, to a breed with ravenous eyes like an animal's that no longer took in the same things which the true human being saw but saw only with appetites that were simple and stringent. Such faces I had noticed in Milan just after the expulsion of the Germans; and I was coming, as they recurred, to recognize them as the type of wartime Europe. On the platform, erect before this woman and all her silent companions, stood Laski, slight, bespectacled, high-browed, making them promises which could not always perhaps be realized, amusing them with wisecracks and stories which were not always absolutely first-rate, talking to some degree the mere cant of politics, yet certainly kept up and held to his post by some tension that magnetized and turned him toward that craning gray-faced chicken-eyed woman.

9

ROME IN MIDSUMMER

ROME, ON MY RETURN FROM ENGLAND, seemed more fetid and corrupt than ever. The whole stretch from the gates of the Borghese Gardens down through the Via Veneto, the Via del Tritone and the Corso Umberto to the Piazza Venezia has been, as Moravia says, converted into one great brothel; and in the evenings of the dog-star summer, we all seem stewing like lumps of flesh and fat in a cheap but turbid soup that washes through this winding channel like the bilge of a Venetian canal. Prostitution, with the Americans here, has become, from the Roman point of view, so unprecedentedly, incredibly profitable that many girls have been brought into the streets who might otherwise have stayed at home or worked at decent jobs. The standard price that they try to keep up seems to be thirty thousand lire—that is, thirty dollars; but in other respects the thing has certainly reached a very low level. Bill Barrett is under the impression that the soldiers go further here than has ever been done anywhere in peacetime in dispensing with even the most sketchy preliminaries: the G.I. simply overtakes the girl, cranes around to get a glimpse of her face so as to be sure she is not absolutely repulsive, then grabs her; she allows herself to be grabbed, but, backing against the wall, makes him stop for a discussion of terms. All the way along the Via del Tritone, these walls are lined with soldiers, who have been watching the parade every evening so that they have got to know the regular girls, and are fishing for the better ones, with whom they will attempt to drive bargains. If a respectable woman goes through here and hurries on without replying to greetings, she is likely to be followed by such jeers as, "She must be a hundred-thousand-lire broad!"

The hotels in the Via Veneto that have been commandeered by the A.C. are picketed by tarts and pimps. The air corps are great spenders on furlough and they are allowed to have women in their rooms, so that the aviators' hotel in this section is the center of activity and gaiety. Women stream through the lobby, perch in the bar and flutter about the entrance like starlings. I saw one little girl coming out, wild-looking, red-haired and slim, who gave me the impression that she was having an intoxicatingly good time as well as making a great deal of money. In another of these hotels, one night, some soldiers threw a girl out the window and broke her back so that she died. Such incidents have antagonized the Italians, and the "better class" of people are disgusted by the spectacle of the Roman women—and many who have come into Rome for the purpose—making such a display of themselves, and by seeing what was once one of the handsomest and most fashionable quarters of modern Rome turned into a squalid market, where the behavior of Catullus' Lesbia *"in quadriviis et angiportis"*—which I have never seen in public before—as a matter of nightly occurrence. There is a sign on an American army club which says, "Reserved for G.I.'s and Their Lady Guests," and the Romans have picked up the latter phrase as a

synonym for tarts. They say that the word *signorina,* from
its constant use by the soldiers, has passed into disrepute.

————

In these days it is always reassuring to find people who
have been working at the arts undistracted by war-work
and unshaken in morale. One of the things I have
enjoyed most in Rome has been calling, from time to
time, on Leonor Fini, the painter. I had seen in New
York a few of her pictures, which were half-Surrealist,
half-Romantic; and to climb up to her apartment in an
enormous old palace in the squalid Piazza del Gesù is to
realize that Rome itself is not only intensely Romantic
but even also rather Surrealist, so that such work loses
the power to shock that was its aim and its pride in Paris.
At night, with electricity economized, the place is entirely
dark, and at first, among the many entrances that open on
all sides of the courtyard, I would always become confused and have to summon the *portiere.* You need
matches to achieve the ascent of the shallow and wide
and deep interminable marble stairs, made for unimaginable grandeur, that the proportionately lofty arched windows illuminate only faintly; and by the glimmer, beneath the stone vaults and among the great funeral vases
and the flower-carved entablatures, one has glimpses of
Roman relics that appear, on their heroic scale, in a
completely Surrealist key: the conventionally statuesque
pose of a white naked hero with a sword would be
followed by a similar figure in an unexpected half-
squatting posture; a single finger from an ancient colossus,
standing upright on a pedestal, loomed as tall as an
ordinary statue; and a bearded man, seated on something
and leaning forward intent on a book, had the appearance
of reading in the toilet. As the staircase goes on so long
that you finally lose count of the landings, you are likely

to try wrong apartments and get the rooms of some lurking nobleman whose old butler peers out through the crack of a door apprehensively secured by a chain.

At last, taking a smaller stairway, you arrive, just under the roof, at what must once have been servants' quarters but is now a duplex apartment. One comfortable large room serves as both studio and living room and looks out, in a commanding view, as I discovered on later visits, over the infinite lines and planes of the roofs and top stories of Rome, all gray-blues and dry pale buffs, which are matched, during the late summer sunsets, by the pale blues and pinks of the sky, in which the eternal swifts restlessly flock and twitter. The mood induced by the stairway and by my previous experience of Surrealists was so strong that when I went there first I mistook for a "Surrealist object" a large cat with a bandage on its head that was lying on the table like an ornament but that turned out to be alive when I tried to pick it up. And, as a matter of fact, the studio is remarkably and refreshingly free from what Signorina Fini, in speaking of another painter, once called the *"voulu"* aspect of Surrealism. Such "objects" as one did find about were mostly things she had used as models, such as a small glass case of moths; and the place, with its disorderly elegance, was quite free from the neo-Gothicism that one associates with, for example, Max Ernst. The pictures by Leonor Fini and her colleagues on the walls and tables and shelves had an element of fairy-tale enchantment and *commedia dell'arte* humor that prevented their being "modern" in the sense that Ernst and Dali are; and, in Rome, it seemed perfectly natural to pass to Signorina Fini's paintings from the late Renaissance patterns, the decorated ceilings and strips of wall, that make a background in the Vatican Museum: hippogriffs that hang in a filigree of scrollery, vine-leaves and tendrils, winged

sphinxes with the curling rears of seahorses, spindle-
legged and needle-billed birds, hawk-beaked and double-
headed eagles, feathery-tongued serpents with twining
tails, cupids holding red spidery lobsters, allegorical figures or Graces that seem balancing like tight-rope
walkers; and the satyrs' masks, the lions' faces, the unidentifiable female beings all compact of imperturbable
complacencies. It was as if into this mythical world,
conventionalized and quietly lively, Signorina Fini had
brought an emotion more personal and more poetic, and
motifs from a later time. Here the sphinxes are leonine,
and immobilized in their first somber broodings or the
maiden surprises of girlhood—a girlhood cut off from the
world and queerly turned in on itself; here great ladies
with dishevelled long hair and long enveloping skirts sit
silent and self-absorbed in the grand but bare rooms of
palaces, from the walls or arches of which big fragments
have sometimes fallen; and a tousle-headed dubious-eyed
girl with a pretty throat and round full breasts has
flowered from a twisted root that sends out fibers and
bulbous sprouts, in defiance of a death's-head moth, two
white paper animal skulls and a dead lizard with its pale
belly up. These contrasts of brokenness and deadness
with a warm and rich physical life that is unable to
extricate itself are characteristic of Signorina Fini's painting; they seem to express a tragic paradox. This is a soul
that is sullenly and fiercely and yet wistfully narcissistic,
self-admiring and self-consuming, at once blooming and
checked in growth. She is entirely a *female* artist, occupied much less with the work, which the man will
approach as a craft but which in her case is unequal in
skill and taste, than with her dreams, her awareness of
herself, her personality and role as a woman. And for this
reason her pictures of men are the weakest part of her
work. With women she sometimes succeeds through

assimilating them to herself; but her portraits of men that I have seen are invariably sentimental: mere images that rise in the mind of the smoldering sequestered girl who, in the other pictures, waits too long.

In one corner, beside her own work, hangs that of the Marchese Lepri, a young man in the Foreign Office, whom Leonor Fini first met in the early years of the war, when he was consul at Monte Carlo and who, more or less under her tutelage, has recently learned to paint. These examples of his painting show that he has been making a rapid development: some of the latest ones seem to me extremely good. Satirical and fantastic, they do not exploit the anomalies which are the tricks of the Surrealist school, but attach themselves to a tradition that is Italian, almost mediaeval. I told him that as I was looking at a picture—done recently and one of the best— in which a party of sodden people in contemporary evening dress are seen gorging at a dinner table that stretches back in a long perspective, while the walls and the floor and the table itself are cracking up below and about them—all painted with the precision and clearness of a loggia in some early religious scene; and he replied that he had hoped he had got into it "a certain actuality, too." On a table stood some drawings by Clerici: a young architect and classical draughtsman who has emerged from months of hiding in Florence to apply his firm and hollow line to violins spilling human intestines and bald indignant wigmaker's dummies.

I did not find at first in Signorina Fini any outward traits that corresponded to the elements of moroseness and frustration that often appeared in her work, nor in Lepri any disgust with the society breaking up around him. Leonor Fini is a handsome and voluptuous, an extraordinarily attractive woman—with large dark round eyes and abundant dark hair, which she arranges in a style that is copied from the ladies in Venetian paintings: gathered up and tied with a ribbon behind, but with a mass of it pushed forward on her forehead; and though she lived in Paris for years before the war drove her back to Italy, she seems always, not Parisian in dress, but magnificently and generously Italian. She was wearing, the first time I saw her, an emerald-green taffeta housecoat with a kind of white-lace filigree bodice, and a pair of very high-heeled sandals. She is quite natural and talks very well—with perfect freedom and ease—about people and pictures and books, too sure of her personal taste, too intent on her own painting, ever to have been involved in that sectarian esprit de corps, that ardor for group promotion, that has possessed some of the other Surrealists. Lepri, in his white summer clothes, is quiet and cool and modest with, apparently, the indifference to current events and the skeptical lack of zeal that are supposed to be typical of Romans of the cultivated upper class. I liked to see them, and they were always most amiable. I would sit turning over the pages of Max Ernst's demonological *collages* of illustrations from nineteenth-century novels or of bestiaries of curious woodcuts showing animals with human heads. It seemed to me that here was a center of real creative life in Rome, a live spirit that had not been extinguished.

It was, then, with rather a shock that I discovered one day that their dearest hope was to get to the United States before the summer was over. "You don't like Rome, do you?" Signorina Fini had suddenly said to me. I confessed, feeling impolite, that I did not like it very much. But, "*I* don't like it," she told me. "I hate it!" She wanted to go to America and live in the country there. She had made a brief visit to the States, and she felt she could find there the freedom she needed—she described herself, I think, as *"sauvage"*—which she implied was impossible in Europe. Her position, as I knew, is, like Silone's, not that of a great figure in Italy. She suffers, like him, from the handicap of having made a reputation abroad while many Italian writers and artists were taking the wage of the Fascists or submitting to the Fascist directives. Such exiles, returning, are met with a mixture of envious malice and of the uncomprehending hostility of an antiquated mandarin culture, which has also been lately condemned, by the restrictions of Mussolini, to a narrow provinciality. As for Lepri, however good a civil servant, he cannot look forward to much of a career in a government that seems likely to remain under the thumb of a foreign power or, if it escapes this, to go to the Left at a rate that he could scarcely follow. They are not at home, not serene—probably almost as uncomfortable as I am. The sullen women in the empty palaces, the swinish crew in the banquet hall, are the realities with which they live.

This is a period that is hard to accept, we are in it but we do not really believe in it. One day Signorina Fini showed me a copy of *Vogue* which she had just received from America and expressed an amused astonishment at an article on Buchenwald, with pictures of human incinerators, piles of tangled emaciated corpses and bodies hung up on hooks, followed immediately by new flowered hats and smart bathing brassières, with an article that ran over into the back among the cosmetics ads. This was embarrassing to me as an American, but her instinctive reaction to it was not itself, I thought, without a certain incongruity, for she had just been engaged in executing, with a good deal of finesse and elegance, a series of pen-and-ink drawings for the *Juliette* of the Marquis de Sade: dim figures of men and women hacking one another to pieces and performing other nasty acts. The Surrealists had cultivated deliberately a sadism of the parlor and the gallery; but now the times had overtaken and passed them in a manner so overwhelming that it was impossible for Leonor Fini not to be shocked by the impropriety of juxtaposing these wretched victims with the refinements of Saks Fifth Avenue. The Surrealist exponent of such horrors who makes out of them objects of art which the lover of art will enjoy, with a shudder of pleasure or pain, cannot help being startled at finding them served up as if they were detective or spy thrillers or merely a whet to the appetite in the enjoyment of articles of luxury.

———

At Leonor Fini's, I met Alberto Moravia, the novelist. He took a gloomy view of the future of Europe. He had had to hide for weeks in a barn which was right on the line of battle, living on bread and the meat of the untended "veals" and goats, which he had had to strangle with his own hands. He had found this extremely distasteful. He was tired of being in danger of getting bombed or shot, and would like to go to somewhere like Greece, but for an Italian now Greece was out of the question. The partisans in the North—though this had not yet been made public—had killed twenty thousand Fascists; eight hundred in one small town. The Italians had been hoping that the Big Three would guarantee peace for a period, but it did not look like that now. Italy was controlled by England, but they might as well resign themselves to this: if the English moved out, the Russians would come in. The exacerbated nationalisms of the various nationalities were at this point making it impossible to have a European federation. It was plain from what had happened in the Soviet Union that you couldn't have socialism without an intensification of nationalism.

———

My hotel, the Hôtel de la Ville, is at the top of the Via Sistina, and almost directly opposite, at the convergence of two streets, stands a curious flatiron-shaped house, in which D'Annunzio lived and to which, in the luscious eighties, the *femmes du monde* of *Il Piacere* are supposed, with faltering or eager steps, to have come to their rendezvous. A little farther down the Via Sistina is the house where Gogol wrote *Dead Souls,* designated now by a plaque with inscriptions in Italian and Russian, that has been put up by the Russian colony; in the next street, the Via Gregoriana, is a house in which Stendhal lived when he was making his *Promenades dans Rome* and which a couple of centuries earlier had been occupied by Salvator Rosa; and in a building just below this, at the foot of the Spanish Steps, is the room in which Keats died and which has been kept as a Keats museum. Not far away are the houses where Scott and Bernini and Goethe lived.

Now, at first I found myself rather stimulated by the thought of these illustrious neighbors—especially since it seemed an environment, this region around the Piazza di Spagna, where men had really lived and worked, not merely a Bohemian quarter where talent went soft or ran thin. But the longer I have stayed in Rome, the more the cultural accretions of its past have come to weigh on me and affect me as cloying. The climax of this feeling was a visit I paid to the celebrated Caffè Greco, which I had been told I ought to explore. Though it went back to 1760 and had been frequented by no end of great people, I could not like the Caffè Greco. Making a plunge through those sordid rope curtains that I always find distasteful in Rome, I threaded my way through three dingy compartments, which were narrow, inadequately lighted and lined with little black horsehair seats forbiddingly and uncomfortably squeezed in behind little gray-veined marble tables. On the walls hung bad portraits and landscapes and not very impressive medallions of famous men who had come to the place. One of the ridiculous little hallwaylike rooms that should all have been thrown into a single one was lit only by a dismal filtration from the dirty gray panes of the skylight. The waiter prides himself on his languages and has a humorous-familiar tinge, as if he were playing a role in some comedy of the eighteen-forties. He will show you the yellow old albums in which the great men have signed their names, if your interest is sufficiently keen and you back it with the hint of a tip. And you can pick up a little leaflet with a description of the place in four languages, each of which contains a list of names of celebrities of that nationality who have been habitués of the restaurant. I learned from this that the Caffé Greco had been visited by the following persons: Goldoni, Canova, Leopardi, Carducci, D'Annunzio, Stendhal, Berlioz, Corot, Gounod, Bizet, Baudelaire, Paul Bourget, Anatole France, Byron, Shelley, Keats, Thackeray, Goethe, Schopenhauer, Mendelssohn, Liszt, Wagner, King Ludwig of Bavaria, Gogol, Thorwaldsen and Mark Twain—as well as by many others only less famous.

But all these names and associations were too much for me to take in at once, and my effort to react to them appropriately had upon me the effect of an emetic and compelled me to disgorge, as it were, the whole mass of lore that I had swallowed before in connection with the genius-haunted past of Rome. For the moment, my only thought was that the Greco was chill, cramped and fusty, that it had no more relation to those artists than the leather of their old boots.

———

I started, before I left Rome, Hawthorne's *The Marble Faun,* which I had never read before, and I was amazed to find how close his reflections—mostly transferred, I believe, from his notebooks—had run to the kind of thing that I was putting down in my own. When I finally left the city, I was feeling, very much as he was, decidedly "tired of the sight of those immense seven-storied, yellow-washed hovels, or call them palaces, where all that is dreary in domestic life seems magnified and multiplied, and weary of climbing those staircases, which ascend from a ground floor of cook-shops, cobblers' stalls, stables and regiments of cavalry, to a middle region of princes, cardinals and ambassadors, and an upper tier of artists, just beneath the unattainable sky [a description which still more or less fitted such places as the Palazzo Altieri where Leonor Fini lived] . . . disgusted with the pretense of holiness and the reality of nastiness, each equally omnipresent . . . half lifeless from the languid atmosphere, the vital principle of which has been used up long ago or corrupted by myriads of slaughters . . . crushed down in spirit with the desolation of her [Rome's] ruin and the hopelessness of her future . . . in short, hating her with all our might and adding our individual curse to the infinite anathema which her old crimes have unmistakably brought down." It is true that I was also to feel—although not until a year or so later, when I was back in the United States—the nostalgia of which he speaks when he writes that, after leaving Rome "in such mood as this, we are astonished by the discovery, by and by, that our heart-strings have mysteriously attached themselves to the Eternal City, and are drawing us thitherward again." But, in the meantime, I was in a position to recognize the perfect accuracy of Hawthorne's description of the effect of modern Rome on a Protestant Anglo-Saxon.

Later on, when I was back at home, I read Norman Douglas' *South Wind*, also for the first time. It seemed to me that this famous novel had been very much over-rated—for though it is clever and fairly well-written, it is really, it seems to me, hardly more than a superior piece of journalism about the life of the foreign colony in Capri. Douglas *is* up to a point successful in dealing with a subject very similar to that of Hawthorne in *The Marble Faun:* the influence on an Anglican bishop of the demoralizing atmosphere of Italy. But if one reads the two books side by side, one is made very clearly aware of the relative superficiality of the later writer's treatment of the theme. The contrast is inescapable because—what I have never seen noted—Norman Douglas has reproduced the central incident of Hawthorne's book and used it in just the same way to create a moral problem. The parallel is so complete that one assumes it to have been the result of some trick of unconscious memory, reviving the impression of a story which had been read and forgotten in youth. Thus in Hawthorne we have a woman, American but perhaps with some non-English blood, constantly pursued and plagued by a rascally discarded husband, who is in a position to threaten her with "blasting" her reputation. The moral crux of the book is the scene on the Capitoline Hill, in which she consentingly stands by while an Italian who wants to protect her pushes him over a cliff and kills him. In *South Wind,* an English woman is similarly pursued and blackmailed by an undesirable husband, and the moral situation is managed by having her push him over a cliff in Capri, where she has lived for so long that she has presumably caught what the author has already shown to be the local point of view on revenge and the taking of human life. In either case, the problem presented is how shall the crime be treated, not only by the persons responsible but also by those, New England or English, who happen to know about it; and the conclusion in either case is that the languor and animality of Italy are capable of dulling the conscience to a degree where such an act of violence does not seem so clearly wrong as it would in another country.

But the difference—a curious one—is that Douglas, the man of the world, who has now been accepted for thirty years (since the appearance of *South Wind*) as the touchstone of sophistication, should have made the whole thing too simple: a matter of black and white, with the two colors simply interchanged. The Scotch moralist in Douglas has always interfered with the epicurean Austrian (to assign, perhaps rashly, his mixed tendencies to the elements of his mixed blood), so that he cannot enjoy the pleasures which he makes it his business to celebrate without at the same time betraying a need to justify his self-indulgence by bringing charges of inhuman or anti-social behavior against people with sterner principles. But a hedonist should not be peevish; and Douglas' doctrine of sybaritic Nietzscheanism, at once too soft and too cruel to catch the real exaltation of Nietzsche, suffers also from the handicap, in a Nietzschean fatal, of being nagged by a bad conscience. In *South Wind*, the point he would like to make is that the sun of Southern Italy puts the morality of the North to sleep and may lead us to regard as quite natural, perhaps even to approve as beneficent, actions that we should elsewhere condemn. But what it turns out that he cannot help doing is so to construct his fable that the killing by the woman of her husband becomes a positive moral act, which her brother the Bishop and the reader must endorse as not merely under-

standable but demonstrably, undeniably *right*—so that,
instead of remaining a comedy or suggesting a psychological inquiry, the book ends as a melodrama, with the
lady as surely a heroine as if she had killed to defend her
honor. In real life, a woman who had done such a thing
would certainly have had some qualms, and her brother
would have at least been uncomfortable and his relations
with his sister affected: the story would be only half told;
and Hawthorne shows his insight and intelligence, his
superior toughness of logic, by giving Miriam a complex
character which makes her behavior plausible as well as a
great deal more interesting (Douglas' lady is all of a
piece), and even partly redeeming the husband, who is
less a Victorian demon than an unhappy and desperate
détraqué where Douglas' husband is simply a rotter; by
having his Italian murderer driven finally to a Catholic
repentance for his pagan Italian crime; and by presenting
the painful embarrassment caused by both parties involved in the crime to their well-meaning American
friends. It is here the provincial puritan, the grumpy
American traveller, who complained about the emptiness
of Italian museums and the shallowness of Italian painting and who wanted the nude statues clothed, who is the
genuine man of the world where the cities of the soul are
in question, and who knows that Anglo-Saxon and Italian
share, after all, the same mixed nature.

Yet *South Wind* may be read with *The Marble Faun*
as one of the best accounts ever attempted of the peculiar
—and, to the Anglo-Saxon, dismaying—alteration in
one's point of view that may result from a long sojourn in
Italy.

———

Philip Hamburger, also here for the *New Yorker,* has
just come back from a trip to Trieste. The British did

their best to dissuade him from interviewing any Jugoslavs or visiting the back-country. If he hadn't had an
American major with him, he believes that he wouldn't
have got anywhere at all. The British called the Jugoslavs "Jugs" and Jugoslavia "Jugland." They talked
about the natives in such a way as to suggest that they
were hairy savages crawling around on all fours—as if
they had once been good police dogs but had now turned
into dangerous wolves, as if Hamburger and his companion were likely to be torn to pieces. The President of
the Trieste Council had been locked up in jail by the
British for reasons of "military expediency," and he was
speechless with indignation. They always referred to him
contemptuously as "the fisherman," because that had been
his occupation—which had finally moved him to protest:
"Well, after all, Christ was a carpenter!" When the
Americans finally, after waiting for days, had been allowed to see a little of the hinterland, a British general
had attempted to brief them. The Jugoslavs, he explained, always carried their politics with them. Hamburger had asked whether the British didn't do that, too.
The American major had become much incensed and
described to Hamburger as follows one of the obstacles he
had had to contend with: "A bicycle drove up, and out
swarmed three top-ranking warmongers, all complete
with pips and squeaks." From Trieste they went on to
Klagenfurt, where they were treated, says Hamburger, at
the British mess, as if they were captured enemy officers.
After dinner, an altercation had occurred. The British
had announced to the Americans that England would
now have to fight the Russians, "and you people will have
to help us." Hamburger and the major emphatically
denied that they would have to do anything of the kind.
One of the British—there is always one Englishman who
is uncompromisingly opposed to what the rest of the

English are doing, but who is helpless to influence the proceedings—suddenly blew up and denounced his fellow officers, telling them that they were two hundred years behind the times. This made things more acrimonious, and the Americans left the next day.

———

A few days before I left Rome, I was taken by American friends to dine in a black-market restaurant. We ate at outside tables in a little enclosure on the street. The clientele all looked more or less as if they were black-market profiteers themselves. We were sitting right next to the rail that fenced us in from the street, and I had my back to this, so that, absorbed in conversation, I did not notice at first that a crowd had gathered behind us and were reaching in to grab things from our plates. But the management soon sent out a bouncer, who knocked down an old woman with a blow on the head, and drove back the mob, mostly women and children, some of whom disappeared, while others, keeping their distance, stood dumbly and stared at the diners.

10

NOTES ON LIBERATED MILAN

WHEN I FIRST SAW MILAN, at the beginning of May, it looked like a slice of Hell. Some of the shabby green trams were running and some of the inhabitants were going about their routines, but the whole place seemed stunned and stopped, and the bloodless undernourished people, wrapped in any old cloth that could protect their skins, seemed to have been reduced, in the course of the German oppression, the bombings by the Allies and the embittered civil war, to a condition of permanent strain. The children, especially, were appalling: they had acquired, as they were growing up, expressions of indignation and apprehension which were now as much a part of their faces as malnutrition was of their bones. The half-grown boys in their teens, exhilarated at getting a chance to let themselves go against somebody, were cruising around in cars with machine-guns, looking for Fascist collaborators to shoot. A hotel in which the Germans had tried desperately to fortify themselves was still surrounded by barricades and barbed wire; and Americans who invaded the S.S. headquarters found their police dogs and pornographic pictures. Over the whole city hung the stink of the killing of Mussolini and his followers, the exhibition of their bodies in public and the defilement of them by the crowd. Italians would stop you in the bars and show you photographs they had taken of it.

The Albergo Diana of those days, taken over for the American Army, had the grisliness of all the reminders of the old holiday tourist Europe as one finds them still clinging to the carcase left by the recent convulsions and blastings. The cool white-tiled corridors of bedrooms, the views of the Villa d'Este, the coy little plaques in the wall that indicated by a series of pictures (thus avoiding complications of language) which button you were to press for the waiter, which for the valet and which for the chambermaid—all these comforts and amenities of the traveller seemed sickeningly stale and mendacious, like the few old shopworn volumes of Tauchnitz novels that some of the bookstores had brought out for the English-speaking Allies. And the desk-clerks, lift-boys and waiters, though they were going through all their old motions and speaking an adequate English, as they had just been speaking an adequate German, were somewhat upset by the new arrivals (they would probably, as Hamburger suggested, not have been at all surprised to receive the Japanese next) and had little to accommodate them with. The maître d'hôtel in full dress was presiding over homely dinners of bully beef and army greens, reinforced by large hard wafers that rather resembled dog-biscuits and were the sole local contribution.

Today, however, two months and a half later, the Diana is completely transfigured. A rest hotel for American soldiers, it must be one of the pleasantest places in Italy. The hotel people have got back into their smooth routine, and it seems quite natural to be well taken care of. The food and wine are by far the best I have had since I have been in Europe, and you eat, to the accompaniment of music, at wicker tables with blue-and-white-checked cloths, in a charming outdoor dining room, full of the leafage of plants and vines and shaded by chestnuts and oaks, in the branches of which is suspended a sort of decorative roofing of Japanese mats. These is an admirably equipped bar and a great atmosphere of dates and parties. The Americans are capturing and bringing to dinner some remarkably good-looking girls.

———

The women here, in general, are marvellous. They don't have the natural chic which is almost universal in Rome, but, in general, the quality is better. They give—like almost everything about Milan, in contrast to almost everything about Rome—an impression of independence and strength. They have broad backs, and there is a splendid blond type—often but not always dyed—who wears a shoulder-length *chevelure*. I was struck by one girl on a bicycle who, riding without hands, raised her arms to smooth back her done-up pale-blond hair; and I passed, at a table on the sidewalk, where she was having a drink with a man, what seemed to me one of the prettiest girls I had ever seen anywhere: another blonde, with lively brown eyes and provocative arched eyebrows, who was wearing on her bare feet, instead of the usual wooden clogs, a pair of high-heeled red-leather shoes that she had somehow succeeded in getting. She made me imagine what would be possible for them if they really had clothes and cosmetics.

———

When I was here before in the spring just after the Allies had arrived, the walls were covered with bills that said in English, "Hurrah for the Anglo-Saxon Liberators." But there were also inscriptions of a different kind, painted, it is said, by the Fascists, and these, I see, have been left up, though the others have disappeared:

"*Museo distrutto*" or "*Casa incendiata dai liberatori anglo-sassoni. Milanesi, riflettete!*" And they have invented a play on words: "*Anglosassoni assassini.*" These reproaches meet you all over the city, wherever there have been buildings bombed. And it is true that the Allies bombarded Milan as cruelly and as indiscriminately as the Germans ever did London. Most of this hideous damage was inflicted in August, 1943, when we were trying to force Badoglio's hand by a series of pure terror bombings aimed at densely populated districts and could hardly have hit more cultural monuments if the policy had been to destroy them. The museum and the Scala have been gutted, the finest churches are half reduced to rubble, some of the best sculpture on the cathedral has been shattered, and of the refectory containing da Vinci's *Last Supper* there is nothing left but a shell.

———

Though the Scala is boarded and silent, the Scala orchestra and opera company are still performing in other places. I went to a Scala concert in the courtyard of the old Sforzesco castle, with its heraldry of gold-crested blue dragons devouring anguished victims and its immense and once formidable moat, now comfortably planted with cabbage and squash. The orchestra played Bloch, Ravel and Debussy, and Hindemith's *Mathis der Mahler;* and the delicate pieces were traced with an exquisite faithfulness that made much music in New York seem vulgar. The concert was jammed, and the *canto funèbre* of the Bloch Concerto Grosso was incongruously disturbed by the roarings of people who were besieging the doors. I got into conversation with an exceptionally well-dressed man sitting next to me. He didn't care much for modern music, and Hindemith was way beyond him. He had been very much alarmed, he said, by a report that the

Allies were to leave. They mustn't go away, he insisted; he was, he explained, *un borghese,* and he knew that if the Allies deserted them, there would be terrible civil war and the Communists would bring in the Russians.

When I got back to the Diana, I went to the bar, which stands at one side of the lobby, and found a very drunk American soldier holding forth in a loud voice in a vein which reminded me of conversations on a supposedly higher level. They said, he proclaimed, that he was a mental case and that he needed psychiatric attention— well, if anything was plain in that unit, it was that the Major was absolutely screwy and needed to be psycho- analyzed himself—and the Colonel, wasn't he nuts!—he needed to be analyzed, too. He went on and on and on, standing at the bar alone, and, though he was using the dirtiest possible language, nothing was done about him, because the policy in these rest hotels is to leave people as free as possible. The two or three other soldiers present occasionally threw a word or a laugh at him. There was a woman across the room, but she must have been an Italian and unable to understand what he was saying, for she sat placidly through it all.

———

I saw another of those horrifying children: a very tall and ill-fed boy in absurd short pants—probably because he had no others—with drawn face, frowning brows, glazed blue eyes. They look as if they had been frozen by the Gorgon.

———

I noticed a book in a bookshop called *Arrigo Beyle, Milanese.* Stendhal adored Milan and wanted this in- scribed on his tombstone. He must have loved the boxes of the Scala, the close, long and solidly built-up streets, the pale pinnacles of lace on the Duomo, the peculiar dry blue of the sky—*"sempre un poco stanco,"* as a poem in a Roman paper said the other day—and the mountains beyond the town, as I saw them the first time that I came here: a purified dimmed slate-blue, sharply outlined like an old engraving, but presented in a softened perspective, with the silvery snow on their ridges, or, as they show on this second trip, scarcely by a shade darker than the blue of the sky behind them, so that the mottlings of snow seem a pattern on a background of taut silk. I forget about Stendhal's adventures in Milan. He came here first with Napoleon's army, and he would have fallen in love with some countess. He would have done his incessant, inexhaustible, illegible, cipher-screened writing that made his secret and personal life, and he would have been sustained from without by the energy, the sound relations, the upright spine of the city. It does not seem out of keeping here to find a statue of Leonardo or a street named after Dante, whereas in Rome the monument to Giordano Bruno seems to have fallen to the utmost ignominy in the squalid and swarming market of the square in which he was burned.

———

Beneath the patched glass of the big Galleria, where the Milanese go in the afternoon for ices, vermouth and cakes, I sat down, at one of the outside cafés, with a young American officer: a tall fellow in a forest-green uniform, who had been hammered into hardness and seriousness by his experiences of the war. He seemed to have been principally engaged in laying mines against the Germans for our side and in detecting and digging up the enemy's mines. I had already some sort of idea of what this exceedingly dangerous work was like, for I had been down along the coast in Littoria, which is still planted with thousands of mines, ours and the Germans' both, so that large areas of that important region are impossible for cultivation. The little pins that explode the caps are so sensitive that the wind bending the grass is sometimes enough to set them off, and the malaria-control workers and the mine-diggers as well as the fishermen and the country people are constantly getting blown up.

This lieutenant explained to me at length the mechanism and technique of mines, drawing me little diagrams and showing a keen interest in the subject. There was the German kind that had two charges, the first of which blew it out of the ground and the second of which caused it to burst in the air and scatter big pieces of shot like ball-bearings. Later, they had improved on this with thick jagged cuttings of wire that gave a "terrible slash." The Americans had taken over this idea and turned out a model that was even worse. Hunting mines was a very delicate business. There was one kind that had a hole in the pin through which you could pass a wire to prevent it from going off, but if they didn't have that, you just had to take a chance. You dragged them out of the ground with long ropes and exploded them at a distance with T.N.T. If there were fragments of shell around, the mine detectors weren't much good, because they registered the presence of any kind of metal. For the "bakelite jobs" that the Germans used later, the detector was no good at all. Then there were quantities of dummy mines that the Germans had put in to fool us and that had to be removed with just as much care as if they had been real ones. In the case of the leaping mines, you had a chance to see what was coming and throw yourself on your face, and one man who had done this had survived and received the Purple Heart. Another had thrown himself against the mine to protect the men who were with him, and they had named one of the new bridges after him.

The lieutenant said that he had once been blown yards away from where he was standing, and that another time, after one of these incidents, when he had gone over and started to talk to his men, he had suddenly fainted away. With booby-traps, you had no guide: you just had to suspect everything. Once a Britisher and an American had gone into a suspected house to search it room by room. The American had sat down on a bed and the whole house had blown up and left him among the ruins holding a piece of the bed; the Englishman, who had been downstairs, had suffocated under the heap before they could get him out.

But in spite of the shortcomings of the Germans, you did have to hand it to them: all these mines and things were wonderful work. The lieutenant told me with pride that he had acquired a clockwork time-bomb of the kind that had destroyed the Naples post office a week after the Germans had left. He talked about it as if it were a rare book or print—said that there were only seven or eight extant. It was made beautifully—all of aluminum. He had set it without the explosive, and it had gone off within two minutes of the time. I realized, in talking to him, how the younger generations of Americans were being affected by the war. During the First War, in which we were less deeply involved, there was, as I have said above, an humanitarian reaction against the practice of war itself; but in this one the German methods have ended by making everybody more callous and by interesting the practical Americans in the technical side of the business, as if mechanized large-scale homicide were a natural occupation.

The lieutenant did not think much of the Italians, who, he said, had laid down on the war just when the critical moment had come. He told me that, a few nights before, he had walked out of a bar with an Italian girl and run into a gang of young men who wanted to grab her and shave her head—a penalty which has been sometimes inflicted for going out with Allied soldiers; but he had called some other Americans out of the bar, and they had completely cleaned up on the Italians. He said that it had been the best fight he had had since he had been in Italy. He told me that American jeeps were constantly being stolen, and blamed it all on the Negro soldiers, who sold them, he said, to the Italians.

———

The following day, in the Galleria, an Italian at the next table spoke to me in very good English. He was neat, precise, gray and well-dressed—evidently some sort of businessman. He felt very strongly that the Allies ought to stay in order to keep order in Italy. The working class were threatening trouble—not because they were naturally bad, but because they were misled by their leaders.

———

A translation of Karl Marx's *Das Kapital* has appeared in almost all the bookstores. It is queer to see it displayed in the windows between a translation of Catullus and a new edition of Rimbaud—and along with Gide's *L'Immoraliste* and Barbey d'Aurevilly on Dandyism. The Italians under Fascism seem to have been completely cut off from the main cultural currents of the time, and their reading is still out of date. It was curious to see, in Rome, how a novelette, the *Agostino* of Alberto Moravia, which deals in the lightest and mildest way with a Freudian mother-and-son relationship, could create a sensation in a city where new editions of Verlaine's pornographic poems and the short stories of the Marquis de Sade were on sale in every bookstore. And here it is as if they had discovered Marx at the same moment as Gide and Rimbaud, and just as, in literature, they regard the *fin de siècle* as very advanced and daring, so in politics they are still in the period when Communism was seriously Marxist: they don't know that in the Soviet Union Marx and Lenin have gone by the board, and that the Russians are unlikely to encourage a genuine working-class movement aiming at bona-fide socialism.

The inevitable class line-up that you find in conversation with the people is evident even in these bookstores. One of the shops in the Gallerìa says, *"Libri socialistici non si vendono qui."*

———

I went to see one of the American officials in the Allied Military Government. He was a Jew, a big agreeable well-meaning man, not quite so well-posted and alert, perhaps, as one expects a Jew to be. I arrived at a moment of crisis. "Here's the story," he said. "There was a jail-break in the prison last Tuesday, and thirty-six men escaped—all Partisans, but none of them political prisoners: they were all in for regular crimes that ranged from robbery to rape. The guards were Partisans, too, and so I'll have to change them for carabinieri, which I've been wanting to do all along. But now, according to the reports we get, there's going to be a demonstration—it's supposed to start at four o'clock right outside in the square, and then march to the prison and protest." Who were doing the demonstrating? I asked. Why, a lot of Italian war prisoners who had just come back from Germany. But what was the point of the protest? "Why, they'll probably be demanding more food. They want to show people they're starved. They certainly do look it," he added. But what was the connection between that and the jailbreak? I did my best to pin him down, but got no satisfactory answer, and I decided that he did not know. "They're always having demonstrations," he said.

At this moment, like a scene in a play, a large British security man entered, with a small red-faced and bewildered American major following in his wake. "There'll be no demonstration," said this chief of the Allied police, a quiet-spoken fellow of enormous girth and menacing strong-arm aplomb. "We've been over to their headquarters—they're just across the square. I told 'em that if they marched to the jail, we'd have a reception committee there, and we'd extend to 'em the hospitality of A.M.G.— we had cells there empty and ready for 'em, where we'd be glad to put 'em up. When we came in, they were loungin' all about, and I told 'em to stand up and show some courtesy. And there's not goin' to be a demonstration. They were buzzin' about after I talked to 'em like a lot of blue-arsed flies. It was just like when we talked to Togliatti [the leader of the Communist Party and Minister of Justice in the new Parri government]. He thought he was goin' to make a speech, and then he decided not to make one."

The security man went off to the prison—just to make sure, as he said—and the major remained behind. The high official showed me a handful of literature which announced a giant demonstration—presented as a public festivity—in celebration of Bastille Day. The invitation to the high official had on it a curious symbol that I had already seen on all the posters advertizing this celebration with which the city was plastered; and it dawned on me now that this curious thing that looked a little like the head of a bird was the Phrygian Liberty Cap, the emblem of the French Revolution, drawn, however, in such a way that it was not necessarily recognizable and might perhaps be explained away as an arbitrary decorative design. The officers, too, had been puzzling over it and seemed to regard it with some suspicion, and when I suggested my explanation, the major, perturbed and dazed, cried, "Does *that* mean the French Revolution?" This major presently left us. "In my opinion," said the Jewish official, "the sooner we get out of Italy, the better for all concerned. When a baby is learning to walk, you have to let it fall down sometimes—you have to let it make its mistakes by itself."

———

I made a point of taking part in the big turn-out in celebration of the Fourteenth of July. While I was sitting on a curb in the park waiting for things to begin, a man came and sat down beside me and immediately began to talk to me volubly in some patois that was hard to understand. I made out that he wanted me to know that he had always been against the Fascists. He showed me his Communist card and told me how he and his father, who was blind, had suffered at the hands of the regime, and how the workers had had their own methods of dealing with the Fascists in the factory. An American journalist said to me that this had several times happened to him: humble people like this think that showing their C.P. cards to Americans will give proof of their sincere anti-Fascism and recommend them to the anti-Fascist liberators.

Suddenly people, with many children, began to troop across the grass from behind me, and I had to get up, as I was in their way, and move in the same direction. But as they swarmed in a thick mass in the vicinity of the triumphal arch, where there was a platform for music and speeches, I worked my way out, and eventually back through the park and home to the Albergo Diana. All the way I had to squeeze through the solid mob pushing in the other direction. It was prodigious: I had never seen a city where the streets seemed so filled with people. There are said to have been a million of the million and a half that populate Milan and its environs. But they were

simply walking around—they were not particularly celebrating anything. There were a prize-ring and a little
circus, some pop-stands and some ice-cream carts, and two
small blimps moored above the park with the inscription
"*Fraternità.*" There was a band, and the crowd here and
there would clear a circle around three or four dancing
couples. But the voice from the loudspeaker sounded
rasping, metallic and grim. "*Attenzione! Attenzione!*" it
would snap out again and again. "*Ballate!*" it would
exhort the people in the tone with which the blood-
freezing voice used to announce to the audience in
Hellzapoppin that the spiders were about to descend on
them. "*Questa è la sera della libertà. Gli uomini liberi
sono allegri!*" But there was little spontaneity or gaiety,
and in that threatening and didactic tone I recognized the
impersonal accent—the same everywhere—of the Communist Party, as I had recognized its efficient direction in
the methods with which the turn-out had been publicized
and engineered.

A young public-relations man, newly arrived in Milan, who took me around in a jeep, kindly explained the
occasion—the first Fourteenth of July that had ever been
celebrated in Italy—as an attempt to make up to France
for the so-called "stab in the back" of Mussolini's attack
upon her. "What are those things they are wearing?" he
asked. It was the Phrygian Liberty Cap, which many of
the strolling citizens had pinned to their lapels or their
blouses.*

————

Sick of contemplating mines and bombings and reading about Italian politics, oppressed by the feeling of
being submerged in the general wreckage and mess, I

* When I returned to Milan in 1963, the municipality was
Communist.

bought a new book on Stravinsky by the Italian composer Malipiero. But what I found in it was disappointing. It has been written to order for a series, and, though Malipiero allows that *Le Sacre du Printemps* has merit, he does nothing but grumble and scoff at the music which Stravinsky has written since. The whole tone is old-fogeyish and grudging, as if Malipiero were peevish with Stravinsky for outstripping him in reputation and engaging in musical adventures which he, Malipiero, cannot understand. The twelve-tone scale of Arnold Schoenberg he says flatly "is not music." You feel the cultural backwater of Fascism rippled and made rather uncomfortable by the presence of live spirits outside.

———

But there are elements of vitality in Milan that you are not aware of in Rome. The young people who have worked in the underground and who have helped to drive the Germans out are perhaps the only group in Italy that is in earnest, energetic and enthusiastic. Two examples: A woman lawyer from somewhere near the Austrian border; she has been studying and doing political work all through these difficult years and now, wiry, quick-eyed and intent, communicates a certain electricity, a certain elation of hope. She says that Italy is not now a great country, but still quite enough to devote one's life to. A young man, a lieutenant of Parri's, who has been trained in high principles of conduct through his contact with that upright and industrious man. As a boy who had grown up under the Fascist regime, he joined the Fascist Youth Organization and went as a soldier to the Ethiopian war. But he saw then that the regime was a "bluff." The soldiers had no food or equipment while the officers were acquiring medals; men were bleeding to death with dysentery for lack of ice to stop the hemorrhage. Later, he joined the anti-Fascist underground and went to do secret work in Germany, pretending to be a Spaniard. If the Italians had become too skeptical, the Germans, he found, were fantastically credulous. A German officer, he said, had told him that they now had a powder a pinch of which would blow up a city block: they would dust it on the United States and the United States would disappear. The women were terribly stupid—especially when amorous, he added, with a delightedly rolling eye: he got a lot of information out of them.

These people may have as little idea of what the Soviet Union has been up to while Mussolini was keeping them blacked out or of what England and America are up to as Malipiero has of the achievements of the later Stravinsky; but there are elements among them who count on the Russians and elements who count on the Americans. Now, dating from the expulsion of the Germans, our main American contributions to following up the "liberation" of Italy have consisted of a few U.N.R.R.A. supplies and calling one of our telephone exchanges Freedom; and, after our arming and encouragement of the Partisans through the period when they were serving our purpose, we are now taking their weapons away from them, forbidding them to make political speeches and throwing them into jail if they give any trouble. It is true that, since the departure of the Germans, the Partisans in the North have been guilty of some ruthless and probably unjustifiable bloodshed: they are supposed to have killed some twenty thousand people. But the new Italian revolution is something more than a savage vendetta, and it is hardly, I believe, a movement whose impetus can be curbed at this point. The Partisans, according to the A.M.G. estimate, have been disarmed only about sixty per cent: they have hidden a great deal of equipment, and we have no means of knowing how much, since they still had the arms that they took from the enemy as well as the ones that we gave them. And they have worked up their own methods for maintaining the strength of their organization.

———

How they were doing this I soon came to see. I had continued to be puzzled by the problem of the Italian ex-prisoners from Germany who had had to be restrained from protesting against the local jailbreak, and I had asked a number of people about it. Nobody seemed to be able to explain, and I began to get a distinct impression that there was something that the Americans hadn't grasped and that the Italians didn't want to reveal. Once when I was talking to an Italian journalist, the young man mentioned above, who apparently knew what was going on and to be just on the point of telling, we were interrupted by someone who came up, and when the other conversation was over, my friend went on smoothly and cheerfully, with the air of returning to our original subject: "And so I hope to go to America as press attaché to the Embassy." At last I found an American correspondent who had been a long time in Italy and was exceptionally well-informed. He had been pondering on similar problems. There had occurred, he said, in the last month or so, a whole series of demonstrations that did not seem to have much relevance to their pretexts: festivities, protests, strikes. Even the undertakers had once been called out. He had finally come to the conclusion that the Left parties of the governing "federation" were systematically organizing the people, who had lost the habit of mass action under Fascism, and exercising them in a series of turn-outs which would prepare them for an eventual crisis. These demonstrations, he said, were always perfectly well-conducted, and if the authorities intervened, as in the case of the protest which I had just seen nipped, they simply called them off. Neither side wanted a repetition of the disaster in Greece last winter.

I put to him another question which I had already tried on Allied officials. Was there anything in the following statement, which I had found in the English liberal weekly, the *New Statesman and Nation,* of June 16, 1945?: "In a revealing dispatch last Tuesday, a special correspondent of *The Times* stated bluntly that A.M.G. has refused to recognize decisions of the local liberation committees [in Northern Italy] which had successfully captured and taken over nearly all the industrial plants before the arrival of our armies. In the cause of 'efficiency' managing directors such as Valetta of Fiat, who collaborated actively with the Germans, are being reinstated, under the threat that the Allies will not release coal and other raw materials to factories run by workers' councils." The amiable A.M.G. official whom I had visited at the moment of the averted demonstration had told me that, whereas he couldn't say specifically about Valetta and Fiat, whose factories were in Turin, he could positively assert that this kind of thing was not being done in Milan, where it was the policy to allow the Italians to purge their Fascist officials. But the newspaperman had just come from Turin and he told me that it was perfectly true that these companies had the same old management. Valetta now sat in an office with a real-estate sign on the door, but from that office he still ran his factory. "The greatest shock I had," said my friend, "was when I found out that the Fiat stock was all owned by the original people."

———

The general impression I got from talking to people in Milan, including two of our top officials, was that the ideal our policy was aiming at was to keep Italian industry going as much as was needed to relieve unemployment, and to weaken the appeal of the Left, but not to allow it to revive sufficiently—since the factories themselves are in excellent shape—to give serious competition to England. Many Italians, I found, were also of this opinion.

———

The morning before I left, I went to see two places of interest which I had not yet visited.

The spot where Mussolini's body and those of his mistress and the members of his staff were exposed after the executions is not one of the city's great squares, as the reports may have sometimes suggested, but a small crossroads in the working-class section. They were hung up by the feet, in a gas station, to the thing under which the cars stop, and the names that indicated which was which are still daubed on it in crude black letters. The station is closed and deserted, and now and then somebody comes up to stare at it.

At the other end of the city, behind a mountainous heap of rubble, is the refectory of Santa Maria delle Grazie, where Leonardo painted his *Last Supper*. It is always being said that this picture was already in bad condition and that the bombing did not do it any harm. But, after all, most of the building was smashed: there is nothing but a husk of four walls, which has been sketchily roofed in for shelter, and an immense amount of debris must have fallen upon the mural, which, with the fresco at the other end, also in very bad condition, is the only object surviving that is even recognizable. The *Last Supper*, at any rate, is little today but a grease-spot—a vague and incomplete phantom, which, however, does assert its reality in a curious and poignant way. From a distance, the three open windows in the wall behind the figure of Christ, dim though they become when you are near to them, do still seem to give a vista on a landscape of peace and shining light. And the subtleties of green and blue, faded and half-effaced, the lovely modelling of an open hand where the faces can hardly be seen, introduce into the bare place that element which, pathetically, we choose to call human because it recreates and ennobles, though it represents relatively so small a part of the activity of human beings and though it appears in any intensity so rarely.

The dead tyrant and the living Christ are today both dishonored in Italy.

11

GREEK DIARY: NOTES ON
LIBERATED ATHENS

It is a piquant and novel sensation to travel from Naples to Athens in an army transport plane. Our airports and planes create a world of their own, an extension of the American system, that has been superimposed on Europe and makes a dissonant contrast with it. Over the blue Ionian Sea, you are handed a neat cardboard box, which contains, carefully wrapped in wax-paper, sandwiches of three kinds, each with a small printed slip that tells what the filling is—beef-spread, melted cheese or marmalade and peanut butter—so that you will know in what order to eat them; a hardboiled egg, with pepper and salt done up picnic-fashion in paper; a cookie; a small container of cut-up peaches and pears, with a miniature pasteboard spoon; a bag of fruit drops of assorted flavors; and a pasteboard cup for water.

When you look down and see the first Greek islands, you are surprised by the difference from Italy, whose dense plantings of parched yellow fields you have so short a time before left behind. Here is a paler, purer, soberer country, which seems both wild and old and quite distinct from anything farther west. The sea is absolutely smooth, sometimes violet, sometimes blue, with a softness of watercolor, glistening in patches with a fine grain of silver; and the islands of all sizes in bulbous or oblong shapes—blobs and round-bottomed bottles and the contours of plump roast fowl—seem not to rise out of the water but to be plaqued on it like cuff-links on cuffs or to lie scattered like the fragments of a picture-puzzle on a table with a blue cloth cover. These islands are a dry terra-cotta— quite unlike the deep earthy clay tints to which one has been accustomed in Italy—almost the color of too well-cooked liver, and the vegetation looks like gray lichens. The marblings on the looping beaches set up a feeling of uncanny familiarity which refers itself, as one recognizes in a moment, to the patterns on the ancient Greek vases made out of this very soil. Even on the large islands and the mainland, there are visible little cultivation and few plainly cut ribbons of roads, and the country, after humanized Italy, seems grander and more mysterious. The haze of the fawn-colored foreground shades farther away into blue, where the mountains stand dim and serene. These are the "shadowy mountains" of Homer.

Swooping down upon the airport at Eleusis, you seem to be heaving among billows that do not really resemble hills, with their dry green of foliage, pale gray of stone and curious pale yellow of clay. There is a special apparent lightness of substance and absence of strong color which characterizes Greece and sets it off from other countries. As you descend into the hot airport, you have a general grateful impression of simplification and gentle austerity.

The transportation truck speeds with jolts along the Sacred Way that leads from Eleusis to the Acropolis. One is surprised and thrilled to see from the street-signs that it is still called the Hiera Hodos. The lavender mountains of Salamis make a contrast that harmonizes with the bright-blue water beneath. Above the low roofs of Athens the Acropolis rises on its pedestal of rock: astonishing, dramatic, divine, with at the same time the look of a phantom.

———

The Grande Bretagne Hotel, the principal hostelry of Athens, which has been taken for a billet by the British and at which transient Americans also stay, has an atmosphere entirely dissimilar from the atmosphere of Italian hotels. In Italy the porters and deskmen still think they are giving service to tourists: they bow constantly, show you places on street-maps. But something is wrong at the Grande Bretagne. You are first told by a slant-eyed Greek that there are no decent rooms left but that he will be glad to give you a room in his house at a price only a little higher than what you would be obliged to pay at the hotel. When you insist on seeing the sergeant in charge of the American side, you find an insolent equally slit-eyed fellow, quite untypical of the American Army, who also seems to be some kind of Greek. "Dere's so many drips comin' in," he says, "so many generals and high-rankin' officers—dat I'm full up all de time. I'll have to put you in a room wit two odder beds in it." I thought he was hoping I'd take the private room, but I insisted on staying here, and he repeated several times, as he reluctantly got a boy for my bag, "Dere's so many drips all de time."

The room with the three beds had been riddled by what I took to be a machine-gun, which had sprayed bullets all around the doorway and made several holes in the door. One of the shots had struck just above my bed and left a scar in the plaster. Out the window I could see blinds knocked askew, snarls of German barbed wire on the roof and other evidences of close-range fighting. The Grande Bretagne had first been occupied by the Germans, who lived in it all through the war; then it was put at the disposal of the British after the Germans had been driven out. At the time of the civil war last winter, the fatal demonstration by E.A.M. (the National Liberation Front), at which the police fired into the crowd, took place in the square just outside it; and when the battle to the death was on and E.A.M. for a time had the British at bay, the Grande Bretagne was one of the only places in Athens which the latter succeeded in holding. The bullet-holes in my door were probably made by one of E.A.M.'s guns. Later, when the royalists had won, Winston Churchill, on his hasty trip to Athens, stayed at the Grande Bretagne and held his conferences there; and some of the Partisans loaded the basement with dynamite and planned to blow the place up—thereby wiping out at one stroke, as a sympathizer with E.A.M. told me, the inspirer of the foreign policy which was backing the monarchy in Greece and General Scobie and Ambassador Leeper, who had been carrying that policy out. But someone gave the plot away, and the wires were cut in time.

The employees of the Grande Bretagne, many of whom have worked there for years, have been through a good deal. One cannot precisely know whether they are sullen or discouraged or stunned, but, with the exception of a few of the waiters, they have neglected to learn any English. They do not even expect tips: they disappear, without waiting a second, as soon as you have succeeded in catching one and inducing him to do something for you. Greek callers at the hotel complain that they are treated by the Greek employees with the utmost impoliteness.

———

One gets a sudden revelation, in coming to Greece from Italy, of all that was vulgar about ancient Rome and all that was trashy in the Renaissance. There is no

Renaissance art in Athens and, except for some Byzantine churches, nothing between ancient and modern Greece. You have no overlay of Catholic history; the Orthodox Church, in general, is singularly unobtrusive; and I confess that it came as a relief not to find the scene incrusted with the three hundred and thirty-six churches that you meet at every turn in Rome. You have, instead, a clean and well-swept city of small buildings, white, pale gray or dry yellow, which are almost never ornate in the Mediterranean manner, but rather simple and uniform, with a dignity of classical taste; and, among these, a few ancient monuments that are perhaps the things of the kind most worth seeing in the whole Western world. You understand for the first time that it is true that, in matters of architecture, the Romans merely imitated the Greeks, and you realize what coarsening and deadening results this imitation produced. The Parthenon itself, the Erechtheum, the temple of the Wingless Victory keep a vitality, a splendor and a grace that I have never seen in any other ruins. They do not seem the bones of perished ages; they still transform the world where they shine—a world of square houses and shops that might otherwise seem chalky and meager but that, beside them, catches something of their distinction.

––––

It has been shown that the classical Greeks had a rather uncertain sense of color. They used the same word for yellow and green, and they seem to have confused red with purple. It was the Romans who brought color into European poetry with the Italian landscapes of Virgil—as well as the sense of materials, of hardness and tightness and weight, with the marbles and bricks and bronzes that Horace and Virgil both describe in their verse and imitate by its structure. The Greeks lacked this feeling for matter, for their very mountains seem immaterial, and they worked in Pentelican marble, which gives the effect of solidified light. As soon as one arrives in Greece, one understands how a native of this country who had never seen anything else might have had no conception of a world that was painted in definite colors. The olive trees, the pepper trees, the tiny firs are indeterminately blue, green and gray; the yellow of the earth is a neutral tint which is always turning pink or brown, and the pinks and browns themselves sometimes deepen or brighten to red. What the Greeks did have highly developed— besides the architectural sense of proportion—was an appreciation of the light and shade that are the main features of visible Attica. You find it in the choruses of the plays, where things are always darkling or gleaming, and in the settings of Plato's dialogues, when they take place on sunny days in the shade; and you find it exploited in the most masterly way in the colonnades and porches of the temples. You still have to learn in Athens to appreciate everything in terms of light.

—

All the American soldiers love Athens: they infinitely prefer Greece to Italy, and I have been trying to figure out why. I remember a man in Rome who kept assuring me that Athens was "a real metropolis," which it certainly is strikingly not. When you ask them why they like it so much, they immediately say that it is "clean," which up to a point is true—that is, the filth of the slums is kept in the back streets as they are used to having it kept at home, instead of, as in Naples, being all over the place. But, for another thing, the Greeks, to an American, seem relatively non-foreign and normal. They are much less theatrical than Italians. They are quieter and do not jabber. They are more independent, have more backbone.

There are few beggars in Athens and few prostitutes—a great contrast to the state of things in Italy. I had somehow got the impression that the Athenian women were still more or less in the harem phase, but, though this really is the case in Italy, I did not find it true in Greece. The Greek women seem remarkably intelligent, and they do a good deal on their own. There are few professional sirens.

But I have finally come to the conclusion that there are other, perhaps less admirable, qualities that recommend the Greek capital to the Americans: a certain monotony of the streets, of which my French guidebook complains, and a certain mediocrity in Athens. It comes back to me that an American who had grown up in Greece once told me that Athens was "a hick town," and I understand now that it looks more like home to the exiled and wandering G.I., because, compared to other places in Europe, it seems orderly, prosaic and new. This is unquestionably what was meant by my friend in Rome when he pronounced it "a real metropolis."

———

In any case, one realizes, as one walks in the streets, that Greece now is really the country where nobody has anything at all. In Italy there are still many commodities that are being produced and sold—striped neckties, pink silk slips and lace brassières, new books in crisp bright covers, perfume and candy and cakes—and that revive some of the brilliance of the shops in places like Milan and Rome. But in Greece there is not much beyond remnants of old stocks that must predate the war, and, in clothing, a scanty supply that only meets rudimentary needs. No woman in the streets wears make-up, and they have only rather dreary cheap dresses, mostly of the national blue; none of the men has a necktie on, even when his shirt collar is buttoned. If you go to a better-class restaurant, you can get little but a slice of fish, a dish of cut-up tomatoes, a bottle of resinated wine and a slice of watermelon. The people are not riding bicycles, as they are in Italy and England; but this fact is due, I am told, not so much to the difficulty of getting them as to the scornful aversion that the Greeks have always felt toward bicycle-riding. They regard it, it seems, as undignified. The one thing that the Athenians have that the Romans and Neapolitans don't have is quite enough light at night. They defended their electric plant and saved it when the Germans were evacuating; and it is very cheerful, coming from cities where the streets are murky and blind, to find Athens twinkling among its hills under the dry clear summer sky.

I got the impression at first of a city depleted of life (though its actual population has been increased by the influx from towns destroyed by the Germans), as if everything that was going on were at once underpatron-ized and understaffed. But I was told by several foreigners who had lived there before the war that this impression was partly misleading: the Athenians had always been frugal and they had never made much of a show; and the lack of organic town-life was not wholly the result of the war, since the inhabitants of Athens had always been, as a Russian lady explained, content with *"une douce an-archie."* But here as elsewhere in Europe the disorganiza-tion brought by the war is generally profound. After all, out of a population of only seven million in the whole of Greece, a million have died during the last five years—six hundred thousand of these from starvation. I had not expected to find whole streets of the city as badly battered as London or Milan—full of walls nicked or speckled with bullets and of the blasted-out husks of buildings. E.L.A.S. (the Greek Popular Liberation Army, the military aspect of E.A.M.) blew up police headquarters and other strongholds of the royalist authorities, and the British retaliated with bombing raids, mortar-fire and tanks shooting-up the streets.

———

I share a bathroom with an American major, a former Standard Oil engineer now engaged in "petroleum rehabilitation," who is eager to talk about his work. He is a tall energetic Westerner who is enthusiastically intent on a purpose—a purpose which is probably typical of the American approach to Europe. There are two main points of which he is anxious to convince me and to which he usually reverts when I meet him, prefacing each step of his argument with an emphatic and cogent *"Aw right!,"* on the assumption that I have agreed with the step before. The first of these points he immediately raised when he saw that I was a war correspondent. He flourished before me a clipping that had just been sent him from home and declared with indignation that the newspapermen had been misrepresenting the situation in Greece. The editorial from his home-town paper asserted that the present regime was a lawless and ruthless tyranny, which was arresting thousands of people on political charges and holding them without trial, and that it ill became the United States to countenance a government by terror that made democratic processes impossible. I told him that this was very much the picture that had been given me before I came, by the American correspondents who had been in Greece, and I suggested that British policy, in its brutal repression of a movement which is generally admitted to have had at the time the support of eighty per cent of the Greeks, and in its backing of the unpopular royalists, had hardly evidenced a serious concern for the extension of the Four Freedoms.

Like most Americans, no matter how predatory, no matter how hungry for power, he was daunted and embarrassed for a moment by the appeal to democratic principles. But he quickly shook off these objections. Political problems did not really exist for him; he was interested in something else. He only wanted me to admit that it was best that the radicals should be kept down—the Greeks needed a period of stabilization, didn't they?—and then to take me up with *"Aw right!"* and expand on the subject that he had at heart.

This subject was the favorable openings for American business in Greece—not for "exploitation" (he always made this disclaimer); no: that wouldn't do!—the Greeks were suspicious of us, "rightly perhaps." What he had in mind was something quite different: to develop Greek water power and oil wells by organizing international companies for which one third of the capital and the technical advice would be supplied by American enterprise, another third of the money by Greek financiers, and the remaining third be put up by the Greek employees themselves, so that they would have some real interest in the project. "Liberal labor and capital" were beginning to get together at home, and he didn't see why they shouldn't in Greece. He beamed with an impersonal elation behind his professional glasses. Volos, to which he had just made a trip, reminded him a lot of the Yosemite; the Greeks were perfectly fine: it wasn't hard to arouse their interest and they would work with you in a wonderful way. When I remarked that I had been told that the government stood in the way of technical training, he violently denied this, assuring me that this was not necessarily true: he had, he said, a young engineer who was a damn sight keener and more competent than the average man at home turned out by the technical schools.

The drive of his point of view—capitalistic and engineering-minded—in the direction of the non-political and the anti-nationalistic was illustrated by a story he loved, about a German who had lived thirty years in Greece in the neighborhood of Volos and whom the Germans put in charge of the oil installations when they arrived in 1941. This oil had been owned by the Shell Company, and the Shell Company manager at Volos had been also the British vice-consul. He was now put on parole by the Germans and made to report to them every day. When the Germans were getting out of Greece and blowing up all the public utilities, the German expatriate went to the military authorities and persuaded them to spare the oil installations, pointing out that the people of Volos had done the invaders no harm and that they needed the oil for their economy. Now the British vice-consul is back in charge, the German has returned to his farm, and the Greeks have refrained from bringing charges against him, as they would have with any other collaborationist, because he has saved their oil.

This major was a likable man and I found his excitement infectious. He referred with pride to his wife, who had been getting a college degree in some such subject as sociology, and who, he said, was "a good-looking little son-of-a-bitch."

———

I was fortunate in having letters from a Greek lady I knew in New York. She sent me to her mother, Mrs. D., who turned out to be in touch with many strata and departments of Athenian life. Mrs. D. is one of seven sisters who came originally from the island of Samos; her father was a classical scholar, the director of a Greek school in Smyrna. She is remarkably intelligent, as well as lively and charming; fair-haired and blue-eyed, with almost the profile of an ancient statue. You do not find

often, among the modern Greeks—who run to round
faces and round black eyes—these types that recall the
great age, but you do see a few startling examples. The
women of Samos are famous for their beauty, and the
pure race is represented by these blondes who have blue
or glaucous eyes, and sometimes look almost English. The
innumerable nephews and nieces of Mrs. D.'s whom I
met were all more or less distinguished by these Greek sea-
colored eyes and these archaic foreheads and noses. They
and their husbands and wives and their various family
connections are active in education, in the government, in
business, in archaeology, in the newspaper world, in the
theater; and they include every degree of political opinion
from Communism to the official conservatism. You run
into them everywhere, and if there is anything I want to
see or anybody I want to meet, one simply passes me on to
another. These relations and a variety of friends are
always dropping in on Mrs. D. When I remarked that I
had met in her family every shade of opinion except
royalist, one of the nieces, at my next visit, came over and
whispered to me that there were two royalist ladies
present—not, she hastened to add, relatives but friends.

I have several times visited Mrs. D. in a house she has
rented for the summer in a residential suburb called
Philothei. It is a well-designed modern villa—a pleasant
refuge from the terrific, almost tropical heat, the worst
they can remember, they say: white ceilings, pale straw-
colored walls, large casements and green latticed blinds,
cupboards of natural wood and green-and-white linoleum
that imitates tiles. Among the barren and sun-baked
mountains, Hymettus, Pentelicus and Parnes, it seems
very much like southern California, with its comfortable
outdoor furniture, its potted ice plants, its collection of
cactus and its dry aromatic smell. There are a turbid
green pool with big goldfish, a garden with dahlias,

petunias and bushes of yellow roses, fig trees with ripe green figs and clusters of heavy green grapes draping the arbor that shades the back porch.

There have always been so many people, and they have all been so familiar and casual, that I have had to ask questions later to identify them and straighten out their relationships, but I have pretty clear impressions of the following:

A nephew, who has qualified himself to teach physics and mathematics but who has been waiting eight years for a job, in the meantime making a meager living by giving private lessons. I got from him for the first time a picture—which was later confirmed by other sources—of the miserable illiteracy of Greece. He told me that seventy per cent of the Greeks have had only the most rudimentary schooling or none, and that there are thirty-two hundred teachers out of work, while it is impossible, with the reactionary government, to establish a democratic educational system. There are only two good public libraries in Greece—one in Athens and one in Salonika— and it is an almost insuperable task to find anything you want in either of them. He is a sympathizer with the E.A.M. movement. He told me that before the war the Greeks had seen so much of the English that they had learned to get on with them and like them, but that, except for those Greeks who wanted the monarchy, the attitude toward the British was now bitter. After all, only seven British tanks—since E.L.A.S. had no tanks—had stood between E.A.M. and victory (they were American tanks, by the way); and, after all, he thought that they, the Greeks, could say that, given their equipment and manpower, nobody else in Europe had done more to stand up to the Nazis than they had and that they deserved the kind of democratic regime that most of them had thought they were fighting for.

A little niece of twenty-two, who speaks French, studies literature and is preparing to be an archaeologist. She is bright and well brought-up and has, I should say, a good deal of character. She has a sister, whom I met later, a year younger than she. This sister was out in the mountains with the Partisans and is a passionate supporter of E.A.M. I told the older one that I got the impression that her sister was a little on the Communist side. *"Pas un peu,"* she answered slyly. *"Assez."* She herself is wholeheartedly pro-E.A.M. but her attitude toward the Communists is critical. The nuance of difference in politics between these two girls is typical of the state of things in Greece.

An old schoolmate of my friend in New York—a young woman who, before the war, had started to study medicine but had given it up when the family fortunes broke down in the general disaster. She ended by marrying a lawyer and going to live in Salonika. They had had to sell their best carpets and such other things of value as they possessed in order to get enough to eat. She seems to me an able woman who would have had a career of her own if she had not been grounded by the war and whose life is rather unsatisfactory.

Two sisters, cousins of Mrs. D. One is married to a man in the government: white suit, tan-and-white shoes, fine Panama hat; very suave, speaks English well. The other sister has all of what I found to be the typical conventional opinions of the well-to-do Greek bourgeoisie. She was appalled by the British elections—was Attlee as "intelligent" as Churchill? Churchill had saved them from the Communists, who would otherwise have won and "shot everybody." E.A.M. had been run by the Communists, and Greek Communism was the fanaticism of ignorant people. She had asked her maid the other day what she would do after the revolution—didn't she see that she would still have to be a maid because she didn't know how to do anything else? The girl hadn't thought of that: she had thought she would be a lady. That was what Greek Communism was made of!

The two royalist ladies. They had got to know each other in jail and had been good friends ever since. They had been sheltering British soldiers during the German occupation and had been imprisoned in a room with eighty women and children—where one had spent six months, the other eleven. They had not been allowed to read and were unable to relieve themselves except when a large pail was put in the middle of the room for everybody to use. Of the British they had been punished for helping, they said that the New Zealanders were nicest, the Australians somewhat "rougher" and the English "very selfish."

Two children: a boy and a girl of about thirteen and ten, who had been left with Mrs. D. for a visit. They were serious and quiet in a way that I have never seen in any other children: it was evidently the impress of the war. I tried amusing them with a jumping mouse made out of my pocket handkerchief, with which I have usually had great success, but it did not go over very well. The boy, at any rate, seemed much more interested in listening to the political discussion. He made two rather acute observations not intended for me to understand but translated by his elders. "The Americans and English," he said, "don't seem to know their own language, because they hesitate and stammer over words," and "It's a funny thing that the English didn't celebrate the English elections—it was the Greeks that did all the celebrating." But when they were sent to bed, they sat up talking and giggling, like all children, and had to be hushed and told to go to sleep.

The person I talked with most except Mrs. D. herself

was her son, who was staying with her, an importer with a business in Bagdad. Unlike most of the rest of the company, he did not belong to the intelligentsia, and his point of view was non political, practical and a little cynical. He spoke English and talked about his experience in the East with the various English-speaking peoples. You were never able, he said, to get on any kind of terms with the English: you might succeed in inducing them to come to your house, but they would never ask you back. They were awfully unscrupulous in business, and his English rivals in Bagdad, finding that they could not compete with his firm, had tried to get him and his associates locked up as Nazi spies. The English, however, were quiet in public, where the Americans were most obnoxious: they apparently regarded themselves as miraculously invincible with women or privileged with some sort of *droit de seigneur,* for they were always coming up to unknown couples and insisting that the ladies should dance with them. (I had to recognize that this was true: I had seen an American soldier in a restaurant in Rome butt in on a party of Americans and make an obstinate attempt to carry off the wife of one of the men in the Embassy.) The Greeks now thought they loved the Americans, but he told them that they only liked them because they didn't know them yet. He had no confidence at all, he declared, in the disinterested pretensions of U.N.R.R.A.: it would turn out that it was being used to put over American products in Europe. He swore that an American had once asked him whether the war between Athens and Sparta was still going on in Greece. The Scotch he considered cruel on account of their treatment of the Greeks at the time of the civil war. The New Zealanders were the English-speaking people who made the best impression abroad: they were quiet, agreeable and decent. (I asked a New Zealand girl in U.N.R.R.A.

about this overwhelming popularity of the New Zealanders, and she said that they had somehow, in Greece,
known how to "take the right tone." They had felt that
Greece resembled New Zealand—it was a small, rural,
mountainous country, mostly surrounded by water—and
they approached the Greeks as people like themselves.)

Young D. had been a sailor in the Greek Navy in
Egypt at the time of the mutiny of April, 1944, and I
asked him to tell me about it. The incident that had set
off this trouble had been the imprisonment by the puppet
Greek government in Cairo of the delegates sent from
Greece by the Free Greek government of the mountains.
This organization, E.A.M., represented the resistance to
the Germans and consisted of a national council which
had just been chosen by underground elections held all
over Greece. It had sent a committee to Cairo to try to
arrange a union between the Greek government in exile
and itself. But the British, intent on the restoration of the
monarchy and wanting nothing so far to the Left as
E.A.M. was threatening to be, had the delegates sent to
jail. The Greek fleet then mutinied in protest and would
not continue fighting with the British. D. was at that
time in training camp, and he and his companions refused to obey orders for thirty-three days. A Scotch officer
who spoke Greek came and pleaded with them and told
them that they were costing the British £25,000 a day
because the Germans were sinking the ships that the
Greeks were no longer convoying. The Greeks laughed
and said that they were glad to hear this evidence that the
English without the Greeks were helpless against the
Germans. Finally, the British told them that they needed
the training camp for something else, loaded them into
lorries and took them to a prison camp, where they were
kept for twenty-six days. At one point the British lined
them up and offered to escort with bayonets any who

wanted to leave. Out of eight hundred and nine men, only seven accepted. The sailors on one of the ships further infuriated the British by cutting the crown out of the Greek flag, as a result of which the British refused to salute it. Then the word got around among the Greeks that the mutiny had been engineered by the Communists, and the morale of their resistance crumbled. Sixty per cent of them, D. included, agreed to go back to the fleet. The British sorted them out in four categories, each of which was dealt with in a way that was regarded as appropriate to it. Category A consisted of sailors who from the first had not approved of the movement; B, of men who had sympathized with it but had taken no active part or whose sentiments it was impossible to determine because they had been in the hospital or on leave; C, of sailors who were definitely known to have "shouted" or done something positive (this category included also all persons who had grown beards, since the Partisans had had beards in the mountains and this was regarded as a proof of Left sympathies). To D category the leaders were condemned. D. told me about this procedure with an irony, amused but mordant, at the expense of British system and stupidity. One man who had written a letter expressing concern lest the people at home were not getting enough vitamins in their diet was consigned on that evidence to C, since it was considered by the British authorities in itself a dangerous symptom to show an interest in the welfare of Greece. A, B and C categories were eventually all set free, but the men in D were sent to the Sudan, where presumably they still were. It was afterwards said that the mutiny had been provoked by the British themselves in order to find out, among the Greek sailors, who were and who were not Communists.

During the early part of this story, D.'s young wife,

whom he had married only five days before—a good-
looking girl, gray-eyed and tanned—listened with the
decorous quietness that Greek women usually show in the
presence of males, but as he was telling of his disaffec-
tion, when he had finally become convinced that the
mutiny was being managed by the Communists, she
began to try to sabotage his story—she was sitting on the
couch beside him—by burrowing under his arm like a
setter that wants to be fed or tackling him around the
waist and making as if to throw him over. "You must let
me tell my version of the mutiny," she said when her
husband had finished. "She's a Communist sympathizer,"
he explained to me. "She doesn't know what to think
about anything till she gets the directive from headquarters." At any rate, she never did give me her version.
Her husband teased her for being a Communist and also
teased her for being the niece of a prominent public man
who had come to represent for more realistic republican
opinion the most obsolete political old-fogeyism. D. himself, in all this talk of politics, was a little bit aggressively
a businessman, but he was not, I think, quite satisfied
with business. He asked me, with Socratic irony, whether
it were possible in the United States to make a lot of
money and still be honest. "It's not possible over here," he
said. "You can make a little money and be honest, but
you can't make a lot of money without cheating or
exploiting somebody."

The atmosphere of the D. household seemed to me
distinctly different from anything I had ever known
before. These Greeks showed profound effects of the
hardships and horrors through which they had passed,
but they treated them with the utmost lightness. It was as
far from the crisp matter-of-factness of the British—their
understatement that is almost ostentatious—as it was from
the historical consciousness which never deserts the Ital-

ians and which, once having allowed them to accept Mussolini as a reincarnation of the Caesars, now leads them to talk about recent events in terms of the age of Justinian, when the Roman general Belisarius had had to invade Italy in order to fight the Goths, and to conceive their hopes for the future in terms of the reappearance of the great figures of the Risorgimento. In the course of my visits to the D.'s, I sometimes heard of shocking incidents of the years of German occupation. There had been a gibbet at the corner of the street where Mrs. D. lived in Athens; the Germans, on one occasion, in reprisal for the killing of a soldier, had stopped a tram full of women and children on their way to the beach for an outing and shot every human being in it; one lady, whose husband had been in hiding, spoke of her nervousness in her house at night as she waited for the doorbell to ring; someone else said it was awfully pleasant to be able to have lights in the evening—the Germans had been in the habit of firing machine-guns at lighted windows and had sometimes killed the people inside; one of the men, as he was taking his leave, remarked that he had still not got used to not having to dodge the Germans when he was going home late at night. But they usually laughed about these things, as if they were speaking of such inconveniences as cranky neighbors or torn-up roads. "One day you would have a friend," said D.'s little wife, smiling, as she told me about what the Germans had done, "and the next day you wouldn't have one." Unlike the Italians and the Southern French, the Greeks do not like to show emotion; and they give you a curious impression of having waited with perfect self-confidence till the barbarian hordes had passed. After all, as someone reminded me, there Xerxes had once been sitting on the top of one of the hills of Salamis waiting to see the Greek fleet defeated. So, one day, as I was walking along the Tritis Septemvriou with the girl who was giving me Greek lessons, and she was showing me how, during the civil war, the Greeks had been lined up on one side of the street and the British with their tanks on the other, she had mildly replied to my expression of horror: "Oh, no: our men showed how brave they were."

Yet these people do differ in certain ways from any other similar group of people whose conversation I have ever listened to. They do not really make a social world, flourishing and complete in itself within its range of relations and interests, as such people usually do. They have good sense and good humor and poise. They joke about Kou-Kou-e's and Chites, the current nicknames for Communists and royalists, accusing one another of extremism. But they have lived through shocking deprivations; they cannot see a year ahead into the future; they do not really have the security that their kind of life ought to imply. And, as one of the ladies said in some connection that I have now forgotten, "We say that we are free, but we are not free."

———

The first night I spent at Philothei, I was awakened at early dawn by a loud, abrupt, strangulated cry that was evidently not human but animal. I went to the window but could see nothing, though the cry came again and again, like the choking of a dog that has swallowed a bone or the convulsive gasps of a man who is being revived from drowning. The best I could imagine was that the sound was made by some kind of monkey, though I had never heard of monkeys in Greece. Later, when the boy came out, I asked him whether he knew what it was. "He shouts like a man," said the boy. "He jumps with his two legs. He is green." I was trying to picture this bandersnatch when the boy, who could not think of the

English word, explained that it was called *vatrachos*. It pleased me to think that Aristophanes' play had been due to the existence in Greece of some species of super-frog. And I was even more charmed in a moment when one of the ladies came out of the house and remarked, "He says *ko-ax ko-ax*."

I went to performances at the principal theaters: the Ethnikon and the Lyrikon. Like a good many things in Greece, they are closer to ancient Greece than you might expect them to be: the audience sits out-of-doors before a small and severe proscenium. At the Ethnikon, I saw Gogol's *The Inspector General*, which seemed to me very well done; at the Lyrikon, which is definitely Left, J. B. Priestley's *And They Came to a City* and a play by a young Greek dramatist, Nikos Tsekouras, called *If You Work, You Will Eat*. The Priestley play is feeble enough, with its watered-down Shavian satire and its thoroughly depressing picture of a well-adjusted socialist utopia where everybody is uniformly cheerful; but the people at the theater say that they have to produce what they can get. They have had almost nothing new from abroad, and they asked eagerly what was interesting in the theater in England and the United States. More than Italy even, and to a degree that has been very damaging, Greece has been culturally cut off from the West since before the beginning of the war. The little Greek play was also in the nature of a socialist fable, but, in a genre which has been standardized by the Russians, it seemed to me, as relayed to me by a Greek companion, partly redeemed by its very naïveté and by a certain unstandardized folk charm. An Athenian stockbroker and his family are stranded on the island of Rhodes and have to depend on the lighthouse-keeper to put them up and give them something to eat. But the old man who attends to the light is an eccentric and a social philosopher. He will not let the city guests pay him anything, because that is the rule of Greek hospitality; but also he will not give them meals unless they agree to work. On the other hand, the arrival of the financier brings a principle of corruption to the island. He is carrying a large sum of money, which the captain of his ship has got wind of and tries to induce the lighthouse-keeper's son to steal. A conflict ensues between, on one side, the power of money and the parasitism it breeds, and, on the other, honest virtue and wisdom. Of course, in the long run, the rich man is cured of his imaginary ailments by his new regime of open air and exercise, while he rather enjoys the discomfiture of his spoiled and disagreeable wife; his daughter, a charming girl, takes to the simple life with delight and shows herself thoroughly competent, converting also the city slicker who is in love with her; and the young wife of the lighthouse-keeper's son frustrates the designs of the captain by blowing up his ship so that the thieves cannot leave the island. The audience would applaud with a crash at every reference to social justice, and my companion laughed like a schoolgirl at every crack at the bourgeoisie—a form of baiting which seems to be new in Greece and these examples of which she would explain to me with evident doubt as to whether I could grasp the joke.

But there was something both serious and important in the atmosphere of the Theatro Lyrikon when this little socialist play was performed. The director and some of the actors were young people who had brought to it the same kind of spirit that one used to find back in the twenties in the Cherry Lane Theater and the Province-town Players; but certain of the older actors were among the best-known in Athens, and one of them, Aimilios Veakis, is the foremost actor of Greece. Veakis had "been in the mountains"; he had lost his daughter there when she had fallen into a ravine while riding. And a month ago the pro-government reactionaries had rioted in three of the Athenian theaters. They had broken up *Julius Caesar* at the Lyrikon at one of the speeches of the regicide conspirators, and *The Merchant of Venice* at the Ethnikon during the scene in which Shylock makes his plea for the Jews—under the impression, I was told, that these passages had been interpolated by the Left-Wing producers with subversive political intent; and they had attacked Miranda Myrat, a well-known pro-E.A.M. actress. They had shot and wounded a number of people. Miss Myrat was still in bed; and Veakis, who had also been injured, was reappearing for the first time that evening and had been hailed with a great ovation. The more radical of Mrs. D.'s two nieces was engaged to the director of the theater and took me behind the scenes to meet Veakis. He had been playing the lighthouse-keeper and had made him remarkably real. Like most good European actors, he had submerged himself in his part without exploiting his own personality, and now, with his make-up half rubbed off, the sensitivity and intelligence of his face were thrown into relief by contrast with the homely old-man mask I had been watching. He made me a little speech: he said that he was glad to meet an American because the Americans today were the only people who knew what it was to be free; the Greeks had fought for their freedom and won it, and now they had lost it again.

It was an embarrassing moment for me. It had become very plain to me since I had been in Greece that the movement which the British had disarmed and which the United States had allowed them to disarm was neither a chess play directed from Moscow nor a foray of bandits from the hills, but a genuine popular movement which had been able to recruit almost all that was generous, courageous and enlightened in Greece, the most spirited among the young, the clearest-sighted among the mature. This movement has been broken: the prisons are crammed with tens of thousands of political prisoners, and the government police have been practicing just such methods of torture and terror as had made the Gestapo hated (they have maintained the same security battalion that formerly worked for the Nazis), while the British, after calling out their tanks against E.A.M. and expressing indignant horror over outrages perpetrated by the Left, have done little or nothing to curb the Right. "What *is* E.A.M.?" I was challenged one day by a rabidly reactionary Greek lady. "E.A.M. is not a party. It is only a state of mind!" That is true, no doubt, but states of mind may prove more powerful than organizations— especially when they are persecuted. The state of mind of E.A.M. has been similar to that which in Northern Italy is uniting diverse elements in a formidable bloc of the Left, and it is similar to the state of mind which has prevailed to such an extent in England that, unexpectedly to Labour itself, a Socialist government has been voted in.

The people at the theater told me that they had tried to get the story of the riots sent through to the outside world, and, like many other Greeks I talked to, they seemed to have the desperate feeling that nobody knew what was happening in Greece. The only thing I could say to Veakis was that I would try to write about it.

Overheard in the open-air café outside the King George Bar: "How were the Indians?" "Oh, they're easy meat for propaganda. They've begun comparing themselves to British troops—wanting to sleep with white women—that sort of thing." A pause. "How did you people take the elections?" "It shocked me to the roots. I didn't know that Labour was that strong."

12

GREEK DIARY: A TRIP TO DELPHI;
NOTES ON THE BRITISH
IN GREECE

I MADE A TRIP TO DELPHI FROM ATHENS with some
U.N.R.R.A. workers in August. The heat was the most
stunning in decades. The U.N.R.R.A. people made me
wear a sun helmet, and the American chocolate bars that
we bought at the PX for the journey were immediately
turned to syrup. No Greek ever understands setting out
on such exploits at noon: they want to eat and go to sleep.
So did we, as a matter of fact. Most things are uncomfortable in Europe; one does not often choose one's
company, and even when one has been able to do so, the
springs of good humor and charm sometimes quickly dry
up in the heat. But before we had gone very far, bumping
and baking in the jeep, I felt that I had fallen by chance
into a fortunate combination.

The sanitary engineer from U.N.R.R.A. who was
taking me and who drove the car was one of those
modest, soft-spoken, shrewd, amiable and very able men
that we like to imagine representing us among the fevers
and confusions of Europe, but comparatively rarely find.
His interpreter was a young Greek woman, who expressed herself so well in both English and French that I

was amazed when she told me later that she had hardly been out of Greece. She had seemed to me, when she joined us, the first really smart-looking woman that I had so far seen in Athens. I had been putting down the absence of chic—very striking when one came from Rome—to the non-availability of attractive clothes; and I tried to figure out whether Eleni, as she was always called by her boss—I had not caught her married name—had somehow managed to get a few things from Paris or whether a natural gift of style were carrying off inferior garments. She was slim, with bare arms and legs, so burned that they were partly purple, and she wore a simple dress of plain yellow, flat-soled sandals and a dish-shaped straw hat. She said that she had borrowed the hat, as she never ordinarily wore one and did not feel natural in them—she had lovely, slightly curly brown hair—but as she held onto the hat with one hand while she laid the other sideways in the crease of her lap to keep her dress from blowing, she would have done as a model for *Vogue*. She was a type of good-looking Greek woman that I was beginning to identify—I had already seen one winsome specimen in the young actress, Stasa Iatridou, at the Theatro Lyrikon. They have dark, very bright and alive but not enormous eyes, and small, round, rather recessive chins that do not challenge attention like Anglo-Saxon and Latin chins and may at first suggest weakness of character, as the eyes suggest extreme gentleness. But one soon feels that this impression is not correct and watches them with increasing interest, and I presently decided that Eleni was not only smarter but prettier than any other Greek woman I had seen. She had a pointed but not salient nose, and she seemed authentically and traditionally Greek in that she resembled—not the classical statues, which we always imagine fair—but the dark women with long hands and feet painted in black on the red clay

Greek vases. Such a woman, however, gives a different impression when we see her alive and in all her dimensions. To an American—in America we have only the grin—the play of her eyes was enchanting: not the animated lifting of eyebrows that one finds in the Latin women and that has something of a routine coquetry, nor the quick narrowing of eyelids of the Slavs that suggests an animal wariness; but a marvellous sympathetic sensitivity, an instinct to respond and to please, that was always self-possessed and quiet, and a power to fascinate that was exerted so unobtrusively, so sweetly, that one felt it must be almost involuntary, as if it were a spirit that lived in her and that could not help looking out.

I was disappointed, however, by Eleni's politics. We passed through a little town that was covered with crosses and crowns, painted in patriotic blue, and I asked her whether this really meant that the place was predominantly royalist. She replied, with childlike confidence, that it did, and added, after a moment, that she must tell her husband about this: it would please him because he was a royalist. She said she was a royalist, too. The town of Thebes, also curlicued with blue, was an abject and sordid place if one had expected a setting for *Oedipus*. We tried to decide which was the least forbidding restaurant—though without any invidious comment on the part of the U.N.R.R.A. man or myself, since Eleni, quite unlike some fine ladies in minor European countries, never apologized for accommodations or commented on the misery of the people. The glasses and decanters were dim with dirt, and most of the tableware showed traces of previous meals. We sidestepped the meat and got a lunch out of sliced tomatoes, boiled potatoes, sawdusty gray bread and a bottle of raw retsina. The tables were out of doors, and while we were eating, some diseased little children came in from the street begging. They were in rags and had sores on their faces. Eleni quietly gave them a good deal of the bread. She had two children of her own, she told me later. The principal feature of the lunch, however, was an English U.N.R.R.A. man whom the American had arranged to meet there. It is always a relief in Europe to find an Englishman who is not in the Army and who is trying to do something to help the people improve their own condition instead of to keep them from making trouble for the English. The most striking thing about such men, in contrast with most other exiled Englishmen, is a spontaneous middle-class cheerfulness which is inspired by the satisfaction of doing good and the excitement of seeing foreign parts. This man was reporting on the progress of a summer camp for Greek children in which U.N.R.R.A. had a hand. It was one of a large number of such camps that had been organized by the Greeks themselves in an effort to supply a ration of normal feeding and play to the starved and scared generation which had come into the world during the war. It was curious to hear this little man describing, with precise matter-of-factness and a kind of school-masterish humor, as if he had been talking of British Boy Scouts, the problems of such work under conditions that must have seemed to him abysmally uncivilized.

We did find the setting of *Oedipus* as soon as we emerged from the town: a row of black mountains, grim and simple, not rugged, not comparable, in the old cliché, to anything so human as the lifted heads of giants, but looking like thin flint blades against the pale and impoverished sky. I remembered that the Theban plague had been attributed to the incest of Oedipus, and reflected that we now even knew that malaria was not due to bad air but to a particular species of mosquito, and that the purpose of our U.N.R.R.A. expedition was to apply a scientific technique to the destruction of this mosquito.

But in Greece such historical contrasts are not really felt as dramatic. The country has remained so primitive since the period of its great civilization that history does not show as a pageant. You do not look back on the landscape of *Oedipus*. You are right in it, and it is grand and uncanny. And those poor country people who were striken by the plague—working with distaffs and carrying clay jars—are still right there around you. They are nice, they are unusually courteous, but they are not at all "picturesque," and it seems just as natural to an American to be trying to do away with their diseases as if they were sufferers from hookworm in Georgia.

We looped at a terrific rate along what the *Guide Bleu* for Greece calls *"les lacets de la Voie Sacrée"*—which also presents itself not as an historical sight but as an unsatisfactory actuality, full of dangerous hairpin curves with no fences to stop cars going over the side, bone-rattlingly rocky with ruts and bumps, and sometimes gnawed away in great chunks by explosions of bombs and shells. Saturated with dust like old carpets and lame and stiff from the jeep, we stopped at a café for a drink. It was several degrees worse than the one at Thebes. The waiter, in honor of Americans, produced a long-unlaundered tablecloth, stained all over with soup, egg and wine, that was dirtier than the top of the table. We picked out, among the people there, the men who looked as if they must be politicos and tried to figure out which parties they belonged to. Eleni told us which papers they were reading. I had been playing a game in Europe of trying to guess from their accents where the Americans I encountered came from. I hesitated, for the U.N.R.R.A. worker, between Missouri and Texas, and told him this but said I had decided on Missouri. "No, sir," he said. "I was born in Texas, but I've been living in Missouri and I may have picked up the accent." I hoped that Eleni was impressed by my feat, but it turned out that her ideas about America were extremely generalized and vague. She had not been able to understand why the Texan and I spoke differently, and she didn't know what Texas was. "Texas is a state," he explained to her, "that's almost as big as the whole Balkans. It used to be a nation itself but we combined with the United States to help 'em against the British." This was not quite historically true, as Texas did not join the Union till almost the middle of the century, but it had perhaps a more general truth and may have reflected a preoccupation on the part of our companion, because he presently told me a story about a scandal in the American PX. In the earlier period in Athens, before there were any Americans, the British had put up a sign announcing that Canadians and Americans were excluded from buying at the British PX. Now that the American U.N.R.R.A. people and the airport personnel were there and the Americans had their own PX, the British had succeeded in obtaining something like fifty PX cards. They had been able to draw on these cards without revealing their nationality by having the supplies sent out to the airport; but the Americans had discovered this ruse and were calling in the cards. This U.N.R.R.A. man's family name was the same as that of a famous frontiersman, and I asked him whether he were any relation. It turned out that he was a direct descendant and had the famous man's first name, too.

Mount Parnassus and the Castalian spring, which we reached in the late afternoon, are gritty, gray and bleak affairs, quite unlike the poetical properties associated with their names; the great temple of the Delphic Apollo you cannot see at all from the road; and the town of Delphi, caught on this road like gobs of mutton on a shashlik skewer, has its center in a group of little inns, which have been turned into British billets and were crammed with soldiers off on holiday. Only the view below of the sweep of the Delphic valley, with its limitless olive orchard, made one expect some unimaginable mystery: all that the name of the oracle implies. No rooms, we thought, were fit for Eleni: the best thing that we could find was a primitive kind of closet, in a house full of British officers, that was imperfectly screened from the room next door to a partition that did not reach to the ceiling. So we drove on down to Itea on the water. The monotony of ruin in Europe becomes sickening and exasperating. Though one has already seen many such places, it comes as a shock to reach the Gulf of Corinth and find a quiet little seaside town in the same condition as Anzio and Naples. While the frontiersman went to see about lodgings, Eleni and I sat down on a bench and, fighting off the malarious mosquitoes, looked out across flat and dull water to where the hills, in the blue-gray air, were growing blurred like a Whistler nocturne, but more massive and more sullen. She had asked me whether Italy resembled Greece, and I tried to explain the difference. The Italian mountains were shaggy and the Italian country was planted. In Italy, there was too much color, too much flesh and too much smell, too many things sprouting and swarming; Greece was lean and bare but somehow on a higher plane. Yes, she said: it was just the difference between the Roman and the Greek Catholic Churches. The Roman Church proliferated madonnas and was preoccupied with sins and pardons, whereas the Greek Church went in for doctrine and tended to turn theology into metaphysics.

The U.N.R.R.A. man brought back a British officer: swarthy, with a dark cropped mustache, shoes and leather belt well-polished, and a smart lanyard, I think green, tucked into his left breast-pocket. His first name was Demetrius, as we saw from his trunk when he took us up to his room, and Eleni, who found that he did not speak Greek, thought that he had the look of an Egyptian; but he had mastered the British manner and practiced it with a consistency more relentless than the native English themselves. And he established the tone for our visit. He took us, with no comment whatever, through a small wooden door in a wall into a yard full of vegetables and chickens, where a mash made of tomatoes had been spread out to dry, and up a tiny outside flight of steps. Then, always with a dazed and indifferent air of not knowing whether he were going to do anything for us or whether we ought to be there at all, he produced a basin of water and—one cannot say that he showed or invited Eleni into a bedroom: she went in because it seemed the thing indicated. He left her with the curt injunction, "You carry on in there." He was depressing: this English world of the war, with its apparently impassive front which actually masked resentment and weariness, I had been glad to leave behind in London, where anyone of whom you asked a direction would tell you to turn to the right and "carry on from there." He continued to stand by detachedly while the U.N.R.R.A. man and I washed in the room across the hall. "How is it out here?" I asked. "Pretty boring?" "No: it's all right," he answered, and then, after a short pause, as if something more were demanded: "Most of the time is spent swimming." I had already had occasion to note this use of the impersonal passive as one of their curious ways—like the use of "one" where we should say "I"—of suppressing the first person. So you will find A. N. Whitehead, in a brief autobiographical sketch for a volume devoted to his work in the *Living Philosophers* series, writing, "In the autumn of 1885, the fellowship at Trinity was acquired, and with additional luck a teaching job was added. The final position as a senior lecturer was resigned in the year

1910. . . ." The trouble about this is that the effort at self-effacement is likely to become conspicuous and betray what the French call *la morgue anglaise,* of which, as a matter of fact, it is not really a corrective but a refinement. And the Lieutenant's next remark seemed to me also characteristic (you had a good deal of time to reflect, because the gaps between remarks were immense, and my commentary expands in proportion): "The works are over there, I believe"—nodding to a corner of the yard which had a primitive and precarious W.C. "I never use it myself." The natural thing to say, I thought later, would have been something like, "If you want to use the W.C., you'd better wait till we get to the mess. I don't recommend the one they've got here"; but, though really, I think, a very good fellow, he was dominated by the British principle that you should never do anything for anyone without indicating a slight hostility.

Later, on the way to the mess, he told us, as if to back up his assertion that the British were quite happy at Itea, that they had been up to all hours the night before, had marched around the town singing, and had finally ducked the "padre" in the water as well as all the top-ranking officers. Coming into the mess from the crumbled town and the dull and stuffy darkness was startling and disorienting: it was as if one had found, in a provincial town, an unexpectedly competent revival of some vivid old period piece. With their red faces, their bright silk lanyards, their batman standing mute like a butler and vanishing in obedience to orders given without raising the voice or looking in his direction, their gin-and-bitters and their bottles of wine, their miraculously complete dinner, the London *Times* and the *Evening Standard* lying on the table behind them—these Englishmen had made for themselves a snug and self-sufficient little world that seemed more obviously anachronistic—because it was self-consciously historical: that is, because it represented the role of a certain nation accomplishing certain things— than the life of the olive-growing and goat-herding Greeks who were still nearly contemporary with Homer. And we did not fit into that world. I was surprised when the American told me later that he had made several trips to Itea and had already met these men. I said that they had all behaved as if they had never seen him before. "Oh, they always do that," he replied, "but I just burst right in and start talking. They always treat me all right." But though blank silence does not matter with men, it seems schoolboyish or boorish with a woman—especially so pretty a woman as Eleni (she had changed into a blue dress), who spoke English perfectly and was obviously a lady. Nobody talked to her or gave her a look; they went on with their own conversation. Only the major who was the ranking officer in the absence of the real C.O. and who had to preside at dinner made an effort to show some polite interest. "Hot drive?" he inquired. Yes. "No top on the car, I suppose? . . . Then why haven't you got a big red beak like me?" One didn't know whether this was self-depreciation, implying an indirect compliment, or whether the implication was that she had no business to look all right when the damned sun of her native Greece had so grotesquely disfigured an Englishman. Yet he was evidently the nicest of the officers: tall and lank, with long straggling mustaches, and with a touch of the Victorian innocence of Major Dobbin or the White Knight.

But it was only a question of moments before, from another quarter, the inevitable British attack on the unacceptable foreigner began. The young officer on my left and just across the table from Eleni, on learning that she was an Athenian, immediately proceeded to tell her that Athens was "an awful place," and that the people there were lazy, untrustworthy, hard to get along with, inefficient and given to quarrelling among themselves. We Americans, I am sorry to say, allowed this rudeness to continue. We were a little in the situation that Hamburger had described to me from his trip to Trieste of being treated like captured enemies, and there was always the danger, between Americans and British, of exacerbated political argument. I had one at an Anglo-American party at the Grande Bretagne Hotel in Athens which culminated in my being asked by an aroused English correspondent what we Americans were doing "messing about in Europe." But the young man who did not like Athens would not let the subject drop and kept going on and on, while Eleni, who had not, I imagine, ever encountered anything like this before, colored and did not reply. He was finally broken up by the chaplain, a sandy-haired little man sitting on Eleni's right, who made some rapid comment in a voice so unassertive and low that I did not catch what he said. "Oh, the padre's off on one of his tirades!" the man sitting next to him said sharply. "Yes, we all know that England has its faults, too!" But now the presiding major felt that some sort of intervention was needed. "We have no manners at this end of the table," he said, with hardly a glance toward Eleni—putting an end to the unpleasant conversation but doing nothing to stimulate a better one.

Soon they were talking about water polo as if they had been dressing in a locker room. They had organized rival teams, which seemed to have become the chief interest of their exile. The U.N.R.R.A. man remarked that he understood that all the officers had been ducked the night before. "No officers were ducked," said Major Dobbin. "Only the padre and the doctor." (The doctor, it appeared, was Demetrius.) I asked the young man sitting next to me what else they did for amusement, and this

started a new complaint. The women made things awfully difficult, he said; you couldn't get a girl to come
anywhere near you unless she brought along her mother
and her father and her grandmother and her grandfather
and her aunt. "Our chaps are livid about it!" he ended.
There was, however, to be a dance that night—arranged
by a Red Cross worker to raise funds for a local hospital—
and they had thought up an ingenious device to detach
the Greek girls from their chaperones. The parents had
always made the girls sit down with them between
dances; but for tonight the frustrated British had had
built along one wall of the dance-hall a narrow forbidding
bench and had had lined up at the end of the room
several rows of more comfortable seats, and they were
going to try getting the girls to sit down with them on the
bench, where there was not room for many people and
where their families might not want to join them.

After dinner, when the table was cleared and we were
confronted by one another without the resource of food,
conversation broke down completely. It was difficult to
talk about England because the officers, apparently to a
man, were opposed to the Labour government; and it was
difficult to talk about Greece because you could not talk
about Greece without "talking politics." "No politics!" the
major would say as soon as anyone grazed the subject.
"Politics are taboo." Demetrius, with the requisite casual-
ness, asked the sanitary engineer about the American
public-health organization that he had worked for before
the war and wondered uninterestedly whether there were
anything like it in England. Apropos of raising money for
the hospital, he said that the medical situation was
wretched in that part of Greece, and that it was odd that
the local doctors had no confidence whatever in themselves and had the habit—though he'd only just been
registered—of coming to him about the simplest prob-

lems. Finally we went to the dance. It was well enough attended and there were people gazing in through the windows, but—partly as a result of the heat, which made everyone exude water like sponges—it was not an exhilarating affair. The Englishmen did induce some of the Greek girls to sit on the narrow bench, but when they had got them there, it was very uncomfortable and did not especially promote better acquaintance. The major asked Eleni to dance. Every time when at the end of one of the dance tunes another was immediately to follow, the bandleader—in a voice that took the heart out of you—would order the dancers to "carry on."

———

The next morning I went up to the temple. An English soldier drove me in a jeep. He maintained at first the same well-trained silence as the batman waiting on table—a silence which is a feature of their caste system but which always seems unnatural to an American. I asked him how it was out there. "Pretty dreadful!" he replied—he did not have to keep up face like Demetrius. It was impossible to get anywhere with the girls, he said; but he did not blame it all on their families. "They're scared to death," he explained, "to be seen talking to an English soldier." I sounded him out on the elections and found that he was all for Labour. "Before the war," he said, "the Conservatives didn't have a very good record, did they?"

I got at Delphi my first intimation of the almost complete class line-up, on the issue of the Churchill government, between the English officers and the English troops. I afterwards talked with a great many English and I found no English soldier who had not voted for Labour and only one officer who had. Class-consciousness in the United States is likely to be sporadic or local: you do not find any social split that runs through the whole people like a fissure; and I was surprised by the uniformity of the class feeling of the British Army and the sharpness with which it was expressed. I had not realized how much Winston Churchill and the War Minister, Sir James Grigg, were disliked by the English soldiers. I learned that there had been some rather scandalous incidents on the occasion of Churchill's appearances among the troops, and I asked one man why the soldiers were so bitter. "Why, Grigg's probably an able administrator, as far as winning the war goes," he said, "but neither he nor Churchill ever cared anything about the troops. They've always been treated like cattle, while the officers lived in luxury." He expressed himself very strongly on the subject of Churchill's cigar.

One factor in the situation which undoubtedly has been stimulating this sentiment on the part of the English troops is the contrast they have lately been making between the American soldiers and themselves. The Americans are better fed and they have more and better clothes. They are better taken care of. An officer who had been in Crete fixing up an old barracks for the American personnel of an airport told me that he was having an awful time because it was swarming with bedbugs and crab-lice, and they weren't sure that D.D.T. would kill those things. "The English," he said, "let their men be quartered in places like that. I've seen English soldiers living under conditions that would cause riots in the American Army. But *we* have to do something about it." The relations between officers and men are more democratic with us—and more democratic than they were in the last war. Saluting on the street, in Italy and Greece at least, has virtually disappeared. I heard complaints about arrogant officers, and Mauldin's observant cartoons are bitter about the officer who exploits his rank without taking its responsibilities. But such men are regarded as exceptional and their behavior as an obvious violation of the normal relations of life, whereas the whole technique of the Englishman in dealing with the men in his command is a traditional part of his system. Whether he is himself an insolent or an amiable man, his tone assumes class superiority. You see the whole situation in that British phrase "other ranks," which, to an American, seems queer and offensive. We talk about "officers," "noncoms" and "enlisted men"; they talk about "officers" and "other ranks." In Athens, you see, for example, a sign on an inferior night club allotting it to "Other Ranks"—as who should say, "This is the place for the nobodies."

What is most important of all, the American soldier is paid a great deal more than the British. This difference has evidently contributed to the extraordinary, the almost complete failure of the English and the American soldiers to establish any sort of relationship outside of their military duties. The Americans can buy more drinks, get themselves better girls and so forth, and this has made the English sulky. In general, they keep to themselves and have nothing to say to Americans. Once in Italy, when I had been visiting Herculaneum with a couple of G.I.'s and was separating from them to go back to Naples, one of them said to me, "There'll be plenty of trucks coming along this road, but don't bother with the British because they won't pick you up." When I asked him why not, he explained that they were like that. The Americans in the beginning had always picked up the British, but when the British wouldn't reciprocate, we stopped. I feel sure that the resentment or envy of the English troops toward the Americans backfired in the soldier vote.*

As for the officers, many, of course, are simply Tories with all the old ideas. There are a few of the younger

* See Appendix A.

men that do not belong to the upper classes and have not been assimilated to them who tell you stoutly that they are backing Labour. I met a few at Labour meetings in England and was impressed by their sober air of knowing what they were about and being determined to put it through. They had nothing in common with the atmosphere of the mess that I visited at Itea, and they probably represent an emerging and important element in the contemporary English world.

But there are other kinds of motivations than the old-fashioned imperialistic ones which impel certain British officers who may once have been liberals or socialists to support the imperialistic policy of the continued occupation of Italy and Greece. A major whom I met in Crete seemed to me an example of these. He was a remarkably able man, well-educated, serious and active. He had been working in the underground in Crete before the Germans left and was on excellent terms with the inhabitants. He spoke Greek, and he had somehow found time to study the Minoan ruins. All this he had accomplished since he came, in, I think, the last year of the war, and he had become, it seemed to me, the Britisher in Crete most respected by both Cretans and Americans. He took me one day to a modest but very clean and decent house where we were given little glasses of ouzo with bits of watermelon, and where he talked at some length with the Cretan family in his exact and fluent Greek. When we were left alone for a moment, he explained, with a shade of a smile, that "an unfortunate thing" had happened: a car had been stolen from outside the house while they were having a party there. I assumed that he had come as an official to investigate the theft of the car. When we got back into the jeep, we were accompanied by one of the men with whom he had been talking in the house. He explained that he was taking him somewhere, and he

drove him almost to the top of a hill, then dropped him
when the road got too bad. The man walked up to some
rudimentary houses that looked as if they were built of
clay and contained only two or three rooms. "He wanted
me to drive him all the way," the Major explained, when
we had turned around—with the usual faintly humorous
attitude toward the childishness of the native—"but I
didn't want to risk it any further." And he added, "People
who live in the town in rather a sophisticated way like that
usually come from houses like those." Then he said
something I did not understand, and I twice got him to
repeat a word. "Of the girl I'm going to marry," he said.
"He's the brother of my fiancée." The old couple we had
seen in the house were his prospective father- and mother-
in-law. I distinctly got the impression that, in marrying a
Cretan girl, he was settling down for a career in Crete.
The completeness of his acceptance of Crete and his
excellent relations with the inhabitants seemed to me at
first surprising for an English officer abroad; but I learned
later on that he was a Scotchman, which explained, I
dare say, his willingness to ally himself with people from
small houses. In Scotland, the serious world, the world of
authority and learning, may have the but-and-ben close
behind it. But he was typical of a whole group of officers
that I met in the Mediterranean who seemed to be
hoping to remain there as administrators. Conditions in
England, as they have heard or seen, are not now particularly inviting: inferior food and clothes, life hemmed in
by ration books, housing shortage, looming unemployment and a socialist Labour government which is not
likely to try to solve these problems by letting up on the
ration books. In Italy or in Greece, a British officer has
the best that can be had, and he occupies a position of
importance that he could hardly hope to find in England.
Some of the younger men, like Bob Leigh in Rome, have

spent five years in the Mediterranean immediately after
getting out of Oxford or Cambridge and are better fitted
for their present kind of work than they would be for
anything else. (With the Americans, it is just the opposite: they are worse off, instead of better, in Europe, and
practically all of them are frantic to get home.) As I say,
these men are not all Tories. When I asked the Cretan
major how he felt about the elections, he said, "It didn't
surprise me. If you followed the soldiers' discussion
groups, it was plain that the trend was that way. It's not
necessarily a bad thing. It will give them a chance to
show what they can do. They've been complaining about
the government. Now they'll have to take some responsibility." But such people as this excellent major cannot
afford to admit that these countries would be better off
left to themselves.

I went one day to the British Army headquarters
building in Athens to arrange transportation for a trip. I
was told to go to Room 47, but when I got there I found
the door locked. An English soldier stuck his head out of
the door of the next office, and I explained my situation.
"It's just down the corridor," he said, and, when I looked
a little astonished, he added, with an hilarious cheerfulness, "Yes: we'll inundate you with 'em! There's another
47!" I was so delighted by this—there is not much of Sam
Weller surviving in bombed and rationed England—that
I was still dwelling on it as I left the building. But as I
passed out into the street, I saw something that affected
me in a different way. There were two sentries guarding
the entrance, standing rigid, heads back, eyes front, legs
straddled apart and a rifle with a fixed bayonet gripped in
the right hand and held out straight from the body as if
by a marionette, with the butt planted on the pavement.

Whenever an officer went in or out, these sentries, instead of presenting arms, would convulsively lift the rifle butt and bring it down on the ground, at the same time stamping one foot—as if they had been mechanical contrivances controlled, like the doors at the Pennsylvania Station, by photoelectric cells. If you watched them, as I did, for a moment, the effect was absolutely gruesome. It reminded me of the goose-step. They changed the guard there, I learned, with great pomp, every Sunday morning, completely stopping traffic on the street, which is one of the most important in Athens. An American in U.N.R.R.A. told me that he had asked an English officer why they persisted in doing this. "We do it at Buckingham Palace," he answered. "But in London it doesn't tie up the traffic," the American pointed out. This made no impression on the Englishman. The truth is, of course, that, like the bayonets, this ceremony is intended to serve as a reminder and a threat to the Greeks. The mood of the good-humored fellow who talks about inundating the visitor with rooms numbered 47 makes no connection whatever with the automaton outside the door, nor have his feelings, his needs and his interests as yet been able to influence the latter's acts.

13

GREEK DIARY: COMMUNISTS, SOCIALISTS AND ROYALISTS

I HAD INTERVIEWS, in Athens, with two remarkable professors who have become political figures: George Georgalas and Alexander Svolos. Both are middle-aged men of top standing in their fields, and they are typical of the Greek intellectuals who have been driven by the needs of their country to take an active part in the E.A.M. movement, the National Liberation Front, which organized the resistance to the Germans and which controlled most of the countryside of Greece before the Papandreou government, an invention of the British, took over. They present the best possible proof that that movement has not been the exclusive creation either of professional agitators or of cutthroats from the mountains. Svolos, an authority on constitutional law, was the president and spokesman of E.A.M. through the period of crisis last winter; Georgalas, formerly the head of the government geological service, is now the director of E.P.O.N., the United Panhellenic Organization of Youth, which is the junior branch of E.A.M.

Georgalas I saw in his office, just off his geology classroom in the Polytechnic School. He showed me the statistics on Greek education with the enthusiasm and

energy of a man who was fighting for reforms that were
obviously needed and that inevitably had to come: the
rudiments of democratic training. The state of Greek
education seems really, to an American, incredible. The
figures for the school year 1937–38 show how bad the
situation was before the general wreck brought by the
war. At the beginning of that year, out of a population of
7,500,000, there were 987,000 children attending the
primary schools, and before the year was done, 80,000
had dropped out. Of 231,000 children who had entered
the first grade in these schools, only 82,000 were surviving in the sixth grade, so that only about a third of the
ordinary Greeks (who did not go to private schools) even
completed a primary education. The teaching, too, was
quite inadequate: one teacher had sometimes a hundred
pupils. In 1937, 3,700 villages had no school of any kind.
In the same year there were graduated from the high
schools only 94,920 students. Of these high schools there
were five hundred to educate the less than nine per cent
of the population who practiced the liberal professions,
and only two to give agricultural training to the more
than fifty-eight per cent engaged in agriculture. The
education in the high schools was mainly based on the
reading of the ancient Greek authors in a purely philo-
logical way and the study of the physical sciences in a
purely theoretical way and with no direct contact with
nature. "Here you Americans," Georgalas said, "are in-
venting an atomic bomb, while our physicists in Greece
have hardly come to grips with any practical problem!"
Among the graduates of the two universities, Athens and
Salonika, in 1937–38, forty-five per cent had become
lawyers, thirty-three per cent doctors, seven per cent
philologists, five per cent chemists, and of the remaining
ten per cent, eight per cent had gone in for the physical
sciences. The men from these schools and colleges that

equipped them with a classical education did not want to return to the towns: they almost invariably remained in Athens to find or look for government jobs and become "parasites on the bourgeoisie." There had in 1937–38 been 11,140 graduates of the regular universities, while at the two small agricultural schools nineteen students had been graduated, of whom only two were of working-class origin. The principal school of agriculture, founded in 1920, had been closed in 1939 by the dictator Metaxas and its faculty obliged to become part of the University of Salonika, where they had been working ever since with no laboratories.

What E.A.M. was aiming at was to provide instruction in agricultural chemistry and other technical subjects which would make it possible for the peasants to develop their barren country and raise their meager standard of living. The reactionaries had never wanted this, because they did not want the common people strengthened. There would be no real education in Greece till the monarchists were removed from power.

E.P.O.N. itself, he told me, had taken in children under fourteen from all sorts of political backgrounds, and had once had five hundred thousand members. It had organized two hundred stations, where the children were fed and given playgrounds; but all this work had been undone when E.A.M. had been outlawed by the British and its public activities stopped.

———

With Svolos I talked mainly about politics, and I put to him certain questions the answers to which I thought he must know. I had in my mind a fairly clear version of the incidents that had led up to the civil war. The British, in their anxiety to bring back the King and to defeat the activities of the Communists, had been alarmed by the Left tendencies of E.A.M. and by the formidable proportions it was reaching, and they had attempted to disarm E.L.A.S., its army. They had announced that they were disarming all units, of the Right as well as of the Left, in order to create a true national army; but when E.L.A.S. in good faith had laid down its arms, the royalist troops—the Mountain Brigade and the Sacred Battalion—were allowed to retain theirs. On December 3 of last year, E.A.M. held a demonstration in Constitution Square in Athens to protest against the policy of the British. They were unarmed, and many of the women had brought their small children. The British had given a permit for this meeting, but they had revoked it at three o'clock that morning in such a way that it had been impossible to call off the demonstration. I have heard the most contradictory possible accounts of how the trouble started. Having the women and children march first, as was done on this occasion, is a familiar Communist trick which makes it more difficult to use violent methods in breaking up a procession but which invites worse consequences if this occurs. The royalists, in any case, claimed that the crowd were trying to rush the guard at the government's headquarters in the Grande Bretagne Hotel. There seems, however, to be no question that the majority of the demonstrators went on quietly marching while the royalist police fired into them and killed and wounded about a hundred people. Funerals were held the next day, and a procession passed through the streets. The royalists fired on the procession from the windows of hotels and killed or wounded between a hundred and fifty and two hundred.

I asked Svolos now whether it were true, as had been said and as might seem to be indicated by the British revocation of the permit at that impossible time of night, that the whole thing had been a British provocation

intended to provide them with a pretext for crushing
E.A.M. before it grew stronger. He answered that he did
not necessarily believe that the British role in the drama
had been so simple or so conscious as this. They had
perhaps not provoked the insurrection that followed these
attacks by the royalists, but they "had not been sorry" to
have it happen. It was an example of the familiar British
practice of half-allowing, half-stimulating actions which,
though carried out by other people, would be advan-
tageous to British interests. He said that the responsibility
had to be shared, in various proportions, by the royalists,
the British and the Communists. Was it true, as I had
been told by an American who had seen something of
what was happening, that at the time of the Lebanon
conference of May, 1944, which was stage-managed by
the British, Svolos had wired to E.A.M. for advice as to
how to proceed in regard to a proposed program for a
"government of National Unity," and E.A.M. had directed him to make certain reservations, but the tele-
graphed answer from E.A.M. had been suppressed by the
British Ambassador? He replied that it was impossible to
say that the telegram had been suppressed but that it had
certainly been sent and had never arrived. Was the
impression I had correct that, at the time of the crisis
last winter, the Greek Communists in E.A.M. had been
acting without the approval or knowledge of Moscow—
Stalin perhaps, at Yalta, in return for a free hand elsewhere, having agreed not to interfere with the British in
the Mediterranean? Svolos said that he believed this to be
true—that the Greek Communists had at that time sent a
delegate to Russia but that Moscow had refused to see
him and dispatched him straight back to Athens, and that
at no time during this period had the Moscow radio made
any mention of what was going on in Greece. I asked him
about the atrocities alleged to have been committed by

E.A.M.—mass executions of civilians murdered with axes and knives, men and women hostages marched barefoot for days in the snow till many had died of exhaustion—of which so much was made by Ambassador Leeper in his reports to Anthony Eden. Svolos did not deny that such things had happened, but said that they were not, as had been declared, mere outrages by ruffians from the mountains but a part of a long and bitter history of private revenges and political reprisals that had begun under the Metaxas regime and gone on through the German occupation, during both of which periods the Greek Fascists had been committing most of the atrocities. After the liberation, the British, who controlled the news from Greece, had succeeded in forestalling or suppressing reports of what the reactionaries were doing to the liberals. At present, as everybody knew, the jails were full of political prisoners, and every day the agents of the government were arresting more people without warrant, shooting them and beating them up on the street and torturing them to extort information. He was worried by Bevin's speech on British policy, which had been delivered the day before. They had been hoping for an amnesty, but now Bevin, it seemed, had announced that this might be difficult, since, according to him, there were "violent criminals" mixed up with the political prisoners, and there was a problem of sorting these out.

I asked Svolos what sort of following he thought E.A.M. could now command if it were free to function politically. It seemed to be generally admitted that at the time of the civil war it had been backed by about eighty per cent of the Greeks. He replied that, since the suppression of the uprising, the Socialists had detached themselves from E.A.M., but that the Socialists and the Communists between them could still, he thought, command a following of seventy-five per cent of the people.

And he pointed out that when these Left elements asked
the British to allow the Greeks to form what was described as "a representative government," they had proposed a combination which did not at all reflect these
proportions but gave undue importance to the Right—the
formula being one third royalist, one third democratic and
center, and only one third Socialists and Communists.

I asked him why he had split with the Communists.
Because their methods were so unscrupulous, he said. No
non-Communist could get on with people who made a
practice of double-dealing; nor could they accomplish
their own aims in that way. He himself had always been
a Socialist—he had been removed by Metaxas from his
university chair; and now, dissociating himself from
E.A.M., he had organized last April a new Socialist Party
by the fusion of three other parties. Georgalas, he told
me, belonged to a small Socialist group which was still a
part of E.A.M. and which he believed to consist of
camouflaged Communists. During my interview with
Georgalas, I had had a very definite impression that I was
talking to a convinced fellow-traveller, and I was interested by Svolos' confirmation. I tried later to put my
finger on the symptoms which had made me feel this. It
seemed to me that I was able to identify them in the
special kind of cheerfulness and certainty with which he
rose to meet every problem. The middle-class C.P. member or sympathizer is transported into a kind of sub-
stratosphere, where, like the aviator who flies too high,
he falls victim to a treacherous euphoria. There is no
question in his mind that he has picked the winning side
and is about to cash in on the stakes, and he does not
need to argue about it any more than a Rosicrucian is
obliged to defend his esoteric doctrine. Georgalas, no
doubt by temperament a sanguine and self-confident man,
had, I felt, succumbed a little to that mood of Communist

blitheness which is not entirely reassuring. He had talked
to me at length and with feeling about the soul-destroying
pedantry with which the ancient Greek authors were
taught: "Why we love Homer and Sophocles," he said,
"they would never find out from their teachers! A little
niece of mine was terribly proud because she had learned
a verb-form which only occurs about once in the whole of
Greek literature and which, as I told her, I had taught
Greek for years without ever knowing about. But that
was what our education aimed at!" I demurred that this
might not be entirely the fault of the reactionary powers
in Greece, that, even in democratic America, Shakespeare
was often taught in that way—that this was a tendency of
the academic profession at all times and everywhere. But
he smilingly shook his head, brushed my interruption off
and went on; and it seemed to me that, in his Marxist
optimism, he was sure that these stupidities would disappear so soon as the Communists should come to power.
This attitude, I think, dates from Lenin, whose certainty
about social developments and conviction of the rightness
of his purpose gave him a kind of ironical good humor
which some people found uncomfortable and which, in
spite of his element of utopianism, had a relation to bitter
realities. It is curious to see in such followers, as in the
sects founded by certain saints, how the faith of a man of
genius, which has first appeared as a natural force,
communicates itself to his progeny as a mere drug that
shields them from experience and enables them to disregard common sense.

With Svolos it was quite different. You could talk to
him as to anyone else. He lived in the same world that I
did, where there were difficulties, doubts, confused issues,
conflicts between expediency and principle. He reminded
me a little of Silone, engaged in a similar task: the
attempt to create, out of the Socialist tradition and the

survivors from the old Socialist groups, a movement that would be tough enough to stand up to the Russians and avert the kind of paralyzing dictatorship which Russian Communism has everywhere brought with it. Such people are anxious and intent; they are never unnaturally cheerful. Just before I had left Rome in July, while the Socialist Congress was going on, I had run into Silone in the street, and he had told me, excited and beaming, that he believed the pro-Stalinist Socialists were certain to be outvoted on the issue of a merger with the Communists. But this was the only occasion on which I had seen Silone look happy.

(Since I wrote this, I have sometimes been taxed with having accepted too readily in Greece the statements of the agents and adherents of E.A.M. I do not doubt that revolting barbarities were committed on the E.A.M. side or that the Stalinists, to the best of their opportunity, carried on their usual practice of murdering and imprisoning Leftists who differed from them on questions of policy. But it was not, so far as I could learn, at that time really a question of choosing between the Soviet domination and the domination of Downing Street. The E.A.M. movement might, I should think, have been detached from the Communist influence—since the Communists, though, of course, very active, were not numerically important—if the British had supported it instead of suppressing it. The Greeks, unlike the Russians, are naturally independent and, what with Metaxas and the Nazis, they had just had a good dose of dictatorship. The radical leaders in Greece were, for the most part, I believe, sincere Socialists, full of ardor for a national new deal. Even the Communists, as in Northern Italy, seemed idealists who still thought that the Kremlin was the carrier of the banner of Lenin. If England had been at all serious in regard to the Four Freedoms of the Atlantic

Charter, she would have helped the leaders of E.A.M. to detach themselves from the Soviet entanglement and keep in order those wilder elements whose fierceness, in the days of the Resistance, the British had been only too glad to abet. But that would have meant on the part of the Greeks, as any advance in Europe must mean, definite steps in the direction of socialism, and such steps were the last thing that Churchill had any desire to back. Nor is it easy to imagine that the United States, with our present administration, will be much more intelligent in Greece.)*

———

When I returned from our U.N.R.R.A. trip to Delphi, I saw something of Eleni and her family. They belonged to the well-to-do Greek bourgeoisie—that is, they had once been well-to-do, for few people in Greece have much money or can buy much with what they have. The V.'s lived in a well-furnished apartment on the Odos Vasilissis Sophias, among the palaces, the fine houses and the embassies of the fashionable quarter of Athens; but three generations and two branches of the family had been obliged to share half a dozen rooms, so that their life was rather hampered and constricted. There were Eleni and her husband, their two children, her mother-in-law, her brother-in-law and her brother-in-law's wife. And they got water only, I think, twice a week and had to save it in buckets and heat it themselves.

Yet this was, for them, a period of relative security. Eleni's husband had worked against the Germans and had had to escape to Egypt, and Eleni had had to spend a couple of years alone with the children in Athens. Their persistence through it all in the habits and the attitudes of comfortable people made rather an odd impression—espe-

* See Appendix B.

cially when one remembered how completely they had been cut off from the rest of their kind in Europe. It was as if they had preserved in a vacuum an abstraction of the bourgeoisie, an essence which had never been troubled by the social upheavals going on in the world or by the ordeals of their native country. Their culture was at least as much French as Greek. Eleni's husband had studied law in Paris, and Eleni spoke French with her children. Her mother and her stepfather, whom I met there one day, also spoke French, they told me, even between themselves. But the effect was not to place the V.'s in a larger international world: it was rather to make the French language seem like something non-conductive and insipid, a medium of intercourse which did not imply any real relation either with actual present-day Athens or with present-day distant Paris.

On the occasion of one of my calls, I found Eleni's mother-in-law reading an old back number of *Les Œuvres Libres,* and she explained that they had not been able, in Greece, to get any new French books since before the war. I walked up to the large glass-doored bookcase and looked in at the paper-backs, which seemed to exhale a peculiar staleness. They were the biographies, the novels and the poetry, including much that was second-rate, of the early nineteen-hundreds and the twenties. I had already been conscious in Italy of the extent to which the war and Fascism had kept the Italians behind the times; but there the crop of brilliant paper covers that had come out last spring, like flowers, in the shop windows and the sidewalk newsstands had been rapidly making up for this. In Greece there was no similar revival. To go into Kauffman's bookstore, the headquarters for foreign books, was almost like exploring an attic; and in Eleutherou-dakis', the Athenian Brentano's, you were shocked to see how rare and how precious modern books on technical subjects, such as medicine and engineering, had become. A look into the V.'s bookcase was a contact, from which one drew back, with a cultural day-before-yesterday that was somehow still a part of the present world. And near the bookcase hung a small oil-painting which seemed to me in key with the books, for it depicted, not a person or a landscape, but what appeared to be a room in a museum—perhaps one of the great chambers of the Vatican—with indistinct paintings on the walls and something in a case that one could not see. It was, I thought, characteristic of the household. Eleni's husband knew an extraordinary amount about an extraordinary variety of things—the history and culture of Greece and European philosophy and music, as well as his profession of law—and wrote more or less on all these subjects; but his opinions (I do not say it invidiously of so agreeable and learned a man) made sometimes as dry eating as must have been the legendary steaks supposed to have been cut by the Russians from the mammoth found frozen in Siberia. He was a royalist, and, as with all such people whose position had been thus reduced, I could not but feel that his politics were founded—however subtly he might justify them—on an identification of his remnants of property and of the social prestige he enjoyed with the cultural interests and intellectual standards which were unquestionably what he most valued. Nor do I mean to sneer at this. How many similar people in the United States, deprived of social standing and financial independence—which is what the Greek bourgeoisie seem menaced with as no group in America is—could be sure of being strong enough to uphold or defend the ideals which they have been taught to admire?

Eleni, who was younger than her husband, did not, I thought, though loyal to Church and King, quite follow all the bourgeois prejudices, for she told us that some friend of hers was taking her to meet the Soviet Ambassador. She had the special sort of elegance and fineness that is not monied or aristocratic in the usual European sense but a part of some old kind of nobility, at once primitive and civilized, that still thrives in the Greek islands. I used to go swimming with them in the afternoons, and it depressed me to contrast with the beach reserved for the military Americans the "plage" at Gliphada, which had once, I was told, been the gayest and smartest of Athens. We U.N.R.R.A. men and soldiers on leave and engineers and war correspondents had a fine row of clean little houses that seemed to have been newly built, with various kinds of service, such as a woman who splashed you with water to wash the sand off your feet and a bar where they opened your PX beer and supplied you with glasses to drink it. But at Gliphada the old casino had been completely dismantled by the Germans, and there was nothing but a sordid little place where you had to take turns in the bathhouses, rather sickening with the smell of the muddy sand with which the floors were caked and of the fish which was always being fried right next to the wet bathing suits. Eleni, against this background, in a faded pink bathing costume that brought out the tan of her arms and legs and showed her slender and sinuous body, all the more attracted one's attention by her naturalness and poise and grace; and two glimpses of her still stay in my mind as if I had brought them home engraved on Minoan seals: one of her figure going quickly up the stairs, obliquely so that I saw her in profile, pressing firmly but lightly on each of the steps with her rather long feet, showing none of the self-consciousness or vanity of a pretty woman at the beach; and the other of her standing in the water and playing with her little girl, smiling so that she made her eyes slits as she splashed with her palm tipped back at the wrist, at every splash thrusting her face forward and hissing, as if she had been some elemental creature—some siren that resembled a water snake. When I asked her what part she was playing, she answered that it wasn't anything.

———

The V.'s invited me to dinner one evening to celebrate Eleni's birthday. It was then that I met her mother and her stepfather, and I was amazed at her mother's youth, as I had been when I discovered that Eleni had children of ten and thirteen. Eleni had been married at sixteen, and her mother when she was not much older. The stepfather was very cosmopolitan and apologized with dignity for the Greeks: they had recently been led to misbehave themselves by certain lawless and alien elements, and it was regrettable that this should have given the world a poor opinion of them. We went for dinner to one of the very best night clubs: a place such as, for gaiety and glamor, I had not seen, since the war, in Europe. It was also the first full-length meal under completely clean and attractive conditions that I had had since I had been in Greece, and for the V.'s, I think, also it was something of a treat. You got just the same dishes as elsewhere: sliced tomatoes, rice pilaff and fish, but you got enough instead of too little. The place was full of well-groomed British officers with Athenian "society" girls, some of them very pretty with their blond hair in two rolls over their temples so that their faces looked like valentines. Eleni and her mother enjoyed themselves recognizing people and gossiping about them. Some of these Greek girls, they told me, were engaged to English officers.

There was with us, also, a youngish journalist who wrote for a royalist paper: he was a tall slim man of the world, very lively and rather dapper, with mustaches in the style of George II—as Eleni said to me later, "always perfectly delighted with himself." He was an old friend of Eleni's husband, who loved to talk politics with him. I had the impression that the combinations and projects which these two were always discussing were among the least realistic of the many schools of café-table politics with which Athens so abounds; but it had to be admitted this evening that their hopes, from an unexpected quarter, were finding the most heartening encouragement. The journalist had just heard over the radio the news of Bevin's speech on British foreign policy, and he relayed it to us with unrestrained glee and much gloating over the chagrin of the Left: "He said that the Labour government would continue to follow the policy that England had already supported, that they could see no good reason for a change in Greece before the Greek elections took place, and that they would make every effort in the meantime to see that law and order were preserved—that they would send a police mission." And he described to us a visit to England, from which he had just returned. He had been gratified unspeakably, at a party, to see a fashionable English lady recognize, by a glance at his insignia, a fellow Greek who was present as an officer of the Greek Air Force. And he went on to tell us a story about another London party, at which he had had *un succès foudroyant avec trois compliments—trois seulement, mais très méditerranéens.* The first compliment I cannot remember, but the second had been detonated at the time when they were playing a game of "What famous person would you most like to be?" The lady whom he hoped to impress had, in his turn, put this question to him, and he had answered, *"La ville de Hiroshima." " 'Pourquoi?' J'ai répondu, 'Je voudrais être la ville de Hiroshima, si vous étiez la bombe atomique pour me tomber dessus!'"* She had later returned and asked, smiling, "*Dîtes-moi, qu'est-ce que vous voudriez être encore?*" "*Cette fois je lui ai répondu—toujours très méditerranéen: 'Je voudrais être une cigarette.' 'Pourquoi?' 'Pour brûler entre vos lèvres!' Le prochain après-midi, à cinq heures, elle m'a téléphoné,*" etc.*

The floor-show seemed to me positively marvellous. I had forgotten how good such things could be, had hardly realized they were still going on. There were a girl who did an Oriental tumbling dance; a girl who sang in Greek and English; a couple who did a folk dance from one of the islands, fresh and animated and gone in a flash; and the great feature: a famous woman dancer who was also a romantic legend. I learned about her from Eleni and her mother. The Germans had had her on the carpet, the elder but far-from-old lady explained to me, for her well-known association with the English. But she had stood up to them with perfect sang-froid: "*Que j'aurais eu un amant anglais—même deux, trois, quatre,*" she was supposed to have replied, "*qu'est-ce que ça fait?*" She had had German lovers, too, Eleni thought; she had run through all the nationalities and always remained herself—and Eleni added with admiration: "*Elle ment avec une facilité inouïe.*" I saw that the myth of this performer, the great dancer who is also a great courtesan, had come to mean a good deal in Athens, which had been so much without the luxuries and so much at the mercy of the war. She was the devotee of art and love who had endured through all the hardship and conflict, and she was almost a sacred figure.

And she *was* extremely good: very beautiful, quick, sure and dashing, and able to get into everything she did a personality of enchanting insolence. Before one knew it, she would have leapt on a chair and would be bending

* See Appendix C.

down and kissing one of the diners, and then would hit him over the head with her tambourine. I had avoided such black-market places, but I succumbed to the brilliance of this night club, and, since I had been there without my long-distance glasses and since we had been sitting in a corner to the rear of the show, I decided to go again and see better. I got up another party the very next night with a man I knew in U.N.R.R.A. and two of the U.N.R.R.A. girls, and this time we had an excellent table in the middle and on the edge of the floor. The girls, who had been there before, said we were right in the spot to be kissed. This time some of the acts, seen distinctly, turned out rather disappointing; but the star dancer continued to be fascinating. Her first appearance was a ballroom number, which had its climax in a piece of business—an ecstatic start and smile as her partner, kneeling, kissed her midriff—that, for daring, style, naturalness and timing, took your breath away. When she came out for the second time, she seemed to be some sort of priestess or idol—possibly Javanese; and, exhilarated as I was by the wine—well-cooled and non-resinated—I was preparing to fall under her spell when she abruptly disappeared from the stage. The music went on playing, but she did not return. "Did you see what happened then?" the U.N.R.R.A. man asked the girls. "Yes: the thing that held her dress behind broke." "Somebody's catching hell back there!" he said.

This was two evenings before I left Athens, and the image was to remain in my mind as my last memory, and something of a symbol, of the world of the Greek bourgeoisie.

14

GREEK DIARY: VIEWS OF BULL-HEADED CRETE

THERE IS AN AREA just outside Heracleion, the principal
town of Crete, which is strewn for a mile or more with
the twisted and rusty shreds from what must have been
some gigantic explosion. I did not find out what had
happened there. This debris may be part of the remains
of the German ammunition ship which the British blew
up in the harbor. So many things have been blown up in
Crete that you come to take wreckage for granted; and,
for that reason, when I look back on the island, this waste
always recurs to my mind. It is a place which has been
blasted to bits, where people are hardly yet rebuilding but
only beginning to pick things up.

When, in the spring of 1941, the Greek and British
forces were driven out of Greece proper by the Germans,
the latter landed their parachutists in Crete and encountered on the part of the inhabitants a terrific and
unexpected resistance. The Cretans have an ancient tradition of pugnacity and independence. In almost every
epoch of their history, the history of their last three
thousand years, they have had to stand up to invaders: in
succession, the Achæans, the Romans, the Saracens,
the Venetians and the Turks. And they did not hesitate

for a moment, imperfectly equipped though they were, determinedly to attack the Germans. They fought so courageously that they enabled the British to get half their troops away and compelled the Germans to maintain in Crete a relatively enormous garrison of sixty thousand men. The result was a series of reprisals designed finally to crush the Cretans. The Scotch major, who had worked on the island as a secret liaison man, described to me the Nazi method as he had watched it, in hiding, from the hills. The Germans would come into a village at four o'clock in the morning and round up all the people in the public square. Then they would sort out and shoot all the men who seemed capable of bearing arms, give the old people, the women and the children an hour to get away with their animals, and, at the end of that time, one by one, blow up every building in the town. They thus wiped out some sixty villages, and in certain cases they killed the animals, chopped down the olive groves for fuel and took away the fishing boats. They kept the people in extreme poverty by making them exchange at a ruinous rate—demanding the better part of their orange crops in return for a little oil; and, by these means and by cutting Crete off from traffic with the rest of the world, they destroyed the economy of the island, which had lived mainly on its export trade. Out of a population of four hundred and fifty thousand, the Cretans, through the fighting and reprisals, lost something like ten thousand men. In spite of all this, one region boasts that, never subdued by previous aggressors, it succeeded in keeping the Germans at bay. An indomitable Cretan woman, who had become one of the leaders of the resistance and who had been taken by the Germans to Athens in an attempt to make her work for their interests, replied, when they told her they were doing her an honor, that no one could honor a Cretan. When finally, at the end of the war, some twelve thousand Germans were trapped in Crete and set to work digging up mines, the Cretans, in acts of revenge, shot down so many of them that the British took the Germans off this job and allowed them to keep their arms, and later on shipped them to Egypt.

A trip through Crete, as the result of all this, never ceases to be the tour of a battlefield. The sights that are pointed out are razed villages, of which the gray stone walls have relapsed into the gray stony mountainside till they are almost indistinguishable from it; a valley across which the Germans and English fought one of their stiffest battles; a pastoral little white house to which all the ablest men in Heracleion, the officials, the lawyers and the doctors, were brought by the Germans and in which they were shot. The drives that one takes through Crete—there has never been a railroad on the island—contribute to the impression of disorder and disaster. A native driver handles a car with all the superb Cretan carelessness of danger: he will skid around terrible curves on a narrow strip of road that borders a precipice, while you alternate nervously between watching to see whether he will turn sharply enough and gazing off into giddy seascapes, ruggedly framed and of dazzling blue, where the mountain drops away below; and he will suddenly pull up short right on the brink of a broken-off bridge to swerve aside down a steep rocky path and make the crossing on a few wooden boards hardly wide enough to accommodate the car. The jeeps are always spinning off these roads; one of the chief events during my visit was an accident in which an U.N.R.R.A. man had his nose squashed sideways on his cheek. And you move, almost everywhere along the coast, in an atmosphere of scattered explosives which keeps everybody slightly keyed up. The beaches and the water inshore are still studded with hundreds of mines, and when you swim in the small sections that are supposed to have been cleared, you pick your way among air bombs and unburied mines scattered about the sand. The Cretans are not afraid of these devils and, in fact, it seems, have some sort of taste for them. The children get hold of bits of cordite and set them off about the streets like firecrackers; the men and boys who go hunting for mines, being unequipped with mine-detectors, persist—to the dismay of the Americans and British—in practicing an intrepid technique of simply beating the ground with long sticks: if they hit something hard, they investigate; if the mine goes off, so much the worse. One man, on the outskirts of Heracleion, had surrounded his house with a fence built entirely out of very large-sized air bombs, which he has planted on their sharp ends and bound together with wire. The British commander in Crete, hearing about this barricade, decided he had better look into the matter and discovered that, with the hot August weather, the bombs had begun to "bleed"—that is, that the chemicals inside had begun to leak out through the shells—so that he could not have the fence removed: the bombs were dangerous even to touch. In the towns, the mornings of boiling heat and the benumbing muted noons were punctuated, from time to time, by casual booms and bangs to which nobody paid any attention.

———

There are no hotels open in Crete. You read in the pre-war guidebook about comfortable accommodations afforded by the Hotel Minos, and then find the sign of the Minos hanging on a gutted wreck. At Heracleion and at Canea, I was put up by the U.N.R.R.A. people. I owe the U.N.R.R.A. workers a debt for their kindness both in Greece and in Italy, and it is appropriate to pay them a tribute here, as they are nowhere seen to better advantage than in their efforts to do something for Crete. They have everywhere the same complaints: that they do not get enough supplies (though Greece is better provided than Italy) and that their organization is a bureaucratic nightmare. It is depressing to see offices full of capable personnel in one of the larger cities supervising a trickle of food, inadequate and intermittent, to a great hinterland of ruined towns; or trained sanitary engineers visiting Littoria or the Gulf of Corinth only to find that the sprayers haven't come, and restricted to inspecting the malarial mosquitoes, establishing the fact that they are present in hordes and going away again. But it is unexpectedly cheerful in Europe to find representatives of the various Allies collaborating in some sort of attempt to get normal life started again. In an American army mess-room, everybody is disgusted with Europe and talks of nothing but going home. But the U.N.R.R.A. people in a place like Crete have really had to settle down to local conditions and problems, and make themselves an existence there. There are places where the professional social worker, with the social worker's special incapacity for coming to grips with human beings, exercises his dampening effect; but the U.N.R.R.A. house in which I stayed at Canea was presided over by a Connecticut Yankee and his Middle Western wife, who spread good will and inspired confidence. In visiting various centers, I was struck by the differences in tone and morale created by the ranking officials. And this was one of the good Allied spots, where the Americans and the British got on together and where both respected the natives. Yet the U.N.R.R.A. worker never, at best, knows quite what he is doing in Europe. Will he ever get more supplies? Will U.N.R.R.A. simply fade away? Will it somehow be used as an instrument to further somebody's political designs? Is it already being so used? The field workers for U.N.R.R.A. themselves are instructed to be scrupulously impartial, to keep clear of local politics. In Crete they are surrounded by the tensions of quarrels in which they cannot intervene and which they do not always understand. It is typical of the situation that, a night or two before I arrived, the U.N.R.R.A. people in Canea should have been waked up by the sound of someone's being pursued and beaten up in the street right outside their headquarters, but should never have inquired what was going on. And the fundamental question always looms whether it is possible, in the world today, for a genuinely non-political organization to obtain from national governments any very large amount of money for disinterested international aid.

———

One day in Canea, in the afternoon hour when attempting to do anything whatever becomes a plowing through sand, I lay down with a book I had picked up: a paper-backed copy of the text of *Arsenic and Old Lace*. I had never gone to see this play, about which I had heard so much that I had thought I should not enjoy it. But I found that it read very well, and late that night, when I got back from an evening at the two local restaurants with music, where the foreigners did their best to generate a little gaiety, I sat up and finished the book, and, stimulated by a good deal of retsina, was visited by a revelation of the true meaning of this sinister farce. It was—I saw it quite plainly—a fable about the war. Germany appeared in it as Jonathan, the fiendish homicidal maniac, who has a demoralized man of science to work for him. The two genteel old ladies, who are roused to compete with their nephew—having themselves put away, for their own good, a few old men, whose corpses they keep in the cellar—are England and the United States (the atomic bombs had just been dropped). The policeman who wants to write plays and talks of nothing but his banal plots, while the actual crimes going on under his nose are more sensational than anything he has been able to invent, is contemporary literature, which is incapable of catching up with reality. And the other insane brother, who thinks that he is Teddy Roosevelt, unconscious of the abysses of evil beneath him and always gallantly rushing upstairs under the impression that he is charging at San Juan Hill, represents, of course, Winston Churchill.

I do not seriously mean to suggest that all this was really intended by the authors of *Arsenic and Old Lace*, but I am sure that this curious piece—like the production of *The Duchess of Malfi* in London and like the Britten opera, *Peter Grimes*—is a work characteristic of our time which could never have become popular, which would not have been imagined, at any other time. It is the kind of thing that makes life easier by giving expression to importunate feelings which officially we cannot admit. The war was over; our side had won. One could afford to see the whole thing now as a fantasy of crime and horror on which a curtain must finally fall. Here in Crete, where the atmosphere is still one of fury, the landscape still scarred and disfigured, my only impression that night was of a vengeful and demented humanity tearing itself to pieces.

———

My identification of Churchill with mad Teddy Brewster may shock the American reader. I learned later from an article by Rebecca West that Churchill's defeat by Labour had brought him a lot of letters from the United States expressing extreme surprise. She explains that this unpopularity is due, in impoverished England, to the survival in Churchill of an insolence toward the people which is inseparable from the point of view of a well-to-do Edwardian aristocrat, and to the impracticability at the present time of a Prime Minister whose domestic policy is entirely directed to perpetuating the privileges of his class. This is no doubt correct, but I believe there is another element in the eclipse of Churchill in England when he continues to arouse enthusiasm in America. Winston Churchill is half an American, and, though he has often been praised for his revival of the glories of English parliamentary oratory and for his grasp of the great tradition of English history, the truth is that his vision and his eloquence have been both, to a considerable degree, the qualities of a romantic American journalist in love with the achievements of England and with no very realistic sense of what they amount to or what they involve. He has always lived more or less in an historical novel for boys just as Theodore Roosevelt did. There was a moment when this melodrama of history coincided with current events, and then Churchill, of course, was superb. Unlike the typical modern politician, he had courage, he was completely incorruptible and he saw politics as a part of something, melodramatic though that was, larger and nobler than the sequence of expedients of the contemporary political careerist. But, for homeless and foodless Europe, already half-socialized and driven in the direction of equality and international federation, Winston Churchill's old Henty story, once the Germans have been definitely beaten, appears suddenly the flimsiest of legends. This was especially striking in England when I was there just before the elections: one never found an intelligent person who trusted Churchill to handle post-war conditions. The reversal of feeling toward him has been one of the most curious examples of that law of historical relativity of which Michelet made so much: the man who has functioned effectively and brilliantly in one set of social-political conditions loses his value overnight in another.

I heard several amusing anecdotes which illustrated

Churchill's tendency to conceive the modern world in terms of an old-fashioned novel, and I may well include them here in connection with Greece, which has suffered so from Churchill's policy. Young Leigh, whom I knew in Rome, had a story about a visit that Churchill had once paid to his mess. "How many Germans have you shot with that?" the Prime Minister had asked in his gruff mumbling voice, nodding toward Leigh's pistol. The latter, who had been in France and through some of the worst of the fighting, replied that he had never shot a German, that he had hardly even seen one; that, under modern conditions of warfare, you only rarely met the enemy at close range. But Churchill rumbled on: "I shot a man with one of those at Omdurman, and I should think it would take you too long to get your pistol out of that holster." Leigh said that he realized then that the Prime Minister had never learned to see war in terms of engineering operations, but was still dreaming of man-to-man encounters of the kind that had occurred in the Sudan, where Kitchener's lancers, with rifles and swords, had fought dervishes armed with spears and sabers. Another story, that I had heard in London, I found that everybody had heard in Athens. At the time of the Greek crisis last winter, when Churchill came on to Athens, he had inquired whom the British could rely on to head a new government in Greece and defend the monarchist interests. Archbishop Damaskinos had been named. "Is he a scheming, ambitious, mediaeval prelate?" Churchill is supposed to have demanded. They told him that Damaskinos more or less answered to this description. "Good!" the great man growled. "We can use him."

———

The museum at Heracleion was closed, but people thought that the curator would let me in. On my way there, I was accosted in very bad French by an officious little man, who said, when I asked him, that there was no question at all that the curator, a man named Platon, would be in his office now, and that he would be glad to show me the way, which I perfectly well knew. He rang at various doors and brought out an elderly sub-curator, who spoke much better French. My guide addressed him in Greek and, after a few moments' interchange, told me briefly that the curator was not there, and immediately disappeared. The assistant turned to me in wonder. "He said some very ugly things about M. Platon," he explained. "He said that he was *un mauvais homme,* that he wasn't attending to his business, and that he'd collaborated with the Germans. Why does he say such things? M. Platon is a professor, a scholar!"

He took me to see M. Platon, who was certainly attending to his business. He was directing the excavations, up the coast, of what was supposed to be a Minoan priest's house. A frail and tiny man, with pale hair, pale spectacled eyes and a thin neck punctuated by a sharp Adam's apple, he stood hatless in the heat of the forenoon, directing a couple of men with spades. He showed me a cache of little clay jars that he had just unearthed in one of the walls, and said that, if I would wait till he had finished, he would come back with me and show me the museum. I wanted to stay there and watch him as, assisted by a girl student of archaeology and with a plan of the place in his hand, he bent his efforts on reconstructing this building which had gone to wreck and been buried a thousand years before. But the sun had really cooked me: I was dozing as I stood, and I took shelter in the taxi that had brought us.

When he joined me, we returned to the museum. The Germans had put three bombs through the roof and smashed a good many ancient jars and stone things, of which the fragments were lying around. They had also, M. Platon told me, destroyed one of the royal Minoan tombs, on which a great deal of work had been spent, taking the blocks to build something of their own. But all the most valuable pieces in the museum had been put away underground. He had a few things brought up for me to see, including a piece of fresco which had been hideously warped and charred in one of the great fires that, in ancient times, had burned down the palace of Minos, and he showed me how difficult it was to get the layers of earth and ashes off without scraping the painting away. He was extremely quiet and dry and only once or twice faintly smiled; but he went to a lot of trouble to have me see not only the museum but also a private collection, made by a well-to-do doctor, of Greek and Minoan objects. I don't believe that M. Platon ever thought about anything but Minoan ruins, and when I remembered the curious incident of the pushing little stranger who had abused him, it occurred to me that one can feel respect for a man who has stuck to his interests and managed to survive and pursue them through the disasters of recent years, and no respect at all for the man who makes a business of being politically on the right side.

———

I went alone to Knossos to see the ruins of the palace of Minos. This great work of excavation and reconstruction, on which Sir Arthur Evans of Oxford was engaged from 1900 till his death in 1941, is one of the most fascinating exploits in the history of archaeology. It revealed, unexpectedly, an unknown civilization, neither African, Oriental nor Greek, which, in spite of the rich materials unearthed, remains for us rather mysterious. In the houses of Herculaneum and Pompeii, we can easily imagine the lives of people more or less like ourselves. But the Minoans are not only more remote in time (the great palace was probably first built about two thousand years before Christ and destroyed some six hundred years later): though a multitude of images and frescoes, amazingly sophisticated and brilliant, bring us close to the Minoan world, we feel ourselves, at Knossos, in the presence of a unique and an alien people.

The Minoans, at the height of their power, were supreme in the eastern Mediterranean. The Greeks of the mainland were afraid of them and probably paid them tribute—which figures in Greek legend as the boatload of youths and maidens who were supposed to have been sent every year to Crete to be victims of the Minotaur. This bull-headed half-human monster was the child of the Queen Pasiphaë and the bull of which she became enamored, and he was kept in a labyrinth, from which nobody ever escaped. The truth behind the legend, the archaeologists have come to believe, is that the labyrinth is the palace itself, enormous and complicated, of an architecture abhorrent to the Greeks, and that the youths and maidens were killed in a peculiar kind of bull-baiting game, of which the record has been preserved by the Minoan frescoes, seals and bronzes. The Minoan toreador had to face the bull in its charge, to grasp its horns with both hands and allow himself to be tossed in such a way that he could right himself by a somersault over the back of the animal and be caught by another performer standing behind. There were naturally a great many casualties, which are sometimes depicted on Minoan seals. One of the curious features of this rodeo was that the girls wore pseudo-masculine codpieces, perhaps intended to impress the bull. The statue of the Minoan goddess which had the place of honor at these sports wore one of these codpieces, too. The great head and neck of a bull that survives from a ruined bas-relief in one of the porticoes of the northern entrance was probably still to be seen aboveground when the Greeks first came to Knossos and built a village near the buried palace, and it may partly, Evans believes, have inspired the Minotaur myth. The Greeks, it seems, avoided these ruins, regarding them as haunted ground, and to the visitor they are still uncanny.

I went late in the afternoon, and it was twilight before I left. The palace is a maze indeed. You wander up and down stone steps, between raised platforms and underground chambers, among the rows of squat red and black pillars and the flocks of enormous jars that, knobbed with the innumerable handles that were required to lift and move them, give the impression, in subterranean vistas, of rows of palace servants that have been waiting through the centuries for their masters. And you come suddenly here and there upon the marvellous bas-reliefs and frescoes done in the brilliant blues and reds of the Cretan sea, sky and earth: the Cretan ladies—with their curled black coiffures and their pert breasts showing through light chemises, chattering and laughing as they watch the sports—who, by the piquant simplicity of their outlines, queerly suggest drawings by Matisse (one of these women is known as "La Parisienne"); the naked priest-king with his triple-plumed diadem, walking among slim-stemmed irises with elegantly scrolling petals; the cup-bearers and saffron-gatherers, the captain with the black slaves; the bluebirds among wild roses, the blue monkeys among crocuses and ivy, the brown partridges with their vivid white throats standing above multicolored eggs against a background of round-leaved dittany: all running

to antennae-like foliage, lily-like flower-shapes, ferny
fronds and delicate sprays—a liveliness, frivolity and
charm which, in spite of some Egyptian influence, is as
far from Egyptian stiffness as it is from the chastity of
Greece. The Minoan civilization has come and gone
without leaving the key to its secrets. There survive over
sixteen hundred documents in their half-hieroglyphic
script, but their language has not been deciphered. A
Czech scholar, just before the war, was supposed to have
made a beginning, but since the Germans invaded his
country, M. Platon told me, nobody knows what has
happened to him.* Says the former curator of Knossos,
Mr. J. D. S. Pendlebury, in his handbook to the palace:
"With that wild spring day at the beginning of the
fourteenth century B.C. [the day when some unknown
catastrophe finally destroyed the palace], something went
out of the world which the world will never see again;
something grotesque perhaps, something fantastic and
cruel, but something also very lovely." How the memory
of it lingered in the ancient world I happened, not many
days later, to have a chance to see in Pompeii in the
House of the Labyrinth. This residence of some rich
Pompeian is decorated with Cretan themes: you find the
design of a miniature maze, now reproduced in shrubbery,
a mosaic of the Minotaur surrounded with human bones,
and a fresco—very curious to come on at the end of this
war of aircraft—illustrating another legend of Crete:
Daedalus and Icarus escaping from Minos with the wings
invented by Daedalus, the father making the flight suc-

* Linear B has since been deciphered by Michael Ventris and
John Chadwick. It turned out to be an archaic form of Greek,
which also appears in documents of the Mycenaean period found
in Pylos on the Peloponnesos, just across the sea from Crete. The
documents discovered at Knossos throw little light on Minoan
history—they are mostly account books and inventories—but do
give some idea of Minoan life.

cessfully, the son fallen, wrecked, into the water. Daedalus, the great artificer, was supposed to have come to Crete and to have invented, under the patronage of Minos, some of his most unholy devices: the labyrinth, the talking statues and the wooden imitation cow in which the king's wife, Pasiphaë, bewitched by a god, had succeeded in making an impression on the beautiful white bull which had been presented to them by Poseidon. Minos was so enraged by this last exploit that Daedalus had to flee for his life and hastily invented his wings of wax. Yes, certainly there was something rather strange about Crete, something insolent and exultant, at once refined and barbaric. The Minos of Greek mythology had a great reputation for wisdom and was famous as a giver of laws. Evans believes, on the basis of what he can make out from the lists and accounts on old tablets, that the regime was even rather bureaucratic. But with this there were a recklessness and a richness that a little recall the Italian Renaissance, a way of life unacceptable and frightening to the more moderate and pious Greeks.

And as I stood before the vivacious fresco of an elongated piebald bull over whose back a team of two girls and a boy are performing their extraordinary acrobatics, I had what seemed to me a flash of insight into the symbolism and spirit of Crete. I had been studying, that afternoon, a large wall-map, and I was struck now by the resemblance of the island to the outline of the bull in the fresco. Crete itself is an elongated bull, facing the same way as the fresco, with Capes Busa and Spatha as horns, an eye just below Phalasarna, and a nose and mouth at Cape Krio, genitals at Cape Littino below, and a tail at Cape Sider on the eastern end. Unquestionably the Minoans were preoccupied with bulls. Not only did the Queen Pasiphaë have a love affair with a bull but the first King Minos was supposed to have been the offspring of Zeus, disguised as a bull, and Europa, whom, in this disguise, he had carried away across the sea to Crete; not only, among Minoan antiquities, do we find the innumerable bulls of the paintings and objects of art, but there is the motif of the bull's crescent horns that stood over the Minoan doorways and that still figures in the architecture of the island. I do not know what the state of mapmaking may have been in Minoan days, but I imagine that it would only have been necessary to ascend the highest mountains of Crete to get a pretty good idea of its shape. The later Cretans saw the outline of Mount Ida as the profile of the sleeping Zeus, and the theory that the ancient Minoans identified their island and themselves with bulls because that was what their country looked like seems as plausible as Evans' theory, based on very slender evidence, that the Minoan obsession with bulls was connected with the periodic earthquakes, which they attributed to the heaving and roaring of a gigantic bull underground. I tried this notion on M. Platon and on several archaeologists in Athens, none of whom had ever heard it suggested. M. Platon said, *"C'est une hypothèse."* In any case, it made me feel a naturalness as well as an appropriateness in the bull that was challenged by man as an emblem for the Cretans themselves; and of the ferocious and bestial bull-man as a bugbear for the outsiders upon whom they preyed. The bull still today in Crete haunts one as the inevitable symbol for their stubbornness, their belligerence and their fierceness.

———

The town of Anogeia, on the top of a mountain not far from Psiloriti (Mount Ida) is the highest town in Crete, twenty-eight hundred feet above sea-level. It is known to be nine centuries old and is probably a great deal older. It was inhabited, at the beginning of the war, by something like four thousand people. When the British, during the German occupation, kidnapped one of the German generals, he was spirited away to Anogeia and the people concealed him there. In revenge, the Germans blew up the town, but they killed only thirty-three men, because the rest of them had all managed to escape and hide out for months in the mountains.

Today, the anniversary of the destruction of the town, a memorial service is going to be held there, and the British commander, the U.N.R.R.A. heads, the Minister of Social Welfare from Athens, the son of Venizelos and the Archbishop of Crete have all been asked and have promised to be present. An English major has offered to drive me up with a Greek brigadier general he is taking. I go punctually to an appointed place at an early hour in the morning and the major is there on the dot. If we could keep to the British schedule, the whole thing would be over by noon and everybody would be back for a nap. But the British have not counted on the Greeks. All seems ready at the Greek Army headquarters. I meet the Greek brigadier, a lean, dark-eyed and gray-haired man, and his young son, an enthusiastic Boy Scout. The tall and heavy-jawed Scotch general, commander of the British troops in Crete, goes striding up the steps in his kilt and the Greek sentries salute with violence, as if he were a magnetic force that brings their arms up without their volition. The Greek officers follow him in. We wait in the car for a time, then the major disappears inside. Presently he sends somebody out to tell me to come in, too. I am informed that there will be a slight wait while the Greek general has his coffee, and am shown into a room where I am introduced to the British commander and others, who are all standing there waiting for the brigadier's breakfast. A small cup of Turkish coffee is finally brought, and the general drinks it up in the three

or four sips it requires, with a nonchalant air of enjoyment that is at once exasperating and engaging. Then we
all go out again.

"There's half an hour wasted for no good reason," the
English major says to me before the general climbs into
the car. I get along well with the Major, a young Yorkshireman who voted for Labour. He tells me a lot of
interesting stories—especially about the Germans. He had
had to drive a German officer who had just been taken
prisoner, and he had become aware that the man was
trembling violently and green with fright: "I said, 'You
may well be afraid. There are some villages burned about
here.'" The man had simply been confined in a prison
camp. Another German had said to the Major, "We
ought to have won the war." "I asked him why he
thought they ought to have won it. 'Why, look at these
people,' he said. 'They're inferior, they're contemptible.' I
pointed out that they had been fighting not only the
Greeks but the Americans and the Russians and a few
other people, but he just kept saying, 'We ought to have
won.'" He told me, also, a story about an English officer
he knew of who had taken some Greek Boy Scouts on a
hike and by mistake had passed the Bulgarian frontier.
They had at once been picked up by the Russians, who
had sent the boys back to Greece but kept the officer
there for days, questioning him as to what he was up to.
When they had finally become convinced that he had
intended nothing more serious than a picnic, they had
decided to let him go but had tried to make him sign a
paper affirming that he had not been questioned. He
refused, and they had to release him. This puzzles and
troubles the Yorkshireman, and his attitude toward the
Russians is typical of that of the English, which has been
reflected, in a stupid way, by the policy of the Tories in

Greece. The traditional English procedure of balancing power in Europe has been up against unfamiliar difficulties in the problem of balancing with Russia, which may promise one thing at Yalta about leaving the Mediterranean to the British, and apparently, through the local Communists, do something quite different in Greece. One cannot ever be certain of anything. In the mind of the Major, the peculiar reception given the Scoutmaster by his Soviet allies is connected with the larger question of how far you can trust the Russians—people who find it natural to hold an Englishman as if he were an enemy and try to make him swear to a lie.

As we pass through the little villages, we are welcomed with handfuls of laurel leaves, which the young girls throw in through the windows. We go as far as we can in the car along a wrecked and precarious road, and then have to get out and walk. It is a steep path up a mountain that hardly threads through the rocks. "The Brigadier," says the Major to me, "is setting a cracking pace." We presently fall behind him, as the old man, erect and lively-eyed, strides along in his polished puttees with a rapid and elastic step. These hills are great gray barren mounds where there is nothing to examine or to look at. A curious little plant with a purple stem and pale waxy perfumeless flowers turns out to be asphodel. The path disappears completely, and we have to clamber among jagged stones. But when we have got beyond this, we find men with donkeys waiting. The Brigadier sees politely that we are mounted. You sit sideways and, since there are no stirrups, you hang on to a wooden handle that sticks out of the front of the saddle. You learn to keep your balance while you look along the path ahead rather than into the abysses below.

At the end of an hour of this, you arrive at the village

of Anogeia (pronounced as if it were Anóya), where you are perched in the Cretan sky and have everything else underneath you. The difficulty at first is to grasp what the condition of Anogeia is. The town, which had been built out of mountain rock, is now mostly just stones like the other stones. The aim of the Germans was not to leave a wall standing, and where the base of a house still remains, it looks exactly like a Minoan ruin. One thinks with a certain affection of good old King Minos, the bureaucrat, who only threw a few maidens and youths to bulls and gave them a sporting chance. The one building spared is the church, not out of reverence, however, but because it had been the German headquarters and might perhaps still be useful as an outpost. The thin dark-eyed women meet us, all in black, with their shawls over their heads, and shake hands with us as we ride. We come to a halt in the public square, where we sit down and are offered refreshments in the shape of little pieces of watermelon and shots of a crude kind of ouzo which is known in the mountains as raki. We shake hands with the men, who have terrific grips and fingers that seem made of flint. Their faces are bearded, their hands are black, and they have piercing black or hazel eyes. The goatherds of this mountain town are the hardest-bitten people I have ever seen. Life is so rugged up here that many of the children die and only the toughest survive. No wonder they could stand up to the Germans.

We have been told that the service is to take place at eleven, but we learn now that it will have to be deferred till the Minister from Athens arrives, and that it may not be held till six. "Isn't that like them?" grumbles the Major. "He was invited a month ago." He does not understand these anniversaries which the Cretans, he says, are always having. "I suppose it makes them feel better," I suggest. "I should think it would make them feel worse," he replies. "I should think it would remind them of the person who was dead and bring back a lot of things about him."

We are shown into a dining room through a smaller room which is strewn with the bones of what has evidently been an earlier repast, and entertained at an Homeric banquet. First they bring on great platters of mutton: simply roast sheep hacked into manageable pieces. You are supposed to eat with your fingers and throw the bones on the floor. And there are also chunks of bread, boiled potatoes and magnificent watermelons. When the melons appear, I assume that we have come to the end of the feast, but they are followed by a delicacy called kokoretsi, which consists of the entrails of the sheep chopped up, stuffed into an intestine, wound around a long skewer and roasted. This fare is a little appalling to some of the British and American guests, but it is very impolite in Greece not to do justice to hospitality, and we are watched by intent eyes looking in on two sides through the windows. "It's important to drink a lot on these occasions," says the Major, who is sitting next to me. They keep refilling our glasses from great pitchers of non-resinated raw red wine, which I get to think rather pleasant. The man on my other side is a British Red Cross worker, another Yorkshireman, who has hardly left his county before and talks with a heavy accent. He tells me about the local diseases: scabies, malaria, etc.: "They say that they never had scabies before the Germans came and conditions got so bad, but I don't know: they're certainly not very clean." A young girl had come to him with a swelling on her neck—"a really beautiful girl, you'd say she was a beautiful girl anywhere—with a wonderful lot of hair. But when I lifted up her hair, it was awful—it was all crawling underneath." We are now becoming talkative and genial. The Greeks are extremely agreeable. There is a handsome old man, a retired official, whose short snowy beard, subtle smile and generous enjoyment of the banquet seem to belong to an heroic age. The brigadier keeps offering us things with his worn but cordial air of a man who has experienced much but has yet remained blithe in spirit.

After the meal, I walk through the town. There are donkeys, chickens and goats, pigs scratching themselves on the ruins, little half-naked keen-eyed kids. I have been warned about Cretan hospitality, but I stop to look at a litter of pigs, which are nursing in a regular rhythm that the mother seems to be directing by an equally rhythmical grunting, as the coxswain sets the stroke for a crew, and I am invited at once into the house beyond, where they offer me bread and wine, and I thus have a chance to see how poor their common nourishment is. After that, I make a point of not looking in the direction of any house, but while I stand gazing out at the dusty hills, a woman in a doorway sends her daughter to give me some watermelon. They are beginning to rebuild the town, but most of the people are living merely between plugged-up and roofed-in ground-floor walls. A little whitewashed cell in a ruin, with grapes growing over the door, seems an attractive and comfortable home.

But I am going to sleep on my feet and I look up the rest of the party. They have retreated into a house to escape the sun and are all sitting together on benches. Some are dozing, with their heads in their hands. The Scotch commander is in this position, and somebody asks him, well, how does he feel? He does not reply for a moment, and then declares, "Bloody awful!" Everybody laughs, then again becomes numb. At intervals they hand us in more watermelon. It seems that a second banquet on the same enormous scale is now taking place in the dining-room in honor of Venizelos' son.

It is not till I have been some time in the little building in which we are sitting that I recognize it as the village store. There is so little left to sell: a small bin of grain, a few tiles, a few jars, a few bony cuts of meat. There are children with bright clear eyes—some of the girls are pretty but, like everybody else in the town, as lean and fibrous and swarthy as if they had grown out of the soil like some kind of meager mountain tree. I make a jumping mouse out of my handkerchief. This did not go over well in Athens, but in Anogeia it is a mad success. The children—what rarely happens—at once discover how the trick is done and demonstrate the principle with their fingers. Then they go and bring in other children, and keep crying, *"Pontikos! pontikos!"* But, in the presence of the severe Scotchman, I feel that once is enough.

Of course the Minister of Welfare fails to come. They wait until six, then start. In the square there is a shaft inscribed with the names of their hundred and one men who have been killed in the fighting or reprisals. One sees on it the word *hoplitai,* which takes one back to Xeno-phon. Here the widows and bereaved mothers have been standing in mourning all day. They have brought most extraordinary wreaths that are wreath-shaped loaves of bread. Now young girls take their places here, in the traditional costume of the country: black blouses braided with gold, reddish snoods with gold embroidery, silver necklaces and strings of gold coins. In the background hangs the blue Greek flag between poles that are twisted with laurel. A procession marches into an enclosed space: a long row of priests in black, the Archbishop of Crete at their head, a patriarchal and impressive old man with an immense and well-cared-for beard spreading across the breast of his robe; the Scotch general and the British delegation; the U.N.R.R.A. representatives and all the rest. There are litanies, sermons, prayers; anthems by a choir. The sun is still stupefying; it is hard to remain on one's feet. We keep wondering how soon it will be over, knowing well it will last a long time. At the sound of the church-bells, a donkey brays, interrupting the reverent silence. When the dead sons and fathers are mentioned, the women raise a chanting threnody. It is a traditional song, not a wail, but it seems to make the Major nervous, for he grins faintly as if to indicate that that it not the English way to behave about men who have been lost in a war. The Mayor speaks and the schoolmaster speaks, and the schoolmaster, who is evidently an E.A.M. man, exhorts them with a radical oration, which the Major is able to follow and which makes him more nervous still. "They're going to boo him in a minute," he whispers to me, but the crowd shows every sign of sympathy. Venizelos the son makes a speech—the Venizeloses come from Crete. Then innumerable wreaths are presented. The Scotch general brings up a big wreath.

By this time the sun is going down. The Americans and the British are in a hurry to get started for home so that they will not have to drive on those roads in the dark. "Wasn't that terrific? I warned you," says the U.N.R.R.A. man from Connecticut. "It wasn't even a good show for that kind of thing." Like the Major, he doesn't understand what they get out of these somber celebrations.

But on our way to the donkeys to carry us back, the Brigadier has to stop for civilities, and we have to drink another round of raki. When we set out in the car again, we are immediately blocked by a row of Greek trucks, which are taking people home from Anogeia but which have for some reason stopped at a small settlement, parking all over the road. No one pays any attention to

our efforts to induce the trucks to move, and the Brigadier
himself volunteers to get out and see what can be done.
He disappears for a long time. The Major by now is
frantic. When we start on, it is almost dark and our
progress is impeded by the trucks, which are ahead of us
and which, on the narrow road, it is impossible for us to
pass. And then, just after we have finally escaped, we
discover with indignant horror that we are in for another
service. In a village at the foot of the mountain, there is a
crowd around a lantern-lit catafalque, and the Archbishop is going into action. I am as eager to get on as the
Major and I urge him to shoot right through. But he
knows that the Brigadier ought to be there and that he
ought to be there with him, so we park and join the
group. They are standing on the edge of a grave, in
which looms a large coffin with trappings. This time the
wreaths are made of cake, clumsily molded and decora-
tively iced. The Major whispers that a man standing near
us was the head of the Resistance in that region. He has a
small curled and pointed black mustache and holds his
hat in his hands. He is clean-shaven and soberly dressed.

But this ceremony is brief and we have come at the
end. Glancing about in the inadequate light, I see that
the Archbishop's cheeks are wet and that the leader of
the local Resistance has tears starting out of his eyes; nor
do they seem to me to be weeping for show. For the first
time in that long day's ordeal and despite my former
impatience, the scene takes me unaware and I am suddenly, painfully moved. Perhaps the Major, too, is
moved: he does not smile and has ceased to fume. A small
band plays the Greek national anthem, and then another,
much more martial tune, which, I am told, is the anthem
of Crete.

And that is how the burning of Anogeia was commemorated by the Allies—not very solemnly or gra-

ciously, but whatever good will we had went into that
trip up the mountain.

———

I lay around dozing at the airport waiting for a plane to
take me back to Athens. The American engineers there
begged me to give them some publicity. The were irked
at having been stranded in Crete, in exile from the main
stream of American troops. It was hard for them, they
said, to "have any initiative," because they didn't know
what they were there for and couldn't see the point of
their work. What did we want with an airport in Crete?

This airport was at Heracleion. At Canea there is a
British one. I had flown over "British" and was going back
"American." There was as usual a striking contrast. On
the British plane, the discipline had been complete. I had
been made to wear my Mae West life preserver by a
sergeant who called me "sir" and respectfully helped me
into it. A security man questioned me politely as to my
purpose in visiting Crete and made certain, when I
landed there, to whom I was going to report. All the
safety restrictions were scrupulously observed. In order to
make the trip at all, I had had to get orders from the
British. But here, when an American plane came in, I
simply went to it and asked to be taken back. The
lieutenant who piloted it was sitting on the ground with
his crew, his hat pushed back on one side of his head, in
the shade of the wing of the plane. He did not ask to see
my orders, but simply said, sure: come along. On the
flight no one wore a Mae West or strapped himself to the
seat; the windows were all left open; and everyone
except the pilot lay down right away on the seats or the
floor and immediately went sound asleep. There in our
bird-body plastered with pin-ups we sailed through the

afternoon—delightfully cool in the upper air—over the misty blue summer sea.

The lieutenant had been some time in Athens, but had done nothing about the antiquities and asked me what he ought to see. Some G.I.'s on leave, on the other hand, who drove with me in the truck into the city, had no interest in anything but eating. They asked whether it were really true that you could get ice-cream in Athens "just the same as they have at home," and that there were doughnuts covered with sugar and honest-to-God beer.

15

STOPOVER IN NAPLES

THOUGH GREECE HAD BEEN A RELIEF after Italy, it also worked a little the other way. It was pleasant, after those arid hills, to see trees and plowed fields below one, and to find, on the road to Caserta, hay-ricks and orchards and gardens, an earth that could be cultivated, again; to speed along a high eucalyptus drive; to smell sulphur and swamp and manure. It was gratifying at first glimpse, after the neutral colors of Athens, to see the ridiculous big pink buildings with their green blinds and their plastery statues three times life-size; the yellow-haired or dark-haired women with their red or white clogs; the queer ornaments on the collars of the horses that the Neapolitans seem to love: silver rosettes, silver bells, silver madonnas, saints and birds. I like to look even at the Bay of Naples, which resembles a colored picture postcard.

But since I was here at the end of April, the Americans have set their mark on the scene. A campaign for improvement is in progress. All along the road from Caserta one is admonished by signs in English which make great play with the letter F: "FLIES FOUL FOOD," "FLIES FEED ON FAECES AND FOOD," "FLIES SPREAD DIARRHOEA," etc. And there are warnings all over

Naples, thought up no doubt by some advertizing man: "DRIVE CAREFULLY. DEATH IS SO PERMA-NENT." In the middle of the Via Roma—for no reason that one can see except that of simple refreshment—a free lemonade stand for Americans has been set up by the Red Cross.

———

Last spring I saw the bombed-out section that extends a good way in from the docks: shapeless fragments of buildings rising like sand-castle stumps out of mounds of pulverized plaster, filthy children playing in the garbage of the pavementless, lightless, policeless streets, the butcher-shops with gruesome cuts of meat, the half-obliterated shrines. I have had enough of ruins now, and I give this a wide berth. But the misery is all through the city. No matter how late one walks out, the ragged little boys are still in the streets. When they get too tired to beg or pimp, they go to sleep on the curbs along buildings or on the running-boards of parked cars. And everybody who has passed the age of puberty seems to be busy making more children: the town is full of pregnant women and of women with wretched little babies that have sores all over their faces or are covered with the pink mottlings of disease. The Neapolitans seem to me some-times to have as little relation to people as small octopi, crabs and molluscs brought in by the marine tide.

———

But the life here is rank and flamboyant, and even in death it exults in the flesh. I have never seen a city in which funerals seem to figure in so important a way. Where so many human creatures are begotten many must be constantly dying, and they like to make a fête of death.

The streets are always full of hearses. There are cheap black ones loaded down with flowers, cheap white ones that look like pastry, more costly ones studded with crowns that give the impression of Christmas-tree ornaments. And I saw one magnificent black one, drawn by eight black horses. With its crown-shaped lamps on the corners, its quantities of spiralled columns and its elaborate jet carvings, it looked like a luxurious Renaissance bed.

———

Yet Count Morra told me in Rome that, when he came here at the time of the invasion, the people had shown great cleverness and courage. It had been "1848 over again." When the Germans had posted an order that all the young men were to report to help defend the city against the Allies, these young men all immediately disappeared, and the Germans could never locate them. Barricades were thrown up in the streets, and little boys went about with hand-grenades strung around their waists. This was not the result of organization, but mainly a spontaneous movement. It was, he said, as if the spirit of a common purpose had run through the city like an electric current.

I liked Morra. He is not one of the Roman nobility, but something more like a country squire. He had, I was told, never left his estate through the whole of the Fascist regime, though he had refused to pay homage to Fascism and had been penalized and ostracized. He is now, though so severely crippled that it is difficult for him to get around, extremely active as one of the editors of the liberal *Nuova Europa* and in various other ways. Though cultivated and cosmopolitan like the more detached people in Rome, I thought him a thorough patriot of the old-fashioned disinterested kind. He obviously took deep pride in this demonstration of Neapolitan solidarity.

———

My earlier visit to Naples is associated with *Lili Marlene*, which I heard being played at a great rate in the enlisted men's Red Cross canteen, where, among all those dazed boys from home crowded together in their drab army clothes and breathing the bad air, it seemed to me, in its prettiness and pathos, its banality that was never too obvious, to carry the experience of war which must so largely remain unspoken but which may sometimes be picked up by a song: the hardships, the changes of scene, the blankness, the longing for home. *Lili Marlene* was originally German, but the Allies had taken it over and the street-singers had learned it in Italy, and everybody had been singing it at the same time. It had sounded through Europe—with no conscious intent on the part of those who sang it—as one of the few human utterances that had no nationalistic animus: it told simply of a soldier's girl-friend who waited for him night after night in the rain by a lamp-post at the barracks gate. A martial step and the echo of trumpets seem to have faded in the wastes of the war-years. The lover may or may not come back: if he does, he will meet her at the lantern; if he fails to, who will wait there then? And this song was all that these soldiers had had to establish human fellowship between them while they were massacring one another and bombing one another's sweethearts! This little memorial to a faith perhaps futile was all they had had to offset the tragedy of manhood destroyed and debased!

———

There were people I knew at Sorrento, but I kept putting off going out there, because my transportation

might come any moment and I might have to leave at
once; so I stayed on from day to day visiting Pompeii and
the Naples Museum and wandering around the city,
where I knew nobody.

The Via Roma at night, in the smell-thickened hot
August air, was the channel for a dense traffic of women
and soldiers looking for women. I spoke one evening to a
very pretty girl, almost the only really pretty one I had
seen, who seemed, in fact, so well-dressed and fresh-faced
that she might have been taken for respectable if she had
not been walking alone at that hour in the Via Roma.
She was conspicuous among the Neapolitans by her type,
which was unusual there: she had yellow hair, brown
eyes and fair skin; and I learned later that she was not
Italian, but half-Polish and half-German. She took me
straight to her place of business, which was in the for-
bidden zone up the hill from the Via Roma. Every cross-
street on this side of the main artery had a sign barring
out the troops; and, exploring this quarter for the first
time, it was easy for me to understand why. The little
girl—who said her name was Giannetta—piloted me by
the arm through the squalidest and most sinister-looking
streets that I have ever seen anywhere. By a maze of stone
steps and blind alleys, a whole world that, besides being
closed to the troops, seemed self-contained in its degradation and partly shut off from the rest of the town, we
arrived at an old dark and stinking house, where the dank
and cavernous stairwell was dripping from thrown-out
slops or a permanent leak in the plumbing.

Here Giannetta and three or four other girls hired the
use of two disgusting rooms from an old woman who
rented a small flat there. When I entered, not without
misgivings, I was somewhat reassured to find a taciturn
American M.P. sitting solidly in a little waiting room
which was also dining room and kitchen. The impression

that I got then and later was that the M.P.'s, instead of keeping out the G.I.'s, were giving the girls in the barred zone protection and getting repaid in kind or by a cut out of their professional earnings; and this conclusion has been confirmed since my return by an American air-transport man who spent a good deal of time in Naples and saw how the system worked. Giannetta told me that if a customer made trouble or become obnoxious in any way, she called the M.P. at once and had the man thrown out. He could always be threatened with arrest for having been found in that quarter at all.

Giannetta first said she was seventeen, and she did not look any older; but, forgetting this, she later made it nineteen; and when one day she showed me her passport, I saw that she was down as twenty-two. She had been married and had separated from her husband. She had been unfaithful to him, she confessed—but then he had been unfaithful to her. She had recently come to Naples from Rome, giving her status—she smiled slyly when I remarked on it—as that of *casalinga;* because Naples was apparently now where the biggest money was made. She charged three hundred lire, so she was earning anywhere from sixty to a hundred and fifty dollars a day. She and the other girls were frantically working overtime to rake in as much as possible before the Americans went away; and when I called on her one afternoon to ask her to dine with me and go to the theater, she told me that she could not do anything except for a flat rate. An evening of mere amusement would mean a loss of hundreds of lire, and I should have to pay her by the hour, if I wanted her to do things outside with me, just as if I were going to bed with her. While I was talking to her in the little anteroom, I could see, in the room beyond, a soldier, fully dressed, lying full-length on the bed. But Giannetta had still another distraction and, in the course of the conversation, would keep running out on a little balcony to watch a street-fight in progress outside. It made the whole thing seem rather childlike. She had none of the marks yet of the professional whore, but a girlish candor and gaiety; and for this reason she was much in demand by soldiers who had picked her out as I had done, and of whom I would sometimes find a whole row sitting on the bench in the anteroom.

Her price for going out was prohibitive, but I dropped in for a call once or twice. I also got to know her half-sister, who was not pretty and seemed rather sensible: she did not look like a prostitute either. It was queer to sit behind the scenes of this business which in its way dealt in glamor. For a man, at least an American, always expects of a woman—in relations however commercial—a touch of romance and passion, and the woman must try to supply it. Nothing has ever brought home to me so sharply the difference, in this connection, between the woman's and the man's point of view as seeing these girls in Naples return to the general conversation after being away in the next room with their customers, laughing about the things that had happened or discussing them in a practical way as if they had been incidents of market-ing. That they were sometimes only half-dressed did not make them self-conscious in the least nor was it intended to appeal to my appetites. Yet they had just lit men's expectations, created a suggestion of mystery and—even in that unspeakable den—gratified them by moments of magic.

Giannetta sounded quite cute in Italian, but when she broke into American the effect was absolutely blood-curdling. She had been able to learn from her customers nothing but the toughest talk: a jargon of male idioms and obscenities that sounded horrible as it came from her good little mouth. The Americans have brought to Italy.

along with their campaign to swat the fly, some of the worst features of American society. There was plenty of racketeering in the army; and that summer the Roman police had been to considerable trouble to round up a gang of American deserters who had been holding people up for months and had committed several murders. It made me uncomfortable in Naples to see shady-looking Italians in clothes that had been stolen or bought from G.I.'s. The Neapolitan and American underworlds had merged in the Via Roma and were sometimes, except for insignia, indistinguishable from one another.

16

HOMECOMING; FINAL REFLECTIONS

FLYING BACK TO THE STATES, I had wonderful weather and great good luck in making connections. I left Naples about 10.30 in the morning and arrived in New York at about 12.30 two mornings later (though the actual flying time had of course been some eight hours longer). The whole Atlantic was as smooth and blue as if it had been the Mediterranean: you could not even see any white-caps.

But, as usual after long flights, I to some extent suffered from shock. It took me days to adjust myself to having travelled so far so quickly. Having grown up in the age of trains and ships, I am conditioned by the old-fashioned journeys that gave you time to prepare yourself for the new continent or country you were visiting. But when you leap across the Atlantic by plane, your reflexes are caught unawares and do not tell you that you are home again. You have the illusion that the country in which you have alighted is not really the country you left, but some sort of mirage or simulacrum.

This was partly due, no doubt, to the fact that I had been thinking, all the time I was in Europe, how much better off we were at home and had created an ideal picture, based on everything most agreeable to remember from the past, which the present in its actuality could hardly justify. And this emptiness of the present was due also to the death of Roosevelt and to the general displacement of activity to Europe and the Pacific. With all this, in that outside world—where we had suddenly found ourselves engaged and exposed as we had never been before—we were still, except as a fighting machine, more or less disoriented. It was as if at one stroke we had been deprived of most of what had been in our minds—our imaginative conception of ourselves, our complex of occupations, all formerly contained in the United States; but had not yet really related ourselves to the developments of the larger arena—so that civilians moved at home in a void and Americans returning from the services found an unexpected relaxation contrasting with the tension abroad.

In any case, I felt for a while almost as if I had merely arrived in yet another foreign country. I noticed characteristics of the Americans of which I had not been conscious when I left. They were much larger than Europeans—enormous, they looked to me now; their faces were insufficiently focussed and their personalities lacking in flavor; they were doing a good many things expertly, but in a way which made them seem rather uninteresting. I had looked forward to picking up my old pursuits, but was baffled and disconcerted to find that these no longer appeared so absorbing as they had before. Then I saw that I had to make an adjustment quite different from the kind of adjustment that is involved in going abroad and learning your way about. I already knew my way about at home, yet I could not find the values I had known, the values on which I depended; and I realized that what made the difference was that, in visiting a foreign country, you were always in the position of a spectator for whom the inhabitants were staging a show. This show consists of their being foreigners and behaving in an unfamiliar way, and it provides you with entertainment without involving you in responsibility as to the progress and outcome of the play. But in America you are no longer in the audience, you have to be one of the actors, and the old drama in which you figured will not get under way for you again unless you go back into your role. You have now to contribute, yourself, to creating the interest and value, and, back in New York, I found myself still in the passive state of mind of the onlooker. I had not begun working yet.

The Careerists. I had, however, acquired or had had strengthened, during my trip and in the war-years before, certain convictions and prognostications which I shall set down here for what they may be worth.

First of all, I have come to believe that the accepted interpretations of history have been failing to take into account one extremely important factor, which I have never seen adequately studied. This factor is the always unforeseen and immediately disastrous results of democratic education and free competition for advancement. The point is that these results have proved to be very much the same in any modern society in which hitherto unprivileged people have been given a chance to do any kind of work for which they can qualify and to go as far as they can get—that is, they have proved the same irrespective of what the Marxists call the specific class character of the revolution that brought them about. The reformers of the eighteenth century were always talking about the desirability of "the career open to the talents." We got it in America and in France when the revolutions in those countries occurred; but we did not get the Reign of Reason that the philosophers and statesmen had hoped for: the career thrown open to the talents very soon turned out to mean that it was the careerists who dominated society and not at all the superior talents of the kind that a Condorcet or a Jefferson prized. In France, the political idealisms of the revolutionary period proper, whether liberal and humane or intolerant and moralistic, gave way to the mad speculation, the exploitation of official position and the general scrimmage for money that were rampant under the Directory and still going strong under the Third Republic; and the patriotism of Valmy and Jemappes that had defended the Rights of Man turned rapidly into the *"gloire"* of Napoleon, who exploited the patriotism of the French to realize his own upstart ambitions. In America, the republican idealism, with no reactionary neighbors to fear and no feudalism at home to undermine it, was preserved in more or less sincerity for longer and with less upsetting vicissitudes; but it was choked, after the Civil War, by the wild and overwhelming growth of the same impulses to self-aggrandizement and appetites for material success that had been taking possession of the French. Our Rockefellers and Goulds and Morgans were the American counterparts of the French businessmen and financiers who had sat for the protagonists of Balzac, and they had operated on the scale of Napoleon. They had just the same relation to the Declaration of Independence, the Bill of Rights and the Gettysburg Address that Napoleon did to the Oath of the Tennis Court and *Liberté, Egalité, Fraternité.*

Now the Marxists have always told us that all this was the result of the capitalist system, which instigated cutthroat competition, and of the merchant and banking class who cared about nothing but money. Marx and Engels and Lenin and Trotsky believed unquestioningly that, in spite of the fact that the rising bourgeoisie, in displacing the feudal nobility, had brought in this murderous commercial age, the overthrow of the bourgeoisie by

the agricultural and industrial proletariat would inaugu-
rate an era distinguished by honest workmanship, human
brotherhood and scrupulous public conscience. The truth
was that the new revolutions of the first half of the
twentieth century were to produce, in their early phases,
even more degrading results than what had happened in
France and America. But there were reasons why Marx
did not foresee them. He made two fallacies, he argued
from two false analogies, in forecasting what might be
expected when the process of scrapping capitalism should
begin. In the first place, being a Jew, from a family that
had included many rabbis, he identified the situation of
the factory worker with the situation of the Jew. A Jew
like Marx, escaped from the disfranchised state, had a
moral authority and an intellectual training that were his
by natural right because they had been bred in him by
Jewish tradition. He concluded from this that the industrial worker, liberated from the capitalist's mill, would
display the same qualities of leadership. Besides, had not
the bourgeoisie, breaking out of the rusty shackles of
feudalism, known very well how to govern and to admin-
ister their affairs in their own interest? This was the
second of Marx's fallacies. The fault of the analogy lay in
the fact that the bourgeoisie, before they took over
officially, had been already a well-educated group, with
plenty of experience of handling property and of dis-
charging public responsibility, who produced many able
and intelligent men and accomplished some permanent
reforms before the rapacities that they were unleashing
began to gobble up everything else. The proletariat,
insofar as it approximated to the impoverished and abject
state to which Marx thought it would have to be reduced
before it could rebel effectively, was as unfitted for the
enlightened statesmanship of which the great bourgeois
leaders had been capable before the era of careerism

swamped them as it was for the lawgiving and vision of the great Jewish radical prophets. Marx and Engels might have been warned by the contemptuous tone into which they themselves often fell in writing to one another about working-class leaders and movements, that the proletarian dictatorship, when it came, would not be of a kind to please them.

It was true that they had been reluctant to contemplate the possibility that the proletarian revolution might first occur in Russia, because they thought the Russians irresponsible and given to overdoing things and did not consider the country industrialized enough to make a socialist economy possible. But their disciples Lenin and Trotsky dreamt of a socialist Russia and willed it and partly brought it about. What they did not foresee any more than Marx was that what happens, when you let down the bars, is that a lot of gross and ignorant people who have been condemned to mean destinies before go rushing for all they are worth after things that they can eat, drink, sleep on, ride in, preside at and amuse themselves with. It may seem that the Soviet bureaucrats who have flourished under Stalin's regime differ greatly from the American millionaires of the big post-Civil War monopolies; but the principle that has produced them is the same: in Russia, though the opportunities for money-making are limited compared with what ours have been, the relative inequalities of privilege and pay are enormous; and the arrogant official in his car, surrounded by his bodyguard, would have been as repugnant to Lenin, with his schoolmaster discipline and addiction to study and his belief that the formalities of government, which bored him, could easily be attended to in the off-moments of serious people occupied with higher things, as the publicity-inflated tycoon would have been to Jefferson, with his ideal of the cultivated country gentleman and his aversion to industrial inventions. Both are single-minded remorseless careerists who do not realize that human beings can want anything but power and possessions. The only difference is that Stalin's machine is a gang that has to work together whereas the American millionaires were usually out each for himself.

Napoleon paid lip-service to the Revolution till he no longer needed its supporters; the American Chamber of Commerce speaks with respect of the Founding Fathers; Stalin, on appropriate occasions, still invokes the name of Lenin at the same time that he is allowing himself to be glorified in the role of Ivan the Terrible. The Nazis in Germany were not the heirs of any revolutionary tradition, but—careerists of the lower middle class, who, due to the bankruptcy of the feudal order and the continued degradation of Germany imposed by the Treaty of Versailles, found themselves at last with a fair field and a free hand—they exploited the prestige of socialism, so largely German in origin, by appealing to the German masses in the interest of a "National Socialism." Like Napoleon, Hitler gratified the hungers of a base but brazen little man by a series of megalomaniac conquests, which—not being founded on anything better than "reeking tube and iron shard"—have not lasted any longer than Napoleon's. Like Stalin, he drove into exile, imprisoned or put to death everyone whose brains or ideals were of a higher grade than his own. It has always been a feature of the careerist regime to suppress systematically that enlightenment which the pre-revolutionary reformers have aimed to cherish and spread. The censorship of Napoleon was less complete than that of Hitler or Stalin, but in its time it was a serious enough nuisance; and though we in the United States, between, say, 1880 and 1910, did not have a literal burning of books, we had a discouragement of non-commercial and non-genteel ideas which made it difficult for unorthodox writers to get read or even printed and sometimes reduced our most important thinkers to the status of nonentities or outlaws, as well as a hostility to aesthetic interests which drove many of our artists to Europe, where they were almost as much refugees as those who have recently come to us from there.

In England it has worked somewhat differently. Here the structure of the feudal caste system, though modified, has been long maintained by absorbing into the "governing class," that unique English institution, as many as possible of the able people who have come up from the lower strata. There are of course in England, too, a certain number of highly successful careerists who have not been influenced by the discipline and style that characterize this governing class; but they have never had quite the same sort of field-day that they have had in the Soviet Union and in the United States. As long as the Crown is at the top of the hierarchy, the rich brewer or newspaper owner may always be tempted to buy a title or have his daughter presented at court, and as long as the public schools and universities are nurseries for most places of distinction, he is likely to want to send his sons there. The British system has thus preserved certain ideals of devotion to the State and of disinterested intellectual activity that during the latter part of the nineteenth century were pretty well obliterated in the United States, and the second of which, the free play of intellect, went up in a holocaust in Hitler's Germany and Stalin's Russia, while the first, the devotion to the public service, appeared in a fanatical or a sordid form which had nothing in common with the tact, the common sense and the careful study that had been brought to it through centuries in England. Yet this system, in adhering to the feudal mold, has cramped the natural development of society and delayed the democratization—or rather equalization—of England in such a way that when it finally arrives, it may produce merely a dreary mediocrity of groups that have been too long kept under and not allowed to find their own way to self-improvement through the scramble for money and power. This we *have* been able to do in America, and my optimistic opinion is that the United States at the present time is politically more advanced than any other part of the world, because we have been through the worst of the careerist phase and are coming out on the other side. We have seen in the last fifty years a revival of the democratic creativeness which presided at the birth of the Republic and flourished up through the Civil War. This began to assert itself strongly during the first two decades of the century, was stimulated by the depression that followed the collapse of the stock market and culminated in the New Deal. It was accompanied by a remarkable renascence of American arts and letters.

This phase seems now to have run its course, and I do not know what is coming next; but I doubt whether it is possible today for us either to relapse in our traditional way into one of those periods of industrial gourmandizing and speculative inflation that have usually followed reform administrations or, in an effort to meet the need for government control of industry, without which modern life is impossible, to reproduce Hitler's brutality or Stalin's bureaucratic nightmare. Our careerism will crop up again, after war service and wartime socialism; but the old kind will be curbed by the demands of labor and the rudiments of community conscience, and we may hope that the new kind, which offers its prizes to labor officials and government clerks rather than to the "captains of industry," will be redeemed by our relatively high standards of security and education.

Democratic Socialism. I do not feel, as some people do, that socialism has been discredited by what has happened in Russia or that socialism is incompatible with democracy. The only thing that can make democracy real is the ability on the part of a people to distribute responsibility; and this ability the Russians have never possessed. An American travelling in Russia a few years before the war was amazed to find in Soviet officialdom exactly the same characteristics of timidity, evasiveness and inaction that one reads about in Herzen's memoirs as prevailing in the reign of Nicholas I. One realized that in the United States the pettiest position of authority involved a sphere, however limited, in which the individual must think and act for himself. The bank teller must decide for himself whether or not your check is good, the ticket seller at the railroad station must be able to proceed unfalteringly in making out however long a ticket—whereas in Russia he immediately appealed to the official just above him, and this official appealed to another. The result of this method in Russia has been that, in order to get anything done, they have had to train a new race of officials who *would* take responsibility and have thus produced the Communist Party, a special élite caste who aimed to be energetic and conscientious and to see that what was supposed to be done got done. Anyone who has ever been stranded in a Russian provincial town and rescued by the local G.P.U. man or ill in a Russian hospital and helpless to get anything done for him save by going to the Communist director or the Communist head nurse, is able to understand perfectly how this state of things has come about. (The Germans, in a similar way, delivered themselves up to Hitler by their incapacity for individual action: they are more practical and systematic than the Russians, but they seem to be able to function only as units in an organizational hierarchy, with the orders coming down from the top.) It is thus not merely socialism which has created Stalin or even Stalin who has created himself, but the Russians who, by default or self-dependence, have allowed him to become their tyrant. In the Soviet Union they have passed the buck till it has become the exclusive possession of a dictator and his gang, and Comrade Stalin is soon Generalissimo Stalin and the only candidate at every election, while the Soviets— which were supposed to be popular councils—soon took counsel from only one source. You cannot expect a people who have always been used to a despotism to produce democratic institutions simply because the power has been shifted to a different class. The Russians still wanted —it had been a part of their religion—the authority of a great earthly father; and Stalin, the political careerist, with those who had a stake in his career and cared nothing about Lenin's socialism, were glad to gratify them in this department.

But we in the United States have had a training in individual self-dependence. We have got along remarkably well in balancing government control between the state and the federal authorities, and our more or less efficient public services such as the school system and the post office have not often lent themselves to serious bureaucratic abuses. Why should not socialized American industries and socialized American institutions be handled by their own staffs in equilibrium with the central authorities instead of becoming enslaved by these? And if we don't like our socialist president, why can we not always refuse to reëlect him?

Better Human Beings. I am beginning to suspect, however, that socialism will not simply go on to its goal of making everybody healthy and happy, but will presently change its object to that of turning out better human beings. In Naples, I had been thinking that such people as the gutter-bred swarming Neapolitans should not be allowed to exist, and that the greatest crime of the Catholic Church, and one of the greatest social crimes possible, was to forbid the use of contraceptives; but, home in New York, I was forced to admit that such people as most of the New Yorkers, pale and high-pressured and underdeveloped, ought not to exist either. The Neapolitans had at least one advantage over them: they were cheerful and able to sing. It may be that these big modern cities are only good to be bombed and destroyed. The respect for human life in itself has, in any case, largely disappeared in the course of this last war, and I doubt whether enough now survives to inspire the organizers of socialism to try to keep everybody alive and see that everybody gets an equal chance. The ideal of equality on a low social level is probably an impossible one, anyway. The only thing, among human beings, that really arouses enthusiasm to the point of effective action is the idea of excelling or making other people excel. Better hygiene and better training will certainly improve the race, but we shall not find this enough. We shall want to *breed* better people, and it is unlikely that, in our kind of society, we shall return in any very intensive way to the old aristocratic method of limiting sexual selection to the members of certain families. We shall rather be coming to apply every device of physical stimulant and mental suggestion, resorting to the techniques of biology, psychology, glandular science and who knows what other methods, in the attempt to produce men and women who are longer-lived or taller and stronger or more intellectual and skilful. People may at first be invited to volunteer for such experiments, but it is certain that, once better-equipped people have really been produced, they will take their place at the top, and it is likely that they will discourage the reproduction of people of inferior stock. We may even eventually have conflicts between the people of different artificial breeds or between different countries or groups who want to breed different kinds of people. This suggestion sometimes rouses the objection that it would be dangerous to give powers of biological control to any mere committee of human beings; but if we accept without question a Board of Health, I do not see why we should refuse in time to accept a Board of Breeding. The worst kind of thing that can happen in the attempt to improve the breed was demonstrated by the Nazis with their mythical Aryan race, their snuffing-out of the insane and the ill, and their mass incinerations of kinds of people whom they regarded as not up to themselves; but it would be just as foolish to allow this to discourage us with eugenics as it would be to give up the practice of medicine on account of the horrible acts that were perpetrated by the Nazi doctors. If we can produce, from some cousin of the jackal or the wolf, the dachshund and the Great Dane, the Pekinese and the poodle, what should we not be able to do with man?

The Anthropoids. I have found it strangely reassuring to read, during the years of the war, the current books about the anthropoid apes. The status of these animals is changing. T. H. Huxley in the last century had already taken account of the fact that the great apes were much closer to men than they were to any species of monkey. Like us, they have shed their tails and, like us, they walk erect. But the age that linked man with the apes also tended to make a sharp distinction between what were called the "animals" and the "human race." The creature that talked about his "soul" and considered that soul "divine" was frightened by the idea of kinship with creatures that could not pronounce words, that were hairier than we and that lived in trees; and even non-religious people in that period of top-hats, straight trousers, trimmed beards and rolled umbrellas, with its background of locomotives and factories, snubbed the anthropoids like country relations. Their doings did not seem compatible with the capitalized abstractions of Empire and Progress in terms of which human beings were still able to think of their own activities. But in our age of mass stultification, wholesale destruction of human works and mechanized civilian massacre, the anthropologist can no longer afford to be snobbish about the anthropoids. Doctrines like those of the American "Humanists" or of Huxley's grandson Aldous that continue to draw a definite line between human and animal kind, or between a part of our nature which is supposed to be human and a part which is supposed to be animal, seem as quaint as the medical analysis which accounted for differences in temperament by ascribing them to the action of four "humors." As humanity has been shedding its religions and discrediting its political myths, as it has been demonstrating its closeness to the brute and making its pretensions to divine origin ridiculous, the higher apes have been taking on an aspect more human and "civilized." The anthropoids are treated in captivity with much more consideration than formerly. The apes in old-fashioned zoos were prisoners that lived in squalor and that deteriorated like the inmates of human jails; but the anthropoids in the Yerkes laboratory are cared for and instructed and made friends with almost as if they were human children, and the result is that they display abilities hardly suspected a century ago, and our picture of them has changed completely. They use tools, we now know; they are able to talk to one another and they more or less understand what we say; they have a family and tribal life which is evidently not very much different from that of primitive human beings. They seem to penetrate situations with what we describe as "insight"; they seem to do what we call "reason"; and the most sympathetic observers believe that they have been able to discover in them the beginnings of the moral and the aesthetic senses. It has even been suggested by Gertrude Lintz, the former owner of the gorilla Gargantua, who has kept and studied apes for years, that chimpanzees—which can be taught to sew—might be trained to do the work of mechanics.

These apes help us to face in a more agreeable way than by contemplating the ruins of Europe the fact that man is himself an animal, not so very far in advance of the anthropoids, and that his problem is to recognize this and the conditions under which he may develop. It is at the same time a relief and a stimulus to read the results of the researches of the scientists who have been working on the anthropoids. These beasts are much cleverer than we realized and more like us in their social habits; but, instead of having the consequence of appearing to degrade human beings, this enables us to relegate to a more rudimentary level a good deal of human activity—sexual, political, economic—that may have seemed to us to have been a part of what we call "civilization," and to understand the relative crudity—relative, that is, in relation to the last century's godlike idea of itself—of the materials with which we have to work. "If," says Mr. Robert M. Yerkes of the Yale Institute of Psychology, one of the foremost authorities in this field, "as servant of science the chimpanzee should help to make clearer and more attractive to mankind [by exhibiting its susceptibility to training] ways for the achievement of greater social-mindedness, dependability and coöperativeness, how immeasurable our debt to it! The really important things for us at present are recognition and active acceptance of the principles of modifiability, controllability and consequent improvability of human nature."

One of the most fortifying experiences of my trip was a visit to Norman Kemp Smith, under whom I had sat at Princeton, where for a time he was professor of philosophy, and who afterwards held for twenty-five years the chair of logic and metaphysics at Edinburgh University. I found him living alone. His wife had died since I had seen him last, and his daughter had married and gone to India. His family were an old Scotch housekeeper, an old black spaniel and a homeless cat who had come one day to live with them. In compliance with the government's request to avoid unnecessary travelling, he had spent the whole war in Edinburgh. He greeted me with his usual impassivity, as if he had seen me that morning in class, and entertained me with his old cordiality. He was over seventy now and had reached the age of retirement; but he was still amazingly active. The night that I arrived he had just got out of bed from a fairly serious attack of grippe, but he took me out in the damp Scotch weather for a brisk and rather strenuous walk which involved a good deal of hill-climbing and clambering over stone fences, while he explained to me the topography of Edinburgh and the various historical landmarks. He had all of his old lively interest in literature, science, ideas and news—in everything men were doing. Philosophy had always meant for him everything that men had thought.

In the morning we had breakfast together, and he insisted on my eating the porridge in the traditional Scottish way: you had to take with each spoonful of porridge a spoonful of cold milk—which he said brought the flavor out better. Then we would retire to work, and the housekeeper brought tea at eleven. In the afternoon people dropped in, or we would do something in the city, to which he was a wonderful guide. He seemed to know every street and took me to see a variety of people in the somber and august old houses. I remember one man especially, who wanted to talk about nothing but Greek. He came from the country and had had few "advantages," but had made himself a formidable scholar. He now lived retired and alone, in shabby high-ceilinged rooms, and devoted himself to Plato. I had met C. M. Bowra in London and introduced his name, but Kemp Smith's friend was positively shocked at Bowra's recent interest in Russian, as if it were a treason to Greek, and said sharply that the understanding of a single Greek writer like Plato made such demands on the reader that one's whole life was not enough to exhaust him. In the evening, if there was no one to dinner, we sat and talked in front of the fire, which, on account of the shortage of coal, could only be lighted at hours when there was somebody in the room. The house would grow cold around us. Kemp Smith always sent me to bed with a handful of things to read, of which I particularly remember a report written down by Boswell after an interview with David Hume. Hume was a great favorite of Kemp Smith's—he had lately done a book about him; and he said that he thought this dialogue showed both Boswell and Hume at their best: Boswell in his portraiture of Hume and Hume in his dry refusal to yield anything to Boswell's almost tearful plea for the immortality of the soul. I remembered how Kemp Smith had once told us at college that if you did not believe in immortality, you ought not to allow yourself to be convinced by the death of a favorite daughter.

One day I remarked that the immediate future seemed to me extremely depressing, and he vigorously took me up, declaring that he thought it looked hopeful. When I asked him how he could possibly think so, he replied: "People's complacency's shaken." A lot of ground had been cleared, he felt; we knew what elements we had to deal with and we should have to come to grips with our problems. A constructive age might well ensue. He often made fun of the theologies and churches; but when I said that I thought it was time to get rid of the word *God*, since we had "no need of that hypothesis" to account for the life that was in us and the coherence of the universe, he said, "I don't know any better word." He was of an older generation than I and had, I suppose, in Scotland, had a more rigorous religious training. For myself, I am extremely reluctant to call anything whatever "God," for the word has too many connotations of obsolete and miraculous mythologies; and what Kemp Smith called God was, I thought, something mainly identifiable with a vigorous physical persistence, a rectitude in relation to others and to one's own work in the world, and a faith in the endurance of the human mind.

APPENDIX A

WHEN THIS CHAPTER FIRST APPEARED in the *New Yorker*, I received an interesting letter from Mr. W. Hanks of Worthing, Sussex, England, which throws some further light on the situation I tried to describe. He has given me permission to quote it here.

I spent ten years in America before the war and I'm half British and half American by birth. Like you, I deplored the lack of friendship between the U.S. and British troops. I have set down some reasons to account for this from the British point of view. Many of them apply particularly to those who were in the Mediterranean campaign. Most of them are unfair.

1. That the G.I.'s were having a whale of a time with the girls in England while the British were doing the early fighting in the desert.

2. That the Americans were playing the same game as in the last war—collect the money and capture the British trade, then come in time for the victory parade.

3. No troops like other bodies of troops, English, American or any other nationality. (If you want to enjoy yourself, it's best to be the only unit in the town.) "Americans no business in Greece—look what they said in their papers," etc.

4. The British troops imagined in Italy that the Americans were all "base wallahs." (A fighting division seldom sees any other division when it is in the line, and it is only when they come out for a rest that they meet other formations.) "There's a hundred men in Naples for one Yank in the line," etc.

5. It was argued that if everyone was putting everything into the pot, the Americans were using up too much war effort on their own comfort. For example, unlimited supplies of clothes and food, "a jeep for every private," particularly in the rear areas, when the British couldn't get them for use in the forward areas. This partly answers your comment *re* the lack of lifts to U.S. troops by British drivers.

6. And the old ones—that the Yanks had too much money, that they didn't know how to drink and that they made too much noise.

I'm afraid that ideas such as the above are firmly fixed in the minds of even the supposedly better-educated British soldiers. I also found that the members of an officers' mess were not interested in hearing about America, although they would condescend to read my American magazines. Of course, they cried out in scorn at those dreadful advertisements of G.I. Joes making Walt Whitman speeches on the beach just after landing, but they didn't care to be told that American soldiers also became slightly sick when they read them.

I was with a field artillery regiment. We were due for a rest after a long spell in Italy when the Greek business turned up. We went to Greece expecting an unpleasant "Black and Tan" job for the rest of the war. As far as we could gather, in the early stages, we were breaking up a riot. I saw a few examples of what the "rebels" had done. It was sufficient to make me feel, at the time, that we were on the right side. At the end of my eight months in

Greece I had given up all hope of ever finding out which side was which. . . .

Entertainment in a British mess is liable to be about as gay as a church supper. One thing you must remember is that in the regular army the junior officers don't speak unless they are spoken to. This goes on for years apparently, although there are occasional lapses when everyone gets stinking drunk, clothes are torn off and drink is thrown. It is talked about for some time afterwards.

You probably did something dreadful in taking a woman into that mess. If you had taken twenty, you would have been more popular.

APPENDIX B

Since my view of the greek situation seems not very widely held, I am glad to be able to quote in support of it (from *Partisan Picture* by Basil Davidson) a letter to the London *Times* of February 24, 1946, by Captain Francis Noel-Baker, M.P., who, says Mr. Davidson, "had been closely associated with Greek affairs during the war and spoke from long experience of Greece."

From 1942 onwards it was difficult to detect either objectivity or consistency in British policy towards Greece, and I believe that I am not alone in thinking that that policy was one of the causes of the civil war in which it culminated. In my view, two cardinal mistakes were made. First, ignoring the popular reaction against the pre-war Fascist dictatorship and against King George for his part in installing and maintaining that dictatorship, the British Government persisted right until the eve of liberation, in "hoping" (and working) for a royal restoration. Second, in their fear of the left wing (which in Greece, as elsewhere in Europe, was the core of the resistance movement), the British authorities did nothing to encourage "moderates" to join E.A.M. in the early days when it was not yet Communist-dominated, but, on the contrary, tried to create a "counter-balance" by building up "na-

353

tionalist" groups of E.A.M.'s extreme political opponents. The tragedy of this policy was that it produced precisely that situation which it sought most desperately to avoid. Baffled and exasperated by British maneuvers, E.A.M. became more extremist, more Communist and eventually violently anti-British; whereas our "national" bulwark soon collapsed.

APPENDIX C

Another favorable greek view of England is to be found in the following poem composed in Greek and translated by the poet.

TO MOST ADORED GREAT BRITAIN

A Hymn

How I admire and wonder thee
o! great Britain country!
as I consider thee holding
the bridles of all the world.

O respectable and glorious
and powerful England
thou art the joy of all the world
and the alone liberty.

Thou art the judge of the world
and police captain for all
and the greatest supporter
of all the weak persons.

According to thy somuch gold
thou art the richest on world
and thy paper money also
has the superior price.

But thou hast and most treasors
by much precious stones,
thou hast too and most flaming pearls
and legendary prices.

In this earth situation
thou hast the superior
and thou doest live the excellent
and much sweetest life.

Thou got many colossal ships
possessions and colonies
and abundant richness and goods
and very solid houses.

                              (it follows)

NOTES FROM A EUROPEAN DIARY:

1963-1964

1

PARIS

The Decline of Glamor. Paris, I am rather surprised to find, has no longer much glamor for me. In some ways it seems commonplace. After the war, one felt that Europe had been wrecked, and this gave it a certain tragic interest, but now a country that has to any extent recovered is inevitably seen as belonging to a more and more standardized, a more and more Americanized world.

I went one night to the Olympia Music Hall, which I remembered from the early twenties as a rather uninspired imitation of the similar theaters in London. I had seen Little Tich there. Now I sat through a first half that consisted of vaudeville acts, some of them very good, but was astonished by a second half which featured American-type entertainment of the coarsest and most raucous kind: a jazz orchestra, a spasm of the Twist, women torch singers, tremendously applauded, who never let up on their nervous Twist steps. They sing into a microphone, which is sometimes held in the right hand and sometimes comes out of the corsage, with a great cable like a garden hose. When a guitarist accompanies the songstress, also with a microphone cable, it looks as if they are going to skip rope. The singers and the *compère* and the comics and the monologist all deafen you and grate upon you with their horrible magnified voices. It is impossible to escape from these voices. If you move to the rear of the balcony, they come out of the backs of the seats in front of you. I had been puzzled by the posters and the names in lights outside, which announced such American-sounding stars as "Billy Holladay," of whom I had never heard, but they all turned out to be French. It was fashionable to be American, and they occasionally sang an American song, which I imagine they had learned by rote. The men often had Beatle haircuts. One called himself Leny Escudero, but actually came from Belleville, one of the more squalid sections of Paris. The teenagers in the audience sometimes made such a row that one could not even hear the blaring voices. When the Beatles appeared at the Olympia, one could not hear a word or a note.

Versailles Under de Gaulle. We took our daughter to Versailles on a holiday. Gray weather; a great flock of *petit-bourgeois* visitors. These French seemed dreary and dwarfed, and so alien to the royal château, with its gardens and its great galleries, its huge portraits and wall-filling paintings of crowded historical scenes, that these latter had themselves the appearance of something discarded and shopworn, shoved away behind museum barriers, no longer felt by the people—who moved past them with no signs of interest—as having any real relation to themselves. The glorious past was no longer there, though, remotely, it lurked in the background in the anachronistic figure of de Gaulle. He seems to make no contact with the people. We encountered no enthusiasm for him. I don't think they particularly enjoy him but they don't know what they would rather have.

Gleams from the Past. I was reminded for a moment, in the restaurant at Versailles, of my winter excursions to

Contrexéville, in the company of army friends, when, at
the time of the first war, I was stationed at Vittel in the
Vosges: the cold tiled floor, the bare winter light, the red
wine that warmed us at dinner, the smell of the cold tiled
toilet; and in Paris I remembered the excitement of my
visits to Paris on furlough, when I stayed at the American
University Club in the Rue de Richelieu, and was
enchanted by the bookshops in the Avenue de l'Opéra,
with big price signs on the second-hand sets, and by the
productions of Sacha and Lucien Guitry, with the delightful *gamine* Yvonne Printemps, at that time the wife
of Sacha. I thought, in the Bois de Boulogne, of a scene
there with my first great love, when I went to France in
the summer of 1921, and this brought back my many
evenings at the out-of-door Théâtre de l'Oasis, for which
Mme Picabia had been able to recruit Yvette Guilbert,
Aristide Bruant and other vedettes of the nineties. And
then there was the autumn of 1935, when I stopped over
on my way back from Russia and saw the Jolases, the
Malraux and the Joyces, and, coming from the Soviet
Union, was charmed by the coiffures and general chic—
so little in evidence now—of the women one saw in the
theaters.

But all such things had now fallen back onto the map
of a much flatter world, in which Washington and Boston
and New York were centers at least as active as Paris; in
which France and England seemed comparatively supine,
while the United States was energetic and aggressive.
Paris now is almost a provincial city, though de Gaulle,
with *la gloire* and *la France*, hovers high in the empyrean
and Malraux tries to make the place shine by cleaning up
the ancient monuments—it is somewhat disconcerting,
however, to find the Louvre turning yellow—and ringing
changes on the opera houses and theaters. The Opéra has
been given a new lease on life; we heard an excellent

Wozzeck, sung in German, and the best production of *Carmen* I remember, realistic rather than romantic, with costumes and sets out of Goya.

French Canada. It is curious to find that French Canada, about which I am now writing articles, does not seem so remote in Paris as I had been expecting it would. In its present nationalistic phase, it makes, in the French-speaking world, a point of intense vivacity. For the first time since Louis XV refused to send the French Canadians reënforcements against the English and sold them out at the Peace of Paris, the mother country has been taking some interest in them. De Gaulle is making passes at French Canada, has established a center there, and Malraux has visited Quebec and orated to the Québecois, telling them that they, too, are French—*démarches* which, however, I gather, have not always been well received; they cannot compensate for two centuries of scornful indifference. We have seen a documentary French film in which the Province of Quebec is presented as a patriotic French colony which ought to be recognized as an integral part of the realm of France. It included a short speech by one of the leaders of the nationalist movement, who aimed, as it was explained, to be President of a French Canada independent of English Canada, and the new big buildings of Montreal were exhibited with the apparent implication that they were the work of French Canadians. There is a French Canadian library in Paris, from which I have been getting books through a young French Canadian friend, who works both in a Paris news agency and on the Larousse encyclopaedia. Professor Étiemble, in his book, *Parlez-Vous Franglais?,"* suggests that the obnoxious *"living,"* now used instead of *"salon"* for "living room," be eliminated by substituting for it the French Canadian word *vivoir*.

The Details of Change. It was some time before I was able to take account of all the things that made Paris seem so different: the abolition of urinals, the prostitutes driven off the streets (both the results of a de Gaulle cleanup), the disappearance of the Paris *Herald,* the absence of that strong-smelling petrol that I had always remembered as of the essence of Paris, the almost total disappearance of the pretty and well-turned-out Parisian women. Then the signs, which are likely to be printed in German and English as well as in French—and there are many American signs. Frenchmen still take hours for lunch, locking up their offices and banks, but they also today have quick-lunch rooms, which they can only describe as "snack bars," since—the institution being quite new—there is as yet no word for this in French. And, finally, the atmosphere of official repression, which, I suppose, has been partly brought on by the struggle against the Algerian conspirators. I have never before felt this in Paris. The government now censors books and papers for both moral and political reasons. De Gaulle's opponent Defferre, the Socialist Mayor of Marseille, is never allowed to be heard on either radio or television. It is dismaying to find Parisians, in a place like the Café de la Paix, looking about them, as people used to do in Moscow, to make sure that they will not be overheard.

The Young People. But perhaps the most striking change is in the attitude of the young toward the old; the traditional submission to parents and acceptance of established conventions now seem largely to have broken down. A young professor at the Sorbonne told me that he

would never, in his student days, have ventured to
address a professor—if you wanted to communicate with
him, you had to write him a letter—but that nowadays
his own students did not hesitate to speak to him with the
utmost freedom; they did everything except *tutoyer* him.
The young people now have for their elders—for anyone,
that is, over forty—a whole pejorative vocabulary. The
first and commonest term was, I believe, *les croulants*
("the *crumbling ones*"), but this is now being improved
upon with more ingenious ideas: *les "son-et-lumière"*
("*Son et Lumière*" is the official name of the program for
lighting up the old châteaux and broadcasting historical
information) and *les pas cotés dans l'Argus* ("not listed in
the *Argus*," a paper entirely devoted to the trade in
secondhand cars). Old ladies are *les viocques*. (This last,
I understand, is not recent.) Other examples of young
people's slang are such superlatives as *formid, sensass* and
bouledum, the last of which, it seems, is a contraction of
bouleversant d'humanité. The equivalent of our "terrific"
is *vachement terrible* or *bovine terrible*. One slang phrase
that particularly amuses me is *les zozoteurs*, for *les auteurs*,
which has a suggestion of *zozoter*, "to lisp."

"*La Reine Verte.*" We took our daughter to *La Reine
Verte*, which sounded like an interesting novelty. It is
amusing in a circus-like way, but not a serious artistic
exploit, as a review had misled me to believe. This
entertainment is simply a concoction of variegated and
now mostly dated clichés: Surrealism, Dürrenmatt, Cocteau, jazz, electronic music, "*toute la boutique.*" After the
first shocks and mystifications, you learn that it purports
to deal with three large and obvious subjects—"*l'Amour,
la Mort et l'Homme.*" Death is also somehow Nature and
Vegetation; the character who represents her has much in

common with both Cocteau's Sphinx and Dürrenmatt's Old Lady. The author or the producer has evidently been carried away by Grandville's illustrations for *Les Fleurs Animées,* and the costumes are straight out of these. You have Grandville's frogs and insects as well as his flowers, and even his elegantly stylized watering pot. L'Homme, like Adonis and Atthis, seems to be a "vegetable god," who, after being slain by Nature-Death, is eventually resurrected. Enough sentimental music to offset the electronic loopings; some bizarre clowning and tumbling in a now rather ancient vein, which would undoubtedly have left Cocteau unmoved. At the close of the first act, somebody yelled something about *"blague,"* but if the producer had hoped for anything like the demonstrations over *Le Sacre du Printemps*—the reviews having suggested audacity—there was no possibility of it. Even for a really audacious talent such as that of Jean Genet, it is probably impossible, in the theater, to become so outrageous as to rouse the public. All the horrors and the moral perversities have become an accepted routine; all the grotesqueries have been calmly digested; no dissonance any longer jars. They have all been absorbed by the boulevard, and *La Reine Verte* is nothing if not boulevard. (Since this was written, however, a semi-private attempt to put on the stage *La Philosophie dans le Boudoir* of the Marquis de Sade has been stopped by the Paris police. The de Gaulle administration has been very strong against pornography.)

Le Doux Train-Train de Notre Vie Paisible et Monotone. Here in Paris, at the Hôtel de Castille, just opposite the Ritz Bar—where Henry James once lived in a building now owned by Chanel, and Turgenev in the Rue de Rivoli, just around the corner—with our daughter away at school, we have settled down to a life which resembles unexpectedly our life in Cambridge. As usual, I read and write and buy the English weeklies, as well as *L'Express, Paris-Soir,* and sometimes *Le Canard Enchaîné,* which is today making fun of de Gaulle in exactly the same systematic and rather monotonous way as, at the time of the first war, it made fun of Clemenceau. In the evenings, we go to the theater or, just as we did on Brattle Street, to some promising French or foreign movie. Usually, we take advantage of our *demi-pension* arrangement by dining at the hotel here. Altogether, it is very pleasant.

For me, it is especially a pleasure—after having, in connection with writing about Canada and our Civil War, had to read a good many mediocre books—to be able to enjoy at last some really well-written ones: Smollett's *Travels through France and Italy,* the excellent selection by Auden of Walter De la Mare's poetry, a volume of Saintsbury's called *Miscellaneous Essays,* which I had never seen before but picked up at Blackwell's in Oxford (Saintsbury at his best, in his middle period: 1892)—a masterly study of the differences between English and French literature, little essays on minor French writers such as Chamfort, Parny and Dorat, and essays on the development of English prose which contain the first sketches of his later long work on the history of English prose rhythm. If these papers were ever read by the *Partisan Review* boys and the other New York critics of their school, they would either not understand them or, if they did, be filled with despair. By the "explicating" New Critics and the academic myth-and-symbol men they could never be read at all. An essay on the English novel is less satisfactory than the others. Saintsbury is supercilious about Howells and Henry James, and seems to believe that the return to romantic fiction—which I think produced nothing lasting except, perhaps, Robert Louis

Stevenson, who is best when he is *not* being too romantic
—is a perfectly splendid thing.

Inedibility of Paul Claudel. I saw that the Barrault
company was doing Claudel's play *Le Soulier de Satin.* I
thought that I ought to go and got the text to read it first.
Though I had never been attracted by what I knew of
Claudel, I had a certain curiosity about him, and especially about this play, which a lady whose taste I respect
had told me she read at twenty, when it made a deep
impression upon her. But I only lasted halfway through,
and I felt I couldn't face a performance. I have rarely
disliked a book so much. There are occasional gleams of
poetry, but the combination of rhetoric and religiosity,
the supersexual and antisexual idealism that seems so
effortful and not quite sincere, was rejected by my literary stomach. The preposterous hero and heroine are
prevented from consummating their passion by the fact
that the latter is married, and they are supposed to be
enjoying a higher bliss through the self-denial this im-
poses. It turned out that what had impressed my friend
was that the heroine had safeguarded herself from temptation by pledging herself to the Virgin. She says that this
had the effect of persuading her not to flinch from exposing herself to temptation.

Yet some passages in *Le Soulier de Satin*—in which
the characters do a great deal of travelling and which does
aim at a certain universal scope—made me feel again the
flimsiness of human life. Surrounded by the void of the
universe, we agitate ourselves, one must sometimes feel,
to very dubious purpose. Our little lives soon go out, and
is it really at all surprising that in order to fulfill our
immediate desires we should not shrink from extinguish-
ing other lives, from sending them into the void
before us? Eventually, *we* shall go blank. What differ-

ence does it make, after all, if we terminate a few other existences in order to prolong our own?

Livid Daylight. The French naturalistic novelists were always talking about *"un jour blafard."* You would find in them such descriptions as *"Un jour blafard était tamisé au travers les rideaux de guipure sale."* You have to spend a winter in Paris really to know what this *jour blafard* is. It is what you get most of the time. I composed a short poem on the subject:

HIVER PARISIEN

Le jour blafard
Donne le cafard.

It makes you, as Elena [my wife] says, sympathize with the eagerness of the boy in Proust to see real sunlight falling on the balcony, which means that he can go out to the Champs Élysées.

Assassination of Kennedy. Elena much upset emotionally. We both had had bronchial and sinus colds, and that weekend we sat dismally in the hotel room surrounded by the ghastly newspapers. The whole thing is sickening: the sordidness of the assassins—a schizoid boy who had thought he was a Marxist, a boastful crook who ran a small night club; the ineptitude of the Dallas police; the humiliating position of the President, who had had to run around the country soliciting political support. I was surprised at the reaction in France and, as I gathered, in Europe generally. The Parisians had been putting on a great show of anti-Americanism. Elena has been more aware of this, in her everyday contacts with people, than I have. She says that when she has asked in a shop for anything that sounded American, the reply was *"Ce n'est pas français, ça,"* but that now the people in shops and even the taxidrivers are likely to commiserate with her. This shows how much, in Europe, they have really been counting on us, with Kennedy at our head, to come to the rescue of the West. Though they rail at us, they have envied and idealized us. They do not know what the United States is like now; they imagine that we are safe and comfortable. And now Kennedy, who had been doing his best, against truculent and well-organized opposition, to establish an enlightened administration—to work for a reduction of taxes, a guarantee of civil rights for the Negroes and a peaceful settlement with Russia—has fallen victim to the worst elements in American society: the gangsters, the delinquents, the baboons of the South. When Kennedy was received in Dallas, according to Henry Brandon, who was there—the Washington correspondent of the London *Sunday Times* —there was a plane overhead with a streamer that said, "Coexistence is Surrender," and pickets protesting against his policy in regard to the Negro. Someone is reported to have said, "Whoever did it, I'm glad he got the nigger-lover!"

"Home Thoughts from Abroad." Helen [our daughter] writes from her school in Switzerland that she has been homesick, since the murder of Kennedy, to talk to other Americans. I feel sometimes—since seeing Don Stewart and Tom Matthews in London—that I need to talk to Americans, but I should dread going back at this moment. I was finding it a strain before I left, and now it seems even more forbidding. Nicholas Nabokov tells me that when he was last—not long ago—in New York, he had a certain feeling of apprehension that he might not get away without being beaten up. A bullying taxi-

driver had tried to convert him to Seventh Day Adventism. I was told by the wife of the Washington correspondent of one of the Paris papers that she had been oppressed in Washington by the fear of she didn't know what and was anxious to be back in Paris.

Lee Oswald's violent acts have obviously something in common with the riotings and wreckings that have been going on at home. The recent student riot at Princeton was one of the worst on record. The students tore down the President's fence and destroyed a lot of other property. When I talked about this with the former Master of one of the Yale houses, he asked me whether I had ever been involved in a riot, and told me about one at Yale. He found that he had lost all authority: if you tried to say anything to restrain them, they would simply throw something at you. There had been, also, before I left, the meaningless outbreak of young people—who did thousands of dollars' worth of damage to an expensive Long Island house—as the aftermath of an engagement party.

Later, in Manchester, when I saw Marcus Cunliffe, one of the Englishmen who knows most about the United States, he was speculating as to whether the very distinction, combined with the advantages, of Kennedy had not aroused an envious resentment in the breasts of a good many of his countrymen. That the President of the United States should be rich, good-looking, full of charm, young-appearing yet extremely competent, married to a beautiful wife—surely all this was hard to forgive. How a Lee Oswald must have hated him! And how relieved many people must have been at seeing this brilliant figure extinguished! I think there may be something in this. There is certainly a sulky rebellion against all forms of seriousness and superiority, the acceptance of standards of excellence. The beatniks represent it in literature, the Abstract and Pop painters in art, and in music you have it in such exploits as those of John Cage, when, for example, he asks people to listen to six radios simultaneously playing different programs. In all this, mediocre abilities or men with no ability at all are trying to divert attention by demonstrating against discipline.

The much advertized film *Cleopatra,* of which, just before I came over, I saw the first half in Boston but couldn't stand to stay for the rest, is so stupid, in such bad taste, and so incoherent and senseless that, made at such tremendous expense, I thought at the time that it indicated some great emptiness and bankruptcy in American life.

Montmartre. On Sunday afternoon, December 1st, we went for a walk on Montmartre—Place Pigalle, Place Clichy—where I don't think I have been for years. There were a good many people out—small and dark and unenlivened, quiet and almost morose, as they strolled past the five-franc strip-tease joints, the booths that sold cheap sausages and pastry, and the posters for movies full of violence and vice. They reminded me of the low-spirited strollers that I had seen in Moscow in 1935, trying feebly to enjoy themselves in the Park of Culture and Rest.

The Rat in the Place de l'Opéra. We have been both more or less ill all winter. The winter weather has always been bad in Paris, but I have never had to spend a whole winter here before. Nowadays the air is bad as well as the weather: impregnated with the damp, it is poisoned by the fumes from the cars and made stifling by the central heating. You wake up half asphyxiated. We went finally to a nose-and-throat doctor. I remarked that the air was bad, and he said yes, of course it was: it had become a serious problem for the city. He told me that an experiment had been performed to find out just how bad it was. A caged rat had been exposed to the fumes of the Place de l'Opéra, very near which we have been living: "He was dead at the end of half an hour." We found that the chambermaids had heard this impressive story. One wonders whether anything more—now that the lethal character of the air has been so definitely *constaté*—has been done about the situation.

Simone de Beauvoir. I have read, or rather skipped through, the second and third volumes of Simone de Beauvoir's memoirs: *La Force de l'Âge* and *La Force des Choses.* She is certainly a very boring woman and a very unattractive writer. She has absolutely no sense of humor and no sense of proportion or of literary form. She tells you about every movie that she and Sartre went to together, very often without adding any comment. Her attitude toward distinguished contemporaries with whom she has been acquainted is entirely determined by their relations with Sartre. Camus did not approve of Sartre's politics, and a serious rupture occurred; Jouvet did not produce Sartre's plays; in the case of Malraux, it is difficult to know precisely what Simone de Beauvoir's grievances are, but it is obvious that the de Gaulle Minister and the obstinate supporter of the Communists must be unsympathetic to one another. It is embarrassing to read her account of her relations with Nelson Algren and of Sartre's requesting her by cable to defer her return to France on account of his affair with someone else. One ends by feeling rather sorry for Mlle de Beauvoir. I do not see why the threnody on advancing age with which the book ends should have made some women readers indignant. I found it quite honest and touching. Elena has read her book *Le Deuxième Sexe* and says that Simone de Beauvoir tells you everything about women except that they are attractive to men.

A Winter Mood. Nowadays, from time to time, in almost any connection, I find myself tending to feel that human works of art are futile because the beings who create them must die. Why go to so much trouble, expend so much energy and thought and taste when we are so perishable ourselves and even the things that we construct to outlast us must eventually perish, too? This mood has just been brought on by reading an essay on the rococo in a book by Cyril Connolly. He tells us to hurry up if we want to enjoy the rococo: "Even as I write some façade is crumbling; a ceiling flakes, panelling is being stripped, plasterwork crushed, chimneypieces torn out, a Chippendale looking-glass cracks and innumerable pieces of china are thumbed and shattered."

"Der Stellvertreter." The great theatrical sensation of the season has been Rolf Hochhuth's *Der Stellvertreter,* done in Paris as *Le Vicaire,* in London as *The Representative* and in New York as *The Deputy* (these names apply to the Pope, "The Vicar of Christ on Earth"). I do not know whether there has ever in the history of the drama been a case like that of this play. Here is a work on so huge a scale that it would take seven hours to perform, and on account of the nature of the work this would hardly be practicable even if it were performed on successive evenings, like *Back to Methuselah,* or in the afternoon and evening of one day, like *Mourning Becomes Electra.* It contains a good deal that is theatrically moving and it is written in a kind of rough free verse, but too much of the dialogue consists of what are really editorial matter and news bulletins, which on the stage would be intolerably tiresome. The subject is the situation in Ger-

many created by the murder of the Jews, and the attempts of a Jesuit priest to induce the Pope, Pius XII, to protest against these massacres. He is unsuccessful in this and decides to die a martyr's death. He puts on the Star of David and allows himself to be sent to Auschwitz, where eventually he is shot. The exploit of Hochhuth's hero was derived from the career of a real priest, whose story was, however, somewhat different, and there are real persons who are presented under their own names: the Apostolic Nuncio in Germany, the Pope, Eichmann and Kurt Gerstein, that mysterious S.S. officer who, wearing the Nazi uniform, worked clandestinely against the Nazis. The play includes a whole panorama of the forces involved in the situation: the Nuncio's house and the Vatican, a Nazi beer cellar, a Jewish household, an Italian religious order which is hiding Jewish refugees, and, finally, Auschwitz in all its horror. One of the author's effective ideas is to have the large cast of characters played by a limited number of actors, who sit at the back of the stage in a kind of drab uniform, only putting on occasional robes and headwear to come forward and play different parts, regardless of the side or faith to which these characters are supposed to belong. The implication is that any one of us might find himself in any of these roles. The play has tremendous dramatic values and is important, like the novels of Günter Grass, in representing the first efforts of German writers to confront and to deal with the immediate past. But its peculiarity is that its producers in the various countries in which it has been performed, with so wide-ranging a text to choose from, and one not well organized, have in each case made a different selection and constructed a different play.

We saw the London and Paris productions and read the original text, and these differences between them were revealing. All the Jews had been banished from the London production, and all the women except the pretty waitress Helga, and she only in the beer-cellar scene. Not to have followed her through makes this character rather pointless, for she turns up again in Auschwitz, still serving and sleeping with the soldiers and apparently hardly conscious of what is going on about her. The Nazis here were merely rowdy officers. The Auschwitz scenes were played down and, with abominable theatrical results, the whole play was bracketed between films of the prisoners and the corpses in the concentration camps. In Paris, there were Jews but no women at all, and the Nazis were as brutal and cruel as the author meant them to be. A cosmopolitan German who had been following the progress of the play said to me that it was quite impossible to induce an English actor to behave like a Nazi on the stage, but that this was not so difficult in France. At the end of the Vatican scene, the Pope, in writing the proclamation in which he fails to condemn the Nazis for their persecution of the Jews, is made by Hochhuth, as a result of nervousness, to get ink upon his hands, and a basin is brought for him to wash them. This is, of course, a reference to Pilate, and though the English included it, the French left it out. In France, there were riots at first, even with this omission, but they did not last very long and finally petered out with the releasing in the theater of a number of mice, which, it was hoped, would create a panic among the women in the audience. A lady who liked animals, however, and was not afraid of mice succeeded in catching a good many of them and put them away in her handbag.

In Italy, we were told that the play could never be produced in Rome. An attempt was later made by some independent group, but the performances were stopped by the police. Yet *Der Stellvertreter*—written by a Prot-

estant and in the spirit of the Reformation—is essentially
a religious play. In Germany, the set was dominated by a
cross at the back of the stage. The interest of the final
scenes is centered on a diabolical "doctor," who is performing anatomical experiments and exults in sending
women and children to their deaths. He is a well-
educated man and has studied for the priesthood, and he
keeps his arguments with the Jesuit, and hence the play
itself, on a theological level by explaining that his present
activities are in the nature of "a question asked of God."
"And so I risked what no man had / yet risked since the
world began to turn. . . . / I took an oath that I would
provoke the Old Man so measurelessly, / so totally beyond
measure, that he would have to give an answer. / Even if
it was only the negative answer, which / as Stendhal says,
is all that *can* excuse Him: that he does not exist." But all
the good people are destroyed, and the doctor, though he
knows that the war is lost and that the Allies, if they can
catch him, will hang him, goes sardonically on with his
crimes. This last act is perhaps too harrowing as well as
too long to be performed on the stage. Hochhuth says
that he has thought about this problem and wants to have
the scenes at Auschwitz as little realistic, as dim and
abstract, as possible, but even so, if performed as written,
they would try the nerves of any audience.

Le Strip-Tease. This form of entertainment—im-
ported from abroad: another case of a foreign word for
something which had not existed in France—has now
become such a feature of Paris that I thought I ought to
see what they were doing with it. This turned out to be
something entirely unlike our old burlesque shows of
Fourteenth Street and Minsky's. I first visited La Tomate, in the Rue Notre-Dame de Lorette. The theater
was small and sordid. The audience consisted exclusively

of rather heavy middle-aged men who sat in their over-coats, as silent, unstirring and solemn as if they were attending a funeral. One man in the front row with thick lenses read a newspaper all the time except when the girls were appearing. The intervals between these appearances were dark and rather long. A piano was played backstage. Then a voice from a loudspeaker would announce, "*Je vous présente la charmante Suzanne.*" But the girls did not dance or sing, as our American girls used to do, and they were not called back by the audience to take off another garment. They were simply revealed in the nude in the poses of the nudes in the cheap magazines. A few obliged with a smile, but most of them were perfectly stolid and seemed to be thinking about something else. When they went through a mild routine, they might as well have been doing setting-up exercises. The applause was no more than perfunctory, and there was something rather awful about these women displaying themselves to an audience with whom no rapport was established.

I went later to Les Folies Pigalle, a smart show with a certain reputation. Here you could order drinks, and the men brought their wives and mistresses. You were re-ceived with an oily obsequiousness which put you at once on your guard. There were two not bad-looking pickups, one blonde and one brunette, obviously attached to the house. The headwaiter tried to put me at a table against the wall next to the one where the brunette was sitting. I made a point of choosing one further away, but the brunette immediately moved in on me. She talked po-litely and sensibly enough, as these girls in Paris often do, and I was almost sorry to disappoint her. She said that she came from Corsica, where she had learned Italian and French at school: Corsican was different from Italian. She was "a dancer," and she had been in Paris only three years. Before that, she had been in Geneva, where business had apparently not been good; she said the town was *"très sévère."*

The show far surpassed La Tomate. There was not, from the American point of view, any real strip tease here, either. The girls would first come on in some enveloping garment, then discard it and appear quite naked. They did not even wear the conventional G-strings but only little patches. One had a pink patch in the form of a rose. The first girls were slim and extremely pretty; they were followed, in order to please other tastes, by more ample blond types with prominent breasts and behinds. The production, like *La Reine Verte,* was self-consciously avant-garde. In one tableau, the girl was posturing in back of a long brown object that looked like a huge stuffed seal. But this turned out to be abstract art. It had vaguely phallic protuberances, which the girl put in juxtaposition to various parts of her body, finally swooning and curling up on her back. In the intervals between the tableaux proper, there was a chorus of men and girls, who did thumping and twisting dances. I decided after a time that I had had enough, but the siren said I mustn't miss the following number, which was indeed worth seeing and which I recognized as a daring novelty about which I had already heard. This was a man on a speeding motorcycle, with a girl riding pillion behind him. She was evidently representing the Spirit of the Motorcycle, for she very soon threw off her cloak and, now nude, floated into the air and stretched out above the cyclist, who from time to time lifted his face and kissed her on the thigh. I have a certain interest in stage "illusions," but I could not see how this was done. The waiter wanted to bring another bottle of champagne, and my companion had of course to beg for it: *"Ça me ferait plaisir."* But, after the waiter left, I told her that if I was going to spend anything more, I'd rather give it to her than to the house. I slipped her something under the table, wished her good luck and left. I was curious now to see what they would do to top the motorcycle, but didn't want to have to be further bothered fighting off the waiter and the siren.

Christiane Rochefort. A new best-seller in Paris was a novel called *Les Stances à Sophie*, by a writer I had never heard of called Christiane Rochefort. A review I read led me to buy it, and it turned out to be remarkably interesting. I later got the author's other books, and I believe she has a certain importance. Mlle Rochefort's three novels are *Le Repos du Guerrier* (1958), *Les Petits Enfants du Siècle* (1961) and *Les Stances à Sophie* (1963). They have all been translated into English, with the titles *Warrior's Rest, Children of Heaven* and *Cats Don't Care for Money*. I have looked into the last of these, made by Helen Eustis and recently published by Doubleday, and was surprised to find how good it was. I had supposed that the novel was untranslatable. But Miss Eustis has not been daunted by the bad language, the Paris argot or the sardonic hipster cracks; she has found American equivalents, and the book reads with perfect naturalness. These novels are three studies of women, each from a different milieu, in every case told by the woman herself and each in her own idiom, which is sometimes, like the point of view, extremely tough. I cannot think of anything to compare them to except such a novel of Dawn Powell's as *Angels on Toast,* in which the antics of advertizing men are mostly seen from their women's point of view, or Elaine Dundy's *The Old Man and Me,* in which a hard-boiled young charmer from New York describes her adventures in England. The second and third, at least, of Mlle Rochefort's novels are not only very amusing but also to be taken seriously as studies of contemporary France.

The first of these, *Le Repos du Guerrier,* has interested

me the least. The narrator is a young woman of the bourgeoisie who has inherited a little property. She falls in love with a brash but attractive man, ten years older, who proves to be an incurable alcoholic. He lives on her, humiliates her, torments her, estranges her from her friends and family, and resists her attempts to reform him. She finally leaves him in a clinic, with no real hope for his recovery. One gets bored by his outrageousness and worthlessness, and by the woman's masochistic loyalty. It is explained on the back of the jacket that they are typical of the postwar world. He, having fought in the Second War, has no longer any vocation or ambition; she "belongs to a generation which has not even learned to hope, which knows of nothing better than Personal Happiness, nor of any other love than personal possessive love, enjoyed in a happy security." But in the novel itself nothing is made of all this. The title has been used for a film featuring Brigitte Bardot. I have not seen this film, but I cannot imagine that it had much in common with the novel. The heroine does not resemble in any respect the types played by Brigitte Bardot.

The heroine of *Les Petits Enfants du Siècle* is the daughter of a fairly well-paid factory worker who describes his occupation as "making a fool of himself all day filling cubes with a lot of nasty mustard." The sole aim of the parents' lives is to acquire the new household devices: *le frigo, la machine à laver, la télé,* and, of course, *la voiture.* (The corresponding acquisitions of the young are *la moto* and *le scooter.*) The parents have as many children as possible because every baby brings a bonus which will enable them to get something new. The narrator is the eldest daughter, Jo. She is obliged to take care of her sisters and brothers, which include a set of twins. One of these children is sickly, another is feeble-minded, one of the boys is a delinquent and goes to jail.

Jo, who is the ablest and brightest, is always carrying on in her own mind a bitterly sarcastic commentary. One of her most devastating soliloquies takes place on a trip to market, when she observes the matrons of the neighborhood all in different stages of pregnancy. A woman who has already acquired a mixer and a fur rug pats her belly and boasts, "And my Frigidaire is here!" "In order to get *our* Frigidaire," Jo reflects, "we'd have to have triplets at least." Another woman, five weeks behind the first, gives her rival a mean look. "And I'll even get to the washing machine." "We've got that already," says the other. "A long time ago. In my belief, it's the most important thing in the house. For the laundry," she makes it quite clear. This woman's children were always boys, of which she is very proud. "She could furnish all by herself," thinks Jo, "an execution platoon for the fatherland; it's true that the fatherland would have paid her in advance, as was right. I was hoping there would be a war in good time to make use of all this material, which would otherwise not be much good, because they were all complete nitwits. I thought of the day when they would say '*En avant!*' to all of the Mauvin boys, and bang, they'd all lie dead on the battlefield, and a cross would be planted over them: here fell Mauvin TV, Mauvin Jalopy, Mauvin Frigidaire, Mauvin Mixer, Mauvin Carpet, Mauvin Pressure Cooker, and with the pension they would get they could afford a vacuum cleaner and a family vault."

Jo is overworked, loudly disdainful. She has never known any affection except from one of her little brothers till she attracts an Italian workman who is employed in building construction. This man becomes genuinely fond of her and initiates a love affair, but when her father's factory shuts down in August, she has to go with the rest of the family for a vacation in a country hotel, travelling in the new car, to the tune of much weeping and quarrelling, because the father is a very bad driver. When she gets back, the buildings are finished and the workmen have gone away. She is desolated, and takes to going out with other teen-agers into the woods, but though all the boys will lend her their scooters, she is longing still for her Guido, and, hearing that Italian workers are now employed by a new housing project, she goes to look for him there. She does not find him, but is enchanted by the suburb. *"Ça c'était de la Cité, de la vraie Cité de l'Avenir! Sur des kilomètres et des kilomètres et des kilomètres, des maisons, des maisons, des maisons. Pareilles. Alignées. Blanches."* Rue Paul-Valéry, Rue Mallarmé, Rue Victor-Hugo, Rue Paul-Claudel. A playground, a library, new shops "in the middle of each rectangle of houses so that each *bonne femme* has the same number of steps to take to go to buy her noodles." Then Mr. Right comes along. Jo's mother has just produced another set of twins, bringing the children to the number of eleven. She is asked whether she is going to complete the dozen. But she now has double phlebitis and cannot attend to the babies. Jo and her father take the new twins to the hospital. The babies are there found extremely cute, and people ask which is Caroline and which is Isabelle, but neither Jo nor her father knows. Jo sees a blond young man admiring her, and later he makes her acquaintance. He is *un monteur de télévisions.* They go for walks in the woods. When she tells him that she is pregnant, he is quite ecstatic: he first saw her with a baby in her arms, and a baby by her is just what he has longed for. They get married, and she suggests that they might go to live in that new suburb which she has thought so heavenly. For her, it is the next step up in technological civilization.

The narrator of *Le Repos du Guerrier* is an educated woman who writes good French. The narrator of *Les*

Petits Enfants is talking her story in the language that she would use if she were telling it to a friend. The author is trying to escape from the literary fashions of French fiction and to show us what life in modern Paris is really like for the ordinary people submerged in it. She continues this in *Les Stances à Sophie*, on a higher social level. This is, I think, the best of her books up to date. The heroine of *Les Stances à Sophie* is a clever independent girl. Céline, who leads a bohemian life, wears her hair short, prefers slacks to dresses and talks the wisecracking slang of Paris. She has a genuine passion for a bourgeois young man who, against her better instincts, puts such pressure on her, threatening to give her up, that, after going through a kind of nervous breakdown brought on by her reluctance to forfeit her freedom, she finally consents to marry him. But she finds that his conventional family drive her to malicious revolt: outrageous opinions, bad language. When she is asked what she was doing before she married, she tells them—although not truthfully—that she was *une strip-teaseuse*. She continues—despite her husband's disapproval—to wear slacks and not let her hair grow long. He begs her not to say *merde* so often. His friends—*les jeunes ménages*—are as bad as his family. They entertain one another, play poker and go out to *boîtes* together. None of these couples has children. Husbands and wives are in general faithful, but occasionally one of the men tries making a pass at Céline. In this case, she simply tells him to go look in the glass or arranges to have her husband find out about it, with the result that he will quarrel with his friend. For this group, the frequenting of strip tease shows is *"notre petit libertinage, avec filet . . . Une façon de rester prudes tout en se donnant des airs."* The couples I saw at Les Folies Pigalle seemed exactly to answer this description, as did those, three or four of them together, that we would see at such restaurants as La Tour d'Argent. So many of the features of the new modern Paris by which we had already been struck are touched upon in this book: the Spanish servants who do not know French; *le living,* which has taken the place of *le salon;* the bad air (Céline predicts that a certain number of babies will have to die before the city does anything about it); the indifference of the people in the shops and the increasing standardization and ugliness of the goods they have to sell. Céline sets out to buy some curtains but cannot find the material she wants. " 'I want some cotton voile, but not dotted Swiss.' 'They don't make that kind, Madame.' 'Why?' 'Because this is the way they make it, Madame.' 'And why is it made like this?' (She's beginning to get sore.) 'There's no demand for it, Madame.' 'But am I not asking for it?' No, that won't get me anywhere: there's no demand for it, so I who am asking for it must not exist. They deny that I exist. They're just waiting for me to go away. A subtle strategy for turning people into sheep. I'll have no curtains if I go on like this. Or else I'll have to give in—then they'll have got the better of me; they're strong. They've decided that this year my saucepans will be tangerine, turquoise or dove's-neck—just like the other ladies'."

But after her first phase of resistance Céline decides to play it the other way. She will go in for wifemanship; she will impersonate the perfect wife. She wears all the right things; *"Je ne dis pas 'merde' en public."* She becomes a great success as a hostess, and learns to pay no attention to the monotonous conversation of the men but to study their expressions and their tones of voice, as if she were an anthropologist. Céline's husband works on the municipal plan in the Department of Decentralization, and his closest friend also works on it in the Department of Regroupment. Like the vacationers of *Les Petits Enfants du Siècle* on their lower social level, these husbands of the young marrieds talk most of the time about cars, and they are engaged in a feverish rivalry. When they go on their vacations, their great idea is to race one another. Céline and her husband pass a smashed-up car, with people standing around it, but do not stop to find out what has happened. When they get to their destination, they learn that this car was that of their friends. The wife is dead and the husband has six broken ribs. This has been his eleventh accident. Céline, out of sheer boredom, having completely lost interest in her husband, has been having a Lesbian affair with the wife. She goes to see the husband's friend in the hospital and brutally bawls him out.

Now her husband decides to run for Deputy. He abandons what he has imagined to be his radicalism in order to get in with the winning group. He tells Céline to make herself attractive and buys her a lot of new clothes. But she feels that he is behaving like a pimp. She has in the meantime met an old lover, who is organizing a chain of strip-tease joints. He has asked her to supply him with new ideas for acts, and she finds that her clever mind is "a veritable fountain" of such ideas. She realizes that she cannot face playing the role of a conservative Deputy's wife, and when she comes to feel reasonably sure that her husband will be elected, she writes him a letter and leaves, explaining that the new clothes he has bought her are for the future *"Députée."* She can count on being paid for her work on the strip-tease show, to which she is now adding the duties of hostess, and takes a room in her old apartment house. She brushes off a would-be lover. "I breathe again. At last. Alone."

The title of *Les Stances à Sophie* is likely to mystify the foreign reader, since there is no one named Sophie in the novel. But *Les Stances à Sophie* is well known in

France as an extremely dirty *chanson de corps de garde,* which deals with the misfortunes of a man who picks up a disgusting and degrading woman. The first line of the song is the epigraph of the novel: *"Quand jt'ai rencontrée, un soir dans la rue,"* etc., and the third line of this stanza is what she and her friend imagine her husband will be saying to himself: *"Ah, si j'avais su que tu n'étais qu'une grue!"*

Bibliothèque Nationale. I had not been in the Bibliothèque Nationale since the summer of 1921, when I was trying to find some biographical information about the novelist Octave Mirbeau. The materials offered were extremely meager, and it turned out to be so hard to get anywhere with the antiquated library system that I had never been able to bring myself to look anything up there again. I now wanted some information about a figure of the same period, the caricaturist Sem, a great admiration of mine, whose albums I had been collecting. These albums are almost never dated, and the names of the people caricatured are almost never given, though occasionally someone has written them in. I was expecting a bibliography and hoping for perhaps a key. But what was supposed to be the great library of France turned out to be just as antiquated and just as unsatisfactory as it had been forty years ago.

You have to get a pass, in the first place, to be admitted to the building at all. But this was the least of my difficulties. Inside, I asked one of the snippy old ladies by whom the place seemed largely to be staffed where I could find Sem's albums and information about him. *"Il faut choisir,"* she enjoined. Couldn't I see them both? *"Pas la même fois."* I consulted the catalogue and discovered, to my astonishment, that the entries had never been typed but were still being written out in an old-fashioned early-nineteenth-century hand, to keep up the tradition of which, I reflected, they must now have to train special scribes. And these entries have not been arranged all in one alphabetical catalogue but are divided up into sections, each of which is supposed to cover books published between certain dates, and I was informed by a frequenter of the library that titles were often assigned to the wrong years. I found only one entry for Sem. I was told to make out two slips. When I handed them in at the desk, the old frustrator presiding there snapped at me with "Comment voulez-vous que j'accepte des fiches au crayon?," so I had to borrow a pen and make out another pair. I was then given information which must have been intentionally misleading, for I was told to go up to the third floor. This involved climbing a high marble staircase, getting sidetracked in an exhibition of the manuscripts and portraits of Alfred de Vigny, for which I had to pay two francs, and making my way through long marble corridors till I finally discovered an elevator, by which I ascended to more marble corridors, and found myself at last confronted by the door of the print department. I inquired of a young man, who told me to go down to the ground floor. I explained that I had been told to come up there. He called up the reading room to check, then said yes, I must go below. There I handed in my slips and was directed to a numbered seat, to which presently my single item was brought by a very old man. It was an article of about five pages, written by a friend of Sem's at the time of the latter's death. The albums, I was now told, were kept in the print department, from which I had just come. I went above again, and the helpful young man got them out, but there were only four or five of them—whereas I had myself a great many. He could throw no light on the dates; he explained that there was no bibliography of Sem.

A woman friend whom I told about this had had an even more discouraging experience and had eventually become so intimidated that she had precipitately escaped from the library, leaving her winter coat. She could not bring herself to go back again, and her husband had had to retrieve it. Now, it is not perhaps a bad idea to scrape the crust off the old buildings in Paris, but if a cultural overhauling is going on, why isn't something done about the Bibliothèque Nationale? France at the present moment is constantly asserting her title to the cultural hegemony of Europe and implying that the other peoples are all barbarians, but the facilities for study in France seem in every way to be wretched. This winter a student riot, caused by the overcrowded classrooms and the deficient equipment of the Sorbonne, was broken up by police clubbings.

2

ROME

Arrival and Relief. I have always had a feeling of liberation in coming from France to Italy. Rome is much more open and cheerful than Paris, and the whole tone of life is more generous. The Romans are hospitable, as the French are not, and drinking and dining out, for one in his late sixties, though delightful, becomes as exhausting as the hospitality of Virginia. And after the gray weather of Paris, the sunlight and spring green are exhilarating. The mimosas are out in their delicate yellow.

But the city is in some ways much changed since I was here at the end of the Second War. There were only jeeps and bicycles then. Now it is full of cars with noisy horns, and the traffic is the worst I have ever seen, even worse than in Providence and Boston. There is almost no effort made to manage it. In Paris, the suspension of traffic so that people can cross the street is accomplished with perfect punctuality, but here, except occasionally on the most important streets, you just have to plunge across and count on the cars' stopping. If you are going out to dinner, it may take you an hour to find a taxi and an hour or two to get there. Since there is usually no one to direct the traffic, there are jams that may go on indefinitely, while more cars are accumulating and making it worse. One particularly bad tie-up, which paralyzed two streets that crossed, held everyone at the crossroads imprisoned till two men in one of the cars got out and took it upon themselves to tell people what to do in order to disentangle.

As in Paris, the old smell of the city—which I remember so well from childhood—is now completely gone. It was made up, I suppose, of spaghetti and cheese, horses and refuse and poverty. There are no longer so many beggars, and I have not seen the formerly familiar sight of small children peeing in the street.

The Museum of the Villa Borghese. The glorification of the body that one no longer finds in art; the dazzling profusion of the Renaissance, an enchantment with all kinds of life—in pictures, in marble, in frescoes, in enormous mosaics on the floor: fowls, dolphins, wild beasts, and dogs as well as human beings; fauns, sphinxes, and centaurs that are half and half; the hermaphrodite that combines the sexes. But when we went to see Sophia Loren in *Ieri, Oggi e, Domani,* it occurred to me that the luscious bodies displayed in the Italian films were carrying on the tradition of that opulence of the flesh in Italian art which seemed to have faded away into the muted still-lifes of Morandi and the cold perspectives of Chirico.

Popular Serials. Two of the great publishing successes in Italy have been, surprisingly, the Bible and the *Divine Comedy,* brought out in weekly installments. The Bible has sold so well that it is now being issued over again. The mad popularity of this newsstand edition of works that one would think must already be sufficiently familiar is no doubt partly due to the fact that this device makes it possible to take these long classics in small doses but principally, I think, to the many brightly colored illustrations. The Dante has been enriched not only with pictures intended for it, from the Middle Ages and the Renaissance, but with others—such as Bosch's *Last Judgment*—that depict somewhat similar subjects. All these red and blue and green devils tormenting the pale sinners, interspersed with equally brilliant saints and angels and ecclesiastics, make the new edition of the *Inferno*—which during my visit was drawing toward its close—rather surprisingly seem quite gay. There is also a *Divine Comedy,* transposed into Neapolitan, which is coming out canto by canto. I cannot make much of this, but the intention is evidently comic.

Lampedusa. In Paris, we had seen the film of Lampedusa's *Il Gattopardo (The Leopard).* I thought it one of the best that have ever been made. It was like a nineteenth-century novel—vast sequences of inter-family relations and a ball that must last half an hour—and so long that it was thought impossible for the English-speaking countries, where it was ruined, I am told, by cutting. But when I read the book in Rome, I found that its effect was different. *Il Gattopardo* is not like a nineteenth-century novel. It goes by much more quickly than the film and is told with an ironic tone that in the film is entirely lacking. Lampedusa's writing is full of witty phrase and color. It belongs to the end of the century of Huysmans and D'Annunzio, both of whom, although their subjects are so different from one another, it manages to suggest at moments. There are also little patches of Proust. The rich *pasta* served at the family dinner and the festive refreshments at the ball are described with a splendor of language which is rarely expended on food but which is in keeping with all the rest of Lampedusa's half-nostalgic, half-humorous picture of a declining but still feudal princely family in Sicily in the sixties of the last century. This family was Lampedusa's own. He was a tenacious yet rather stranded Sicilian prince, who, though much travelled, went on living in his native Palermo. He was married to a Baltic lady, who has survived him and is now the head of the international Theosophical Society as well as a vice-president of the Italian Psychoanalytical Society. They had no children, and Lampedusa adopted a son, creating a situation from which seems to have been derived the situation in the novel between the patriarchal uncle and his favorite nephew. Lampedusa was extremely cultivated and had always been much occupied with literature, but had apparently till *Il Gattopardo* written almost nothing. There is an odd and attractive picture of the muted retired life that Lampedusa led in Palermo in *Ricordo di Lampedusa* by Francesco Orlando. Orlando, when he first met Lampedusa in 1953, was a nineteen-year-old law student. Lampedusa's daily routine had been to go to a café in the morning, have breakfast there and linger reading; then, later, to visit the bookshops and move on to a second café, where he joined a group of *conoscenti,* men of his own age. He made young Orlando's acquaintance and offered to teach him English and give him a course in English literature. He was distinguished, says Orlando, by a special sort of simplicity which the young man had never encountered in anyone else—"a simplicity trans-ferred, of course, to a high plane of mental insight, and nourished without effort by a wealth of ideas; a simplicity which may best be compared to that which, as a mark of excellence, is usually attributed to the art of the epochs that we call classic." They talked of nothing but litera-ture. Among Lampedusa's favorite writers were Mon-taigne, Shakespeare, Pascal, Racine, Swift, Saint-Simon, Goethe, Stendhal, Dickens, Dostoevsky and Proust. He worked systematically at his English course, which ex-tended from Anglo-Saxon poetry to T. S. Eliot and

Christopher Fry, and his outline and disquisitions for this are, I understand, soon to be published. He found other pupils as well, and Orlando believes that Lampedusa "was glad to have broken his intellectual solitude, to be able to talk so much about literature, to get to know some young human specimens and to be able to transmit to them something." He spoke of Sicily as "Peru," and "would add every month to his list of the horrible things that only take place in Palermo."

It was precisely at the time which Orlando describes that Lampedusa, who was then sixty, was moved to write *Il Gattopardo*. According to the legend I heard in Rome, he had, in 1954, attended a literary congress with a cousin who wrote poetry. The cousin won a prize for a book of poems, and this seems to have surprised Lampedusa, who had no very high opinion of his cousin's talents, and made him wonder whether he could not do better himself. He then produced *Il Gattopardo*. He died in 1957, before he had seen the book published. He had sent it to a well-known publisher, who returned it, with, it is said, suggestions for making it into a conventional commodity. Now, one of the great distinctions of *Il Gattopardo* is that it could not have been produced by a "pro." Lampedusa, who has written to please himself and has not given a thought to the public, does none of the things that a pro would do. In the year after the author's death, the manuscript was sent by a friend to Feltrinelli, the publisher of *Doctor Zhivago*, who had the good taste to appreciate it. In 1959, it won the Strega Award, the most important Italian prize for literature. Not everyone approved of this. Lampedusa, for one thing, was not a member of the professional writers' brotherhood; for another, he was dead. The feeling was, I was told, that "the money ought to be kept in the family." But everybody read the book; it immediately became a classic.

Feltrinelli a few years later published a volume of Lampedusa's miscellanies—*Racconti*—collected from among his papers. All the pieces in this book are interesting. The first is a fragment of a sequel to follow *Il Gattopardo*. The drama of *Il Gattopardo* hinges mainly on the decision of the Prince's nephew—who has become a supporter of Garibaldi—to marry the daughter of the Mayor, a handsome girl who comes of peasant stock but has been sent to school in Florence. Her manners, even so, from the point of view of the family, are likely to give them the shudders, but the boy is infatuated by her beauty, and she will bring him a considerable dowry. The Prince dislikes this alliance but he sees it through with princely dignity. (His dancing with the girl at the ball is one of the great scenes of the picture.) He cannot help being aware that his class is being supplanted. And in the sequel, this *dégringolade* is seen to have gone a good deal further. The rising power in Palermo is now a very low-class *mezzadro*—that is, a kind of sharecropper—who is gradually getting into his hands a good deal of the nobles' property. Beside him, the Mayor's family look almost distinguished. The disgruntled nobles sit around their little club, obsessed—though they do not know him and would not think of going near him—by the idea of the money he is piling up, as to the amount of which they argue bitterly, either wildly overestimating it or contemptuously trying to belittle it. One swears that this entirely crass character has built himself a luxurious pleasure villa, embellished with erotic paintings specially done for him by a Paris painter, where he "entertains women by the dozen"—in other words, the kind of thing that this gentleman would like to have for himself. There occurs in this fragment, also, the description of a rich dinner, but this time a dinner of *maccheroni* that "literally swarm in the oil of their sauce and were buried under avalanches of *caciocavallo* cheese" and of meat "stuffed with incendiary salami." But all this to Ferrara, the *mezzadro*'s accountant, seemed "exquisite and the height of really good cuisine; the rare meals he had eaten at the Salina house [that is, at the house of the present Prince] had always been disappointing in their insipidity." This is all very like the ascendancy of Faulkner's unspeakable Snopeses.

There are also memories of childhood, which deal with the town house and the country mansion already described in the novel, but here in a quite different way, as seen through the eyes of a child. Lampedusa's youth, he says, was enchanting. The "mastodonic" country place was provided with so many rooms—as well as having attached to it a theater, a church, enormous stables and a very elaborate garden—that one never got to the end of it, never had it completely explored. "It will be seen that the Santa Margherita house was a kind of eighteenth-century Pompeii, in which everything had been miraculously preserved intact; something that is always uncommon but that is almost unique in Sicily, which, on account of its indifference and poverty, is the most destructive country that exists." The town house in Palermo, he says, was bombed by "the liberators" in the Second War; the great palace had been sold by a Socialist uncle just after the preceding war, and is now an unrecognizable ruin. He mentions that no eyes but his own will ever see what he is writing, but these memories are done with the brilliance and love of an unfailingly first-rate writer and make one regret and wonder that Lampedusa had not recognized his métier.

One regrets and wonders even more when one encounters the long short story *Lighea,* which was the last thing Lampedusa wrote. This story seems to me a masterpiece. It is so beautifully built up and written that it is impossible to give any real idea of it by attempting to summarize it. A young man of a noble Sicilian family is working on a newspaper in Turin. He frequents a limbo-like café, where he makes the acquaintance of another Sicilian, an old Greek scholar of tremendous reputation. This scholar has degrees from all over the world, has been a pre-Fascist senator, and "finally—his greatest glory—is not a member of the Accademia d'Italia." He is arrogant and eccentric. He reads learned papers and spits on the floor. This annoys the other habitués, and they present him with a brass spittoon. The young journalist asks him why he does not do something to cure his catarrh, and the old man haughtily answers that he is not suffering from catarrh: he is spitting on the opinions of the idiots whose papers he is always reading. He remarks that the Greek professors do not have the faintest notion of how ancient Greek was pronounced. The young man reflects that the scholar, whose name is La Ciura, cannot know about this, either. La Ciura likes to taunt the young man about what he imagines to be the sordidness of his love affairs. The other indignantly declares that there has been nothing sordid about them. When La Ciura refers to the ignoble pleasures that he probably enjoys between dirty sheets, he protests that his sheets are clean. The old man keeps saying mysteriously that the other—whom he persists in addressing as "peasant"—does not "know," does not understand. But the two Sicilians make friends, and the younger is finally invited for an evening to the scholar's apartment. He is shown an old photograph of his host in his youth, and he sees that "the poor Senator in his dressing gown had once been a young god." He sees also Greek bowls and amphoras, which show Odysseus tied to the mast in order to be restrained from going overboard after the Sirens, who are dashing themselves on the rocks in chagrin at the loss of their prey. "All nonsense," La

Ciura assures him, "petty bourgeois nonsense of the poets; no one escapes from them, and if anyone did, they wouldn't die for such a trifle. And, besides, how *could* they die?" The young man notes in the bookcase the *Undine* of de La Motte Fouqué, as well as Giraudoux's *Ondine* and the works of H. G. Wells. "There's a little novel among them," the Senator says of these last, "that if I should reread it, would make me want to spit for a month."

The reader will soon be aware that this novel is *The Lady from the Sea,* but he is only gradually prepared for La Ciura's final revelation, on the eve of his starting on a voyage for a Hellenists' congress in Portugal. In his apartment, on his last night in Turin, he tells his young friend a strange story. When he himself had been a young man getting ready to try to pass a terribly stiff competitive examination for the University of Pavia, he had had to stuff himself with Greek and, in order to pay his rent, had also been obliged to give lessons. He had taxed himself to the limit when, that summer of 1887, the eruption of Etna occurred. The sirocco was blowing. You could not touch the railing of a balcony without having to run for first aid, and the pavements made of lava seemed about to melt. A man who knew him came upon him one day distractedly roaming the streets and stammering Greek verses which he no longer understood. The friend saw that the boy was about to break down, and offered him a shack on the coast which he himself was not going to occupy that summer. There the student lived in austere solitude and, though the sun was still brutal even there, he recovered some equilibrium. He hired a little boat and would row about on the water reciting Greek poetry and reviewing the names of the gods.

One morning, when engaged in this exercise, he felt

that the side of the boat was being pulled down behind him. He looked around and saw an adolescent girl holding on to the side of the boat. She smiled with pale lips and sharp white little teeth like a dog's—a smile which was not "adulterated with any accessory expression, of benevolence, of irony, of piety, of cruelty or whatever; it expressed only itself—that is, a joy in existing that was almost bestial, an almost divine happiness." He helped her into the boat. He had imagined that she was a bather, but he saw now that she had a fish tail, covered with blue nacreous scales, with which she slowly thumped the bottom of the boat. The water from her dishevelled and sun-colored hair dripped into her wide-open green eyes, her flesh had a greenish tinge, and she exhaled a strange, voluptuous sea-smell. She spoke to him in ancient Greek, which at first he had some difficulty in understanding. Her voice was a little blurred and guttural; one felt behind it the lazy summer surf, the swish of the last foam on the beach, the sound of the wind over the moonlit waves. The Sirens do not sing, says La Ciura; it is the sound of their voice which enchants. She tells him that she has heard him speaking a language that resembled her own. "I like you, take me," she says. "Don't believe those stories they've invented about us; we never kill anybody, we only love."

So began their three-week affair. She stayed with him in the shack. She would leave him for the sea from time to time, but would always eventually reappear. Once, as a special present, she brought him a huge branch of coral encrusted with seaweed and shells. He had to help her up from the beach, for on land she could only crawl and, though so active and swift in the water, gave the impression of a wounded animal. Her diet was live fish. When eating them, the blood would run down her chin, and after a few bites she would throw them over her shoulder and submerge to wash off the blood. She told him of her lovers in the course of the centuries: fishermen, sailors, Greeks, Sicilians, Arabs, Capresi, occasionally ship-wrecked men. All had responded to her invitation, and all, either sooner or later, had come to seek her again. All, that is, with one exception—a handsome young man so drunk that he could not have known who she was and must have taken her for a fisherman's girl.

But I must not attempt too detailed a paraphrase, which would not do this episode justice. The young journalist says that when he heard it told, he could not doubt a word of it, and it actually transports the reader, in a way that few fairy tales do, to a state of things beyond our world. This story is perhaps more intense than anything in *Il Gattopardo,* for, in creating an imaginary experience, it produces heightened emotions that never cease to seem real. Lampedusa has concentrated here all his feeling for pagan Sicily, which has hardly emerged from an antiquity as abysmal as its sea. La Ciura's relations with the Siren in some ways, he says, suggest to him the solitary goatherds' amours with their goats. "I am immortal," the Siren says, "because all the dead beings flow into me, from that of the codfish that I ate just now to that of Zeus himself, and, united in me, they return to a life that is not merely individual, deter-mined, but Panic and therefore free. . . . I shall always be with you: I am everywhere, and your thirst for sleep will be satisfied."

As the summer comes to an end, the weather clouds and it begins to rain. The sea becomes dove-colored and mourns like a dove. In the evening, it roughens a little. Then the winds assail the further waters; near the shore, leaden billows swell. She tells him that her comrades are blowing their conchs to call her to the revels of the stormy season. "Goodbye," she says. "You will not forget me." A great wave breaks on her rock. She dives into the irised spray and seems to dissolve in the foam.

The Senator leaves the next day, and his young friend sees him off at the station. The old man is as sarcastic and cantankerous as ever, but when the train begins to move, he puts his head out the window and pats the young man on the head. A week later, the newspaper office gets a telephone message from Genoa informing them that, on the voyage to Portugal, La Ciura has somehow gone overboard and his body has not been found.*

The Language. There is always something festive about the Italian language, even when what is being said is not. Those verbs that crackle and sparkle: *zampillare, spezzare, spruzzare, luccicare*—I have just encountered these in *Lighea,* where they bring to life the salt summer sea. Even the cadences of sorrowful poetry may have a kind of juicy exuberance.

Hazards for Jesuits. I was told by Silone some extraordinary stories of the inroads of Communism among the priesthood. The Vatican had established a department, with a Jesuit at its head, for the purpose of studying and combatting Communism. It was noticed that a Communist paper was printing exclusive news about the Vatican which could have come only from an inside source. It turned out that his researches into Communism had led this Jesuit—no doubt attracted by what the Party had in common with his order: dedication to an all-demanding cause, concentration on a long-term task, strict obedience and rigid discipline, secret manipulations—to become

* I find that the greater part of these *Racconti* has been translated, with an introduction by E. M. Forster, as *Two Stories and a Memory.* One of the original stories has, for some reason, been omitted, and *Lighea* has been stupidly titled *The Professor and the Mermaid.*

converted to it. He was expelled, and he joined the Party as an expert on Vatican policy. But then the Party changed its line: it thought it wise to try to conciliate the Vatican, and the ex-priest was no longer needed. He disappeared from Rome. Some time afterwards he was recognized by a journalist in a restaurant in Albania. Asked what he was doing there, he explained that he had been sent by the Party to lecture to the Albanians on the incomparably better life now enjoyed by Albania under Communism—*"le dernier des pays!"* said Silone—than that of the wretched Italians, still shackled by the capitalist system. *"Le pauvre homme!"*—a dismal story. There had also been two Jesuits in China who were brainwashed into Communism. When they returned, they were taken in hand. Their order has confined them in a monastery and is brainwashing them back into the Church.

Galileo. Bertolt Brecht's *Life of Galileo,* done by the Piccolo Teatro of Milan. Extremely disappointing. I am really not qualified to appreciate Brecht. I only know him in German through the libretti of *Mahogonny* and the *Dreigroschenoper,* which are certainly well turned and witty, and I have never seen a first-rate Brecht production—actually, the best I have seen was that of *The Caucasian Chalk Circle* done by the Harvard students at the Loeb Theater in Cambridge. But I do not care, in his more serious plays, for the mixture of musical comedy with more or less straight drama, and I somewhat distrust his Marxism, as I do that of Sartre—the Marxism of a bourgeois who pretends that his Communism has been able to survive Stalin and who is still trying to hew to the line. Sartre attempts to be rigorous and lands himself in impossible positions; Brecht gives the impression of wobbling. The *Galileo* is primarily derived from Shaw—

history with modern comic irony and contemporary implications—but Shaw, in his plays, at least, always keeps
to a clear point of view; he knows what points he is
making. One cannot be sure about Brecht: the dramatist
seems to be one thing and the doctrinaire another, and
they rather get in one another's way. The social and
political situation has, between Shaw's generation and
Brecht's, of course very much changed. Shaw is an
educated man writing for an educated audience; Brecht is
an educated man trying to write for a popular audience—
ideally, a proletarian audience. He attempts to amuse this
audience by interpolated songs and buffooneries and to
make sure that it doesn't miss the point by inserting little
explanations at the beginning of each of the scenes. But
what is to be the point of the whole thing? What is to be
the moral? The first version of the *Galileo*, written in
1937–39 in Denmark, whither Brecht had gone to get
away from Hitler, made the scientist an intellectual who
retreated from an oppressive regime by repudiating his
own conclusions but by doing so secured his survival in
order secretly to develop his ideas. The second version,
written in the United States in 1945–47, must be a
product of the atomic bomb. In this version, Galileo is
cast somewhat in the role of Einstein, about whom, it
seems, at this time Brecht had also contemplated writing a
play. The man of science is here made culpable for
having allowed his discoveries to be exploited by the
bourgeoisie. There is apparently an analogy intended
between the use of atomic research in warfare and the
practical uses of Galileo's discoveries in facilitating navi-
gation, hence trade. In a perhaps too prophetic final
speech, Galileo is made to declare that the scientist must
not let his instruments fall into the hands of the ex-
ploiters but must reserve them for the betterment of the
human race. I have not seen the original text of this play,

but from reading the text used here I get the impression that the Italian translators have made for themselves a version which is clearer and more consistent than Brecht's own rather cockeyed propaganda.

The Piccolo Teatro of Milan has high pretensions and considerable prestige, but if its performance of *Galileo* really represents the best of the Italian theater, that theater is low in vitality. The performance began at four and dragged so that at nine it was by no means over. Even so, the scene in which Galileo is shown carrying on in spite of the plague was omitted—a cut which I did not regret, since I had dreaded having to sit through this. The actor who played Galileo was intolerably slow and monotonous. Certain scenes are bound to be effective: A monk who is a student of physics is convinced by Galileo's ideas but cannot bear to upset the world that his poor peasant parents live in, to which Galileo replies that he ought to want to put an end to their miserable way of life; the interview between the Pope and the Cardinal Inquisitor, in which the Pope, who knows very well that Galileo is "the greatest physicist of his time, the luminary of Italy," is putting on his sacerdotal robes and, by the time he is fully attired and has assumed his official role, acquiesces in the wishes of the Cardinal and tells him to bring pressure on Galileo by showing him the instruments of torture. The production given the play by this Milanese company is not at all appropriate to Brecht, whose action always moves very quickly. We were bored and hungry, and left.

Italian Love Songs. They are still singing *Oi, Mari,* as they were in 1945 and as they were in 1908, when I first heard it, on a steamer of the old North German Lloyd line. It was sung by a man in the steerage, which was then at the back of the ship, shut off by a barrier from the rest of the deck. Italian songs never die: *Santa Lucia, Torna a Sorrento.*

Punch and Judy and Pulcinella. I made a point in Rome and London of looking up street puppet shows. I have been since an early age an amateur Punch-and-Judy operator and have given the subject some study. The Punch-and-Judy show seems almost to have died out in the United States, but it is still going strong in England. There are supposed to be in Britain about fifty performers. The tercentenary of Punch was celebrated in London in 1962. The date of this celebration was fixed by the first performance of which there is a definite record: an entry in Pepys's diary of May 9, 1662, which mentions that he has visited Covent Garden; "thence to see an Italian puppet play, that is within the rails there, which is very pretty, the best that ever I saw, and great resort of gallants." A plaque with an engraved inscription commemorating this occasion was put up on the wall of St. Paul's Church, opposite Covent Garden, and a huge Punch-and-Judy booth was erected. Forty professional Punchmen assembled, and forty Punches appeared simultaneously, followed by forty Judys, who cheered the unveiling of the plaque. An immense birthday cake was cut, and crocodiles and dragons leaped out. The crowd sang *Happy Birthday* and *For He's a Jolly Good Fellow.* The Rector of St. Paul's, the Reverend Clarence May, walked up the aisle of the church, cradling a puppet of Punch in both hands, and preached a "special Service of Praise and Thanksgiving for Punch's 300th Birthday."

This last feature of the celebration was particularly significant and interesting because Punch is, of course, par excellence one of the most immoral figures of drama. He came to England from the Catholic countries of the

Continent, following immediately the return of Charles
Stuart, in 1660, and there is a tradition in the Punch
profession that Charles himself gave the showmen li-
censes. The play of Punch and Judy is thus in some sense
a naughty Restoration comedy. After disposing of almost
everyone else, his family and the agents of law and order,
Punch must always in the end beat the Devil. One finds a
few records of performances in which the Devil carries
Punch off, but these are in the minority; the tradition is
all the other way. Dr. Johnson, writing in 1765, remarks
that "in rustic puppet plays I have seen the Devil very
lustily belaboured by Punch" and that "in modern puppet
shows, which seem to be copied from the old faces,
Punch sometimes fights the Devil and always overcomes
him." The crocodile which afterwards devoured Punch in
the versions I saw in my youth is said by Mr. George
Speaight, the leading authority on the subject, to have
been introduced only in the middle of the nineteenth
century. My theory about it is that though the tradition
did not make it possible for Punch not to vanquish the
Devil, Victorian morality demanded that the sinner
should not go scot free. (J. M. Barrie seems to have
borrowed this crocodile for the crocodile in *Peter Pan*.
The audience of children would have accepted it as
something already familiar.) But that the Devil should
get the worst of it was essential to the real story. At the
end of the old productions, Punch used to proclaim
triumphantly, "Hurrah, boys, the Devil's dead!" The men
who had been watching the show were sometimes so
enthusiastic that they would go up to shake Punch's hand
and offer to buy him a drink.

Now, why did Punch become for the English, like St.
George and John Bull, one of their mythical heroes, a
national symbol? He had originally been the boastful
Neopolitan in the Italian *commedia dell'arte* (he is

supposed by some to go even further back, to the Fabulae
Atellanae and the Fescennine buffooneries of Rome). He
was brought to France by the Italian players sometime in
the sixteenth century. They played the *commedia
dell'arte*—that is, partly improvised comedies with a traditional cast of stock characters: Harlequin, Columbine,
Scapin, Pierrot, Pantaloon, who turn up later in the
English pantomime, as several of them do in Molière—
and became extremely popular. But in 1697, as a result of
some satirical cracks about the King's mistress, Madame
de Maintenon, the Italians' theater was closed and the
troupe was expelled from Paris. The French comic performers at the fairs then took these entertainments up
and were eventually so successful in Paris that the actors
of the Comédie-Française got the police to prohibit the
performance of comedy except by the members of this
official company. The definition of the kind of performance banned was "any spectacle in which there is dialogue," and *les forains* evaded this by having only one
actor on the stage at a time. He would deliver a line and
withdraw, and then another actor would emerge from the
wings and reply. There were police raids in 1709, in
which the theaters were burned and wrecked. The producers resorted to puppet shows for which permits were
given only on condition that there should be no speaking
except through *un sifflet-pratique*—an instrument I shall
explain later—and that is how Pulcinella-Polichinelle-
Punch arrived in a puppet booth. Pulcinella first modu-
lated into Polichinelle, then in England had a new
incarnation as Punch. Both these Continental personages,
however, are quite distinct from Punch, yet the description of Polichinelle in Maurice Sand's *Masques et
Bouffons* does show that they once had a good deal in
common: a hump, a big belly, a stick, a temperament of
extreme truculence and a tendency to unscrupulous phi-

landering. During the Terror of the French Revolution, it was one of the features of the executions, which became public entertainments, that Polichinelle in his booth should also be guillotined as the other heads were falling; but then, when the Terror relaxed with Thermidor, he would turn, like Punch, on the executioner and hang him and the Devil by the same rope. Polichinelle in France was something of a popular hero, but he never became so important as Punch has been for the English. One can understand Punch's first success in the reaction against Puritanism, and I used to believe that the brutality of the puppet, who is always knocking people on the head, appealed to the brutality of the British. But a more satisfactory theory—which does not, however, exclude the other—has been suggested to me by Mr. John Wain, who pointed out to me that Punch was allowed to give way, and allowed to give way with impunity, to all those impulses of violence and defiance that had usually to be repressed by the common man. He throws the baby out the window; he disposes of his scolding wife; he murders the complaining landlord (there was sometimes also a tradesman); and when—scared to death by the ghost or believing himself to have been injured by Judy—he resorts to calling in the doctor, he gets out of paying the fee by annihilating him, too. When Punch has at last been arrested and tried and sentenced to be hanged, he manages to hang the hangman by inducing him to put his own head in the noose on the pretext that he, Punch, does not know how to go about it—"I've never been hanged before!" When the Devil eventually comes for him and puts up a stiff fight, he escapes eternal punishment, too. In the intervals between his crimes, he merrily sings and dances, and he formerly flirted with a Pretty Polly, a figure who seems now to have disappeared. The monotony, however, of his misdemeanors is sometimes

varied at Punch's expense by his failure to get even a
crack at an elusive Negro or Clown, who plays him
embarrassing tricks, and he is powerless against the ghost,
the only creature of whom he is frightened.

Punch-and-Judy shows in England and the Pulcinella
shows of Italy are usually performed out-of-doors, in parks
or other "pitches," in summer, when the children are out
of school. They stop when school starts again. (The well-
known Guignol of France has nothing to do with Polichinelle, except that he knocks people about with a stick.
He dates only from the end of the eighteenth century,
but has quite displaced his predecessor. Guignol was
created in Lyon—he was originally an innocent silk-
worker, and he is still more or less of a simpleton, though
he is capable of clever tricks and always comes out on top.
His comedies are likely to hinge—which is characteristic
of France—on the possession or the acquisition of money,
a subject which never figures in Punch and Judy. The
Guignol shows spread all over France and gave their name
to the Grand Guignol in Paris.) Since I only arrived in
England in October and left Europe before school was
out, I had difficulty in seeing these puppets. I found one
show on the Pincio, in Rome, but a very inferior one.
The spectacle had no structure and never came to an end;
it was continuous and always going back on itself to
scenes that had been done before. What I had taken at
first for a wolf, or a crocodile disguised as one, turned out
to be meant for a dog, a mispronounced "Lassie" from our
movies. When she fixed her teeth in Pulcinella, her
owner put his price up and up before he would call her
off. Most of the rest of the show was simply banging
about, which was no substitute for imaginative drama. I
had somewhat better luck in London. I found there a
Punch operator of high reputation, who was about to give

a show for children at a Friends' recreation center. The performance was first-rate, but, to my disappointment and the operator's, it had to be cut short when the lady presiding at the entertainment explained that the parents had come for their children and that they had to go home to their suppers. The Devil had not yet appeared. I asked whether he was not to be vanquished and was assured by the operator that he was. I did not see any crocodile.

The name Punch comes from Puncinello, who nevertheless in Italy, so far as I heard, is always called Pulcinella. It is supposed to be a diminutive of *pulcino,* "chicken," and to refer to the character's peculiar voice. This voice is produced by a device called a "swazzle," the nature of which was for decades kept a secret by the Punch showmen. A Punchman interviewed by Henry Mayhew, who tells about it in his *London Labour and the London Poor,* published in 1851, referred to the swazzle as "an unknown tongue, that's known to none except those in our profession." It was evidently never described in print till 1866, when it turned out to be two pieces of metal, bent out from one another in such a way as to leave a small channel between them, and fastened together by tape. It is held by the tongue to the roof of the mouth, and the performer, when he is doing Punch, speaks through it in a whistling squeal. The swazzle is quite difficult to manage—especially since the showman must use his tongue in the natural way when he speaks for the other characters. There is a saying in the profession that one must have swallowed the swazzle three times in order to qualify as a Punchman. The dose recommended for expelling it was "plenty of plum pudding." One that I recently purchased was accompanied by a warning that, when practicing, it was as well to have a heavy thread attached to it. I have never mastered the swazzle. In my youth, I had a simpler device—a double disc, with a hole in the middle—which does not now seem to be on the market. There is a story of an eighteenth-century French nobleman of fashionable and frivolous tastes who became a great amateur of these puppets and delighted in giving shows himself. One day he swallowed the swazzle, which is called *la pratique* in French, and was thought to be choking to death. A priest was immediately summoned, and the gentleman was heard confessing his sins in the voice of Polichinelle. Then suddenly he coughed up the instrument and sent the priest packing. Besides the difficulty of manipulating the swazzle, the Punchman has other problems. He is obliged to perform standing up and holding both hands above his head. This position requires endurance and the handling of the puppets great dexterity. The operator must take special exercises to discipline his fingers and wrists.

The puppets made now in the United States—procurable through dealers in magicians' supplies—are of rather inferior quality. The heads are not carved out of wood but molded in some hard kind of papier-mâché, which makes them lighter but much less impressive than the old-fashioned wooden kind. In England, the production of these puppets is an ancient handicraft, and you can have them made to order. One of the best of the English puppetmakers is an old man who lives in Gravesend. He does not have a telephone, and you have to go to Gravesend to see him. He made me a beautiful Punch, Judy and Baby fitted to the size of my hands, and charged me an incredibly low price for them. My coarse American Punch has no hooked nose and no hump and is otherwise also entirely uninteresting; but this English one is quite traditional: he has the right kind of Punch personality. (The big, sagging belly of Punch which used to balance the hump and which is prominent in Tenniel's drawing for the cover of the humorous weekly has been abandoned in practical puppetry. It makes it too difficult to wield the stick with which Punch has to knock out so many people. I have one old example of a Punch with a paunch in a small set that came from Saratoga, but I do not see how it could have been used for the purposes of the regular drama.) The costume of my English Punch is brilliant; a great deal of pains has been taken with it. The coat, with its ruff, is red, with a dark-blue velvet facing; the hump is of the same velvet. The peaked cap is pink and green, with a pompon of yellow. The knee breeches are a lighter blue; the stockings are painted on the legs in yellow, with tops of some pink material, and the red shoes have black and pink bows, secured with a large brass button. The face of the American Punch which I have had to use for years has no well-defined expression—its bulbous red nose and pop-eyes might be those of a glaring old drunk—but the other has sharply carved features and that "frank" and "glad" smile of which Max Beerbohm says so well that it is that "of a great sinner well-knowing himself to be also a great force for good." The Judy, as is proper for an English wife, is much more plainly dressed than her husband. The Baby shows the influence of the well-known drawings made by George Cruikshank from the most popular London Punch show of his day. These were published, with the dialogue, in 1828, and the book has several times been reprinted. It is one of the most important sources for the Punch-and-Judy tradition. Here the Baby is not a true puppet but a small inanimate object, with a Punchlike tall cap which gives it a shape rather like an hourglass. It hardly looks human, but is easier to handle and less susceptible to damage when thrown around than the more convincing full-sized model, whose pink cheeks are likely to get chipped. My new one, a block with a head, is red-haired and blue-eyed, with a red cap, orange hands, a red belt with a green bow and a pink flowered gown. The old man who made these figures was extremely friendly and was pleased that I was so pleased with them. He had his wife bring me tea and taught me a trick that I did not know. He also presented me with one of his swazzles—he was a performer in a modest way himself—and a script prepared, with strict expurgation, to be performed before Queen Victoria, for which he would not let me pay. He referred me for ready-made figures to a dealer in magic supplies, whom I found in an old building in a very Dickensian basement at the approach to London Bridge. There I bought a splendid purple-robed Beadle, with a somewhat birdlike beak and wide-open blue English eyes. The maker of this figure had recently died, and his work seemed to be highly valued.

I have a collection of Punch-and-Judy scripts and several books about glove puppetry. The most complete and authoritative work is *The History of the English Puppet Theatre,* by George Speaight, himself a puppet-master and one of the organizers of the Punch tricentenary. The first Punch-and-Judy I ever saw—it must have been before 1900—was a sideshow in the Barnum & Bailey Circus in Madison Square Garden. The Punch was dressed in red and was extremely loud and dynamic. He would plunge around the stage after every outrageous exploit, singing that favorite song of the Spanish War, *There'll Be a Hot Time in the Old Town Tonight.* I was fascinated but also frightened, and when I revived the puppet theater for my children, I was afraid the real Punch and Judy would be too alarming for them, and, instead, gave them a kind of soap opera—improvised from night to night—in which the Punch and Judy were transformed into a comfortable domestic couple who never quarrelled about anything but were plagued by a mischievous devil. Later, I acquired new puppets of the kind that were then coming over from Germany. These were made not for Punch and Judy but for such fairy tales as *Hansel and Gretel,* and they enabled me to extend my serial to the scope of a small kingdom, the king of which was always asleep, so that it had to be run by the princess, very pretty and dignified and always wearing a small crown. The devils became more and more a nuisance—I had by this time collected several of them—and the Princess was now ably served by a guard of loyal animals. (The Germans have excelled at these animals and now offer a considerable variety, though their puppets are not so well made as they were just after the last war.) But this taxed my creative powers, coming at the end of the day, and I decided to reconstruct the true Punch, with his "That's the way to do it!" and his roistering Spanish War song, and it was now as if more than I had thought I remembered were emerging from buried impressions, perhaps from a racial subconsciousness. I discovered, on consulting my litera-ture on the subject, that lines and business I imagined I had just made up had been part of the performance for centuries. I also began to feel—I suppose, like an actor playing Hamlet—that I understood the character of Punch as something with an uncanny life of its own that had always been in existence and only needed to be revived. One episode I was sure was an innovation. I provided a happy ending. When Punch had sent the Devil back to Hell, I had the latter, as the result of a council, decide to hire a floozy seductress to lure him into the Crocodile Swamp. This gave me an opportunity to exploit my by then large and varied collection of dragons and crocodiles. These monsters become ever more formidable, but just when Punch has lost his stick, undoubtedly a phallic symbol, which has been swallowed by one of the crocodiles, and, trembling and helpless, is being dragged down by the most ferocious of these, poor old Judy pops up and rescues him. She explains that she had only been pretending to be dead to see how Punch would take it, and when she heard him dancing and singing, she swore that she would never go near him again. But she had realized, seeing him in the jaws of the dragon, that she could not let him be devoured. I found, however, in Speaight, that this resuscitation of Judy has also been sometimes used.

The puppets that I bought in Rome in a toy store on the Via Veneto were decorative and rather expensive. They are closer to the characters of the *commedia dell'arte* than to the more ruffianly types of the Punch show. The women play a much more attractive and more important role in Italy. There is no shrewish Judy, no German witch. In the show I saw on the Pincio, Pulcinella had a great love, the beautiful Rosalie. I purchased another beauty—a brunette with a high-built black coiffure, lashes of black gauze, a lace collar, a pearl necklace and pearl earrings. Also, a carabiniere, with a cockaded bicorne, and what I take to be a Crusader, gray-eyed and fair-haired, clad in a befeathered and bejeweled, somewhat beret-like soft red cap that droops dashingly over his left ear. All have gray or black glass-bead eyes, and the men mustaches and eyebrows finely embroidered in silk. I bought also a Pulcinella, who could not differ more from Punch. It is clear from Maurice Sand's book that the several variations on this name cover two quite distinct personages: one the braggart who turned into Punch and the other a mere playful imp. My puppet

closely resembles Sand's drawing labelled Polliciniella:
a slight figure with a black half mask, a white foolscap
and a white pierrot costume.

The Italians, of course, also excel at the more complicated marionettes, and the shops are full of puppets on
wires and threads, of all sizes and prices. One of my
vividest childhood memories of Rome is of buying, together with my cousins, some cheap marionettes, which
included Roman gladiators with swords, and of staging
plays for one another—when we had tired of being taken
to churches—in a theater improvised in the hotel room
from a chair laid on its back and draped with towels. But
even though the Venetian puppeteers can make marionettes do the most wonderful things and almost seem to be
living actors, no genuine glove-puppet fancier has any
real use for marionettes. The fact that they are worked
from above and that in the more ambitious performances
several people may be needed to animate one puppet,
while the voices are supplied by still others, makes them
seem much too labored and mechanical. I agree with
Frank Peschka of the New York Little Players, the
greatest master of glove-puppetry whose work I have ever
seen (who, however, does not do Punch and Judy but
puts on more elaborate productions created by himself in
collaboration with his stage manager, Wilbur Murdock),
when he says that its satisfactoriness lies in its not being
an engineered group effort but a performance which
without machinery—all the characters, all the voices—
comes straight out of the performer himself, who becomes in his own person an organic drama.

I also agree with Sand, whose mother was George
Sand, that a puppet theater in a household may prove a
delightful resource and give life a kind of new dimen-
sion. He tells of a family—his own, one supposes—who,

obliged to spend their winters in the country, rigged up a charade theater and produced in it little plays. The story would be invented every night at dessert, then the lines would be improvised as they acted it. They began with the characters of the *commedia dell'arte* but mixed them with other things. "Pierrot, now a choirmaster, was sent to the court of Prince Irenaeus, by the way of the Tales of Hoffman; Scaramouche, become a brigand, to the palace of the Sleeping Beauty by way of Perrault's fairy tales." One winter there were only four actors, so they could not provide an audience. They resorted to a theater of glove puppets, with two watching and two performing, and instead of restricting the entertainments this led to more interesting developments. They acquired some fifty puppets, and permanent characters came into being. They adopted a soap-opera technique, like mine, of making each episode at the end lead on to the one to follow. When they were able to go back to a real stage, their *commedia dell'arte* had come to life and taken possession of them—as I found, in my own experience, when my daughter was old enough to collaborate with me, that our version of Punch had done with us. Sand says that when professional actors were invited to participate, they found it excessively difficult; they were supplied with no written roles, whereas the young people were living theirs.

Farewell to Rome. It is impossible for an American not eventually to feel frivolous in Rome. He eats and drinks well, he listens to Roman gossip, he meets charming writers and artists and scholars who are among the most cultivated and the most cosmopolitan in the world. He has a choice of the relics and monuments and master-pieces of two or three millennia. But expeditions among these—like a trip that we made to the Etruscan tombs—are likely, with the heat and fatigue, to give way, before

the ground has been covered, to gay and prolonged
lunches. I am now going on to Budapest, where I suppose
that life is "real and earnest"; where the breaking of the
old system and the problem of adaptation to the Communist world are imposing more hardship and demanding
more effort.

3

BUDAPEST

Impressions of the City. I flew to Budapest from Milan on the Hungarian Malév line. The only other passengers were three or four men. The stewardesses handed around a Hungarian Communist paper. It was just after Khrushchyov's visit, and I was able to make out an announcement which was featured on the front page: "Everywhere and at all times, Hungary and Russia must be friends." No one bothered to read this paper, and the men spent most of their time in gay conversation with one of the stewardesses.

In Budapest, I found that the current joke was that Khrushchyov had come to Hungary in order to cure his *sárgaság*, which in Hungarian means both *yellowness* and *jaundice*. He had actually just had an attack of jaundice, and the point of the pun was that he was trying to consolidate his position with the West in order to offset his break with China. It was hoped he would withdraw the Soviet troops which are still garrisoned in Hungary, but he did not do this, and he annoyed a good many Hungarians by decorating Kádár for his services not to Hungary but to the Soviet Union. At the same time, in certain quarters, not necessarily Communist, the Hungarians had looked to him with a certain hopefulness. They had seemed to think that he and Kennedy between them might stabilize the unsteady West. The assassination of Kennedy had been felt as a setback in Hungary, as it seems to have been all over Europe.

I stayed at the huge Hotel Gellért in Buda, at the foot of St. Gellért's Mountain, named after a Venetian missionary who was brought on by the Christian King Stephen I, at the beginning of the eleventh century, but very badly received by the intractably pagan Magyars, who rolled him down this steep hillside, in a barrel lined with spikes, into the Danube. The Gellért is comfortable, and the food very good. I order something different almost every night just to see what it will turn out to be, since the names are sometimes quite fanciful, and even by consulting the dictionary you cannot always be sure what they represent. An odd feature is cold orange soup. This, I am told, is a variation of the traditional cold peach and cherry soups. Some of the best dishes are made from *ponty*, the carp from Lake Balaton. A good deal of the clientele consists of what I take to be rather crass Central European businessmen and fat Germanic women. The orchestra, for the benefit of foreigners and to the distress of the Hungarians who dine with me, plays the flashy Hungarian gypsy music, sometimes breaking into song, and almost invariably Brahms' Hungarian Dances and Liszt's Hungarian Rhapsody. The waiters, regardless of sex, address foreigners as "M'sieu, M'dame." They did this, also, in Rome, and I wonder whether the current incomprehension of the real meaning of these service words may not be an indication of a loss of prestige on the part of the French. Papers from the "bourgeois" countries have only recently been made available at such hotels, but they often take a long time in coming. They have to be bought at the desk. There is nothing to be had at the newsstand but the international boilerplate of the Communist press, which I never saw anyone buying.

I take long walks along the Béla Bartók Út, on which the Gellért stands. The Hungarians, who, as I have seen them abroad, have always seemed so dynamic, here give me the impression, after their recent misfortunes, of being stunned and rather stupefied, of purposelessly walking the streets or going listlessly about their work—in striking contrast to busy, brisk and swarming Milan. They seem not to know quite where they are or what has been happening to them. Almost all of them have the look of belonging to about the same social level, a kind of shabby middle class, though I am told that there are working-class people among them.

There is plenty to buy in the shops, but some of it is very inferior; I bought a suitcase manufactured in East Germany that might almost as well have been made of pasteboard. But one advantage of a Communist country is that new books and handicraft products—such as the gay embroidered Hungarian tablecloths—are much cheaper than they would be elsewhere. The liquor is sold in the grocery stores or combined with confectionary and pastry in the Édesség Boltok, sweet shops. The bottles of plum, cherry and apricot brandy, and Tokaji (which we call Tokay) look quite pretty and tempting in the windows, among the fancy displays of sweetmeats, with bows of pink ribbon about their necks.

I had heard Budapest described as the most beautiful city in Europe. It is strange and dramatic, to be sure, but there is something rather barbaric about it. It wants to belong to the West, but one remembers the Mongolians and the Turks. It is a mixture of baroque and Gothic, a spiky and hispid city: churches with high, sharp spires, minarets with needles like stings. An element of the goblinesque: the porcupine dome of the

Parliament House, which stretches along the Danube its weighty and enormous length; the ubiquitous unendearing cupids; the curious pronglike shaft in front of the Mátyás Church, on which a bulging mass of these cupids seem swarming like torpid bees, an exercise in the same kind of baroque bad taste as the monument to the Plague in Vienna, with its gruesome mess of tangled corpses. Of course, the city has been badly battered, especially in this neighborhood of the Mátyás Church, where the metallic scaffolding on the buildings in process of reconstruction adds to the bristling effect. The royal palace in Buda was wrecked; it has to be rebuilt after every war. In the last one, when the Russians had come, the Germans barricaded themselves in it, and they blew up all the six bridges to keep the enemy from getting across—one of them without warning, though it is said that this was accidental, with all the trams and cars and pedestrians on it. Then the palace was bombarded by the Russians and finally burned down by looters. One young man told me of his horror when, as a boy, just after these events, he had someone ferry him across the river and found Buda strewn with corpses. The Hungarians had been proud of their bridges, which bind Buda and Pest together—the first one dates only from 1848 and the two cities were incorporated in one only in 1871—and they started at once to rebuild them. They are working now on the last. But this capital, at the present time, is still rather sad and empty.

Buda, on its steep hills, includes most of the old part of the city; flat Pest is the modern commercial part. Behind the Mátyás Church in Buda is the Halászbástya, "Fishermen's Bastion," to which one ascends by a high flight of stairs. Though built in the last century, it presents, with its stone walls and turrets, a somewhat absurd and yet somehow formidable belated mediaeval aspect. It does not appear to serve any purpose except to afford a platform from which to admire the view. One can look down on ancient Buda, with its domes and rectangular square-windowed façades, that seem to belong in eighteenth-century engravings; the big old palaces and public buildings in bad repair, with much yellow and orange, which I found attractive, but to which a Hungarian-American friend objected on the ground that the prevalence of yellow and orange was due to their having been Maria Theresa's favorite colors, and so reminded him disagreeably of the Hapsburgs. I stood on the bastion at an hour when an august gray and smudged-yellow sunset was spreading behind the abrupt Buda hills, which were sprinkled with the first magnolia and apricot blossoms, and with the villas of those fortunate enough to be able to have villas, scattered on their steep slopes; on their summits, rather awkward-looking monuments unidentifiable at that distance.

The many public statues in Budapest are of a special Hungarian species: convulsive, frenetic, full of desperate effort. There are a few fierce and rearing equestrians from the fabulous monarchic past, but these memorials are mostly of patriots who were fighting against oppression: heroic highbooted hussars, warriors with erectile manes and the long defiant mustaches that challenge like taurine horns. One of the poets is fixed in a permanent seizure of composition; a giant figure of Endre Ady, the great modern poet-patriot, is at once Promethean and Byronic. The male caryatids on one of the old palaces—now turned into offices and shops—are agonizedly straining with their muscles and necks to uphold the heavy stone front; the female figures on a public fountain are apparently equally taxed to maneuver their ponderous urns. Another fountain is guarded by bears. In the midst of a busy square, a group of beatific saints look out with a strange concentration into the vision of another world. The towering statue of Kossuth in front of the Parliament House had originally a tragic character: he was shown in the dejection of exile and failure, but he has now been redone as a conqueror, imperious in a gesture of accusation. A more modern but still rather romantic note is struck by a statue of Electric Power: a madly speeding female figure accompanied by a zigzagging lightning shaft.

But the oddest of the Budapest statues is in the Városliget, the big public park. The author of the first Hungarian chronicle, who is supposed to have written at the end of the twelfth century, is referred to, since his name is not known, as Anonymus Belae Regis Notarius, the Anonymous Scribe of King Béla, which is usually shortened to "Anonymus." He is commemorated, in a curious statue, as a shrouded and seated figure, whose face is so enveloped in a hood that even when one comes quite close to it the features cannot be distinguished. The grass has been worn away by people who have approached to peer at him, but one can only catch a vague deathlike visage—meant, I suppose, to be as mysterious as the origin of the Hungarians itself. This statue stands beside a vast replica of a feudal Transylvanian castle, which was erected for the exhibition of 1896 and is now used for an agricultural museum and other prosaic purposes. The Liget is a charming and entertaining resort, one of the most agreeable parks in Europe. The city is painting and repairing it for the spring, and one remembers the first act of *Liliom,* which is supposed to take place in the Liget. There is Gundel's elegant restaurant, with a white-whiskered Franz Josef porter, which cannot have changed much since the old regime; a zoo of considerable size and range, and a circus connected with it. The animals have been badly neglected. They are boxed up in small filthy cages, and it is painful to see wolves and bears pacing glumly in their stinking prisons. But with the housing situation for humans as difficult as it is, it is impossible, I suppose, to provide anything better for the animals.

The American Legation. A spooky place: no American Minister, only a chargé d'affaires, and the imprisoned Cardinal Mindszenty walking back and forth on the top floor. The front door is guarded by two glaring soldier-policemen. Since they had red stars on their caps and otherwise seemed dressed like Soviet soldiers, I assumed that they must be Russians, but it turned out that they were actually Hungarians in uniforms that differed from the Russian ones only in color and a few details. In the reception room are two sets of photographs—one of the Kennedys and other American officials and one of young Hungarians engaged in skiing and other sports—that give an impression of not having been looked at by the visitors of either country. Unless you are a certified American, you are not, on account of Mindszenty, allowed above the ground floor. The Cardinal's meals are sent up to him, and he gets a little exercise in the courtyard. A small room has been fitted up as a chapel, and he holds Mass there for American Catholics. "That albatross around your neck," a man in the British Embassy said to me. I did not find Mindszenty popular in Hungary. He courageously stood up to the Russians, but in doing so caused unnecessary trouble for many Catholics whom he led to support him and who were penalized by the Communist authorities. In regard to social reforms, he had been flatly reactionary—had been opposed to popular education and to breaking up the big estates. It is asserted—I do not know how truly—that he would now be free to go to

Rome or, if he were willing to relinquish his office, to retire in Hungary itself, but he insists on maintaining his primacy. "He wears—what you call it?—blinders like a horse," one Hungarian said to me. It is a pity that we have sent no Minister, and that our relations should still be strained. It was only a short time ago that the official prohibition was lifted which made it impossible for the Legation staff to travel more than twenty kilometers beyond the city limits, and they are still rather restricted and uncomfortable. As a result of this, I could not get them to send my books to the United States. The whole situation is disheartening, since the Hungarians seem to idealize America. But it was, I thought, a sign of enlightenment on the part of our State Department—whose personnel have not always been so competent—that five out of the nine of the Legation staff were able to speak Hungarian. The chargé d'affaires did not, but the cultural liaison man did, having studied it before he came, in Washington.

The Russians. I heard little said about Russia. But my personal reaction in Budapest was a rearoused antagonism toward the Soviet Union such as I had not experienced since the banning of *Zhivago* and the death of Boris Pasternak. One felt that an energetic people had been bludgeoned and partly crippled by an alien hand, that they were still, in decisive ways, at the mercy of a great stupid power—plagued by the insincere cant of the Soviet ideology and harassed by restrictions which, so far as I could see, hid nothing from, and inhibited no thinking on the part of, the alert Hungarians. A lingering resentment against the Russians dates from 1848, when Franz Josef got the Tsar to send troops to help him put down the Hungarian rebellion. This was at first rekindled by the Russian invasion at the end of the last war. I was told a curious story of the arrival in 1945 of an officer of the Red Army at one of the cultural institutions. He began, *"Messieurs, Mesdames, les barbares sont ici,"* and went on to explain that, regrettably, the Russian soldiers would not all be like him, but that some of them were pretty rough customers. There followed days of robbing and raping—the usual indulgence of victorious troops. But the Russians had got rid of the Nazis; the Hungarians were grateful to them for this, and, during several years of transition, they were hoping for national autonomy and for the democratic regime that had always been the goal of their patriots. But what they got was the Communism of Stalin, and when they revolted against this, in 1956, the suppression of the rebellion by Soviet tanks.

Russian language in the schools was made compulsory, and was mostly, I gather, detested. A young woman I know, who was old enough to have had her schooling before the war, started in to study Russian, but found it made her mother so uneasy that she dropped it in a moment of repulsion when she discovered that the word for *paper* was *bumaga,* which sounded to her particularly outlandish in the coarse pronunciation of the Russian soldiers —so remote from Hungarian *papir,* which associates itself so naturally with *papier, Papier* and *paper.* But that was in the nineteen-forties. Now that Stalin is dead and the revolt that followed has had its effect, the objection to compulsory Russian is rather that, as a first foreign language, it is too difficult and discouraging for small children. For in spite of the reputation of the Hungarian language for difficulty, it is a great deal less difficult than Russian: an almost perfectly logical instrument codified as a literary language as late as the eighteen-thirties by a practical committee of scholars, whereas Russian was developed in a hit-or-miss fashion—a language composed of idioms, with a queer and irregular grammar. There are, however, in the universities some students who go on with Russian, and there is still the strong interest in Russian culture—Russian music and literature—that was felt before the last war. (English, which is of course not compulsory, is the second most cultivated foreign language.) I was assured that the renaming of a street after the Soviet poet Mayakovsky and the inclusion in the ballet of numbers by contemporary Russian composers was not necessarily due to the pressure of the Soviet Union. When I spoke to a Hungarian friend of their harsh treatment at the hands of Russia, I was told that the country had suffered far worse at the hands of the Western Allies when it was deprived by the Treaty of the Trianon of two-thirds of its territory. Hungary now finds herself midway between West and East, and though she does trade to some extent with Western Europe, she is mainly—as a result of our panicky prejudice against all countries that call themselves socialist—forced eastward into doing business with Russia. The feudal system in Hungary had to go—it was one of the most antiquated in Europe—and one would think that even without Russian intervention a native revolution would in the long run have been inevitable. If the Russians should pull out tomorrow, I am sure, the country would adopt some such compromise between what we have been calling "socialism" and what we have been calling "capitalism" as is now seen, in various versions, to be taking shape throughout the industrialized world.

Hungarian Ambiguity. I discovered, in speaking English, that the word *ambiguous* was likely to crop up as often as in one of those American literary quarterlies that are always talking about different "levels." I was told, for example, that at present the attitude toward the churches was "ambiguous." The policy of the government is, of course, supposed to be anti-religious, but no one, I was given to understand, necessarily pays any attention to this. Both the Catholic and the Protestant churches, though their property has been taken by the State, are actually subsidized by it. In reading contemporary writing, one sometimes gets the impression that though the writers are obliged to pretend to be following the official ideology, they tend actually, from their taste and intelligence, to give expression to a different attitude. A little history of Hungarian literature which has come out in both Hungarian and English strikes me as an amusing instance of this. It is divided into three sections, written by three different men, and I have not read in it enough to distinguish between them, but it is plain that in keeping up the show of analyzing literary history in the set terms of capitalism and socialism, proletariat and bourgeoisie, they sometimes treat the Marxist thesis in a rather cavalier fashion. They will speak of some writer's associating himself with the sufferings of the people and describing their condition in his work and for a time becoming a socialist, but then, coolly and without condemnation, go on to record that he came later on to lose his faith in "the masses."

I was told that a prominent Hungarian writer declared publicly, on a visit to Paris, that the thing about Hungary he regretted most was its now being cut off from Transylvania. The official reception of this at home was like that of the autobiography which Yevtushenko had published in *L'Express,* but I gathered that in this case the public rebuke was not made with the same sincerity. People seemed to be sure that this writer had been put up to his impious statement—which it was hoped would ricochet on the Russians—by the Communist authorities at home.

If this is true, it is a good example of Hungarian "ambiguity."

Cirkusz a Varietében. This was a kind of revue, a very Central European affair, which seemed to me really to date from just after the last war. One is likely to find such old-fashioned entertainments in the Communist countries cut off from the West. There was a sort of Marlene Dietrich *commère,* with a jaunty top hat and a tight-fitting gown that was designed to show her admirable figure. The acts involved parodies of the circus just opened in the Városliget. First, someone emerged from behind the scenes and told the Marlene Dietrich *commère* that the black panther was loose and had eaten several members of the cast—an announcement that left her unmoved. Then a man came up from the audience and attempted to start a flirtation with her, but he was presently interrupted by a snarling and roaring offstage. The man at first showed signs of fright, but then decided to face the beast, and a horrible struggle was heard, at the end of which he returned with his clothes in shreds, holding up a limp dummy tiger. "You idiot," the lady said, "that's not a black panther. You've got the wrong animal!" This was followed—after a stupid act in which a female lion-tamer lashed her whip at a man disguised as a lion—by a comic organ-grinder, with a jaunty long cigar and an old-fashioned Magyar mustache, who entertained us with a series of gags such as taking off the mustache with the cigar attached to it and walking away from the organ while it went on playing by itself. It eventually, however, stopped playing, and the organ-grinder was tinkering with it when suddenly the top flew open and a heavy thick-ankled woman popped out and turned back-flips and cartwheels all over the stage. This acrobatic ballet worked up to the climax of what was apparently to be a strip tease. The lights were slowly turned down, and her garments were seen to be luminous. By the time there was nothing but a bikini left, the stage had become quite dark. Someone exclaimed, "It's not going to be true!," and, sure enough, the bikini went out and the woman disappeared. There were, however, pretty, slender girls who danced the first-act finale in bikinis.

On the Fringes of the Language. It is a tight, crowded, hemmed-in language. In spite of its element of Slavic vocabulary, it is otherwise quite unlike Russian, which has the looseness of a large half-empty country. A danger in writing Hungarian without due exercise of taste is that the adjectives and nouns, with their prefixes and endings, are likely to get jammed together—"agglutinated"—in such a way as to make dense reading. A foreigner may sometimes feel that the language is musclebound. To this foreigner, the *megs* and *mags* may at first give an ugly impression. *Meg* is the commonest prefix for verbs—it is the sign of a kind of perfective aspect—and there are also *meg, and; még, still, yet; mag, seed;* and the common *maga,* which means *self* and is also the most frequent form for *you.*

There is an interesting characterization of Hungarian by Gyula Illyés, the dramatist and poet, who seems to be regarded in Hungary as at present one of its ranking writers. I translate from the French version given in an *Esquisse de la Langue Hongroise,* by Professor Aurélien Sauvageot:

"It is not the language of trade, of persuasion, of weighing things, but rather that of pronouncement, of judgment. It is a language which articulates, strongly emphasizing every word. Foreigners, when they first hear it, feel that it is a language of command. But it is not. It does not evoke commands or troops that are waiting to obey, but, on the contrary, a free solitude, with two men quite remote from one another, each of whom has to wait when he has sent out a word till the resistance of nature has been overcome, the verbiage of the trees and the waves. It evokes a solitude from the beginning of time! And the protest against that solitude. Those who forged it have communicated only thoughts that are completed, already chewed, and then they have said no more. Each of their words has its value. Behind each thought is a real experience, if not a real sorrow. The very word for *thought* [*gondolat*] is derived in this language from the word for care [*gond*]."

I said something in English to a friend with whom I was reading Hungarian about the room's being rather warm, and she asked me whether I knew how to say "I am warm" and "I am cold" in Hungarian. I supposed they were *Meleg vagyok* and *Hideg vagyok*. That, she said, was what a foreigner would think, but if you put it that way, people might laugh. *Meleg vagyok* implies that you are Lesbian, *Hideg vagyok* that you are frigid. What you ought to say is *Melegem van* and *Fázom*. A tip for foreign visitors.

I had already known about Gábor Devecseri and made a point of being taken to see him. He is a poet and a classical scholar of a kind that could exist only in Hungary. The reason for this uniqueness is that it is only the Hungarians, so far as I know, who can claim that their verse is, like Latin and Greek, both accentual and quantitative. We do not really know how Greek and Latin verse were read. The meters, as they have come down to us, are based on long and short quantities, and these do not correspond with what are supposed to have been the stress accents—so in reading we have had to resort to substituting stress accent for quantity, emphasizing the long syllables and leaving the short ones unemphasized, as the meter seems to direct. (There are those, to be sure, who contend that the accents written in Greek are indications not of stress but of pitch, though in modern Greek they indicate stress.) Now, in Hungarian the length of a vowel is as important as the stress on an accented syllable and does not necessarily coincide with it. If, in trying to read Hungarian aloud, you pay more attention to one than the other, you will immediately be corrected, and I have found it a painful ordeal to try thus to read Hungarian poetry; it reminds me of attempts I have heard to read aloud ancient Greek poetry in such a way as to give value to both stress accent and quantity—in fact, it resembles those feats of performing conflicting movements with the right and left arms or legs. But this does make it possible, as their poets have been boasting ever since the eighteenth century, for a Hungarian to translate Greek and Latin poetry and reproduce—as is not possible, so far as I know, in any other modern language—both quantity and stress accent. There are also double consonants by which they seek to give the effect of the Latin and Greek double consonants which make a vowel "long by position." Gábor Devecseri has thus translated many of the classics, and he has spent years on a translation of Homer, which has now come out in paperback and has had an immense circulation. It was odd to find that Devecseri had been surprised that a young Englishman he had met should be able to recite passages from Homer. This visitor had told the Hungarian poet that his activities in his school and university days had been divided between classics and athletics. Devecseri had innocently commented, "Then half your time was well employed."

He evidently did not know the traditional attitude of the English in regard to the Greek and Latin classics.

Another feature of Hungarian verse that makes it uncomfortable for the foreigner is the fact that, since Hungarian words are all accented on the first syllable, it is almost impossible to produce true rhymes. A true rhyme, from our point of view, can only occur when two lines are made to end in words of which the stressed syllables correspond. But this is almost impossible in Hungarian. There are assonances, not real rhymes, and they constantly pair endings in *m* with endings in *n*. Devecseri said that they now and then do introduce true rhymes—sometimes for humorous effect—"like a pinch of salt," and he showed me an example of what he believed to be a true rhyme, but this (*unalom* and *malom*) turned out to be, from our point of view, not a true rhyme at all but as impossible a combination as if one should try to make *boringly* rhyme with *singly*. Final syllables that rhyme exactly are regarded by Hungarians as easy and cheap, undoubtedly for the reason that the prepositions and pronouns in Hungarian are likely to be written as suffixes at the ends of the words, so that the effect of trying to rhyme them would be clumsy. The Hungarians, Devecseri said, were "a nation of translators." He read me translations of Shelley and Keats, which sounded very beautiful, and it was curious to hear the lyric effects of these poets reproduced by such different means. Someone had claimed that the translation of Shelley's *Ode to the West Wind* was the finest Hungarian poem. Poe's *Raven* had been translated some fifteen times. Devecseri showed me several of these, and I found that various devices had been resorted to for "Nevermore." Later on, in talking of this with someone else, I tried on a deadpan joke: I said that there was one translation in which the refrain was

"Nem nem soha." *Nem nem soha*—which means *No, no, never*—was the great Hungarian slogan when the country, by the ruling of the Treaty of the Trianon, was being reduced by two-thirds. (I have known a Hungarian of American birth who told me that his parents in the Middle West had this motto up over the fireplace.) "Oh, yes," said my companion in Budapest, "but that was a satirical parody at the end of the first war." I did not know whether there was such a parody or whether, without actually knowing of one, he had taken me at my word.

How to Say "You" in Hungarian. One of the first and most baffling problems that the student of Hungarian runs into is what word to use for *you.* When he asks a Hungarian to explain this, he finds that he has created a situation similar to that which arises when the beginner in Russian asks his teacher what the verbs are for *to go* and *to come.* In this case, the Russian teacher is put to the embarrassment of breaking it to the student that there are no such verbs in Russian; that there exist, instead, innumerable verbs for different kinds of going and coming, depending on means of transportation, on frequency and regularity, on completed or continued action and even on length of stay at one's destination; and that the student can only hope to gradually get the hang of these. But, in spite of this proliferation of what seem to the foreigner two simple ideas, it is possible to give a definite explanation of the function of any of these words; whereas, if you ask a Hungarian what to do about saying *you,* he is likely to be nonplussed. There are four words for *you* in Hungarian, and each of them has a plural. Their nuances are a very important part of the same Magyar ceremoniousness which, before the present regime, embroidered personal relationships with a system of class honorifics that seems almost as complicated as the Japanese; but though the hierarchy of honorifics has officially been abolished by the Communist administration, the different ways of saying *you* still remain, and one can still admit another person to varying degrees of familiarity or keep him at varying degrees of distance by addressing him in different ways. This may raise serious issues of a kind that does not exist in English or even in those languages that make a distinction between the formal *vous* or *Sie* and the familiar *tu* or *Du*. What corresponds in Hungarian to *tu* and *Du* is the somewhat similar *te*, but what corresponds to the more formal counterparts is *maga* (literally *self*), which is respectful, like the Italian *lei*, and, like it, takes the verb in the third person. The difficulties created by *te* and *maga* have been amusingly satirized in an imaginary dialogue by the humorist Frigyes Karinthy:

Two men meet on the street. They have known each other for ten years; they have never been particularly intimate, and if they have happened to meet, they have been in the habit of exchanging a few politely cold words and immediately separating. But five days before this meeting, they have attended a banquet together, and in the course of it drunk champagne and addressed one another as "te" [this implies, it seems, a special ceremony like swearing "Bruderschaft"]. Now both of them remember this, but one of them is not altogether sure as to whether on this occasion they had been really on a basis of "te" or had only seemed to be. The situation is difficult, because, if they have really been on terms of "te," one of them will be offended if the other fails to remember it and will suppose that he now regrets it. If, however, this was not the case, how will the other be able to handle the situation if one of them now suddenly begins calling him "te"? Nevertheless, they will have to converse, because both have stopped on the street, and each decides at once that he will wait till the other addresses him and take his cue from that.

ONE (*shakes hands with the other and looks at him encouragingly*). Uh . . .

THE OTHER (*looks at him in the same way*). Uh . . . well, well . . . (*He does not let go of the other's hand.*)

ONE. Well, well . . . this is pleasant . . . uh . . . our meeting again. (*He looks at his friend smilingly and pressingly.*)

THE OTHER. Well . . . which way are . . . Are we going in this direction?

ONE. I'm going, precisely, in this direction . . . This is where I am going. Well . . . uh . . . how are we?

THE OTHER (*glad that he can speak of himself; there is no doubt that for the time being he must speak in the first person*). Oh, I'm getting along all right. The heat is awful, but otherwise I'm feeling well . . . uh . . . One does feel the heat, doesn't one?

ONE (*eagerly*). Oh, yes, terribly. And the sun is broiling, besides!

THE OTHER. Yes, of course, that's it! It isn't merely that it's so beastly hot, the sun is broiling, besides.

ONE. At a time like this in summer everything seems to combine.

Painful silence. The situation is putting a strain on both of them, but they do not dare to separate before the problem of "te" has been solved, since in order to be able to part, one has to say either "szervusz" [which implies "te"] or "your humble servant" [which implies "maga"]; no third course is possible.

THE OTHER. Well, what is . . . uh . . . the family doing? This kind of weather is hard on the family, isn't it?

ONE (*stupidly*). Hard on what family?

THE OTHER. Why . . . (*jokingly*) Our family? The lady and the children?

ONE. Meaning my children?

THE OTHER. Uh . . . Yes, of course, of course. The children.

ONE (*not quite understanding*). Is it *my* children— or . . .

THE OTHER. Yes, of course—just what I said. Our family, as they say jokingly, ha ha ha.

ONE (*chuckling*). Oh, jokingly!

Long silence, at the end of which they warmly shake hands and laugh. Suddenly the first man notices that a bug is crawling on the other's jacket.

ONE. Look out—we must look out. There's a bug crawling here . . . uh . . .

THE OTHER. Where?

ONE. On the thingumabob . . . on the jacket.

THE OTHER. What jacket?

ONE. Uh . . . on this one here . . . uh . . . (*jestingly*) not on mine, ha ha.

THE OTHER (*staring at him*). Well, whose?

ONE (*painfully facetious*). I'm not saying.

THE OTHER. On mine? (*He keeps staring*).

ONE (*after some cogitation*). Yes.

THE OTHER (*grasping the situation and brushing off the bug*). Thanks. It's most kind of . . . of people to be so attentive to one another.

ONE. Oh, it's nothing.

THE OTHER. No, but I'm very grateful.

ONE. Nothing at all, a mere trifle.

Long silence.

THE OTHER. Well—I'll be getting along now.

ONE (*frightened*). Already? . . . Is it really so urgent? Can't—can't we chat a little still?

THE OTHER. It's just that I'm not sure that . . . that it isn't inconvenient. . . . One . . .

ONE. Not at all, not at all! I'm really very glad that I've had a chance to see . . . that we've had a chance to see one another . . .

THE OTHER. I, too, am very glad . . . that . . . one has had a chance to see one another.

ONE (*resolutely*). I'm going toward the boulevard. Won't . . . shan't we go together?

For no reason at all, they go together and talk about all sorts of subjects—politics, philosophy, poetry, business, pure generalities—simply because they must not address one another directly. Each is painfully waiting for the other to address him first.

ONE (*It is now twelve o'clock and all the bars are closed*). Well, where—where do we live? Where do we live?

THE OTHER. Who? Where does who live?

ONE (*submissively*). I.

THE OTHER. How should I know that?

ONE. Why, of course . . .

He steps on the other's toe.

THE OTHER. Ouch!

ONE. What's the matter?

THE OTHER. Nothing . . . just a little accident, ha ha . . . we stepped on my toe.

ONE (*pale with anger*). Who did? Who?

THE OTHER (*absentmindedly*). I don't know.

ONE. You don't? (*He slaps him.*) Take that, you damned idiot! *Now* do you know? (*He is addressing him at last as* "te.")

He takes out a revolver.

THE OTHER (*happily*). Yes: of course I know! . . . Szervusz! . . . Te, te, te. . . .

They fall on each other's necks.

But then there is also the problem of *ön*. When I asked my Hungarian friends at home how this pronoun was

properly used, they reacted with something like horror
and advised me never to use it. It was pompous and
appropriate only in some such situation as that of a
teacher addressing a pupil. When I went to Budapest, I
used *maga* to the people in shops, but was then told that
this was incorrect, that I ought to have said *ön,* since the
relation between customer and shopkeeper was a strictly
impersonal one. A Hungarian lady in Boston recommended, after some thought, simply putting the verb in
the third person and using no pronoun at all—*ön* and
maga both take the third person. A Hungarian lady in
Cambridge, also after some reflection, suggested that I
might try *kegyed,* a pronoun I had not yet encountered. I
found that it, too, took the third person and was described
in László Országh's dictionary as "the most formal way of
address." *Kegyed* means *kind, merciful,* and *kegyelmes* is
a high honorific. But I was then told by someone else that
it had been used only by peasants, and when I inquired
about it in Budapest of somebody close to the Party, I got
the rather scoffing reply that—presumably because I was
an American—someone might possibly call *me* that. "Are
you ever addressed as *kegyed?*" "Oh, no!" he said. He
admitted, however, that although an attempt had been
made to cut down on the old distinctions, they seemed to
be reappearing. He said further that it was really no use
for a foreigner to try to get these things right. Age, rank,
intimacy, sex were involved; one had to have grown up in
Hungary. And it was true that I never ceased to be
astonished by the unpredictability of the words for *you.* I
noticed, in one of the scenes of Molnár's *The Devil*—a
conversation between an artist's model and a rich young
lady who have met for the first time—that they said
sometimes *maga,* sometimes *kegyed,* and sometimes *ön* to
one another, and I assumed that this must indicate
nuances of friendliness and respect, but when I inquired
about it I was told that in spite of the honorifics which

the model bestows on the lady, the pronouns, in the kind
of language the two women are using to one another, do
not have any special significance and are actually inter-
changeable. An American woman who, before the last
war, had been married to a Hungarian nobleman told me
that she and her husband had always called one another
maga, not *te*, but that her husband had called his men
friends *te*. A young Hungarian professor resident in the
United States described to me his difficulties with the
forms of address on a visit to Budapest. He found that
whereas in the United States the émigrés among themselves
called one another *te*, the scholars in his native country—
as it seemed to him, rather stiffly—addressed one another as
maga. He addressed them as *kolléga úr* (*Mr. Colleague*)
or *kollégém* (*my colleague*) and began letters "*Kedves kolléga*" (*Dear colleague*). In the official Academy of Science, the woman secretary always called him *elvtárs*, the
Hungarian word for *comrade*, the required use of which
is evidently repugnant to the traditionally ceremonious
Hungarians and seems now to have been largely dropped.
They made fun of it by saying *elvtárs úr*, and when my
friend protested that he was not an *elvtárs* but a citizen
of the United States, she replied that so far as she was
concerned everybody in that office was *elvtárs*. (The
awkwardness and absurdity of *tovarishch* has also become
a problem in Russia. According to a recent bulletin, the
old-regime words for *sir* and *madam*—*sudar'* and *sud-
arynya*—are now to be readmitted.)

Bartók and Kodály. It was delightful, in Budapest, to
see the ballets and operas of Bartók and Kodály so
spiritedly performed in their land of origin. You can get
no idea of Kodály's *Háry János* or Bartók's *Miraculous
Mandarin* from the sketchy orchestral suites that have
been put together from their scores, or even, in the case

of the former, from hearing a complete recording. I attended a matinée for children of *Háry János,* which began at eleven o'clock in the morning. This opera, in actual performance, has something in common both with the Rimsky-Korsakov of *Le Coq d'Or* and *The Tale of the Czar Saltana* and with the English Christmas panto-mime. It is full of animated toys and astonishing fairy-tale tricks. Háry János is a boastful old soldier romancing to a friend in a tavern, and the story of the opera is the fantasy he spins—by implication, a benevolent satire on the romantic self-infatuation and extravagant boasting of old Hungary. Háry, according to his story, has stopped Napoleon's army singlehanded; and the Empress Marie Louise, who, disgusted by Napoleon's cowardice, has divorced him and returned to Vienna, has fallen in love with Háry and takes him to live in the palace, with the intention of making him her husband. But Háry ends by marrying the peasant girl to whom he was already en-gaged. In the meantime, all kinds of wonders and farcical incidents occur. Háry performs the heroic feat of moving the customs house, which was holding up the Empress's coach, so that she finds herself beyond the frontier, and when a great village clock strikes, each of its numerals opens up a round shutter and a little bugler pops out, after which a parade of mechanical figures takes place on the balcony underneath. The soldiers of Napoleon fall dead when Háry János brandishes his sword, and Örzse, the peasant sweetheart, also taken into the palace, is as-signed to the menial task of feeding the two-headed eagle of the Austro-Hungarian Empire, which is made to stretch down from its perch and peck at the corn that she brings it.

The composer himself was present at this matinée, in a bottom-tier box—a tall distinguished old man, with drooping eyelids and myopic eyes. When the audience recognized him at the first intermission, they applauded, and he modestly rose and bowed. He left before the next intermission. He had come on account of the children. One could not but be moved by this evidence of the honor in which—even in a communized country, and in spite of the example of the Soviet Union—an artist is still held in Europe.

I had already seen *The Miraculous Mandarin* several years before in Frankfurt—a stylized expressionist performance, which made little impression on me. But in Budapest it was terrific, and I saw it twice. The first time, it was part of a mixed ballet program, which included an aged pair doing the Blue Bird *pas de deux* decrepitly, and a ballet by Khachaturian—one of those things about a wild semi-Oriental tribe, with much whirling and leaping and brandishing of knives. There was also a remarkable number in which a piquant little girl did a stunt—to tremendous applause—that I had never seen in ballet before: she would roll herself up in a kind of ball and hurl herself backward, to be caught by her partner. If she had fallen, I should think she would have broken her back. In another number, the men, holding the girls horizontally, would throw them up into the air, and before they were caught again the still horizontal ballerinas would have made a complete revolution. What distinguishes the Hungarian ballet from any other I have ever seen is its atmosphere of unruly tumult and dangerous acrobatics. This comes to a shattering climax in *The Miraculous Mandarin*. You have a prostitute who is managed by three pimps. She hails in men off the street from her window by waving a handkerchief. The first is a fat bourgeois, who is murdered, robbed and thrown down a trapdoor. The second is a young man who has no money, so they simply put him out. But now a huge shadow is thrown against the glass of the door. A gigantic

Chinaman appears, and at first sits perfectly silent, disregarding the enticements of the girl, who was played with much vivacity by the little reckless hurtling dancer. She eventually becomes frightened and wants to give up, but her companions, peeping out from their hiding places, insist that she persevere. Then, suddenly, the Chinaman goes after her, so violently that she runs away. He pursues her, and the pimps become frightened. A tremendous roughhouse occurs. They bop him on the head with no effect, and throw a chest at him, which he catches against his breast. At last, they overcome and stab him and throw him down the trapdoor. Grinning, they congratulate themselves; but the lid of the trap opens, and the Chinaman's great hands are seen powerfully clutching the floor: he is pulling himself up. His pursuit of the girl begins again. He chases her upstairs and knocks one of the pimps off the staircase. A second time, they overpower him, and hang him by a rope out the window, but even this does not take. He releases himself and returns. But he has now been too badly injured to renew his pursuit of the girl. After a few convulsive efforts, he dies in her arms. She has come to admire and pity him.

The *Mandarin* invariably gets wild applause. I thought at first, because of a backdrop with high buildings and winking signs which was evidently meant to represent New York, that the Mandarin had been made a symbol for Capitalism, which took a long time to kill. But then, might he not as plausibly be Communism, which heroically resisted being killed? I was not, however, left in doubt, after seeing the ballet again, that the Mandarin was here intended—and had probably been intended by Bartók—to represent simply Hungary, who shook off all attempts to suppress her. The set was a false lead. It seems characteristic of Hungary in relation to her present

regime—as it had been, I suppose, under the Austrians—
that her people will make some pretense of obedience to
their directors, then behave in such a way as to defy
them. Under pressure to produce Russian plays, I
thought they felt a certain satisfaction in performing
one—Leonov's *The Blizzard*—that has been denounced
by Russian critics and is at present, I believe, banned in
Russia.

The second time I saw the *Mandarin* was as part of an
all-Bartók bill, with *Bluebeard's Castle* and *The Wooden
Crown Prince*. I do not think that, except in the *Mandarin*, this composer is naturally dramatic, as Strauss and
Berg and Britten are, in the practical theatrical sense. The
second of these pieces—which I have heard only once—is
a kind of subjective fairy tale, and *Bluebeard*, Bartók's
only opera, though it has indeed its spooky beauty if one
merely hears it on records, did not seem to me effective on
the stage. It has been compared to *Pelléas et Mélisande*,
but I have always felt that this has a similar weakness:
you are not interested in what is happening to the
characters. Like everything else of Bartók's, *Bluebeard's
Castle* is extremely subjective. It is supposed to be preceded by a spoken prologue, the text of which I have not
seen but which explains, one is told in a description
which comes with a German recording, that the meaning
of the opera "must be sought in another and hidden stage
within the mind." But I cannot make out this meaning.
What is the significance of the visions that Bluebeard's
most recent wife beholds when she unlocks the seven
chambers, and why are her three predecessors identified
with morning, noon and evening, and herself put away
by them as night? Bartók *is* capable of drama, but it is
mostly inside himself, as in the startling Concerto for
Orchestra, with its alterations of uneasy melancholy and

furiously assertive passion, and the eruption into its Fourth Movement of a banal popular tune, which—this work was composed in America—seems at once nostalgic and mocking.

There is very little motor traffic in Budapest, and it is comic, after Paris and Rome, to see a taxi driver, held up very briefly at the entrance to one of the bridges, grin sarcastically and throw out his hands. There are not very many taxis, and I had often to walk home from the theater along the broad and interminable boulevards. At night, these were almost empty. There was, I heard, a fairly lively night life, but I made no attempt to explore it. I never saw anybody at night who had the appearance of going anywhere to amuse himself—a few straggling old men and women. Even the most important streets were badly lighted. I was told that these lights in the streets had been getting dimmer for months, and this seemed to make the people dimmer. Everyone is gentle and polite. I hardly heard a disagreeable word all the time I was in Hungary.

Molnár's Theater. I have read in Hungarian three of Molnár's comedies: *Az Üvegcipő* (*The Glass Slipper*), *Úri Divat* (done on Broadway as *Fashions for Men*), and *Az Ördög* (*The Devil*). I did not care much for the first of these, though it has its amusing patches. I am told by Molnár's widow, Lili Darvas, that Molnár declared it was based on his early relations with her—which seems to me, on Molnár's part, something of a piece of impertinence, comparable to the statement by Bernard Shaw that the relations between Higgins and Eliza in *Pygmalion* were based on his own relations with Mrs. Patrick Campbell. The Irma of *The Glass Slipper*—Miss Darvas insists that she was not very good in this part—is a pathetic but impudent little slavey who devotedly waits upon and is hectored by a middle-class maker of furniture (perhaps a joke by Molnár about his own craft). The J. M. Barrie side of Molnár—the Barrie of *A Kiss for Cinderella*—is too much in evidence here: the poor, quaint and wistful little girl who is designed to bring on smiling tears. And the last act is terribly padded—as is likely to be the case with Molnár—with unnecessary characters and incidents contrived to fill out the evening. The furniture manufacturer, as we have clearly foreseen from the start, will marry the little girl.

Úri Divat is, however, much better—is, in fact, it seems to me, something of a comic masterpiece. The first and last acts take place in a shop which—as one would not gather from the Broadway translation of the title, which really means "Clothes for the Quality"—deals in women's clothes as well as men's. In the first act, a terrible triangular crisis is going on between the owner of the shop and his wife and a scoundrelly assistant. The situation is just about to come to a head, but this is always being postponed or interrupted by the necessity of looking after the customers, and the shopkeepers and their assistant are always being forced to alternate between serious personal scenes and obsequious professional ones in which they have to try to please these customers. The dramatist exploits, to great comic effect, the social discriminations, with their corresponding usages and honorifics, of the old Hungarian society: the *nagyságos asszonyom* and *uram* (appropriate to the middle class), the *méltóságos asszonyom* and *uram* (appropriate to certain officials), the *méltóságos báró* and *kegyelmes gróf* (when it is necessary to deal with a title), as well as the formulas of abject deference with which the language of such people as the shopkeepers was encumbered in addressing their social superiors: the incessant *kérem, tes-*

sék, kezeit csókolom, parancsoljon méltóztatni. It is not at
all surprising that this comedy should have had no success
on Broadway. Only the great popularity of Molnár's plays
in the United States in the twenties could have led to the
folly of attempting it. The force of the comedy partly
depends on the contrast between the language that the
shopkeepers use to the customers and the language that
they use to each other, and the former almost entirely
evaporates, I find, in looking up the translation, when all
the gentlemen are addressed as "sir" and all the ladies as
"madam." Then there have to be nuances of deportment
in relation to the elderly Count, the Nervous Gentleman,
the Noble Lady, the Shy Lady, the Anxious Lady, the
Efficient Lady, the Dissatisfied Lady and the Patient
Lady. The whole play is really a study in the shopkeeper's
profession—some have the qualifications, some do not—in
a city such as old Budapest. It reminded me of the shopkeepers in Karlsbad, in my childhood, who would greet
one, if one stopped to look into the window, with a bow
and an *"Ich habe die Ehre."* The play has a curious
resemblance to an Elizabethan comedy—Thomas Dek-
ker's *The Honest Whore*—of which the subplot depends
on a similar character: a linen draper so meek and
subservient that he will stand for any insolence from his
customers and from any provocation on the part of his
contemptuous wife. I was struck by a typically Magyar
reaction on the part of a Hungarian lady in Cambridge to
whom I gave *Úri Divat* to read. "That man is a fool!" she
said. "Such people ought to be exterminated! The people
who always submit do just as much harm as the aggressive people." I suggested that the character was amusing.
"He is not amusing at all!"

I was not able to see this play in Budapest. Nowadays
it would never do. The gentle, self-effacing shopkeeper
who allows himself to be swindled by his wife and his

shop assistant but who emerges as almost a saint, with the
love of his once discontented but later adoring cashier, to
return to his Heaven-sent vocation could hardly today be
tolerated as even a comic hero. But I did see another play
of Molnár's which had for me a special interest. Ferenc
Molnár made his first international reputation through
The Devil, which was produced in Budapest in 1907 and
reached America the next year in—I learn from S. N.
Behrman's chapter on Molnár in his book *The Suspended
Drawing Room*—no less than four simultaneous productions: two in English, one in German and one in
Yiddish. I did not see either Edwin Stevens or George
Arliss in the title role but only a road company in Red
Bank, New Jersey. The play had such a sulphurous
reputation that—I was then thirteen—it rather fright-
ened me, and I was curious, in Budapest, to find out what
all the fuss had been about.

There was a very creditable revival going on in the
repertory of the Vigszínház (the Comedy Theater),
where the play had been first produced, and I took the
precaution of reading it first in order to be able to follow
it. Two young people, a boy and girl, have been brought
up, as protégés and hangers-on, in the house of a rich
family. They had always loved one another, but the girl
has married the rich man's son and the boy has become a
successful painter, who has been having an affair with his
model but is engaged to a society girl. János and his
former sweetheart have now been seeing each other on
social occasions, but no move has been made to revive the
past. The husband of Jolán, the young woman, however,
a stock odious husband of the period, a pretentious
parvenu, stupidly unaware of the inflammable situation,
brings his wife to the painter's studio and insists on his
painting her in décolleté. For this, she has to take off her
blouse. The husband then leaves her with the artist, and,

after a scene in which the two young people intimately discuss their old love, the painter leaves the young woman alone. Shyly and hesitantly, she makes herself unbutton the blouse, and as she is about to hang it on a throne for models which is standing with its back to the audience, she suddenly screams and drops it. The Devil appears from the throne, where he says he has been asleep, and politely hands her the blouse: *"Pardon,* Madam. You have dropped something." All this I remember quite clearly; but I could not have been interested in the rest, for what happened after these first provocative scenes I found that I had almost completely forgotten. I could only remember the Devil, in a later act, walking past a window and flashing the red lining of his cloak at a moment when Jolán is struggling with her temptation. I cannot imagine that the long speeches in which the Devil expounds his immoral moralities were not cut for the productions in English. It is worth noting that *Man and Superman* was first produced in New York in 1905, and that there had hardly been time in the theater for Shaw to have set a precedent. In any event, the "diabolonian ethics," as Shaw called it, was prevented from outraging the audience by his sending them out of the theater reassured by an ending which, if not quite conventional, was calculated to gratify the ladies. And Molnár's Devil, for all his ostensible cynicism, is bringing Boy and Girl together. The scruples that Jolán feels about succumbing to János and that are steadily combatted by the Devil are of so purely conventional a character—since her husband does not deserve her and there are no children to complicate matters—and János's relations with his fiancée are based on such mistaken motives that the Devil seems right to discourage them. His role is very much like that of the old gentleman in George Arliss's *Disraeli* or one of those other romantic comedies, who disentangles the young lovers' difficulties and ultimately effects their union. As someone said to me in Budapest, Molnár's Devil—especially as played by a stout actor of amiable appearance and of by no means towering stature—really should have been called Onkel Teufel. But the play—unlike such trade goods as *Disraeli*—does have some psychological interest: the Devil is more or less made to represent the hidden impulses of sincere passion which are at war with the social exactions.

One of the cleverest scenes is that in which Jolán is made to write a letter for the purpose of telling János that he must never see her again. She hesitates as to how to go about it: she is aiming, she tells herself, at something extremely severe, "brief and dry and final." But the Devil is there and takes over. He dictates a flaming epistle in which he makes her declare that her friend must never see her again, because if he did their love would go up in a holocaust, they could never control themselves, they would kiss as they had never kissed before. "What have I written?" she asks, in a daze. Says the Devil, "Something very severe, calculated to banish him." This is followed by some hanky-panky about the delivery of the letter, which the Devil does not at first give János and which János tears up without reading it, thus sparing the woman the embarrassment of her overheated avowal. But they finally go into the bedroom together, and the Devil, after listening at the door, turns to the audience and announces, *"Voilà!"* The crispness and the point of this did not quite spark off as it should have. The theater of Budapest is now perhaps further away from Paris than it was in Molnár's time, and the actor stressed the first syllable as it is stressed in all Hungarian words and gave the *-là* a long Hungarian *á*. The artist, in the meantime, has made things all right for an audience of the early nineteen-hundreds by announcing that Jolán is his "future wife."

The Vigszínház is huge, and though *The Devil* had
been in the repertory ever since January—this was May
—it was still packing the house with a most sympathetic
audience, who, in spite of the official pretensions to
Communist austerity and discipline, were delighted by
the Devil's worldly cracks and applauded the outburst of
Jolán's letter. The production was full of color: the
glittering lights and gay waltzes of the big evening party
at the house of the millionaire, the elegant gowns of the
women, who were good-looking and excellent actresses.
The dramatic critic of a literary paper associated with the
Party said to me that though it ought to be possible to
make Molnár acceptable to modern Hungary, that was
not the right way to do it. He particularly seemed to
object to the grandeur and glamor of the party. That
kind of thing, he said, had nothing to do with the
way people had to live now. I got the impression that he
thought that all this ought to be made ridiculous, but
though it is true that Molnár liked to exploit the attrac-
tions of nobility and luxury, it is true, also, that his own
origins led him to satirize the upper classes and to enjoy
making his humbler characters eventually come out on
top. Not, of course, that this would satisfy the doctrinaire
Marxists, because what they come out on top of is the old
smart upper-class world. I assured him that the audience
at *The Devil* was still, after five months, house-filling and
enthusiastic. "That's a rather special audience at the
Vigszínház." I hope I have not misunderstood him. I
found that when he reviewed the play he had not taken
this banal line, that he had written about it rather favor-
ably. But he may have been class-angling for a foreigner.

I was sorry, in Budapest, not to be able to see more of
the theater. The variety it offered was astonishing—especially after the poverty of Rome. Besides Hungarian

classics and modern Hungarian comedies, they were do-
ing foreign plays which ranged from Shakespeare, Mo-
lière and Racine, through Diderot (a dramatization of *La
Religieuse*), through Büchner, Shaw and Pirandello, to
O'Neill (*"An American Electra"*), Tennessee Williams,
Anouilh, Noël Coward and Cole Porter.

The Franz Josef "Image." I had inquired of a Hungarian psychoanalyst who has long been practicing in
New York how analysis had been doing in Hungary.
"Oh," he said, "all the Hungarians have a Franz Josef
complex"—that is, I concluded after I had been for a time
in Hungary, a kind of father complex which made Franz
Josef either a great paternal authority who had to be
obeyed and revered or a tyrant who had to be challenged.
I put this to a friend in Budapest, expecting a scoffing
reply, but he answered that there was something in it,
and the more I heard of the Hungarian past the more I
came to believe it. The paternal figure of the Emperor—
though it may not haunt the younger Hungarians—still
lingers in all this part of the world. In Vienna, I went to
a musical show called *Frühjahrsparade,* which gave Viennese and foreigners the complete Viennese works:
waltzes, the Prater in spring, an appetizing Viennese
bakery, pretty women in chic costumes of the early
nineteen-hundreds and, as a climax, Franz Josef in his
palace. The Emperor, a very brief part, was played by a
leading actor, and his appearance was hailed by an
applause which seemed to include the Emperor with the
actor. This Franz Josef was very *bon enfant.* He kindly
receives the young girl from the bakery, who appeals to
him to help to get a hearing for a waltz song which her
fiancé has written. Amiably disregarding her gaucheries,
the Emperor arranges this, and the song is of course a
great hit. The finale is a spring parade, at which the tune

is played by a military band, with a filing-past of many
bright uniforms, including a detachment from the Tyrol,
now partly separated from Austria—a feature patriotically
applauded. You cannot have it quite this way in Budapest, but I saw an amusing Hungarian film in which
Franz Josef, though treated humorously, was no less in
the background of everything. (I had been told that the
Hungarian films were poor, but this was extremely good
—well acted and well produced.) It was called *A Pénz-
csináló* (*The Counterfeiter*) and was adapted from a
short story from the days before the last war. A vulgar
lower-middle-class man discovers that he can imitate exactly the bills with the head of Franz Josef; he passes off
his counterfeits and becomes very rich. He makes connections with the world of the nobility and is able to get his
daughter married to a young man of good family.
Through all this, the visage of Franz Josef on the bills is
constantly present to his consciousness and, according to
the counterfeiter's mood, eyes him dubiously, frowns
severely or winks in a kind of connivance. The counterfeiter gambles with the nobles and loses—I believe they
are supposed to be cheating—and the winner demands
prompt payment. But the man has sent his family to the
country, and along with them the counterfeiting machine, in order to get it off the premises, and he is in
desperation to meet the emergency. He is rescued by a
nouveau riche snob, who has heard about the counterfeiter's having forged a coat of arms for his family and
will pay him a high price to have one forged for himself.
The counterfeiter's noble friends, impressed by the upstart's resources, invite him to come in with them on a
project for which they need a great deal of capital, but he
explains to them the source of his money, and they
summon him sternly to a meeting. He goes to it with
apprehension, but it turns out that his only punishment is

to be made to drink a huge goblet of wine. They all get drunk together; the nobles do not care where the money comes from; they go through with their scheme, and it prospers. The end is a fantasy of the counterfeiter's, which begins with the kicking legs of a line of chorus girls and goes on to a reception by the Emperor, who greets him in bad Hungarian and accepts one of the cheap cigars that have figured in his relations with the nobles, and which ends in a snowstorm of counterfeit bills, with Franz Josef's face on every one. The corruption of the monarchy triumphs. Yet, even in satirizing the monarchy, the film has a certain amount of ambiguity: the nobility are all rascals, and the detective who has been after the counterfeiter is finally himself sent to jail by the powers who have an interest in concealing the fraud; but—especially in connection with the daughter's wedding, at which a Hapsburg is present, not caricatured but played straight—there persists a certain exploitation of the traditional Hungarian snobbery.

The bitterness against the Emperor is seen at its most intense in a legend that followed the Hungarian defeat after the uprising of 1848. Thirteen Hungarian generals were executed in one day by the Austrians, and the Hungarians are supposed to have put a curse on the family of Franz Josef, who were to pay, man for man, for these executions. Ludwig of Bavaria went mad—a Wittelsbach, not a Hapsburg, but the Empress's cousin; Maximilian was shot by the Mexicans; the Empress Elizabeth was stabbed by an anarchist; the Crown Prince Rudolf shot himself and his mistress; the Archduke Ferdinand was assassinated at Sarajevo, etc., etc., to the number of thirteen. But Franz Josef in 1849 had only just ascended the throne. He was nineteen years old at that time, and he was to live to be eighty-six. The Hungarians got used to having him there as both a butt and a presiding presence. The confusion of feeling about him is illustrated in a family anecdote told me by a Hungarian friend. This lady's mother, she said, was an out-and-out anti-Hapsburger, but her father was a person of sufficient importance to be asked to the royal receptions when the Emperor made one of his brief visits to the palace reserved for him in Buda. On one of these occasions, the husband came home to announce that his pocket had been picked. "What do you expect," said the wife, "when you go to meet Franz Josef?" The husband left the house in a rage.

Art Galleries. The Hungarians excel in literature, in music and in the theater, but they lack the vocation of painters, as seems to be the case with all the peoples in this Eastern part of the world, including the whole of Russia. There is a large National Gallery in Budapest which is entirely devoted to the native art and in which its qualities may be studied. It is true that there are only occasional exhibitions of the work of contemporary artists —there has lately been a very strong protest against the museum's slighting of modern art—and that it is impossible to judge recent achievements from the contents of this old gallery. It is true, also, that almost all the religious paintings have been collected in a museum at Esztergom, the ancient cathedral town which is the residence of the primate of the Catholic Church. But the general lack of taste of the varied collection in Budapest seems to indicate—at any rate, for the centuries it covers—an absence of natural talent. The sculpture here is mostly clumsy, highly dramatized—like the public statues—but less acceptable when not seen out-of-doors, where it represents the actors in the national epic. The dominating impression that the paintings make—from the lowering blacks

of Mihály Munkácsy to the half-Cubist browns of Der-
kovits—is one of dark dull colors and rather coarse tex-
tures. Among the most attractive pictures are some early-
nineteenth-century portraits of piquant black-eyed personalities that could not be anything but Magyar. The
situation is very much the same as in the Tretyakov
Gallery in Moscow: the interest lies for the most part in
carefully executed genre pictures of typical scenes of
Hungarian life and in ambitious historical illustrations
that commemorate famous events. These latter run to
painful subjects: revolutionaries in prison and tragic
farewells. The underground struggle against Austria
which followed 1848 was a stimulus to this kind of painting, at a time when it was possible to express that
struggle only by implication, through incidents of the
struggle against the Turks: the militant Franciscan monk
who fell to his death in defending a fortress against
them; the indomitable women of Eger who astounded the
harem-keeping Turks by fighting like demons with the
men at the gate of another fortress. The pictures of
country life, with their murky embrowned landscapes,
are influenced by the Munich School. The murkiest pictures of all are those of Munkácsy, the great reputation
of the nineteenth century, whose work is here displayed
on a gigantic scale. He strikes me as a third-rate Rem-
brandt: large, somber, yet not solidly built canvases, in-
teriors with many figures that usually have some social
significance, or towering Biblical tableaux. Also trained
in the German School, he was the most ambitious of the
nationalist artists. His canvases are deteriorating from
his use of asphalt in his paint, which has lately been
flaking off.

There are some very odd, cmbarrassing things among
the other paintings. The pseudo-classical imaginings of a
kind of Magyar Golden Age that entirely lacks Hellenic

refinement: "Paganism," "Sleeping Bacchante"; an extraordinary Cupid and Psyche, with Cupid suspended
just above his love in such an awkward position as to
seem to be not hovering but performing a balancing act.
An astonishingly elaborate still-life of rich Hungarian
pastry that makes one think of gluttonous eating rather
than of serious art. Landscapes derived from Corot, but a
little too stiff and bristling. The equivalent of scenes
from Victorian novels in the manner of Augustus Egg
and Holman Hunt's *Awakening of Conscience:* a fashionable married couple, sulking on the verge of explosion;
honeymooners of a humbler level embracing on the couch
of a dark inn room, a table set at hand for their supper,
with simple plates and a pitcher of wine; a tragic brother
and sister, *Orphans,* both in dark mourning clothes—he
with his head in his hands on the table, she with her
hands in her lap brooding in blank desperation. They are
confined in a bare room, lit only by a single lamp, with
darkening windows behind them. But the painting seems
to become somewhat worse—instead of being illuminated
and aerated—when, at the end of the last century, they
began following Paris instead of Munich. There is a
rather messy *Picnic in May,* which must have been to
some extent inspired by Manet's *Déjeuner sur l'Herbe*—
the ladies in blue and pink gowns, the men in what look
like velvet jackets, on a background of Paris-green grass.

The Szépmüvészeti (Fine Arts) Múzeum, which
stands just outside the gates of the Liget, is an enormous
old-fashioned marble palace with a classical columned
front, up the steps of which, the day I visited it, a
procession of small schoolchildren—a now familiar sight
—was being led. It contains a large collection of non-
Hungarian art, which includes some excellent things:
Grecos, Goyas, a good many Cranachs. But the selection
of these pictures, I thought, had not been made with very

much taste. There were second-rate specimens of good painters and an admixture of abominable Böcklins and other inferior German stuff. Here, too, a discouraging darkness, but mainly due to the weather. The only light came through a large central skylight from a heavily overcast sky, and one could not see anything satisfactorily. It was only just as I was leaving that someone turned on the electric lights. This situation, however, is much worse in the galleries of Paris, where, even at the Louvre, they do not have any artificial light at all but simply let the people leave when it is getting too dark to see anything.

Debrecen. I wanted to visit this old university town, which lies in the extreme east of Hungary, not far from the Rumanian border, and the Institute of Cultural Relations was good enough to put a limousine at my disposal. This enabled me to see the country between Budapest and the border which is known as the *Alföld* or the *puszta*—that is, the lowland or the waste land. I was surprised, after reading about the horrors of the Old Hungarian life, to see how well the countryside looked, and that the peasants' houses—at least along the road— were clean and freshly painted. This had once been a desert, with not even trees, only used for grazing. It has never been densely populated since the Turkish occupation of the sixteenth and seventeenth centuries, when the natives fled to other parts of Hungary. Now eighty per cent of the Hungarian land is under collective cultivation: miles and miles of smooth green fields, all sown with crops in green strips and not divided off by fences. Along the roads, they have planted some poplars. There are also a few large pig farms, and still some goatherds and shepherds with their flocks. Hungarians who have not been in Russia will tell you that it is just like the steppes, but actually the steppes seem flatter. On the steppes, as far as the eye can reach, there is sometimes nothing but grass and no landmarks upon the horizon. Here the country is bristled at intervals by the queer long-handled high-legged "heron wells," which one of the Hungarian poets has likened to gigantic mosquitoes that suck the moisture from the arid soil.

The Turks left the *puszta* also culturally arid. There is almost nothing here now except the University. A theological school was founded at Debrecen in 1531, before the Turkish conquest, and the town first acquired importance as a center for the refugees who had been driven out of their villages by the Turks. It later became Calvinist, and is now the headquarters of Protestantism in Hungary, which was at one time thirty per cent Protestant. (Many of the children nowadays are not even baptized.) Debrecen is very rich in cultural and historical associations. There are the usual statues to writers. The early Calvinist lyric poet Csokonai was born here in 1773; so, also in the eighteenth century, was Fazekas, the author of a famous humorous poem, *Ludas Matyi,* of which I was given by a professor there a new beautifully illustrated edition. Petőfi lived in poverty here, and Endre Ady studied law. There is a curious Calvinist museum, full of manuscripts and first editions and archaic scientific apparatus. Another museum, the Déri, founded by a rich collector, has an admirable exhibition of costumes, utensils, weapons; a reproduction of a bedroom in a peasant's cottage and another of an ancient pharmacy; a room devoted to the work of a bad Debrecen-born sculptor named Ferenc Medgyessy—the approach to the museum is ornamented by four of his atrocious statues, which represent Art, Exact Science, Ethnology and Archaeology. The old hardly-decorated Calvinist building which houses the scientific and literary collection contains the revered meeting hall in which, in 1849—since the Austrians had taken Budapest—Kossuth and his followers met, preparatory to going to the adjacent church and declaring Hungarian independence. When the Germans had been driven out at the end of the last war, the new Hungarian government was organized in this same room. The wooden staircase up and down which Kossuth and his group had walked in connection with their historic meeting has never been allowed to be touched; it is unpainted and rather broken down. There is a pathos about these steps preserved thus as holy relics. People talk as if Kossuth's defiance of the authority of the Austrian Crown had been a real declaration of independence which, like our own, had had permanent results. But the immediate consequence was that Franz Josef brought in the Russian troops, that Kossuth had to flee to Turkey, that the army surrendered to a Russian general and that an Austrian terror followed. It was to cost Hungary much further struggle and blood to arrive at the Dual Monarchy of 1867, which still left the country, however, by no means free from interference and repression by the Austrians. But the earlier rebellion had had its effect in validating the claims of Hungary and procuring later reforms, as did that other suppressed rebellion of 1956, which partially relieved the oppression of Stalin.

The modern University of Debrecen, which dates only from 1914, is one of the chief centers of Hungarian intellectual life. It is based upon an impressive large new building, which contains most of the offices and classrooms. I met several of the English faculty. One was translating Steinbeck and taking her students through *Tom Jones*, another was doing work on Poe's influence in Hungary. A middle-aged lady, who had visited England, took me around the town. The main street is ill-paved and ill-kept. In the residential streets, the houses reminded me of provincial Russia—a succession of one-story dwellings with bluntly arched windows and yellow or red fronts. Though the façades were very narrow, I was told that these houses extended far back from the street and had long courtyards behind them.

The housing situation presents one of the most difficult problems in Hungary. The country people—partly because of their hostility to the collectivization—are moving into the cities by the thousands, and Debrecen is as crowded as Budapest. Few families have more than one room. I was told by someone close to officialdom that it would take at least ten years to provide adequate housing facilities.

I stayed at the Golden Bull, the best hotel in Debrecen. It was in a state of mad confusion, owing to special preparations for a visit by Walter Ulbricht, the Secretary of the Communist Party of the East German Republic— repainting, moving furniture, climbing ladders, all remarkably inefficient and messy; the elevator always out of commission.

In saying goodbye to the friend who had been helping me with Hungarian—also a member of the English Department—I said that it was sad to think of all the brilliant Hungarian scientists and writers and musicians that they had lost through emigration. "We have hidden resources," she said.

What is tragic about Hungary is that its history of stubborn and energetic effort, of intellectual genius, should so often end in abortion. Kossuth died in exile, Széchenyi went mad. The 1848 revolution was crushed, the 1956 revolt was crushed. Petöfi, fighting the Russians, was killed at twenty-six; Ady died of syphilis; his successor, József Attila, went mad and committed suicide; Bartók was half-extinguished by exile.

When I was just about to leave, it was explained to me that somebody would have to ride with me—I couldn't go in the car alone, because the time of my arrival would have to be checked by a responsible civil servant. I was accompanied by an agreeable young man, who had to go to Budapest. He was teaching French literature and writing about Blaise Cendrars. The river Tisza was overflowing, as it always does every spring when the snow on the Carpathians melts. It was silvery and winding, quite lovely in its setting of the new green of trees and grass, among which it spread silver ponds. We had to wait to cross it on a narrow railroad bridge—an unsatisfactory arrangement. When a train had gone by, we followed it, and at one point the car stumbled over the tracks. I had so far escaped official sightseeing, but my companion stopped the car at a restaurant in a large collectivized area. This, I afterwards learned, was the Hortobágyi Csárda, a famous inn on the largest Hungarian steppe. "During Horthy's Fascist regime," I find in a recent Hungarian book, *The Geography of Hungary,* "the Hungarian gentry brought here their guests from abroad to show them the *fata morgana,* the 'true *puszta*' and the 'csikós' [cowboys] clad in colorful national costumes. This aura of cheap romanticism artificially cast around the *puszta* had the result that in West European geography books Hungary is often represented as a country of semi-nomadic shepherds. Since then, the 'world-famous *puszta*' has assumed a thoroughly different aspect as the inferior grasslands and barren alkali grounds have given way to giant irrigated model farms." I went first to look at one of those heron wells, which turned out to be broken down. A stork flew up from a field with a wad of dry grass in its bill and carried it up to a roof to be applied to its nest. Some of the people there, I was told, were living in their own houses, others in a small community building. We went into the celebrated restaurant, which was remarkably clean and attractive. On the front porch, a girl was posing to be photographed in a long overcoat of wool called a *suba*—the same word as for a fur coat in Russian—that hung down to her feet and enveloped her whole figure. Such young people—although I was told that there were still peasants living in poverty—were certainly far from the days when officials were under the impression that *büdös paraszt* (*stinking peasant*) was all one word.

What have been the effects of the collectivization? It was not inevitable for a Communist regime, since Polish agriculture has not been collectivized, and it has certainly not been popular with the peasants. A few have held out against it. I was told by an Americanized Hungarian who had recently revisited Hungary that so many of the young people had gone to the cities that it was hard to see how it would be possible to get a new generation to work the land. But when one reads—and in non-Communist sources—of the previous condition of the peasants: sometimes twenty or twenty-five servants on one of the big estates housed in a one-room hut and getting one piece of bread a day—one realizes that any regime which finally did away with the old feudal society could not but have been an improvement. Reforms had been attempted from time to time, but they had left things pretty much as they were. Between 1880 and 1907, emigration to the United States had so much increased that in 1907 alone one percent of the population left the country. There was in Hungary even less of a middle class than there had been before the revolution in Russia, and both the industrial workers and the peasants inhabited a world quite apart from the often absentee landowners. At the end of the century, when upper-class Budapest was supposed to be at its most brilliant, many people were living in dark basements, sometimes a family of five in a room; in the country, after the First World War, the factory workers

sometimes lived in caves. I remembered the stories I had
heard about the old upper classes. I had been told that at
house parties given by one of the richest families, the
Festetiches, the guests had been received with a lackey
holding a torch on every stair; an American girl I know
who married a Hungarian nobleman discovered that her
husband and his shooting friends amused themselves,
when not on the hunt, by using the Sèvres china for
targets.

Approaching Budapest, we had the Gödöllő hills on
our left, dark and sudden after the flat even green of the
Alföld. They looked a little menacing until, coming closer,
one could see through the thickening day that their sides
were covered with vineyards, and they thus made an impression more genial. When we arrived at the door of the
Gellért, and before I said goodbye to my companion, he
had to make out a slip, authenticating the time when the
car had arrived at its destination.

Hungarian Character. From my experience of Hungarians in the United States, I had expected to find them
in Hungary tumultuous, self-assertive and talkative. I
was surprised to see in Budapest so little of what I had
assumed to be inalienable qualities of the national character, and I came to the conclusion that many of the old
emotional demonstrative kind must have been shot or
subdued or have left the country after 1956. But I was
told by a younger man than most of my Hungarian-
American friends, who had emigrated long before this
and become an American citizen, that his own generation
had never much resembled the older Hungarian emigrants. The ideal of the swashbuckling braggart of the
type of Háry János, of the flamboyant Hungarian patriot
made famous by the age of Kossuth, of the frenetic
musician still inspired by Liszt, had almost completely

faded. And so had the ideal of the grand seigneur with a feudal castle in the background—an ideal about which I used to have the feeling that even the Hungarian Jews, and even when they had left Hungary, felt some obligation to represent. This must have been finally discredited by the reactionary regency of Horthy, which followed, after the First World War, the brief Communist regime of Béla Kun and lasted for a quarter of a century, destroying for all youthful aspiration the glamor of the feudal past and inciting an anti-Semitism which was enough to somewhat dampen the enthusiasm of the brilliant Hungarian Jews who had played so important a part in the intellectual life of Hungary and who had found in Hungarian nationalism an outlet for the then homeless Jewish patriotism. The Hungarians I met in Budapest and Debrecen did not rant and did not romance. They were sober, serious-minded, discreet; they said exactly what they meant. I had thought that Hungary resembled Ireland—always boiling, with much rhetoric and exaggeration, against the oppression of a foreign power, to which it had adapted itself with some flattery and much sly duplicity. But Ireland's liberation from England has left the Irish Republic at the mercy of one of the narrowest of the branches of the Catholic Church. Hungary, detached from Austria, is now partially at the moment controlled by the policing of Russia; but the Communism of Hungary today is not really the same as that of the Soviet Union. The Hungarians have been through a series of murderous and crushing ordeals—with the war, the Nazi occupation, the Stalinist occupation and the revolt against Stalinism after Stalin's death—and they are obliged to think cleverly and carefully as to how to salvage their country and to adapt it to its neighbors and the modern world. And yet I found on further acquaintance—behind all this chastening, still, banked—

the passion, the dynamic force which have made Hungary, in its strange isolation, its strategic position in the center of Europe, such a continually erupting crater, such a constantly humming powerhouse, which is also such a constant exporter of power.

I was a prey to the inevitable delusion to which the visitor from the United States falls a victim in this part of the world. I remarked in Budapest one day that it seemed to me the logical thing that the countries there, whether socialist or non-socialist, should eventually consolidate themselves as a Central European federation. It was replied that this conception was a very old story. But who was to head such a federation? I could not answer that nobody need head it, since the North, in our Civil War, had imposed its hegemony on the South. I knew that at the time when Hungary had been something of a dominant power she had not been at all liked by the Rumanians, the Slovaks and the southern Slavs, and that she had not been particularly kind to them. Later on, an American friend, a retired professor of government, told me of visiting Hungary before the last war and making the same kind of hopeful suggestion. He had said to a young man he met—I am not sure of what national stock—that what seemed to be needed in that part of the world was a new University of the Danube, which should admit all nationalities and solve the language problem as best it could. "You don't understand, Mr. ——," the Central European had replied. "We *hate* one another!" Such hatreds, of course, still exist. One must add to the antagonisms mentioned above the hatred of the Slovaks for the Czechs, which has evidently been intensified since the Allies, after the First World War, decided, rather unrealistically, to combine them in one national package. (The Poles, the Hungarians and the Jugoslavs do, however, appear now to be more or less friends; they have to deal with the same problems.) I repeated this story to another young Hungarian, now resident in the United States and of a more objective intelligence. It was not so much hatred, he said, that prevented these states from combining as the lack of a lingua franca. Before the last war, the German language had to some extent provided this, but where were they to get one now? The second language in the "satellite countries" is now supposed to be Russian, but anyone who has studied Russian must feel that as a second European language this complicated illogical tongue must be hopelessly impracticable. "A language," said one German-speaking Hungarian, "where you have to decline the numerals!" He had never gone so far as to find out the worst. His English is quite perfect.